JOSEPH P. LASH

ELEANOR: THE YEARS ALONE

Foreword by Franklin D. Roosevelt, Jr.

———

W · W · NORTON & COMPANY · INC · NEW YORK

Grateful acknowledgment for permission to reprint the photographs appearing on the endpapers is made to the following: Acme, Agence France-Presse from Pictorial Parade, *the Board of Education of the City of New York, the* New York Daily News, *Franklin D. Roosevelt Library, Henry Grossman, David A. Gurewitsch, Mac A. Shain. Grateful acknowledgment is also made to the United Nations Association of the USA for permission to reprint the Leo Rosenthal photographs.*

Library of Congress Cataloging in Publication Data
Lash, Joseph P   1909–
    Eleanor: the years alone.
    Continues the biography of Mrs. Roosevelt which began in the author's Eleanor and Franklin.
    Includes bibliographical references.
    1. Roosevelt, Eleanor (Roosevelt) 1884–1962.
I. Title.
E807.1.R574   973.917′092′4 [B]   72–2674
ISBN 0–393–07361–0

To Mrs. Roosevelt's grandchildren
and our own

Contents

Photographs appear following pages 128 and 240

Foreword by Franklin D. Roosevelt, Jr.

There is not much to be added to the introduction that I wrote for *Eleanor and Franklin*. The reviewers of that book shared my judgment that Mr. Lash had made exemplary use of the private papers that Mother had left to me as her literary executor and that I had asked Mr. Lash to examine with a view to writing a biography.

A surprisingly large number of readers of *Eleanor and Franklin* wrote to express the hope that Mr. Lash would go on to write a sequel to that book covering my mother's years alone. Here is that sequel. It will be up to the readers to say whether it maintains the high standards of the earlier book; in my view it does. It is the story of my mother alone, but even more, it is the story of those years in which her internal development and her work and experience with my father come to full and creative maturity. We, her children, watched with pride as she won the love and affection as well as respect of people everywhere and truly earned the title of First Lady of the World.

I hope this book will be read by the generation that came to intellectual and political maturity in the sixties and early seventies. They will then better understand their parents. Here in Mr. Lash's careful and detailed documentation of Mother's encounters with the Communists at the United Nations, they will see her moving from the belief that our good will and readiness to compromise would be reciprocated by the Communists to the realization that Stalin's emissaries respected strength alone. Those who speak critically of the West's "cold war" mentality in the years that followed Father's death should examine closely, as Mr. Lash's chronicle enables them to do, my mother's experiences at the United Nations.

Equally illuminating, and singularly moving, is the book's account of Mother's role in helping establish a homeland for the Jewish people. If young people today want to understand why both my mother's generation and mine invested this cause with the passion and faithfulness that liberals in the thirties gave to Republican Spain, they should read Mr. Lash's account of the birth of Israel.

Of course, there is much more in this book. My mother described her work in the years after my father's death as the work that she did on her own. She dealt with the most powerful men of the postwar world—presidents, cardinals, commissars, political bosses, and Wall Street tycoons. She did so with such self-confidence, authority, independence, and astuteness that she demonstrated anew, if it needed another demonstration, the rightness of woman's claim to equality with man.

Yet she also led a very private life. Despite her involvement in public affairs, she always attached a larger importance to the personal and private side of life. Her children, grandchildren, great-grandchildren, and a few close friends always had first claim on her time. The importance that she attached to success in private functioning is attested to by a letter she wrote on October 3, 1949, to the wife of George C. Edwards, then a candidate for mayor in Detroit and now a federal judge:

The cost of being in politics is fine for one's ideals but it is very high in personal sacrifice, I think. No matter what happens, win or lose, I do not think a woman ever feels that the loss in personal relations is compensated for, but when a man makes up his mind to go into politics, I think that is the only thing he can do. It is in his blood and if he is at all successful he will go on all his life and one must make the best of it, and somehow try to have some of the things one wants for oneself, as well as serving the higher purposes which are pretty tough taskmasters.

This book is going to press just as the Eleanor Roosevelt wings of the Franklin D. Roosevelt Library at Hyde Park are being opened to the public. As visitors enter the library they will be confronted by two busts on either side of the entrance hall, one of my father and the other of my mother. The two figures are symbolic of history's recognition that not only were they a team, but a team of equals. What is made visible in the splendid displays and exhibits at the library is given life here in these pages.

Author's Note

I must again acknowledge my indebtedness to those who assisted me with *Eleanor and Franklin* and who also helped with *Eleanor: The Years Alone*. In connection with this book I am particularly grateful to David A. Gurewitsch, who made his files and his splendid collection of photographs available to me. Maureen Corr, who became Mrs. Roosevelt's private secretary after Malvina Thompson's death, was generous with her recollections, as was Mrs. Roosevelt's old friend Esther Lape. I wish also to thank the friends who kindly read these pages, including Dr. John P. Humphrey, and Egon Schwelb and Giorgio Pagnanelli of the Human Rights Division of the United Nations.

I am happy to record my obligation once more to the Franklin D. Roosevelt Library, whose present director, Mr. J. C. James, was as cooperative as his predecessors, and to Mr. Jerry Deyo, audio-visual archivist, and William F. Stickle, staff photographer.

My sister Elsie Lash typed this manuscript as she did the earlier one.

It was my editor at W. W. Norton & Company, Evan Thomas, who felt that the first volume should end with the death of FDR and that Mrs. Roosevelt's years alone should be written as another book. He was right about this, as he was about so many other matters connected with the Eleanor Roosevelt volumes.

Finally, I wish again to record my indebtedness to my wife, Trude. How much she has been a companion in this enterprise is suggested by a letter that I wrote in 1967 to Franklin Jr. and to the publisher and placed alongside my will in which I expressed the hope that in the event I was unable to finish this book they would ask her to do so.

Preface

A few days after Franklin's death, a newspaper-woman intercepted Eleanor Roosevelt at the doorway of her Washington Square apartment in New York City, the one which she had selected with an eye to Franklin's using it after the White House years, and asked her for a statement. "The story is over," Mrs. Roosevelt said quietly and hurried on.

If precedent was any guide, the story would be over. Previously, presidential wives, after the death of their husbands, quickly sank into obscurity and were seldom seen or recalled except on ceremonial occasions. But this presidential wife was different. It was a measure only of Mrs. Roosevelt's lingering insecurity and modesty that after thirteen strenuous years in the White House she could still believe that she was so widely admired—and hated—not in her own right but because she had been FDR's wife, and could still wonder whether with his death her public career might not be finished.

Yet, the same qualities that had turned this protected daughter of old New York into an uncompromising champion of the poor and oppressed, that had transmuted her beloved but alcoholic father's letters into a primer of youthful virtues and strengths, that had enabled her to remake her marriage after the discovery of her husband's unfaithfulness into a journey of self-discovery and a partnership of immense usefulness to America foretold that Eleanor Roosevelt, now standing alone and speaking for herself, would leave her mark on the times.

She had overcome so much, turned so many difficulties into points of growth. She had emancipated herself from the insular and caste-minded society into which she had been born and, in a relentless battle of wills, had freed herself from the domination of a strong-minded mother-in-law who had embodied the values of that society. She had established a unique relationship of independence and partnership with her husband. A homely adolescent with a deep sense of inadequacy because of her physical plainness, she had grown into a woman of poise, dignity, and gracious beauty. She who had been anti-Semitic and prejudiced against "darkies" had become the epitome of a concern that excluded no one from the circle of its compassion and love. Although she had opposed the woman's suffrage movement, she was now a tough-minded and astute political figure in her own right. She for whom speaking had been an ordeal had become one of the most self-possessed and moving speakers in public life.

She had even learned to cope with the sense of alienation, of being an outsider, that she had acquired in childhood with the death of her parents. Work and loving people no matter what they did were her formulas for transcending loneliness and disappointment.

Could the story be over? She was only sixty-one, full of vitality, at home in the corridors of power, and adept at using power to help others. She had a vast political constituency and felt an obligation to promote her husband's objectives, especially the achievement of peace through the United Nations. Before long the realization would come to her that the story was far from over.

ELEANOR:

THE YEARS

ALONE

I. Champion of Her Husband's Ideals

She had not quite realized how much she had relied upon her husband intellectually, Eleanor Roosevelt wrote Walter Nash, New Zealand's minister of finance, adding, "I shall hope to continue to do what I can to be useful, although without my husband's advice and guidance I feel very inadequate." [1]

It was the old ambivalence. She belittled her powers at the very time she was astonishing the world by her stoutness of heart. Franklin Roosevelt's death occasioned an overwhelming sense of personal loss. "I am frightened," wrote Helen Wilmerding, Eleanor's Roser classmate. "Who will take care of us now?" Strong men felt the same. "What a void has been left for the nation and the world," commented Justice Wiley Rutledge, and over in the House office building, a young Texas congressman, Lyndon B. Johnson, with tears in his eyes, exclaimed to a newspaperman, "God—God how he could take it for us all." [2]

She sensed the country's feeling of rudderlessness and loss but instead of yielding to it sought to convert the nation's grief into an instrument for her husband's objectives. "Perhaps in His wisdom," she said in her column "My Day," which she resumed writing the Monday after her husband's burial,

the Almighty is trying to show us that a leader may chart the way, may point out the road to lasting peace, but that many leaders and many peoples must do the building. It cannot be the work of one man, nor can the responsibility be laid upon his shoulders, and so, when the time comes for people to assume the burden more fully, he is given rest.[3]

Franklin's death seemed to have united the country, she wrote her Aunt Maude:

We knew of course Franklin had aged & no longer felt very strong but everyone, including himself, felt that with care he could carry through these four years. He wanted to see a good peace made but perhaps a better one will come through his death. The upsurge of love & realization of how much they had depended on him & left to him has I think made many people feel that they want to see his objectives succeed where before they were critical on many points & might have been apathetic or really obstructionist. One feels in the San Francisco conference that a strong hand is missing. I am sad that he could not see the end of his long work which he has carried so magnificently but I am thankful that he had no pain & no long lingering illness in which he would have watched others not doing as he would have done.[4]

Throughout the years in Albany and Washington Eleanor had had to fight Franklin. His very strength and magnetism had required a special effort of will to keep her own ideals and personality from being smothered. Now she presented him in a different perspective. Beneath all the compromise, she wrote, there had been a steadiness of purpose which was to give the average human being "a fairer chance for 'life, liberty and the pursuit of happiness.' " His political-spiritual legacy to the nation lay not in particular statutes or appointments, but in an attitude, so she advised John Gilbert Winant, U.S. ambassador to Great Britain, a year later, when he was scheduled to deliver an FDR memorial address in Congress at a time when New Dealers had begun to turn against Truman because he was not Roosevelt. Winant's good friend Belle (Mrs. Kermit) Roosevelt came to Eleanor for suggestions for his address because "he is now feeling a desperate loneliness which comes inevitably to all those who loved Franklin." "It seems rather late to have this memorial," she replied immediately,

and so I think the only thing to do is to point up the fact that as time passes, the perspective of what a man has lived by is probably more important than the actual things he did, because new situations necessitate new answers and one can not apply the same theories or exact methods. The background of a man's thinking and acting is at all times a living thing.

If you can in some way touch on this, it might help a lot of the progressives who are feeling rather lost and friendless at the present time.[5]

In life she had been, Henry L. Stimson wrote her, her husband's "worthy helpmate"; in death, she now emerged as the principal champion and interpreter of his ideals, and by the time she wrote her account of the White House years and had dealt with most of the nation's and world's leaders as a colleague and co-worker, she could testify about her husband, "I have never known a man who gave one a greater sense of security." [6]

The first week after the funeral was taken up with the melancholy business of moving out of the White House. Although the amount to pack was "appalling" and President and Mrs. Truman told her to take all the time she needed, she managed it in a few days. "This is the last evening," she wrote a week after the president's death, "and I have a great sense of relief." She held her last press conference, had dinner in the family dining room with Belle Roosevelt, Tommy (Malvina Thompson, her personal secretary), and Tommy's friend, Henry Osthagen, and, before climbing into bed, took a last look at the Washington Monument with its little red light on top which had always seemed to twinkle at her "in friendly fashion." The next morning she breakfasted on the sun porch, went through some busy hours of saying good-bys and thank-yous, and then was driven to the train.

The return to Hyde Park was even sadder. For a few days, with trucks disgorging barrels and packing cases and a beginning made in the business of sorting and dividing possessions, with James and Elliott in and out, the loneliness was not so acute. But Hyde Park without Franklin as its center and children about was a different place. She was not only on her own but alone. Tommy helped, but there was a vacuum which time and other people would never fill.

She might write her old friend Esther Lape, as she did, that love for Franklin had died long ago, but that by believing in his objectives she had rendered him a service of love in helping him achieve his purposes; but her melancholy and loneliness belied such protestations. She had been hurt anew by the discovery that Lucy Mercer Rutherfurd had been at Warm Springs at the time of Franklin's death, Lucy's presence having been kept a secret from her. She had gone to Anna's room after her return to the White House from Warm Springs, her face and manner as stern as they could get when she was angry, and had asked Anna why she had not been told. Anna assured her she had not known Mrs. Rutherfurd was at Warm Springs. Had Mrs. Rutherfurd also been at the White House? Anna explained that one morning when she was with her father, taking notes on things that he wanted done, he had asked her if she would object to inviting an old friend, Mrs. Rutherfurd, to dinner. Did Anna know who Mrs. Rutherfurd was? her father had asked. Deadpan, Anna said she did. Had she objected to having her invited? No, she had not. She had thought of her father, immured in the White House, the only women around to amuse him being his cousins Laura Delano and Daisy Suckley, oppressed by world cares, and had quickly decided that it was not her responsibility to object. Never had she discussed with her father or anyone else the relationship that she knew there had been between the two many years earlier. It was all aboveboard; there were always people around, she assured her mother. That was how it had happened. "Mother was so upset about everything, though so cool on the exterior, and now so upset about me. I was upset enough to wonder whether it would make my relationship with Mother difficult. It did, for two or three days. That was all. We never spoke about it again." Yet sometimes Anna wondered whether her mother had ever quite forgiven her.[7]

Eleanor was vulnerable, and her sadness at Hyde Park bespoke that vulnerability. But Hyde Park was home for her as no other place would be. The president had often spoken of his rootedness there. She, too, became aware, in the course of a battle with the president's executors, insisting that they not sell off the president's woods and fields, of how deeply she was attached to Hyde Park's rural loveliness and memories. Daily she slipped into the hedge-surrounded rose garden to place a spray of flowers on FDR's grave. Spring, too, had a healing power. When she awoke on her sleeping porch, the birds were twittering, the air fresh, the tree a haze of tender greenness. Her spirits lifted. "Perhaps nature is our best assurance of immortality," she wrote. She even enjoyed listening to the farmer's hour on the radio. She was, at heart, a country woman.[8]

Fala, Franklin's dog, was a great comfort to her. He had originally been taken by Margaret Suckley to live with her because Grace Tully (the president's secretary) had reported that that was what the president had intended, but James Roosevelt asked her to send the dog back to Hyde Park: "In talking to my sister and brother, we all feel very disappointed that Fala is not staying with Mother," he wrote. Fala was really "part of the family," and it would make his mother "very happy to have Fala back at Val-Kill." Miss Suckley agreed immediately.[9] Fala and Mrs. Roosevelt became inseparable. He accompanied her on all her walks through the woods, and when he wandered off the path to pursue a scent, a high-pitched "Faa-la" summoned him back. When he covered himself with mud she bathed him, getting as wet as Fala in the process, and when she fed him, she made him do all his tricks—stand up on his hind legs, roll over, beg—as he had done for his master.

On V-E Day the messages and telegrams poured into Hyde Park telling her how much the senders wished that the late president might have been alive to see the end of the European war. When she heard Truman and Churchill proclaiming Germany's unconditional surrender, she could almost hear Franklin's voice making the announcement "for I had heard him repeat it so often." She spoke over WNBC, expressing what she felt would have been the late president's gratitude to the soldiers, war workers, and civilians who had made victory in Europe possible and urging them to go on and "win through to a permanent peace. That was the main objective that my husband fought for. That is the goal which we must never lose sight of." It still was difficult to believe "my husband is not off on a trip," she wrote President Truman.[10]

A photographer caught Eleanor's picture at the WNBC microphone. It showed a face drawn and strained. The black dress and hat, the straying wisps of hair, all contributed to an effect of gauntness. It was the face of a strong woman, but of a woman acquainted with grief.[11]

Old Josephus Daniels came into the *New York Times* building, to see its publisher. The librarian, Freeda Franklin, was asked to bring him a copy of FDR's undelivered speech about the United Nations. "How is she?" Miss Franklin asked Daniels as she handed over the clipping. Daniels immediately understood to whom she was referring. "Bearing up very well," he replied, and added, "she's just as great a woman as he was a man." [12]

Under the president's will Eleanor and her children had a right to live in the Big House during their lifetimes. All agreed, however, with the letter Franklin had left for his wife, urging that it be turned over as soon as possible to the government. He hated to think of them—it amused him to tease them even after death—having to take refuge in the attic or cellar, which they might very well have to do in order to have some privacy.[13]

Disentangling and dividing Franklin's possessions would be "the hard thing," she predicted. She had in mind the difficulty of distributing those possessions in a way satisfactory to all of her five children. But going through her husband's belongings occasioned a renewed stab of anguish about Lucy Mercer Rutherfurd. There was, she found, a little water color of Franklin that had been painted by Mme. Elizabeth Shumatov, an artist whom Mrs. Rutherfurd had brought along on her visits to Franklin in Warm Springs. With what feelings, one wonders, did Eleanor ask Margaret Suckley to send it on to Mrs. Rutherfurd in Aiken. She had long wanted to tell her, Mrs. Rutherfurd replied gratefully, that she had seen Franklin and how helpful he had been during her husband's illness and how kind he had been to her husband's boys. She could not get Mrs. Roosevelt's grief out of her mind, Mrs. Roosevelt whom she had always considered to be the most fortunate of women.[14]

After Franklin's executors consulted the government, Eleanor's son James, who was one of the executors, told her that the Big House had to be emptied of everything they wanted by June 15— linen, china, silver, glassware, jewelry, furs, furniture, books, ship models, paintings—and either shipped to the children or stored. She had the first choice, but decided to take very little. She had never "worked harder physically," she confessed after a few weeks of sorting, unpacking, and packing.

I took the china and glass as my share and divided it equally among you with the exception of a very small amount which I kept and certain pieces of Dresden china which belonged to me anyway and I have just added a few pieces which Granny had. That you will all have to fight over when I die, but I assure you that there will be much less trouble when I shuffle off this mortal coil, than going through the Big House. I got myself into the eaves today to discover the old swinging cradle Pa used and which I used for all of you and I sent those over to the Library on loan. I also sent his baby clothes in a box and some of his early essays as I did not think they would be considered valuable documents.[15]

A decision that shaped the rest of her life was to use all of her own money to buy Val-Kill and about 825 acres of farm lands, woods, and buildings from the president's estate. She did it on the basis of Elliott's willingness to settle there: "I will be very glad to have you here to supervise some of the men on the place," she wrote him in California. "They are getting me down and I can not keep track of what everybody ought to be doing and I know I am not doing the right thing." Elliott and his wife (the former Faye Emerson) arrived the second week in June. They were to live in the president's top cottage.* "We are getting the top cottage in order & I take my hat off to Faye. She works!"[16]

She wanted to rent from the executors, but they told her they had to sell the land and buildings, except for her cottage at Val-Kill, to the highest bidder. "I have to buy the Hyde Park land because when it came to selling it all at once I could not bear not to try to hold it in the hope that some child would want to run it some day. I'm sure that is what Franklin wanted." Franklin Jr. vehemently urged the executors to hold onto the land. He thought his

* "Father said several times," Anna Halsted recalled, "that once he stopped being president he would no longer be afforded privacy through the Secret Service. It would be quite natural for people to come up the driveway to look at the house of an ex-president. He wanted privacy—to be able to go out driving without braces or being watched. He wanted to live in a house of his own, close to Mother's cottage and really in the woods. It had to be away from any kind of main road and small enough so that a small staff could manage it. So he designed the Top Cottage, probably with the help of Henry Toombs. He also had it in the back of his mind that if he could persuade the family, the Big House would be turned over to the government even before his death. He must have realized that Mother would never be happy living in the Big House."

mother unwise to use her own capital to buy the place. He "told me capital was a sacred trust," she wrote this author, "& I said 'Nonsense!' Work was sacred not money & you can imagine the rest!" [17] *

"How I hate 'things'!" she wrote in midsummer. "When it is all done & the business settled I will feel as though I might be able to breathe again. Now I walk on eggs!" She vowed to reduce her own possessions while she still lived so that her heirs would not be burdened with so depressing a task.[18]

After the memorabilia and special bequests had been divided there were other violent quarrels among the children over an intangible but weightier inheritance—the movies and books that people clamored to do about their father, and, most important of all, the dividing up of the political legacy—which son was to have precedence in running for political office in New York and California.

Family conferences turned into angry shouting matches among the boys that were more than she could bear. After one particularly uproarious session, all turned to her and begged her to act as arbiter. She knew her children and doubted that they would be willing to be guided by her views. In any case she did not want to make decisions for them. But she was willing to serve as a clearing house for the family, she said, adding,

> I want you to agree that you will never say anything derogatory about each other or make any kind of remarks that can be so construed, and you will never allow people in your presence to say anything which will reflect on the integrity and character of the family.[19]

In 1940 Geoffrey T. Hellman had ended his profile of Mrs. Roosevelt in *Life* with the prediction that at the end of the Roosevelt administration the United States was going to face a new problem:

> . . . what to do with an ex-First Lady. This question has not existed before because no President's wife has ever before made a career of the

---

* Franklin's will provided that the income from his estate, which was valued at roughly $1,200,000 at his death, went to Eleanor during her lifetime. At her death the estate was to be divided into five equal parts. Each of his children was to get half of his or her one-fifth share as well as the income from the other half of the one-fifth share, which was to be held in trust during their lives and to go per stirpes to the children of each of the five.

First Ladyship. In any case, Mrs. Roosevelt can be counted on to solve the problem better than most ex-Presidents have solved the problem of what to do with ex-Presidents.[20]

On the funeral train returning to Washington from Hyde Park Henry Morgenthau, Jr., had come into her car and urged her to get her business affairs "rounded up as soon as possible so that she could speak to the world as Eleanor Roosevelt. . . . She sort of questioned whether now that she was the widow of the President anybody would want to hear her." [21]

Even while she was settling the estate and working out a way of life at Hyde Park without Franklin, her mind was busy with thoughts of what she might do once she returned to public activity. There had been proposals, just before the San Francisco conference, that President Truman appoint her as a special delegate, but she had begged Congresswoman Mary Norton, who was about to make a speech to the House to that effect, not to do so. There were two jobs that she was obligated to do and that she wanted to do, she wrote at the time: her question-and-answer page for the *Ladies' Home Journal* and her daily column. She had always wanted the latter to be considered on its merits. "Because I was the wife of the President certain restrictions were imposed upon me. Now I am on my own and I hope to write as a newspaperwoman." [22]

She was not fooled by the rise in the number of papers buying her column immediately after the president's death. "Of course, it is curiosity as to how I handle this period and will soon wear off." By the end of the year, Lee Wood, editor of the *New York World-Telegram*, the New York outlet of the Scripps-Howard chain, who did not approve of Mrs. Roosevelt, relegated her column to the rear of the paper, except on the occasions that she made news, and that was to be quite often.

One line of activity she ruled out immediately—running for political office. Harold Ickes very seriously urged her to do so. He came up to Hyde Park to look over the Big House, which was to be under his jurisdiction. During the two days that he and his wife Jane spent with Mrs. Roosevelt they pressed her to become a candidate for the U.S. Senate in New York State, and Ickes followed up the visit with a letter that forcefully embodied his views. Nothing should be left undone to defeat Governor Dewey in 1946 so as to dispose of him as a possible candidate for the presidency in 1948. A ticket on which Sen. James M. Mead ran for governor and she for senator was the strongest available to New York Democrats, he thought. "You would be unbeatable and you would help greatly to defeat Governor Dewey." [23]

She had not decided what she intended to do in autumn, she replied, but running for office

is not the way in which I can be most useful. My children have labored for many years under the baffling necessity of considering their business of living as it affected their Father's position and I want them to feel in the future that any running for public office will be done by them.

Although she wanted to work with the Democrats, she did not want to have to follow "the party line." She intended to help "the liberals in the country and if I can write interesting columns and do an article now and then my voice would not be silent." [24]

Mrs. Roosevelt was already being heard. An intimate, sympathetic correspondence had sprung up between President Truman and herself. During the week that she was still in the White House she had given him her evaluation of the men and women around FDR. "She told me," a friend wrote in April, "that she would tell Truman what she thinks of people (like Byrnes, Hannegan, Pauley, etc.) but that she will tell him only once,—after that the responsibility will be his." [25]

Her column of May 10, 1945, expressed surprise that the Russians had delayed their announcement of the end of the war almost a day after the simultaneous announcements by Truman and Churchill. Truman, upset lest she think he was not keeping U.S. engagements with Russia, promptly sat down and wrote her an eight-page letter in longhand, giving a detailed account of the surrender arrangements and adding that his difficulties with Churchill were almost as irritating as those with the suspicious Russians. [26]

She was touched and somewhat appalled that he should have spent so much time writing her:

Please if you write again, do have it typed because I feel guilty to take any of your time.

I am typing this because I know my husband always preferred to have things typed so he could read them more quickly and my handwriting is anything but legible.

Your experience with Mr. Churchill is not at all surprising. He is suspicious of the Russians and they know it. If you will remember, he said some pretty rough things about them years ago and they do not forget.

Of course, we will have to be patient, and any lasting peace will have to have the Three Great Powers behind it. I think, however, if you can get on a personal basis with Mr. Churchill you will find it easier. If you talk to him about books and let him quote to you from his marvellous memory everything from Barbara Fritchie to the Nonsense Rhymes and Greek tragedy, you will find him easier to deal with on political subjects. He is a gentleman to whom the personal element means a great deal.

Mr. Churchill does not have the same kind of sense of humor the Russians have. In some ways the Russians are more like us. They enjoy a practical joke, rough housing and play and they will joke about things which Mr. Churchill considers sacred. He takes them deadly seriously and argues about them when what he ought to do is to laugh. That was where Franklin usually won out because when you know when to laugh and when to look upon things as too absurd to take seriously, the other person is ashamed to carry through even if he was serious about it.

You are quite right in believing that the Russians will watch with great care to see how we keep our commitments.

A rumor has reached me that the message from Mr. Stalin to you was really received in plenty of time to have changed the hour but it was held back from you. Those little things were done to my husband now and then. I tell you of this rumor simply because while you may have known about it and decided that it was wise just not to receive it in time, you told me in your letter that you did not receive it and I have known of things which just did not reach my husband in time. That is one of the things which your Military and Naval aides ought to watch very carefully. . . .

I will, of course, keep confidential anything which comes to me in any letter from you and I will never mention, and I would not use, a private letter in any public way at any time.

I would not presume to write you this letter only you did say you would like me to give you some personal impressions of these people, gathered from my husband's contacts, before you went to meet them and as I realize that may happen soon, I thought perhaps you would like this letter now. . . .[27]

She had given him much information that would be helpful, he replied. Elliott had been in to see him, as she had urged, as well as Anna, and both had supplied him with information that he thought would come in handy.[28]

In June she went down to Washington for a couple of days. She lunched with the president. It seemed "a little strange to go to the White House as a visitor," but Truman could not have been more gracious. There was some talk about politics. The president expressed his concern about the situation in New York, where Ed Flynn was the Democratic national committeeman; and thus encouraged to express her views, she gave voice to her misgivings about the national party picture under Robert Hannegan, chairman of the Democratic National Committee. She had sent the president a copy of a three-page letter on the subject that she had just addressed to Hannegan. That blunt missive said that the president himself was doing well from the liberals' point of view, but in Congress, especially in the Senate, if the southern Democrats managed to kill the fair employment practices (FEPC) and the poll tax bills without record votes, large numbers of Democratic supporters would be alienated. The party no longer could rely upon city machines such as Tammany in New York and Pendergast's in Kansas City to swing elections. Program and policy were the keys. She was concerned also about the party's disregard of women: "There will be no woman in the Cabinet and there has been no suggestion so far of any woman or women in comparably important positions." [29]

Frances Perkins had confirmed her fears in regard to Hannegan's reluctance to push women for jobs, and other women who had served the government under Roosevelt wrote nostalgically of the support Mrs. Roosevelt had always given them: "Yes, you *are* missed." [30]

"I have no idea whether you agree with me or not," her letter to President Truman, accompanying the copy of her letter to Hannegan, said, "but all I can do is send you the results of my observations and my conversations with people in the last few days." A few days later the president issued a public statement in favor of the FEPC. "President Truman did a courageous and wise thing when he came out in favor of the FEPC Bill," she wrote in her column. And Truman evidently spoke with Hannegan, as she learned from Doris Byrne, the head of the women's division of the New York State Democratic party. Although Hannegan was still afraid of Mrs. Roosevelt, Miss Byrne reported, she was the only woman in politics whom he took seriously, and the president thought so highly of her that Hannegan was now trying to mend his ways.[31]

Mrs. Roosevelt reciprocated the president's feelings. "I think President Truman is doing extremely well," she wrote her son James after her visit to Washington. "I also think that Mr. Stettinius brought the San Francisco Conference to a very successful conclusion. I suppose now Jimmy Byrnes will become Secretary of State and Mr. Stettinius will go to London and Heaven knows what will happen to Winant."[32]

While she was in Washington (perhaps Truman mentioned the subject to her) she wrote a column about Earl Browder's demotion by the Communists for "revisionism." Her column was clearly intended to be read in Moscow. Browder, in the interests of Big Three cooperation, had been helpful to Roosevelt in preserving domestic unity. Eleanor knew of that helpfulness because Browder's messages to the president had been routed through her. Suddenly, in May, Jacques Duclos, a leader of the French Communists, acting, it was assumed, on directives from Moscow, wrote an article criticizing Browder's collaborationist policies, calling instead for a Marxist revolutionary program. Within a few weeks the American Communists had repudiated Browder, declared U.S. "imperialism" again to be the enemy, and portrayed Browder's collaboration with the New Deal as collaboration with capitalism.

The actions of the American Communists, Mrs. Roosevelt wrote in a column datelined Washington,

have added fire to the general fear of Communism as an international force. Earl Browder has been reprimanded for an attitude which many of us believed had represented the attitude of the Soviet government.

. . . The American Communists had been co-operative where they could be, but now, as we understand it, they are out to force communism on our democracy. That we will not tolerate. . . . The sooner we clear up authoritatively the whole situation of Communists outside of the Soviet Union, the better chance we will have for peace in the future. The Russian people should know this, and so should the people of the United States.[33]

In July, Sidney Hillman invited her to head the National Citizens Political Action Committee, the mainstay of which was the CIO. Organized nationally, as it was, it could sway political parties —"and they need to be swayed," she conceded. But she also knew that NCPAC was infiltrated with left-wingers. "The meeting with NCPAC last night left me torn in my mind. I don't know how useful I will be to them. I have an aversion to take on responsibility except individually and this is a big one. . . ." A week later she turned Hillman down:

I have decided that if I became chairman instead of being helpful with the Democratic Party it would alienate the Democratic Party and I think it important to keep the Democratic Party close to both the CIO-PAC and the NCPAC.

For the present she intended to confine herself to writing and radio work. Also, she might be doing "a considerable amount of travelling," which was an added reason, she told Hillman, why she did not want to be tied down by administrative responsibilities.[34]

The traveling related to the long-hoped-for trip to the Soviet Union. After Franklin's death, as Big Three unity began to founder, she became more eager than ever to see this vast, mysterious, troublesome country with her own eyes. Ed Flynn brought back word from Russia, which he had visited after Yalta on assignment from Roosevelt, of how much the Russians had hoped she and the president would visit their country. He felt she should go on her own. He also reported that he had "told His Holiness the Church should change their tactics and stop attacking the Soviets." George Carlin, the head of United Features Syndicate, suggested that she go as a correspondent. She liked that idea and thought she would go in March, 1946. But Flynn urged her to go immediately as did Harry

Hopkins, who had returned from his mission to Moscow for Truman deeply troubled by the growing division between the United States and the Soviet Union. The Russians would let her see "everything you wanted to see everywhere in the country," Hopkins assured her. She wanted to go "purely as a correspondent" for the syndicate "and not as Franklin's widow," she wrote back a little unrealistically, and she "would not want to do a lot of parties, etc. except of course, for calling on Marshal Stalin." She should go as a correspondent, Harry Hopkins agreed, "although, of course, the Russian Government and the Russian people would receive you as the widow of the President and there is just no way out of that one." [35]

She consulted Mr. Truman:

I haven't spoken to the Syndicate about going at any immediate time because I wanted first to make sure that it would meet with your approval to have me go to Russia, either now or in the spring.

I would not want in any way to complicate anything that you may be doing. . . . [36]

It is not clear when Truman, who was about to leave for Potsdam, replied to her, but judging by subsequent letters, when he did, he counseled her to postpone her visit until the spring of 1946.

She still was looking for a job to do, groping for the assignment that would bring all her interests into a single focus. She had been deeply conscious during her White House years of how her energies had been scattered among a thousand enterprises. After Franklin's fourth-term election, Esther Lape had implored her to think over carefully the best ways to make use of the powers and opportunities that were so peculiarly hers. That involved a "selection and decision," Esther had cautioned her.[37]

Now she was determined to do just that, and she was going to do the selecting. When two long-time friends, Maj. Henry S. Hooker and John Golden, the theatrical producer, proposed to appoint themselves a committee to pass on the jobs suitable for her, she interrupted them, Tommy looking aghast, and, scarcely able to suppress her laughter, said, "I love both of you dearly. But you can't run my life." [38]

She agreed, at the request of Mrs. David M. Levy, with whom she had worked closely in the International Student Service, to join the board of the newly formed Citizens Committee for Children. In addition, she spent more time helping the Wiltwyck School for delinquent children. When the Union for Democratic Action, spearheading the campaign for the full employment bill, asked her to write Truman, she did so.° She became the honorary president of committees for Yugoslavian and Greek relief. She continued her work with Walter White and the NAACP. "When I warn my friends," she wrote on her sixty-first birthday,

that I am going to sit by the fire with a little lace cap on my head and a shawl about my shoulders and knit baby things for the newest generation, they look at me with some incredulity. The day will come, however, and when it does I think it will be rather pleasant.

She was more realistic when S. J. Woolf, who had interviewed and sketched her regularly since the twenties, came to see her. He recalled that ex-President Theodore Roosevelt had once said to him that many people did not have to worry about him in retirement. "I can always find something to keep me busy." Mrs. Roosevelt laughed and answered, "I suppose that is true of all the Roosevelts. They can always keep busy." [40] What she really wanted to do was to make some contribution to what had been Franklin's main wartime objective—the establishment of machinery that would help ensure a lasting peace. As long ago as 1939 she had read Clarence Streit's *Union Now* and had had the author dine at the White

° This was an old and overriding objective with her. A few months before Franklin's death Chester Bowles, administrator of the Office of Price Administration, had come to see her on a Sunday afternoon while Franklin was in Warm Springs. Bowles had helped FDR draft his "economic bill of rights" and was unhappy about Roosevelt's failure to make plans to fulfill the pledges contained in the bill, including the commitment to "60 million jobs." He confided his anxieties to Eleanor, who had spoken "of her own frustrations." Franklin's mind was focused on the war, and almost all of his visitors were diplomats, generals, and admirals. She considered it her responsibility to bring another point of view to Franklin's attention and told Bowles that she called the president on the telephone every morning to urge an immediate beginning to postwar planning. "I have learned by experience," she explained to Bowles, "to recognize the point at which the President's patience is about to give out and he will begin to scold me. At that moment I hurriedly say, 'Franklin, my car is waiting. I must be on my way. I shall call you again tomorrow.'" [39]

House in order to explain his plan to Franklin. She had kept Franklin informed of the work of Clark Eichelberger's Commission to Study the Organization of Peace. All through the war she had argued for a "United Nations" rather than an Anglo-American approach to peacekeeping. In July, when the UN Charter was before the Senate, she had pleaded for immediate ratification, saying her husband thought it most important to write the Charter and have it accepted while the exigencies of winning the war still kept the Allies together.[41]

The dropping of the atomic bomb on Hiroshima and Nagasaki in August and the revelation of the awesome force that had been let loose in the world underscored the indispensability of the United Nations. That had been her reaction when, in July, 1943, she had fortuitously learned one of the most closely guarded secrets of the war from a young nuclear physicist working on the project. "He was convincing and rather frightening and we must have peace in the future." [42]

Although Mrs. Roosevelt did not question the decision to drop the bomb—indeed, welcomed the news of the first bomb as meaning the war must come to an end more speedily and bring the men in the services home sooner—she immediately lent her support to the remarkable movement that developed among the atomic scientists to educate the public so they might see that there could be no national monopoly of the bomb and that U.S. security, therefore, would require international control under adequate safeguards. She saw two of their representatives, Harrison Brown and Eugene Wigner, and, according to them, was "very nice" and offered to help them with introductions in Washington. Their visit was reflected in her column. She was disturbed, she wrote, by the talk in the press about keeping the secret of the bomb. The sovereignty the United States would have to renounce to achieve international control would be a small price to pay for the avoidance of a nuclear arms race. In a transatlantic interview with Dr. Lise Meitner, the shy German refugee who had first grasped the significance of nuclear fission, both women said that the bomb posed a challenge to mankind to ensure that this awesome force was used in the future "for the good of all mankind and not for destructive purposes," and that this would require international control.[43]

The United Nations, regardless of its imperfections, now seemed more important than ever. Mrs. Roosevelt considered it her husband's most significant legacy to the world and wanted his name to be associated with it. She enlisted the help of Truman and Hopkins to get the United Nations to consider the possibility of using Hyde Park as the permanent site of the new organization. She even thought that she, too, might be of help in carrying forward her husband's work.[44]

Truman yielded to no one in his admiration of Mrs. Roosevelt, whom he still addressed as "First Lady," just as he still thought of Roosevelt as "*the* President." There were two people, Truman had told James Byrnes sometime in November, that he had to have on his political team—Henry Wallace, because of his influence with labor, and Mrs. Roosevelt, because of her influence with the Negro voter. He could "take care of Henry" but wanted Byrnes to find an appointment for Mrs. Roosevelt in the field of foreign affairs. "The following week," Byrnes said, "in recommending a list of delegates for the first meeting of the United Nations Assembly in London, I placed Mrs. Roosevelt's name at the top of the list, expressing the belief that because of her husband's deep interest in the success of the UN she might accept. Truman telephoned to her immediately, while I was still in his office, and she did agree to serve."

Franklin Jr. was at her Washington Square apartment when the president telephoned her in early December. He heard his mother protest she had no experience in foreign affairs; she did not know parliamentary procedure; she could not possibly do it. Truman refused to be put off, she told Franklin Jr. when she came back to the luncheon table.[45]

"You have to do it," her son urged. Tommy agreed, as did her other children and the close friends to whom she mentioned the president's call. She decided finally that she had a duty to accept. Mr. Truman was wise, she said, in thinking that her presence in London, because of her connection with FDR, would remind delegates of his hopes for the new organization and would help to keep the Assembly's sights high.

Truman asked Senate Majority Leader Alben Barkley to sound out his colleagues for their reaction to the appointment. A few days later, her nomination was approved with only one dissenting vote cast by Sen. Theodore G. Bilbo of Mississippi, who noted that he had been severely critical of her statements on the American Negro.

"She has convictions and does not hesitate to fight for them," wrote Scripps-Howard columnist Thomas L. Stokes. "The New Deal era was richer for her influence in it. That influence was far greater than appeared publicly." Other women could represent American women, but this was a good appointment because "she, better than perhaps any other person, can represent the little people of this country, indeed of the world." [46]

In her own response to the appointment she spoke of it as an honor and responsibility that had come to her "largely because my husband laid the foundations for the organization through which we all hope to build world peace." The novel note here was the word "largely" with its implication that her own merit and point of view had played a part in her selection.

Some things I can take to the first meeting: A sincere desire to understand the problems of the rest of the world and our relationship to them; a real goodwill for people throughout the world; a hope that I shall be able to build a sense of personal trust and friendship with my co-workers, for without that understanding our work would be doubly difficult.[47]

II. The Hardest-Working Delegate

A few days out at sea on the liner *Queen Elizabeth,* which was carrying the United States delegation to the first session of the United Nations General Assembly in London, Mrs. Roosevelt was persuaded to hold her first formal press conference since she left the White House. The United Nations might not be "final and perfect," she told the reporters, but

I think that if the atomic bomb did nothing more, it scared the people to the point where they realized that either they must do something about preventing war or there is a chance that there might be a morning when we would not wake up.

One comment she put off the record, "For the first time in my life I can say just what I want. For your information it is wonderful to feel free." [1]

It was a sign that she was emerging from the shock of April 12. So much had happened since then—the atom bomb, the growing split with Russia, civil war in China, the Pearl Harbor inquiry, the renewal of domestic bickering. "We have all been plunged into a new world." She would have liked to have drawn upon Franklin's thinking, but she also valued the feeling that she was on her own now, able to speak her own mind in meeting the problems of this new world. And she had an astute appreciation of just how much influence she might be able to wield. "The delegation won't follow me dear," she wrote an overenthusiastic friend, "but I think they won't like to propose anything they think I would not approve of!" [2]

The delegation was a prestigious one. It consisted of five

representatives—Secretary of State James F. Byrnes; Edward R. Stettinius, Jr., who was the U.S. representative on the Security Council; Sen. Tom Connally (D-Texas), chairman of the Senate Foreign Relations Committee; Sen. Arthur H. Vandenberg (R-Michigan), ranking Republican member of the Senate Foreign Relations Committee; and Mrs. Roosevelt. In addition there were five alternates—Rep. Sol Bloom (D-New York), chairman of the House Foreign Affairs Committee; the committee's ranking Republican member, Charles A. Eaton of New Jersey; Frank Walker, former postmaster general and former chairman of the Democratic National Committee; the former chairman of the Republican National Committee, John G. Townsend, Jr., who also was an ex-senator from Delaware. The fifth alternate was John Foster Dulles, chief foreign affairs adviser to Gov. Thomas E. Dewey in the 1944 presidential campaign.

Mrs. Roosevelt had boarded the war-gray giant troopship (for the *Queen Elizabeth* was still unreconverted) at 7:30 the night before it sailed, a lonely figure in black who stepped out of a small car, waved the reporters aside, and began to come up the gangplank by herself until someone on board spotted her. Most of her colleagues had boarded several hours earlier, having come from Washington on a special train and having been driven to the pier in a dozen Army limousines and buses preceded by motorcycle outriders, their sirens moaning and red lights blinking.

"I breakfast alone at the Captain's table each morning," she noted on New Year's day, the second day out, in the diary which she sent back to Tommy to circulate among her children and a few friends, "as the senatorial families do not arise and shine early." She had decided not to take Tommy. She had thought the mail would drop off after she left the White House "but I have never had less than 100 a day and frequently 300 and 400 a day," and if Tommy had come along, they would never catch up.

"A curious New Year's Eve!" she had recorded in her diary. "I went to bed at 8:30 and was glad to be oblivious to the ship's roll at midnight. I did think of you all at home before I went to sleep and

wished for each one individually a happier New Year than the last."
John Golden, the producer, sensing how lonely she might feel had
sent a collection of gifts with a card that read:

> *Here's a little game to play*
> *Just because you go away*
> *One to open every day*
> *Keep or give or throw away.*[3]

She worked hard on shipboard. Even on the "mammoth"
walks, as Dr. Ralph Bunche described them, that she determinedly
took around the deck in fog or sunshine, she was usually accompanied by a fellow delegate or adviser. "That was the best way to talk
to her," Bunche said. "Mr. Dulles and Mr. [Abe] Fortas joined me,
and continued a discussion on trusteeship. Mr. Fortas wants us to
make the proposal that all territories shall have the right of appeal
to the Assembly when difficulties arise." After her breakfast and
luncheon walks she settled down to studying the massive briefing
materials that the State Department had prepared for the members
of the delegation. "I read till I had to get ready to go to a party Mr.
Stettinius gave for the whole delegation at five o'clock. More reading, dinner, more reading and ten-thirty bed." There were briefing
papers and briefing sessions. Alger Hiss, "Principal Adviser," went
over the conference agenda with the whole delegation. Dr. Bunche
"went over questions of trusteeship with me," and later that day
"the State Department boys" discussed questions connected with
the United Nations' specialized agencies. Then back to reading
"and fell asleep occasionally." She decided that she liked the Van-
denbergs better than she did the Connallys, "but I don't like any of
them much." She had another session with Hiss, this time together
with Leo Pasvolsky, who had been Cordell Hull's principal deputy
in the drafting of the UN Charter. Pasvolsky was "a smooth article,
but Hiss I am inclined to like." [4]

So the days on shipboard passed. The night before they disembarked she talked with Stettinius, whom Truman had replaced as
secretary of state with Byrnes. "The tears came to his eyes when he
spoke of Franklin and the ideas which he had talked over with him.

I believe it is a sense of loyalty to F.D.R. which keeps him on the job." [5]

As the delegation disembarked at Southampton, James Reston cabled the *New York Times* that Mrs. Roosevelt had impressed her colleagues "by her industry in studying the technical details" of the approaching Assembly. The reporters had noted that not only had she attended all delegation briefings but she had sat in with the reporters during their interviews with State Department officials. [6]

Westbrook Pegler did not think the country was getting its money's worth. Back home he attacked her appointment, calling it "a political job paying $12,000 a year, which is $2,000 more than the salary of a Senator or Representative, plus expenses at the rate of $25 a day and other perquisites." Actually the government only paid for the days she worked. Congress had authorized her to send out her mail under government frank and this she accepted, but she had refused the lifetime pension of $5,000 a year that it had wanted to vote her as it had done with other widows of presidents. "I won't need any money from home," she informed Tommy, "as I find I have some in my account here with Barings. I must have left it since the trip I made with the boys. I can't take it out of the country so I might as well use it." [7]

They disembarked on a Saturday. On the way to London Senator Connally kept repeating to her, "Where is all this destruction I've heard so much about? Things look all right to me." She started to point out the telltale signs "but soon found he just wasn't interested." "Cliveden," she added, referring to an invitation from Lady Astor that she had declined but most of the others had accepted, "probably did nothing to change their point of view." The delegation was lodged at Claridge's. She had scarcely removed her coat when an old friend, Lady Stella Reading, head of the Women's Voluntary Services, knocked on her door. Then the Noel Bakers came in. As minister of state in the British Labor government, Baker headed the British delegation to the Assembly when Ernest Bevin, the foreign secretary, could not be present. His chief concern was to impress upon Mrs. Roosevelt his belief that the League of Nations had not failed since it had laid the groundwork for all that was being done today. "He was a great League man and they tell me feels called upon to defend it at every turn." American Ambassador John Gilbert Winant was another visitor. "The tears came to his eyes in talking of Franklin." Dorsey Fisher, a member of the embassy staff who had traveled with her during her wartime trip to Great Britain, arrived, as did her young friend Louise Morley Cochrane, whom the embassy had sent to show her how to get to the necessary places in London. The three of them went for supper to the embassy canteen, "which is a godsend since we get army foodstuff which is really good."

There were scores of "welcome" letters—from the queen, from the Winston Churchills, from Allenswood classmates, from old family friends such as Hector Ferguson and Sir Arthur Murray, from Lady Pethick-Lawrence of Peaslake, who was president of the World Women's Party for Equal Rights, and from Lady Eva Reading, who wanted a little of her "precious time" to talk to her about the problems of world Jewry. All the world sent flowers, including the Emir Faisal Alsaud. Sunday night she dined with Adlai Stevenson. "He has headed our work on the temporary [preparatory] commission . . . so I hope to learn something about the people on the other delegations who are still not even names with which I am familiar." Stevenson had been to Cliveden with the senators, who, he told her, had made much the same remarks there about the lack of signs of destruction that they had made to her. She and Stevenson got along well.[8]

By Sunday, too, she had visited her office and established a morning routine. From nine to ten she intended to do all the personal work—"columns, notes, telephones"—but when the delegation meetings began she would have to move "the personal stuff" to eight to nine. Although it was a five-minute walk from hotel to delegation offices, she would have to leave at nine sharp to make the 9:15 delegation meetings because "we meet on the seventh floor and the lift runs more slowly and far less reliably than the one in our old apartment house here."

The first delegation meeting confirmed her view that senators were an egotistical breed. The issue was whether the delegation should speak with a single voice to the press. Vandenberg especially did not take easily to such discipline. Before leaving for London he had "very nearly resigned" from the delegation because he thought the wording of the Moscow Communiqué of the Foreign Ministers agreeing to the establishment of a United Nations Atomic Energy Control Commission could be interpreted to mean that the United States might be obliged to disclose its atomic secrets before there was agreement on adequate inspection and controls. He had sailed with the delegation after receiving assurances from Truman on the matter, but on the boat he slipped several of the newspapermen a memorandum stating his objections to the Moscow wording. "He gave it to the press, in confidence," Mrs. Roosevelt scornfully noted. "Tonight it is on the front pages of the New York and London papers." [9]

Since the press was full of stories about division in the American delegation, Stettinius scheduled a meeting of the delegation with reporters to show this was not the case. But ten minutes before the conference began, Dulles informed Stettinius that he and Vandenberg would not attend. Not having much of a choice, Mrs. Roosevelt and Stettinius went into the meeting alone where "all went well," she later recorded, "till the inevitable question came: 'Where are the two Republican members of the delegation? Does their absence indicate a split in the delegation?' Mr. Stettinius said: 'Certainly not, you men who were on the boat know that is not so. I think Senator Vandenberg is probably at a committee meeting.' Then we left quickly." A few moments later Vandenberg walked in and "took some of the remaining press people up to his room. It seemed to me pretty shoddy behavior, though I was in sympathy with parts of his memo. I think he is right that language should be clear." The U.S. delegation met the press today, Reston cabled his paper, and appealed for unity and peace, "but two members of the delegation were absent from the conference."

The next day Byrnes arrived and saw the senators, "and all seems serene on the atomic bomb statement which stirred up such a rumpus with Senator Vandenberg," she noted. "I am not sure the gentleman does not like a little newspaper publicity." [10]

She was told at the delegation meeting that she had been assigned to Committee III, which—scheduled to deal with humanitarian, social, and cultural matters—was supposed to be a relatively uncontroversial and, therefore, it was thought, safe berth for her. Durward Sandifer was her chief adviser. Short, sandy-haired, dryly spoken, he had been an assistant on legal matters in Pasvolsky's office. She quickly came to depend on him. "I went with her to all the sessions," he recalled. "I started carrying her brief case as well as my own—over her protests." She invited him to Claridge's to dinner. She had half a dozen people there, including a cousin. "I rushed home to write a long account of this dinner to Irene [Sandifer]." By the end of the Assembly they were good friends. He should come to lunch at Washington Square once they were back in New York, she urged. He did. "I was so nervous at having lunch with Mrs. Roosevelt," he confided to Tommy afterward, "that I put salt in my coffee." Mrs. Roosevelt overheard him. "You—nervous at having lunch with me? I am the one who should be nervous at having lunch with you. You will never know how frightened I was getting on that boat. I knew what the British thought of Franklin and what they expected of me. You don't know what a help you were to me." [11]

The General Assembly opened. She drove to Westminster with Stettinius—"How your husband planned for this day," he said to her—and in Westminster's Central Hall as the delegations filed in, most of them led by their foreign ministers, and the temporary president mounted to the high podium which was framed from behind by a huge map of the world on a blue and gold background with two great olive branches below it, she felt that FDR's spirit "must be with us." She noted the flowing robes of the Arab representatives and also that there were "very few women on the delegations." She was seated at the end of the U.S. delegation, next to the Soviet group. By mistake she took the seat of V. V. Kuznetzov, who gallantly invited her to join the Soviet delegation, and relations between them got off to a good start.

The business of the first meeting was to choose a president of the Assembly, and Paul Henri Spaak, Socialist and foreign minister of Belgium, was elected over Trygve Lie, Socialist and foreign minister of Norway.° Spaak won by a vote of 28 to 23, and Lie, who had originally been urged to run for the position by the United States, was angry with the American delegation for its failure to support him openly. "*If* the United States had spoken out in the Assembly in support of my candidacy as it had spoken out to me in August, in December, and that very day, *if* Mr. Byrnes had not sat there tight-lipped, then, the result might well have been otherwise," Lie wrote. "We were very stupid over the election of President of the Assembly," Mrs. Roosevelt felt, but in her column describing the impressive opening of the Assembly she struck a more edifying note. The job before the United Nations was too serious to feel exhilaration over victory or disappointment over defeat. As she left Westminster Hall, she overheard a woman, standing in the rain, say, "They must succeed, the future of the world depends on it." 12

On the carbon of the column that she sent in about the Assembly's opening, Mrs. Roosevelt noted, "For this column the United Press men here have given me great praise." Her account had omitted one of the Assembly's most solemn moments when Spaak, in his speech of acceptance, taking note of the large number of delegates "who have done much more for peace than I have," went on to speak of Mrs. Roosevelt:

Among them there is one delegate to whom I wish to extend particular sympathy and tribute. I refer to her who bears the most illustrious and respected of all names. I do not think it would be possible to begin at this Assembly without mentioning her and the name of the late President Roosevelt and expressing our conviction that his disappearance was a great grief to us all and an irreparable loss.13

There was one tribute to FDR about which she could say nothing —that dealing with whether or not to locate UN headquarters at Hyde Park. "I have been particularly careful to express no preference on the subject whatsoever," she advised her Hyde Park neigh-

° Lie was a candidate both for president of the General Assembly and secretary-general of the United Nations.

bor Gerald Morgan, "and to stress that the Government is the owner not the family." She doubted the choice of Hyde Park, she wrote her aunt, Maude Gray, "because the Republicans are so opposed. They are afraid it might perpetuate FDR's name." In the end the site committee recommended selection of a location as close to New York City as possible and the establishment of temporary headquarters at Lake Success.[14]

"You know I don't like sitting and doing nothing," she noted in her diary as business sessions began and there was an endless number of speeches on rules of procedure all of which had to be translated from English into French or vice versa. "I notice that men always feel passionately about these rules, and on our own delegation Congressman Bloom keeps impressing upon us how very important it is to get these rules just as you want them." She agreed it was wise to have the rules of procedure thought out and accepted in advance, but it did not seem to her "quite as desperate a question" as it did to the men. She informally inquired at the delegation meeting whether she might bring her knitting. The men looked nonplussed, so she left her knitting bag at the hotel.[15]

Despite the tedious stretches devoted to the counting of ballots, the voting behavior of the countries—especially the USSR— were interesting.

I wish you could have watched the Russian faces when New Zealand apparently opposed Great Britain's choice of Canada for the Security Council. They would feel such behaviour among their satellites showed weakness & it is going to take time to realize that when you are sure of fundamentals you can differ on non-essentials. Great Britain had told the Dominions to decide and they could not agree. S. Africa and Canada chose Canada, New Zealand & India and Australia wanted Australia. We had told Great Britain we'd vote for Canada & we did but Australia won! [16]

More than any other member of the delegation she was drawn into jobs unrelated to her UN assignment. There were endless delegations calling upon her, starting with a group of GIs who wanted her to find out from General "Ike" whether there was a demobilization policy for 45 to 60 point men. She went down to Waterloo Station to counsel some GI wives. At Louise Morley's request she talked to nearly a thousand British brides and fiancées of American servicemen and then to seven hundred enlisted men and officers stationed in London. Almost every day, and sometimes more often, she had to dash off to the BBC studios to broadcast. She was fascinated by the conversations that went on between the men in the London studios and those in New York. Once Edward R. Murrow walked into the New York studio as she was preparing to broadcast, and she sent him a message that she had seen his wife Janet and their nine-week-old son and had thought him a beautifully healthy baby.[17]

She lunched with the Churchills, with the leaders of the Labor and Liberal parties, and with the royal family.

Yesterday I lunched alone with the King & Queen & Elizabeth & Margaret Rose. It was nice & they are nice people but so far removed from life it seems.

Teas, cocktail parties, and dinners, the delegations wanted her especially. She went to the Byelorussian party, she noted, and "said some pleasant things. Tasted Vodka and don't like it." "I am seeing all the deposed kings, this week," she noted another time.[18]

She preferred her work in Committee III, but other members of the delegation took more happily to the social end.

My buddy, Sen. Townsend, and Dulles went to Germany on Sat. a.m. and today I got a message they were grounded in Paris. The boys, no matter what their age, can't resist a good time.

There were so many speeches at public meetings that her voice finally gave out. "For two days I've had no voice," she reported. She hoped it would return in time for her to speak at the Pilgrim dinner. (The Pilgrim Society, dedicated to Anglo-American friendship, was one of the most prestigious in the realm.) It was the first time in forty years they had invited a woman. Perhaps that was why her voice had fled, she speculated. The diagnosis was fatigue, not fright. "Frank Walker seemed pleased with my speech; I was the *only* woman!"[19]

Her other big public meeting was at Albert Hall, where she

was the main speaker at a ceremony welcoming the delegates to the
General Assembly. It was in connection with her speech at this
meeting that Noel Baker was concerned she do justice by the
League of Nations. Robert Viscount Cecil, who had drafted the
Covenant of the League of Nations, sat next to her. "He is very deaf
but has transferred his allegiance from the League to the UNO." He
had attended the first session of the Assembly, but since no one had
recognized him and he was unable to hear he did not go again.
"Old age is pathetic," she noted in her diary and paid tribute to him
in her column, which during the Assembly appeared in many British papers. Albert Hall was filled to its topmost gallery. Field Marshal Sir Harold Alexander presided, which brought from Cecil the
whispered comment, "We go about peace in a very belligerent way,
don't we!"

"We must be willing to learn the lesson that cooperation may
imply compromise," Mrs. Roosevelt said in her speech, "but if it
brings a world advance it is a gain for each individual nation. There
will be those who doubt their ability to rise to these new heights
but the alternative is not possible to contemplate." [20]

Some, like Noel Baker, looked backward to the League. A
more numerous group wanted to transform the United Nations into
a world government even as the first session was demonstrating the
reluctance of nations to compromise or to yield any authority to a
higher international body.

I gather Mike Straight * must have talked as many people write to me.
They beg me to stand now for world government, and seem to ignore
the stark reality that Russia would be out at once and our Congress
would never have let us go in. We couldn't get any one of the big three
powers to give up their veto. We will have to crawl together, running
will be out of the question until all of us have gained far more confidence in each other than we now have. I can't even get Byrnes to agree
that we might do better if he talked at one time to Bevin, [Andrei] Gromyko, [Georges] Bidault, and [V. K. Wellington] Koo on the Secretary

---

* Michael Straight was the son of Mrs. Leonard Elmhirst and one of the heirs
to the Whitney fortune. Golden-haired and idealistic, a brilliant writer and orator,
he was at this time publisher of the *New Republic* and a leader in the American
Veterans Committee.

General. There are too many old League people here and far too many elderly statesmen. They are accustomed to diplomatic ways, secrecy appeals to them, and this will only succeed if everyone says what they really think. Perhaps the biggest job to be done is to make the people at home feel this is their machinery which they may use to build peace, but they will have to keep it oiled and make it run. Oratory ended Saturday and tomorrow committee work begins. I'm curious to see how that works. I've certainly been briefed on all the agenda that may come up tomorrow.[21]

There were more moderate proposals for changes in the structure of the United Nations that had been agreed to at San Francisco and in the Preparatory Commission. "At 6:30 Lady Pethick-Lawrence (nice old lady) and Mrs. Gram Swing (very high-powered) came to persuade me to back a woman's group in UNO with special privileges and I was noncommittal as I don't think it should be done but I must, of course, look into it." Mrs. Roosevelt was dubious about the particular suggestion of these two women who came to her representing the World Women's Party for Equal Rights, but she was acutely conscious of the underrepresentation of women at the Assembly. Women delegates and advisers—they numbered eighteen in all from eleven countries—met at her office under her chairmanship to discuss how women might achieve a larger role in UN affairs. They issued a discreetly worded manifesto that called

on the Governments of the world to encourage women everywhere to take a more conscious part in national and international affairs, and on women to come forward and share in the work of peace and reconstruction as they did in the war and resistance.[22]

Lady Pethick-Lawrence and Mrs. Swing had pushed ahead in the meantime with their demand that the United Nations establish a permanent commission on the status of women to implement equal rights. Mrs. Roosevelt would serve as the first U.S. representative on this commission, but she never manifested much enthusiasm for this aspect of UN activity. She preferred to do her politics with the men. "I am sorry that Governments in all parts of the world have not seen fit to send more women as delegates, alternates or advisers to the Assembly," she wrote in her column. "I think it is in these positions that the women of every nation should work to see that equality exists." She did not want women represented as a special group. She wanted them working together with the men on an equal basis to frame the policies of the organization.[23]

The more she saw how the men in the U.S. delegation worked, the more certain she was that women could do as well, if not better. "He is able," she wrote of one of her male colleagues, "but so many foibles! All these important men have them, however. I'm so glad I never *feel* important, it does complicate life!" But that was Eleanor Roosevelt—not women as a breed. More distressing to her was the reluctance, at times, of the men to move boldly. Four of the members of the delegation—Vandenberg, Connally, Bloom, and Eaton—were members of Congress. Byrnes, although secretary of state, was also a product of the Senate, as was Townsend.

I am interested in the way all the legislators react. I think not having strong convictions they doubt their ability to defend a position which they may take, so they can not decide on any position and go on arguing pros and cons endlessly.

She was harsh in her judgment of Byrnes.

I watch our delegation with grave concern. Secretary Byrnes seems to me to be afraid to decide on what he thinks is right and stand on it. I am going to try to tell him tactfully that everyone has to get the things they need from us and that is our ace in the hole. We could lead but we don't. We shift to conciliate and trail either Great Britain or Russia and at times I am sure a feeling that we had convictions and would fight for them would be reassuring to them. Secretary Byrnes is afraid of his own delegation. He has held very few meetings and now we begin to need them and yet we have to ask to see him in separate groups. It isn't that he is leaving me out, for the others complain to me.

Her British friends urged on her the necessity of cooperation between the United States and Britain against Russia.

I'm not so concerned that Great Britain and ourselves must line up to keep the Russians in hand. I think we must be fair and stand for what we believe is right and let them, either or both, side with us. We have had that leadership and we must recapture it.[24]

A key issue at this organizational Assembly—and it was a troublesome one—was the election of a secretary-general. Lie of Norway was a candidate, but during the session some members of the U.S. delegation who had favored his election as president of the Assembly had cooled toward him considerably. They were fearful that Norway, sharing a border with Russia, might fall under its domination and influence Lie's policies as secretary-general. Eleanor thought they were wrong both about Norway's vulnerability to Soviet pressure and Lie's staunchness. The United States' first choice for the post was Lester B. Pearson of Canada, but when he proved unacceptable to the Russians, who countered with the candidacy of the foreign minister of Yugoslavia, the United States switched to Lie and persuaded the British to do so as well.

It was well done I think and we took the lead and though our first choice was Pearson of Canada, when we found the Russians wouldn't consent, but would compromise, we proposed Lie. The papers should not be pessimistic, progress is being made here. Vandenberg and Dulles are largely responsible for pessimism, I think. These representatives of ours don't build friendship for us. They have no confidence, so they are rude and arrogant and create suspicion. Honesty with friendliness goes down, but they haven't the technique. Jimmy Byrnes' overcordiality isn't right either. Why can't we be natural and feel right inside and just let it come out? [25]

She was having her own difficulties with the Russians. Contrary to the expectations of the men when they assigned her to Committee III, the hottest East-West issue of the Assembly boiled up in it. "A new type of political refugee is appearing," she noted in her diary after studying a memo on the refugee question, "people who have been against the present governments and if they stay at home or go home will probably be killed." There were approximately one million such refugees in displaced-person camps, most of them from the East. The Communist position was simple, brutally so. They could not see why the refugee question should be a matter of international concern. There were only two categories of refugees in their view: those who wanted to be repatriated and those who did not because they are "quislings, traitors, war criminals or collaborators," and the international community should waste neither sympathy nor resources on this latter group.

She wanted to avoid a collision with the Communists, but drafting a resolution acceptable to them proved impossible:

I have spent 9 hrs. of meetings these last two days to try to frame a resolution on refugees to which the Russians & ourselves can agree. The Dutch, British & ourselves reach agreement fairly quickly but the Jugo-Slavs & Russians start from different backgrounds. Everything must be in terms to cover their point of view, their needs, no one else's situation is ever considered! I've learned so much, I'm not sure what they are learning! [26]

A week later she was still at it.

Committee meeting was one long wrangle. Finally at one I asked for a vote. The Russians who always play for delay asked for a subcommittee to try to get a resolution we could agree upon. It is hopeless as there are fundamental disagreements, but Peter Fraser (New Zealand, Chairman of the Third Committee) is fair to the utmost. He asked if I would withdraw my motion and then appointed a committee. I was a half hour late for lunch with the Anthony Edens in the House of Commons. At 2:30 I opened a doll show. At 3:10 we sat down in the sub-committee at Church House and we got up at 6 having agreed on 25 lines! [27]

Debate was endless "and so many words," but finally a vote was reached.

We defeated the Russians on the three points we disagreed on, they were all fundamental, and I'm afraid while I was brief I was clear in my opposition. Wise Mr. Sandifer of the State Department seemed pleased but whispered "The Russians won't like that." [28]

The Communist amendments would have curbed "propaganda" in the refugee camps and placed the latter under the administrative supervision of officials from the refugees' countries of origin. The item came up again in plenary when Andrei Vishinsky, the head of the Russian delegation, challenged the committee's recommendations and announced he would make a speech on the subject.

The British had their representative ready to speak but I saw all the heads in our delegation come together because nobody was ready to speak except the woman in Committee 3 whom they had put there, thinking she would be harmless. Finally Mr. Dulles asked me to say a few words and I agreed to do so.[29]

Behind Mr. Dulles's request was a great change in attitude toward Mrs. Roosevelt. New Dealer Benjamin V. Cohen, who was in London as counselor to the State Department, had lunched with Dulles and Vandenberg. While talking with him they also talked to each other, exchanging expressions of amazement at Mrs. Roosevelt's good judgment. They really had not known her before, writing her off as an emotional, rattle-brained woman. "One of the most solid members of the delegation" they now agreed, as Ben Cohen chuckled to himself.[30]

The exchange between Mrs. Roosevelt and Vishinsky, the Soviet Union's wiliest and most formidable debater, provided a moment of high drama. He was the grand inquisitor, the relentless Stalinist prosecutor in the Moscow purge trials, arguing with the twentieth-century embodiment of humanitarianism before a world jury. If democracy had saints, Adlai Stevenson would later say, Eleanor Roosevelt would be among the first canonized. Vishinsky was not happy, Mrs. Roosevelt's aides thought, to find himself ranged against a woman revered for her goodness, who, moreover, bore a name still highly respected in the Soviet Union. His argument was low-keyed. Mankind had paid too much already for tolerance and the right of asylum, he contended. There were limits to liberty. He refused to accept a tolerance "which is known in history by the name of Munich."

She talked over the points she intended to make with Sandifer, but she spoke extemporaneously—"the most important speech ever given by an American delegate without a prepared text," Sandifer later said.[31]

Where Vishinsky sought to exploit the emotional symbolism of Munich, she countered with an equally potent symbol—Spain. Forced repatriation from the refugee camps, Mrs. Roosevelt began, might mean forcing Spanish Republican refugees to return to Spain, "a fascist country." Refugee camps should not be used for political activity, she agreed, but she upheld the right of the refugees to hear good or bad against any UN member. "Are we so weak in the UN that we are going to forbid human beings the right to hear what their friends believe? It is their right to say it and their right to hear it and make their own decision. To say otherwise," she added, would be like saying "I am always right," but "I am not sure my Government or nation will always be right, and we should aim at being so right that the majority will be with us and we can stand having among us those who do not agree."

She recognized that some European countries torn by wars that were both civil and international might take a different view of human rights and human freedom than the United States which, since the Civil War, had no political or religious refugees fleeing its borders, but it was the task of the United Nations "to frame things which will be broader in outlook, which will consider first the rights of man, which will consider what makes man more free: not governments but man!" [32]

The Soviet amendments were again voted down, and afterward she wrote home:

Yesterday we fought the whole battle over again in the Assembly on refugees which we had fought in Committee & we won again hands down. This time Mr. Vishinsky & I fought it out, evidently they, the Russians, don't let any but delegates speak in the Assembly! The Russians are tenacious fighters but when we finally finished voting at 1 a.m. last night I shook hands & said I admired their fighting qualities & I hoped some day on that kind of question we would be on the same side & they were cordiality itself! Also you will be amused that when Mr. Dulles said good-bye to me this morning he said, "I feel I must tell you that when you were appointed I thought it terrible & now I think your work here has been fine!" So—against odds, the women inch forward, but I'm rather old to be carrying on this fight! [33]

III. A Magna Charta for Mankind

On a Monday morning late in April, 1946, a tall woman in black, black stockings, a black gauzy scarf around her neck, emerged from the last stop of the Bronx subway and with swift stride began to cross the Hunter College campus (Hunter has since been renamed the Herbert H. Lehman College). Behind her, an impeccably dressed gentleman in a dark suit tried to catch up with her without breaking into a run. This was James P. Hendrick, Wall Street lawyer during the thirties, War Department aide during the war, and now assistant to the chief of the International Affairs Division of the State Department. Both were on their way to the first meeting of the "nuclear" United Nations commission on human rights.[1]

In Mrs. Roosevelt's clash with Vishinsky over forced repatriation, she had cited the guarantees written into the UN Charter of fundamental human rights. The trampling upon those rights by Nazism and fascism, especially Hitler's persecution of the Jews, was considered by the drafters of the Charter as among the underlying causes of the catastrophe, and a major respect in which the Charter was an advance over the League Covenant was its provision for the establishment of a commission "for the promotion of human rights." It had been the American hope to annex to the Charter a Declaration of Rights, and Durward Sandifer had been assigned to draft such a document. But there was no time before San Francisco to obtain agreement on a Declaration, so its drafting was assigned to the human rights commission as its first order of business.[2]

No delegate in London had more eminently personified the cause of respect for human dignity than Eleanor Roosevelt, and it was not surprising that the Economic and Social Council asked her to serve on the "nuclear" human rights commission whose job it would be to prepare a plan of work and the permanent setup of the Commission. The choice was as widely acclaimed as her appointment as delegate to the London Assembly. Senator Vandenberg, who immediately after FDR's death, had been alarmed by reports that Mrs. Roosevelt might be added to the U.S. delegation to the San Francisco conference, was now enlivening Washington dinner tables with his paeans of praise for Mrs. Roosevelt. "I want to say that I take back everything I ever said about her, and believe me it's been plenty." [3]

"I have cabled Mr. Lie that I would accept," Mrs. Roosevelt informed Secretary Byrnes. "The cable stated that we would meet here in New York City and the meeting would last three weeks and my compensation would be $15 a day and travelling expenses." Would the State Department provide her with an adviser and with secretarial assistance? [4]

Finally catching up with Mrs. Roosevelt, Hendrick introduced himself as her adviser. "I was pretty scared. I didn't know how she'd take to me personally. As an expert picked by the Economic and Social Council she was not under U.S. instruction—and my job was to see to it that she took the State Department line." She quickly put him at his ease. "She was just as kind and hospitable as she could be, welcomed me, and said that what she needed was advice and I was her adviser from then on in human rights meetings." They got along very well. She liked Hendrick, who was a quiet-spoken man of patrician background with a gentle sense of humor. "I don't think there was any time when we had a serious disagreement over what the policy should be," Hendrick asserted.[5]

The meeting of the "nuclear" commission, as it was called, took place in makeshift quarters in the Hunter College library. The furnishings were of hewn oak, and the delegates sat around tables which had been arranged in the shape of a hollow square in the middle of which sat the interpreters and secretaries.

Henri Laugier, assistant secretary-general for social affairs, opened the meeting and Mrs. Roosevelt was promptly elected

chairman by acclamation. She accepted the post with obvious pleasure. "Although my knowledge of parliamentary law is limited, I
shall do my best." Fluent in both French and English, she kept the
proceedings moving, on occasion even aiding the interpreters, some
of whom at that time were not quite as accomplished as they were
later to become. Prof. René Cassin, the French representative, a
white-bearded jurist, voluble and swift in technical discussion,
spoke once for twenty minutes without a halt and then with a
courtly gesture to the interpreter said "traduction, s'il vous plaît."
The young woman began, stammered, flushed red, and ran from
the room. When it became clear she was "gone for good," Mrs. Roosevelt, hoping no one would say no, asked, "Did everyone understand what M. Cassin said?" When several said they had understood nothing, she undertook the translation. "I can't give M.
Cassin's speech verbatim, but I can render the essential meaning."
She gave the commission a competent summary.[6]

She was a vigorous, businesslike, although always gracious,
chairman. She was four minutes late the second day. "I got mixed
up on the subway again," she explained to her colleagues, "but it
won't happen again." The second week a case of the shingles, which
explained why she had been wearing a gauze scarf, "got a little the
better of me," so she turned over the chairmanship to Professor
Cassin. "But by Wednesday, I was able to start out again at 9:30,
stay at Hunter College all day, and even keep my speaking engagement for the evening." By the end of the three weeks the group had
gotten through its agenda, which included proposals to the Economic and Social Council on the setting up the permanent eighteen-nation Commission on Human Rights and on the drafting and
implementation of an international bill of rights. At the very end of
its deliberations, the Soviet delegate, a young man from the embassy, was replaced by the permanent representative on the commission, Alexander Borisov, who had just arrived. He asked Mrs.
Roosevelt to fill him in and she carefully went over the points that
had been accepted, with the concurrence of the Soviet delegate,
and asked the interpreter to translate. He did, but Mr. Borisov said
he did not understand and asked her to go over the points again.

She did so patiently and carefully. Again he claimed he did not understand. She made a third try but still without success, and it finally became clear to her that Mr. Borisov did not want to understand because not only did he refuse to join in the recommendations, but he wanted changed those records showing how his predecessor had voted on those recommendations. This, as chairman, she refused to do. She was "quite annoyed" with Borisov's performance, she confessed a few months later.

No amount of argument ever changes what your Russian delegate says or how he votes. It is the most exasperating thing in the world, but I have made up my mind that I am going through all the arguments just as though I didn't know at the time it would have no effect. If I have patience enough, in a year from now perhaps the Russians may come with a different attitude.[7]

Borisov's abstention was a portent of things to come, but did not affect the commission's proposals. "I think we have done a helpful piece of work," she summed up. "The real work, of course, remains to be done in the next series of meetings, when the actual writing of an international bill of rights will have to be undertaken." [8]

President Truman had said he wanted her to continue with the delegation when the General Assembly reconvened in New York City in October. She had a busy summer ahead. The estate was still unsettled. Tommy was not well. George Bye, her literary agent, was pressing her to go to work on her autobiography for the White House years. She worried about her children, all of whom faced problems of adjustment and settling down. She had financial problems. Her total income, including $30,000 from her husband's estate, would come to $80,000 annually, she estimated, of which taxes would take $54,000. She needed $30,000 a year for living expenses, charities, pensions. She must not incur additional expenses, she told herself, and try somehow to bring her budget into balance.[9]

She had kept her summer calendar free in order to work on the autobiography, but by Labor Day had managed to get drafts of only two chapters written. It bored her to write about herself, she told friends. Her memory no longer was any good, she insisted. But basically what held her back was a fear she might not be able to do a good job. Many of FDR's associates, meanwhile, were coming to her with their drafts of books and articles, asking for her help and imprimatur. Henry Morgenthau, Jr., wrote into his *Colliers* contract that not one word should be printed without her approval. He did so out of loyalty to the president and Mrs. Roosevelt, but she did not wish to be saddled with such responsibility. And all the time she claimed she could not do a book, she was regaling guests and family with stories and evaluations of the White House years that seemed to them clearly to have the makings of a book. Labor Day week end she decided that it might be fun after all to go ahead. She had read Frances Perkins's third installment of *The Roosevelt I Knew* and felt it gave an inaccurate account of Franklin's third-term decision and failed to do justice to the president's background in economics. She began to see she had something to contribute toward history's appraisal of her husband. She would get to work on it, she promised her household.[10]

In August, 1946, she had an automobile accident while driving down from Hyde Park. It was a sign that even she was vulnerable to the ravages of age.

. . . I must have become drowsier than I realized and, before I knew it, I had come head on with another car in a collision and then sideswiped a second one. I was terrified to think that someone else might have been hurt.

There were some injuries but none serious. She had never had a motor accident before, she wrote in the column, which she insisted on filing, despite her shock and bruises. The sun, "together with the fact that I had no one sitting by to talk to me," had combined to make her sleepy. "My eyes are black and blue. In fact, I am black and blue pretty much all over." Her two front teeth had broken off about halfway. "Now I shall have two lovely porcelain ones, which will look far better than the rather protruding large teeth which most of the Roosevelts have." [11] She had to cancel several meetings and engagements, but by the end of October, when the General Assembly reconvened, she was ready again for the diplomatic fray.

Daily her tall, black-garbed figure could be seen at Lake Success and Flushing Meadow, slipping in and out of committee rooms, toting a worn briefcase, a fur scarf dangling over her arm, "the only delegate who is familiar with all the background material of her committees," said a colleague. At lunch time she queued up in the large, noisy cafeteria, passing up the privacy and exclusiveness of the delegates' dining room, talking animatedly with her State Department advisers, who, in addition to Sandifer and Hendrick, included Marjorie M. Whiteman, a willing, always cheerful State Department adviser on international law.[12]

Again, as the U.S. representative on Social, Humanitarian and Cultural Committee of the General Assembly, she crossed swords with Vishinsky. Again, the issue was forced repatriation of refugees. There were still one million displaced persons in Europe, and Committee III debated the charter of an international refugee organization whose function it would be either to help repatriate, if that was what the refugees wished, or to resettle them. "Mr. Vishinsky's view is that the problem is very simple and can be solved by repatriating all the displaced persons," she said beginning her rebuttal. "This thesis ignores the facts of political changes in the countries of origin which have created fears in the minds of the million persons who remain, of such a nature that they choose the miserable life in camps in preference to the risks of repatriation." Mr. Vishinsky wanted to know who these people were who, for political reasons, felt unable to return to their country.

I visited two camps near Frankfurt [she replied], where the majority of people had come from Estonia, Latvia, Lithuania. They did not want to return because their country no longer belonged to them. They did not appear to me to be fascists and Mr. Vishinsky's assumption that all people who do not wish to return to the country of their origin because those countries are now under what is called "a democratic form of government" does not seem to allow for certain differences in the understanding of the word democracy. As he uses it, it would seem that democracy is synonymous with Soviet. . . . Under that formula I am not very sure that he would accept some of the other nations in the world who consider themselves democracies and who are as willing to die for their beliefs as are the people of the Soviet Union.

The delegates from the non-Communist countries forgot diplomatic decorum to applaud her. The "Gibson girl" had again worsted the commissar, or so it seemed to one observer.[13]

In January, 1947, the eighteen-nation Human Rights Commission held its first plenary session. Mrs. Roosevelt was the U.S. representative, appointed by President Truman to a four-year term. Again she was chosen chairman by acclamation. The other officers were a vice-chairman, Dr. Peng-Chun Chang, a scholarly Chinese diplomat, and the Commission's *rapporteur*, Dr. Charles H. Malik of Lebanon, a Christian humanist with an ever-ready reference to Thomas Aquinas.

The initial debate was somewhat philosophical. There was a time, Dr. Chang challenged his European colleagues, when Chinese philosophic writings were well known to all the thinkers of Europe, but in the nineteenth century, Europeans became parochial and self-centered. Now, after the global war mankind must again think on a global scale. The Declaration should incorporate the ideas of Confucius as well as those of Thomas Aquinas. Later, when the professors tended to wander into the byways of abstraction and philosophic discourse, Mrs. Roosevelt would promptly call them back to the business that had to be accomplished, but at those first sessions, as she heard her learned colleagues argue the source and validation of human rights, she looked across at the visitor's section, filled with high-school students, and wished she were "young again with years ahead of me to acquire knowledge!" [14]

A more difficult task of intellectual reconciliation soon revealed itself in the remarks of the Yugoslav representative, who said that the emphasis in many of the bills of human rights that had been assembled by the Secretariat reflected the social and political ideals of the middle classes and were, therefore, obsolete. New trends in the world made it impossible to consider individuals except collectively. In the modern world the social principle should have priority. Dr. Malik challenged the collectivist thesis with his own set of dicta: the "human person" is "prior" to any group to which he may belong whether it be class, race, or nation; his "mind and conscience" were the "most sacred and inviolable things about him";

the group "can be wrong, just as the human person can be; in any case it is only the human person who is competent to judge." That touched off a philosophic Donnybrook Fair, with Russian Communist, British Socialist, and American democrat all entering the debate. "We're living as individuals in a community and society," protested the Soviet delegate, "and we're working for the community and society and the community and society are providing the materials for existence." The British spokesman, a trade-unionist, representing a Labor government, tended to agree:

There is no such thing as complete personal freedom. . . . If freedom or complete detachment from society were possible it would provide a very poor life indeed. We must all pay the price for advantages resulting from calling upon the state to safeguard our liberties both in the sense of personal freedom and also in the direction of the minimum degree of economic security.

Mrs. Roosevelt sided with Dr. Malik. She considered his statement "of particular importance. . . . It is not that you set the individual apart from society but that you recognize in any society that the individual must have rights that are guarded." Malik got in the last word: "I'm not arbitrarily setting the state against the individual. But which, I ask, is for which? I say the state is for the individual." [15]

The debate had revealed two schools of thought within the Commission. "Our policy was to get a declaration which was a carbon copy of the American Declaration of Independence and Bill of Rights," said Hendrick. The Soviet stress was on the need to include all sorts of economic and social rights, "and the less said about freedom of speech, the right to a fair trial, etc., the better." The State Department was lukewarm toward the inclusion of the newer rights. Mrs. Roosevelt, however, saw no reason why such rights should not be incorporated into the draft, and she succeeded in pulling the department along with her.[16]

Policy was formulated by an interdepartmental committee. But, in effect, Mrs. Roosevelt set the policy. She was a presidential appointee, a woman of world stature; and the State Department was eager to do what she wanted. Hendrick kept her advised on what was going on in the policy-committee meetings, "I tried to be watchful that nothing went into the instructions that she would not go for." [17]

Hendrick sat behind her during the meetings of the Commission. He started in by trying to whisper into her good ear ° his suggestions on the best way to handle matters that came up in the Commission, but since that proved unsatisfactory, he took to writing her notes—the speeches in the Commission tended to be lengthy and there was plenty of time to do so. His notes, in addition to suggestions for replies, included advice on how to vote, whom to appoint, resolutions to be submitted:

On the Belgian resolution we have no position, so use your discretion. See no objection to it.

On Philippine resolution, assume you will vote yes.

If there is a sub-committee of three, suggest—Malik, Dukes [Lord Dukeston of Britain], Mora [José A. Mora of Uruguay].[18]

The Commission set up a drafting committee of three to prepare a text for their next session. Mrs. Roosevelt felt "ill-equipped" compared with such "learned gentlemen" as Dr. Chang, Dr. Malik, and Dr. John Humphrey, the United Nations' Human Rights director, but perhaps she could help her colleagues put their "high thoughts" into words that the average person can understand. "I used to tell my husband that, if he could make *me* understand something, it would be clear to all the other people in the country—and perhaps that will be my real value on this drafting commission!" [19]

The drafting committee met in Mrs. Roosevelt's Washington Square apartment. While she poured tea, Chang and Malik argued philosophy. The group finally agreed that if a draft was to be prepared by June the responsibility for doing so would have to be taken by the director of the Human Rights Division, Dr. Humphrey. He should first spend a year in China studying Confucianism, Chang grinningly admonished Humphrey, which was his way of reminding the UN official that something more than Western rights would have to go into the Declaration.

"I get more and more the sensation of something happen-

° Mrs. Roosevelt was deaf in her right ear, and, after a plane descent, even her left ear was none too good, as she explained in a 1944 column in reply to a woman's complaint that she had ignored the latter's question.

ing in the world which has a chance to override all obstacles," Hendrick wrote her after the session, "and more and more that this 'something' could never have come into being without you." [20]

In June, an enlarged drafting committee went to work on the draft prepared by Humphrey.

They should write a bill, Mrs. Roosevelt told the drafting group, that stood some chance of acceptance by all fifty-five governments. As she said this, some of her colleagues wondered how explicit a statement of the state's responsibility for full employment the United States was prepared to accept. At the February session Mrs. Roosevelt had not been sure, but in the intervening months she had overcome resistance within the U.S. government and now said the United States was prepared to support not a "guarantee" of full employment, but an undertaking to "promote" it.

The Soviet representative thought this a pretty feeble affirmation of the right to work. "It would be incorrect for him to ask the U.S. representative to undertake to eliminate unemployment in the United States," he said scornfully. "The economic system in the United States made that impossible. . . . He could, however, ask that something concrete should be done. Instead of making a general statement about the right to work, the relevant article should list measures to be taken to ensure that right." "The right to work in the Soviet Union," Mrs. Roosevelt replied,

means the assignment of workers to do whatever task is given to them by the government without an opportunity for the people to participate in the decision that the government should do this. A society in which everyone works is not necessarily a free society and may indeed be a slave society; on the other hand, a society in which there is widespread economic insecurity can turn freedom into a barren and vapid right for millions of people.[21]

At her urging, the drafting committee did not spend too much time on the precise wording of the articles. A touchier issue had arisen and was dividing the committee—the binding character of the rights that were to be listed in the Declaration. The small nations in particular wanted something more than a moral manifesto. They wanted states to assume a treaty obligation to grant, protect, and enforce the rights enumerated in the Declaration. Neither the United States nor Russia favored this, but the United States, chiefly as a result of Mrs. Roosevelt's pressure, deferred to the views of the majority. There would be two documents, the committee decided, one a relatively brief declaration of principles that would provide "a common standard of achievement," the other a precise convention that would constitute a treaty binding on the states that ratified it and become a part of their own law. It was largely owing to Mrs. Roosevelt, wrote Marjorie Whiteman, that the Commission gave priority to the Declaration. "In her view the world was waiting, as she said, 'for the Commission on Human Rights to do something' and that to start by the drafting of a treaty with its technical language and then to await its being brought into force by ratification, would halt progress in the field of human rights." René Cassin was asked to rework the Humphrey draft with a view to determining which rights should go into a declaration and which into a convention, and by June 25, with Mrs. Roosevelt insistently pressing her colleagues on, the committee had gone over the text presented to them by Professor Cassin and had authorized the Secretariat to forward the draft to member governments for their comments.[22]

The moment had arrived when the U.S. government had to define its attitude toward the two documents that were in process, the Declaration and the Convention. She explained the situation to Sen. Warren R. Austin, the amiable Vermont Yankee who headed the U.S. mission at the United Nations. The United States had wanted to move slowly on the Convention, but a strong majority on the drafting committee demanded that a convention be written at the same time as a declaration and the United States yielded. What Mrs. Roosevelt wanted to know from Senator Austin, who before his appointment to the UN post had been part of the Senate leadership, was whether a convention would be acceptable to the Senate at this time. He could not say, Austin replied.

We should be perfectly willing to enter into a Convention as well as a Declaration, but we must be reasonably certain that the country will back us up. We should not try for too much. It would be most unfortunate if we were to take a lead in forcing a Convention through the General Assembly and then be turned down by the Senate.[23]

Public opinion in the United States and the mood in Congress were turning hostile toward additional UN commitments. In part, this was a response to the fact that the end of the war, instead of ushering in an era of peace, order, and friendliness, had brought almost chaotic conditions as well as a perilous confrontation with the Soviet Union. In part, it reflected domestic developments—the postwar swing to the right that culminated in McCarthyism and McCarranism. In part, it was a reaction to Soviet behavior in the United Nations. The readiness of the Soviet Union to exploit the platform and high principles of the United Nations in order to abuse the West and to boycott and paralyze the organs of the United Nations when those principles were invoked against Russia's mundane interests turned congressional sentiment against a legally binding convention, which, it was said, the Russians would disregard, even as they did their own constitution.

Another factor, perhaps the decisive one, in hardening congressional opposition to the Convention was the rising tension over civil rights inside the United States and the fears of the southern whites that the United Nations might help American Negroes in their struggle against discrimination. Black Americans had already appealed to the United Nations Human Rights division for redress of their grievances against American society. An NAACP petition to this effect was submitted to the United Nations in 1947. It was a carefully researched brief prepared under the direction of Dr. W. E. B. Du Bois with the assistance of distinguished Negro and white attorneys and scholars.

The petition was to be presented to Henri Laugier and Dr. John Humphrey, Walter White notified Mrs. Roosevelt. "Would it be possible for you to be present as demonstration of deep concern of responsible American opinion with the problem which is international as well as national?" She wrote White:

As an individual I should like to be present, but as a member of the delegation I feel that until this subject comes before us in the proper way, in a report of the Human Rights Commission or otherwise, I should not seem to be lining myself up in any particular way on any subject.

It isn't as though everyone did not know where I stand. It is just a matter of proper procedure.[24]

On her way to the first General Assembly she had exclaimed on how wonderful it was to feel free and to be able to say just what she wanted. But she had learned after a year's service with the delegation, that in a way she had less freedom than when Franklin was president:

I am on an entirely different basis. Now I am obliged to carry out the policy of the Government. When my husband was President, although I was the White House hostess, I was, after all, a private citizen, and for that reason I was freer than I am now. . . .[25]

The Soviet double standard and the hostility of the southern bloc in the Senate to any international undertaking that might bolster the Negro drive made the State Department warier than ever of the Convention. Hendrick went up to consult Dr. Humphrey, director of the United Nations Human Rights division, on whether in realistic terms a declaration might not be as effective as a convention in the protection of human rights. Although Dr. Humphrey agreed with the United States that the Declaration should be the starting point in the UN approach to human rights, he did not believe, Hendrick advised Mrs. Roosevelt, it would have legally binding force.[26]

Although the department policy group had prepared a U.S. version of what should go into a convention, there was no agreement, as Mrs. Roosevelt prepared in November, 1947, to leave for Geneva, on whether this document should even be circulated to the other members of the Commission as a working paper and basis for discussion. Robert A. Lovett, the hardboiled international banker, conservative in outlook, who was undersecretary of state, was a little skeptical of Mrs. Roosevelt and even more so of the Convention. When Hendrick conferred with him just before taking off for the December session of the Human Rights Commission in Geneva, Lovett expressed, as Hendrick informed Mrs. Roosevelt, "a very real objection to the implication which he got from the Declaration that all the rights therein contained were immediately enforceable." On Lovett's insistence, Hendrick, subject to Mrs. Roosevelt's concurrence, agreed to soften the Preamble so that it called upon members to "promote" rather than to "enforce" the rights enumerated in the draft Declaration. That was acceptable to Mrs. Roosevelt provided the United States supported a covenant,° but she knew that this would mean ultimately overcoming Lovett's doubts on the subject. He had expressed those doubts to Hendrick after he had finished on the subject of the Declaration. "We don't want to have a document which will be happily adhered to by a number of countries which have absolutely no intention of living up to certain of the provisions, and where the violations will be so widespread the UN will be completely powerless to do anything about the matter." [27]

She arrived in Geneva, after a plane trip that, because of "freakish" weather, took four days, to find the Russians on the offensive. For the first time, Moscow had assigned someone to the Commission who was an experienced diplomat, a legal scholar, and a debater. He was Alexander E. Bogomolov, Russia's ambassador in Paris. In the Subcommission on Minorities and Discrimination, where Jonathan Daniels served as the U.S. expert, the Soviet delegate wanted immediate investigation of the conditions of Negroes

---

° Covenant and Convention were used interchangeably for the legally binding instrument, and in time Covenant became the preferred term.

in the United States on the basis of the petition of the NAACP. And in the Human Rights Commission itself Bogomolov demanded that priority be given to petitions relating to violations of human rights in the non-self-governing trust territories. "Listening to the Russian speakers," commented a *New York Times* reporter, "one gets the impression that they believe they have found the Achilles heel of the U.S. and Britain." Although Bogomolov gave the United States "a very hard time," the *Times* reporter felt that "the Russians seem to have met their match in Mrs. Roosevelt. The proceedings sometimes turn into a long vitriolic attack on the United States when she is not present. These attacks, however, generally degenerate into flurries in the face of her calm and undisturbed but often pointed replies." [28]

"Now, of course, I'm a woman and don't understand all these things," she would begin a reply and further baffle her Communist opponent with the acknowledgment that there was a good deal in his argument. Then, having smothered her antagonist in these placative preliminaries, Mrs. Roosevelt would quietly state America's readiness to have Soviet experts examine U.S. practices, if American observers could do the same in the Soviet Union; or she would acknowledge U.S. shortcomings, note U.S. efforts to do better, and finish her rebuttal by observing mildly that it took maturity in nations as well as individuals to admit mistakes and deficiencies. "Never have I seen naïveté and cunning so gracefully blended," a State Department advisor commented.[29]

At the outset of the Commission's session, she voted for a Soviet resolution to give priority to the Commission's consideration of the draft Declaration. But only the United States and the USSR favored such an ordering of the agenda. When this became clear the United States bowed to the will of the majority, which felt, she noted, "that the world is expecting a definite commitment which would force the governments to change their laws, if necessary, to conform to an international bill or covenant, and they wished that to be considered first, or at least simultaneously with a Declaration." [30]

A cable arrived from Washington authorizing the U.S. delegation to submit the U.S. draft Covenant as a basis for discussion, and Hendrick turned the document over to the Secretariat for distribution. At three in the morning his telephone rang in the Beau Rivage. Walter M. Kotschnig, his superior in Washington, was at the other end. "He bawled the hell out of me for having had the draft Covenant circulated, because in the meantime Lovett had instructed him to kill the Covenant. That was the way we got started with the Covenant at Geneva." [31]

Unexpectedly, a prodigious amount of time was spent on the first article of the Declaration. That article, modeled on the American Declaration of Independence, read, "All men are created equal." That would never do, protested Mrs. Hansa Mehta of India. "All men" might be interpreted to exclude women. In vain did Mrs. Roosevelt argue that the women of the United States had never felt they were cut out of the Declaration of Independence because it said "all men." The women felt strongly. It became a minor *cause célèbre* in the Commission on the Status of Women, which voted unanimously to ask the Commission on Human Rights to substitute "all people" for "all men." [32]

Mrs. Roosevelt did not resist. While she had not objected to being assigned to the Social, Humanitarian and Cultural Committee (III) in the beginning, she had come to resent the automatic assumption on the part of the men that women were not to be trusted with political issues.[33] Many of the women in the United Nations had reached the top in countries where women had very little recognition. They were afraid of the phrase "all men": "Oh, no," they protested, "if it says 'all men,' when we go home it will be all men." So it was finally changed to "all human beings," and subsequent articles began "Everyone" or "No one." Occasionally, in the body of an article a lonely "his" was allowed to remain because that seemed a little more elegant than saying "his and hers."

This same article also substituted the phrase "are born free and equal" for "are created," the latter formulation implying a Divine Creator and a divine spark in man, Mrs. Roosevelt said, which made it unacceptable to the Communist representatives. When you write an international document, she explained, you try not to let the words interfere with getting as much agreement as possible and as much acceptance as possible to obtain the ends you want. Now, we wanted as many nations as possible to accept the fact that men, for one reason or another, were born free and equal in dignity and rights, that they were endowed with reason and conscience, and should act toward one another in a spirit of brotherhood. The way to do that was to find words that everyone would accept, and so that is why it says "are born" instead of saying "are created." [34]

As chairman, she pushed her Commission relentlessly at Geneva. "I drive hard and when I get home I will be tired! The men on the Commission will be also!" she wrote. Her colleagues called her "a slave driver," the delegate of Panama at one point begging her not to forget the rights of the human beings who were members of the Commission. She was not unresponsive to the beauties and distractions of Geneva. "At last I have seen Mont Blanc!" she exclaimed as the clouds finally rolled away, but they had agreed to work overtime if they took Saturday afternoon off, she reminded them, and kept them in session until seven. Why didn't they shorten the length of their speeches, she suggested, if they objected to the length of the sessions. "No one can ever tell me that women like to talk longer than men!"

A week before Christmas the Declaration was approved by a vote of 13 to 4. Mrs. Roosevelt was not satisfied with the language. It was too professorial, too lawyerlike. "All my advisers are lawyers or I would be lost," she advised a friend, adding, "common sense is valuable now & then I find however!" The Commission approved her resolution asking the drafting committee to prepare a short text, "which will be readily understood by all peoples." On this resolution there was neither abstention nor dissent. [35]

The delegates said good-by. Bogomolov came up to her to report that his wife, who had assisted him as a translator, was practically dead "and I am very tired while you look fresh as a daisy." That compliment, coming from a country whose representatives were known for their willingness to outsit and outtalk the representatives of the "decadent" democracies, pleased her.

"I'd love to slide on these floors," Mrs. Roosevelt had confided to Jim Hendrick at the beginning of the session, when she felt their polished marble under her feet. "Now you can take your slide," Hendrick solemnly advised her as they walked away from the Palais des Nations chamber in which the Commission had been meeting. Whereupon Mrs. Roosevelt gave a little run and slid, ran again, and slid once more.

"I've been thinking about the meeting here," she wrote in a more serious vein to a sick friend that same day.

At first it seemed sad to me to go into that beautiful building built with love & hope by nations who thought they had found the way to peace & understanding. Now I think it gives me encouragement & I wish more meetings could be held here for when you see the present activity you realize that perhaps man's spirit, his striving, is indestructible. It is set back but it does not die & so there is a reason why each one of us should do our best in our own small corner. Do you think I'm too optimistic? [36]

Would the Commission, in the end, be able to produce a draft on which both the Soviet bloc and the United States could agree, she was asked at a final press conference before departing for the States:

I think this is quite possible. They like greater emphasis on the authority of the state, and when it comes to social and economic rights, they are most anxious to spell them out in detail. The rights and freedoms of the individual, and religious and spiritual questions, don't seem to them as important in a draft of this kind. But certainly a balance can be achieved. [37]

The revised drafts were forwarded to the member governments for their comments before a final session of the Commission on Human Rights, after which she hoped the documents would be ready for consideration by the 1948 General Assembly. The United States no longer had any problem with the Declaration since it would not require congressional approval.

But there was furious debate inside the administration over whether to go ahead with a covenant under which nations would assume a legal obligation to protect the rights enunciated. Officials on the working level in the field of human rights favored a covenant, but would Congress ratify such a treaty? Mrs. Roosevelt came down to Washington after the Geneva meeting to confer with the president and the State Department. Truman's Committee on Civil Rights had just submitted a hard-hitting report that listed ten recommendations to secure minority groups rights in the United States, and southern demagogues, in full cry against those recommendations, were threatening to bolt the Democratic party in 1948. Lovett doubted that the Senate would ratify a covenant that included strong stipulations against discrimination.

To win Lovett over, the Hendricks gave a dinner in Mrs. Roosevelt's honor while she was in Washington at which the Lovetts were guests, as were the Sandifers and the Kotschnigs. After dinner the ladies of the party went off to make small talk; but that was not what Mrs. Roosevelt was interested in, and she soon had the ladies rejoining the men. The discussion was about the Covenant and the prospects for Senate ratification. "We talked and talked and talked," said Hendrick. Finally Lovett sought to bring the evening to a close. "A most interesting conversation," he said to the guest of honor, "but I know you are such a busy person with so much to do, I don't want to keep you here any longer." Oh, Mrs. Roosevelt protested, she was quite prepared to stay and go on talking. But Lovett, although affecting to make a joke of it, was equally determined. "You know perfectly well you have to leave now. I appreciate your position perfectly." Mrs. Roosevelt knew then she had to say good night. But she still pressed him, writing afterward:

I do not know why I did not think of it the other night, but one of your best arguments to use when the discrimination clause has to be discussed with Congress, is that in this country the people who are the most open to Soviet propaganda are the Negroes because of discrimination. In the international picture this is something we have to consider, in our own world attitude and therefore in our domestic attitude.

It was "a sound suggestion," Lovett replied, and he was passing it on to Dean Rusk who was working on this matter. There were other consequences to the Hendrick dinner. Lovett advised Rusk that he thought the Declaration a horrible document, unacceptable to the United States. When Rusk discussed this with Hendrick, the latter said he thought Lovett's ire had less to do with the

Declaration than with the effort to sell him on the Covenant at a social dinner. Despite Lovett's hostility, Mrs. Roosevelt's authority was such that it became the department's policy to push on with the Covenants as well as the Declaration.[38]

Before the June, 1948, session of the Commission, she wrote the secretary of state, Gen. George C. Marshall, that she felt the United States should do its utmost to obtain the best possible drafts both of the Covenant and the Declaration. He agreed, but with a realistic *caveat*. "The Covenant as a binding legal document must conform fairly closely to the constitutions, laws and practices of all the countries which ratify it. Either this, or it will be a dead letter treaty." When the drafting committee reconvened in May, 1948, she was able to say, "My Government wants a Declaration and it wants a Covenant." [39] Four lawyers sat behind her at that session.

Today was the first day that I began to understand some of the legal points we are now dealing with & when I am not clear myself I cannot make it clear for others. I am not a lawyer & four have to sit behind to guide me & they all see different pitfalls in every phrase & I am sometimes in a complete daze!

The Russians were represented at the 1948 session of the drafting committee and the full commission by a new man, Prof. A. P. Pavlov. He had a large black beard and pink cheeks, and was "by far the most civilized" of the Soviet delegates to the Human Rights Commission as well as the most polemical. He was an authority in the field of Soviet jurisprudence, was Soviet ambassador to Belgium, and was nephew of the great Soviet psychologist of the same name. Instead of proceeding to perfect the Geneva documents, he announced in his introductory speech, the drafting committee should begin the debate anew of basic principles. Slightly appalled, Mrs. Roosevelt replied that "we shall gain very little by discussing general principles at this session." The committee should confine itself to specific drafts and avoid "theoretical conjecture." The committee supported her. One of the general principles Pavlov wanted to stress was that the Declaration must clearly define the citizens' duty toward the state. Indeed, it seemed to Mrs. Roosevelt, as she studied Pavlov's amendments to this effect, that the USSR, at bottom, was dubious about the whole enterprise of drafting a declaration because, in the end, the rights that were asserted therein were rights against the state and the duties that were proclaimed were, in the main, duties the state owed to the individual. To almost every article in the Declaration Pavlov wanted to add either one of two amendments. He wanted a phrase that, in effect, said that the state would see to it that the specified right was observed. Such an exaltation of the state did not sit well with Mrs. Roosevelt, who was reared in the individualistic traditions of the American Revolution and the Protestant ethic and who was sure that "certain rights can never be granted to the government, but must be kept in the hands of the people." [40]

The other amendment that Pavlov sought to add was the "little, rather tricky" clause, "corresponding to the laws of the State." Article XIII of the Declaration, for example, provided that "Everyone has the right to leave any country, including his own, and return to his country." To add the phrase "according to the laws of his state" would have nullified the article because Soviet laws did not permit free departure and return. In fact, Moscow at the time was outraging western opinion by its detention of Russian wives of foreign citizens, as Mrs. Roosevelt pointed out.

It was an effective thrust, blunted somewhat when Professor Pavlov at the opening session of the full Commission charged that the United States had delayed the arrival of the Byelorussian and Ukrainian delegates by holding up their visas and requiring them to fill out an elaborate questionnaire, both in contravention of the UN headquarters agreement. She sent General Marshall a private protest. "I regret the embarrassment caused you," he replied. The problem arose from a conflict between the UN Headquarters Site Agreement and the revised visa requirements mandated by Congress. "The Department will make every effort to prevent unnecessary delay in the granting of visas to authorized individuals coming to UN headquarters." Some good might result from the incident, the general added. "There is now some prospect of working out with the USSR a more liberal and reciprocal form of visa procedure." [41]

"Reciprocity" was becoming a key concept in U.S. response to Soviet attacks. The Russians, she wrote Walter White, wanted to accept for discussion only those petitions that were critical of the United States. She took the view that the Commission should accept all or none. When the Commission discussed the Declaration's draft article on the right to adequate housing and medical care, Pavlov, who always arrived at sessions with two bulging briefcases, delivered carefully researched speeches on American housing shortages and soaring medical costs. In reply, Mrs. Roosevelt invited the Soviet Union to send a group of experts to the United States to examine housing and medical standards, provided an American team was given the same opportunity in the Soviet Union. Pavlov did not accept the offer.[42]

She discomfited him on another occasion when he grandiloquently asserted that with the outbreak of the war Russia had been able to increase its medical facilities, including the supply of doctors and nurses, by 50 per cent. She cornered him after the meeting and innocently asked—in French—how it had been done.

"Oh, it is the system," said Professor Pavlov. "We just plan."

"I see. Then you must have known when the war was coming."

"No, we didn't know when the war was coming."

"Well, then did you take student doctors that had one year of training and suddenly graduate them overnight?"

"No, it takes five years to make a doctor."

"That's interesting—I still don't understand how you produced 50 per cent more doctors, nurses and hospital facilities overnight."

"I am sorry, I do not understand," he said, moving away.

And Mrs. Roosevelt, in reporting the conversation, added after a pause: "and his French is perfectly good, too." [43]

Although Pavlov was brilliantly polemical and propagandistic, much more so than any previous Soviet delegate, he was always careful to conclude his attacks on the U.S. approach with a conciliatory statement that despite the different views the two could come to some understanding. On June 18, late in the evening, the draft Declaration was finally adopted. No vote was cast against it, although the Soviet bloc abstained and Pavlov submitted a minority report calling the draft "weak and completely unacceptable." When the vote was announced the Panamanian delegate, expressing the sentiments of his colleagues, paid tribute to Mrs. Roosevelt, and the United Nations Department of Public Information, in its subsequent account of the writing of the Declaration, departed from its usual style of bland impersonality to declare that from the Commission's first meeting she had "guided and inspired the work of the U.N. in the field of human rights." [44]

The 1948 General Assembly met in Paris at the end of September. It was a moment of tense confrontation with the Communists, who were on the offensive throughout western Europe. Soviet Russia's blockade of Berlin was being abetted by Communist-instigated strikes, street demonstrations, and violence inside France and Italy. At the heart of the confrontation, in the view of the West, was the issue of human liberty. The Assembly would have before it the draft Declaration. The president and General Marshall thought Mrs. Roosevelt should give a major speech in Paris.

I saw both the Secy of State & the Pres. on a flying visit to Washington the other day. They are putting considerable responsibility on me in this session. Dulles has suggested that we point out that all our troubles are rooted in a disregard for the rights & freedoms of the individual & go after the U.S.S.R., not, thank heavens, claiming perfection but saying that under our system we are trying to achieve those rights & succeeding better than most. They want me to make an opening [address] to set this keynote outside the Assembly & I am trying to plan it now. I feel as you do, there cannot be a war but strength & not appeasement will prevent it.

She accepted René Cassin's invitation to come to the Sorbonne and talk on "The Struggle for the Rights of Man." She arrived at the Sorbonne accompanied by General and Mrs. Marshall. The amphitheater, which held 2,500, was packed and many hundreds were unable to gain admittance. The French minister of national defense presided, the French foreign minister was in her audience, and the French Broadcasting System broadcast the entire proceedings. The basic obstacle to peace, she said, sounding her central theme, was the different concept of human rights held by the Soviet Union. It was the battle of the French and American Revolutions all over again. "The issue of human liberty is as decisive now as it was then." Her excellent French and extreme graciousness of manner charmed her audience, as did her ad-libbed departures from her text. Her audience "was particularly delighted when she said she thought she had reached the limits of which human patience is capable when she brought up her family, but that since she had presided over the Commission on Human Rights she had realized that an even greater measure of patience could be exacted from an individual." So the foreign service officer who was assigned to cover the meeting reported to the State Department.

There is no doubt that the speech, far from being submerged by the more immediate and critical international political issues, benefitted from the current feeling of apprehension and nervousness in Paris. The words of the speaker seemed to evoke a response from the audience and to make everyone feel that the fundamental principles of our civilization were still uppermost in the mind of, and being defended by, the United Nations.[45]

The greatest test of patience was still ahead. The Declaration was on the agenda of the Committee III of the General Assembly. To Mrs. Roosevelt's dismay the Committee insisted on debating the Declaration "exactly as though it was all an entirely new idea and nobody had ever looked at it before." It devoted eighty-five meetings to the subject, "considerably more time than any organ of the General Assembly had spent on any other subject." Again the Soviet bloc delegates sought to delay and postpone, but they met a worthy antagonist in Dr. Malik, chairman of the Committee, who, commented Sandifer, was "the only person I ever knew who succeeded in holding a stopwatch on Pavlov."[46]

The debate was repetitive and tedious. Patiently, she sat through the usual Soviet bloc onslaughts "telling us what dogs we are," happy, she confessed, to escape the "wordy atmosphere" occasionally to do a little Christmas shopping, leaving Sandifer to sit in for her, until finally the Declaration was approved by Committee III and forwarded to the Assembly plenary. "I hope," she wrote Maude Gray, the last lap of my work on the Declaration of Human Rights will end to-morrow & that we get it through the General Assembly plenary session with the required ⅔ vote. The Arabs & Soviets may balk—the Arabs for religious reasons, the Soviets for political ones. We will have trouble at home for it can't be a U.S. document & get by with 58 nations & at home that is hard to understand. On the whole I think it is good as a declaration of rights to which all men may aspire & which we should try to achieve. It has no legal value but should carry moral weight.[47]

The Moslem defection did not materialize. Although the Saudi Arabian delegate abstained because he did not think the king of Saudi Arabia would agree that one could change one's religion, the minister of foreign affairs of Pakistan, Sir Mohammed Zafrullah Khan, considered it a misinterpretation of the Koran. "I think we are permitted to believe or disbelieve. He who will believe, shall believe; he who cannot believe, shall not believe. The only unforgiveable sin is to be a hypocrite."

At 3:00 A.M. on December 10 the Assembly adopted the Declaration and she could write "long job finished." The final vote was 48 countries in favor, none against, 2 absent, and 8 abstentions, mostly of Soviet bloc countries. The Assembly delegates, in recognition of Mrs. Roosevelt's leadership, accorded her the rare personal tribute of a standing ovation.

She glowed when General Marshall told the delegation that the 1948 session would go down in history as the "Human Rights Assembly." "I do not see," commented Charles Malik, who succeeded her as chairman of the Commission, "how without her presence we could have accomplished what we actually did accomplish." Helen Keller, after reading the Declaration in Braille, wrote her, "my soul stood erect, exultant, envisioning a new world where the light of justice for every individual will be unclouded." She was being proposed for the Nobel Peace Prize, Clark Eichelberger of the American Association for the United Nations informed her, but the French felt she and Cassin should share the award. Would she object? He could go ahead, she wrote back, but she did not see why she should be nominated at all. Dulles sent her a copy of a letter he had sent the American Bar Association defending the Declaration and her role in drafting it:

As regards Mrs. Roosevelt, she has worked loyally and effectively on this matter for two years and, while herself without legal training has had the assistance of competent draftsmen. It is to be borne in mind that the Universal Declaration of Human Rights is not, at this stage, primarily a legal document. It is, like the French Declaration of the Rights of Man, a major element in the great ideological struggle that is now going on in the world, and in this respect Mrs. Roosevelt has made a distinctive contribution in defense of American ideals.[48]

Some were cynical about the Declaration, stating there was "an inherent absurdity" in an "organization of governments, dedicating itself to protect human rights when, in all ages and climes, it is governments which have been their principal violators." But this was precisely the value of the agreement on the first intergovernmental bill of rights and fundamental freedoms. "Man, the individual human being, has emerged on the international scene which in the past was the jousting ground only of States." [49]

"The first step has been taken," Mrs. Roosevelt replied to Helen Keller. "We shall now go ahead with the work on the Covenants." Progress would be very slow on the Covenants. For a time after Mrs. Roosevelt had left the delegation in 1953, the United States declined to take any part in their drafting. In 1966 two Covenants, one on civil and political rights and the other on economic and social rights, were approved by the Assembly and opened for ratification, but as of this writing fewer than twenty countries have deposited such ratifications and neither of the Covenants has gone into effect.

The Declaration, meanwhile, demonstrated an influence far beyond expectations. It has proved to be "a living document," Dag Hammarskjöld observed on the tenth anniversary of its adoption. "It has entered the consciousness of the people of the world," Adlai E. Stevenson wrote in 1961, "has shaped their aspirations, and has influenced the consciences of nations." The European Convention on Human Rights was a spin-off effect of the Declaration, even going beyond it, since it established a commission to hear complaints and a court to adjust them. The Declaration has found its way into many constitutions and is increasingly cited in domestic court decisions. Its provisions often have been invoked in General Assembly resolutions and by Soviet dissenter and black resister. Pope John XXIII, in his encyclical *Pacem in Terris,* called the Declaration "an act of the highest importance," an "important step on the path towards the juridical-political organization of the world community."

Most international lawyers now think that, whatever the intentions of its authors may have been, the Universal Declaration of Human Rights is now binding on states as part of the customary law of nations.[50]

The decision of Mrs. Roosevelt and her advisers to give priority to the Declaration was vindicated. The first United Nations Human Rights prize was awarded to her posthumously.*

But more than the prize, she would have enjoyed the knowledge that the Declaration was slowly working its way into the ethical conscience of mankind. For as she wrote in 1958:

> Where, after all, do universal human rights begin? In small places, close to home—so close and so small that they cannot be seen on any maps of the world. Yet they *are* the world of the individual persons; the neighborhood he lives in; the school or college he attends; the factory, farm or office where he works. Such are the places where every man, woman and child seeks equal justice, equal opportunity, equal dignity without discrimination. Unless these rights have meaning there, they have little meaning anywhere. Without concerned citizen action to uphold them close to home, we shall look in vain for progress in the larger world.[51]

---

* In 1962 President Kennedy nominated her for the Nobel Peace Prize for her work in connection with the Declaration. She was "overcome," she wrote him, and "grateful . . . but I shall not be surprised in the least if nothing comes of it. . . ." Nothing did come of it, but in 1968 the Norwegian Parliament awarded the prize to René Cassin, primarily for his work in the field of human rights. See Appendix A: "Eleanor Roosevelt and the Nobel Peace Prize."

IV. Reluctant Cold-Warrior

The Soviet bloc's abstention on the Declaration of Human Rights, after all her effort as well as that of others to find language that would be acceptable to the Soviet group, confirmed anew for her the difficulty of dealing with the Russians. She was not prepared to say that agreement was impossible and certainly she was not resigned, as some Americans were, to the inevitability of war, but she no longer believed, as she did at the beginning of her career as an American representative to the United Nations, that at the heart of Soviet aggressiveness were insecurity, fear, and a misunderstanding of U.S. intentions that genuine dialogue with her Soviet colleagues might help to overcome. Real communication, she found, was impossible, no matter how hard she tried.

A letter that she received from Harry Hopkins just before she left for the London General Assembly and her first encounter with the Russians represented the view of many of Roosevelt's New Deal associates about the breakup of Big Three unity.

I cannot say I am too happy about the way the atom bomb is being handled. In fact, I think we are doing almost everything we can to break with Russia which seems so unnecessary to me.[1]

Her run-in with Vishinsky in London over the issue of forced repatriation gave her a taste of how difficult it was to reconcile the outlooks and interests of East and West; yet she thought that with patience, firmness, and a willingness to look at Russia's economic and security needs without self-righteousness a harmonization of interests might in time be achieved. When, during the quick trip that she made to occupied Germany after the London meetings,

GIs asked for her ideas on how to deal with the Russians, she crisply ticked off four points:

> Have convictions.
> Be friendly.
> Stick to your beliefs as they stick to theirs.
> Work as hard as they do.

The Russians had "an inferiority complex," she went on, and also "tenacity."

We shall have to work very hard to understand them, because they start from a different background. They have a great belief in their own reasoning and if we don't have just as great convictions, they won't understand.[2]

Unlike Vandenberg, who had captured the headlines on his return from London with a speech to the Senate on "What is Russia up to now?," she did not believe there was any mystery about Russian behavior, telling Truman as much when she saw him shortly after Vandenberg's speech and giving him her own assessment of Soviet policy.

Soviet agitation in Iran and the Dardanelles, she thought, reflected at bottom a reaching out for "security in the economic situation," which the Russians evidently felt could only be secured through political control. In eastern Europe she thought Russia was "chiefly concerned with military security. That is why she will try to control the governments of the nations in all those areas and why she dreads seeing Germany built up as an industrial power against her." Russia had not yet learned how to live with an opposition at home, and this was reflected in her foreign policy. "This is largely a question of maturity and of course, trust in the people themselves and not such great dependence on the absolute control of the head of the government.

"It will take some time for Russia to achieve this." America, meanwhile, must act out of affirmative belief, not fear. The United States was the strongest country on earth. "The whole social structure in Europe is crumbling," she counseled the president, "and we might as well face the fact that leadership must come from us or it will inevitably come from Russia." The key to the future was the economic situation in Europe. "I feel very strongly that it cannot be handled piecemeal. . . . The economic problem is not one that we can handle with a loan to Great Britain, a loan to France, a loan to Russia. It must be looked on as a whole." [3]

Above all, American leadership meant vigorous support of the United Nations in order to keep the world from dividing into armed camps. In this respect she found herself at loggerheads with Winston Churchill, who, on March 5, 1946, in Fulton, Missouri, in the presence of President Truman, delivered his "Iron Curtain" speech calling for an Anglo-American military alliance and a showdown with Russia.

Even before that speech she had been afraid of his influence over Truman. She intended to see the president as soon as she returned, she had written from London, "It seems to me he is being too attentive to Churchill. I fear Winston will make him believe certain things which just aren't so." [4] Elliott agreed with her. He had attended most of the wartime conferences as his father's aide, and he recalled many bedtime conversations with his father in which the latter had spoken of his differences with Churchill. When Elliott proposed to write a book reporting those conversations she encouraged him to do so.

Churchill came to Hyde Park after his "Iron Curtain" speech to lay a wreath on his wartime comrade's grave in the rose garden, and, of course, Mrs. Roosevelt received him with respect and affection. "No matter how much any of us may differ at times with the ideas which Mr. Churchill may hold," she wrote, "none of us will ever cease to be grateful to him for the leadership which he gave during the war." Having paid her respects to the great man, she proceeded to take issue with him:

Unless we build a strong United Nations Organization it is fairly obvious that the U.S.S.R., the United States and Great Britain, the three great Allies in the European war, are each going to become the center of a group of nations, each building up its individual power.

All three countries wanted peace,

but the old way of counting on our own individual force seems still to have a strong hold on us. We have not worked together enough really to feel that we understand each other. We still question whether our different political and economic systems can exist side by side in the world. We still suspect each other when we belong to different racial and religious groups. We are still loath to give up the old power and attempt to build a new kind of power and security in the world.

I am convinced that this timidity is perhaps the greatest danger today.[5]

Part of her suspicion of Churchill stemmed from a fear that he spoke for a group in the United States and Britain that wanted to rebuild and rearm Germany "as a buffer in Central Europe against the spreading out of the Soviet Union and its influence over neighboring states." An American official, whose business it had been during the war to keep track of the international cartels and their efforts to circumvent the blockade, sent her a report on proposals to rebuild German heavy industry. She sent it on to Truman:

Mr. [Bernard] Baruch tells me that what he has to say is undoubtedly true. I have always known that a certain group in Great Britain would try to bolster Germany's economy as they are really less afraid of a strong Germany, in spite of the wars which we have had, than of a strong Russia because that group in Great Britain is more afraid of an economic change than anything else. I am also afraid that Mr. [Robert] Murphy, our representative in Germany, has always played with this group and this line of thought. From my point of view it threatens not only the peace of Europe but of the world.[6]

Yet, uneasy as she was over some of the developments in western policy, she did not exempt Soviet Russia from its share of responsibility for the breakup of wartime Big Three unity: "We must get together with Russia, but it must be a two-way matter." Her cousin, Joe Alsop, sent her an article that he and his brother Stewart had written for *Life*. It was called "Tragedy of Liberalism," and its theme was that "by ignoring the challenge of Soviet imperialism, U.S. liberals are destroying their nation's chances of building a peaceful world." Soviet *realpolitik*, the Alsop brothers argued, could not be handled by "loving kindness." He was sending the article to her, Joe Alsop wrote, "because with perhaps less patience and good temper than you, I think along precisely the same line that you do."

"Slowly I have been coming to much the same feeling that you have on Russia," she replied two days later,

with one exception, namely, that I do not feel there has been enough plain speaking among the people in our countries. Since Harry Hopkins, I do not believe that anyone has talked "turkey" to Mr. Stalin personally, and certainly most of us haven't talked honestly with people like Mr. Gromyko, Mr. Vishinsky, etc. I am going to make a great effort to get to know Mr. Gromyko and tell him a few of the things I feel.

I think the difficulty with them is to make them see that they have to trust for safety to the United Nations. Otherwise there is no safety for anybody. They are doing exactly what you describe but I think they are doing it because they have no conception of what a strong UN might mean in security for all, and no trust in any one. However, we have no more trust than they have and neither has Great Britain.[7]

The Soviet government still wanted her to visit the Soviet Union. But U.S. officials feared, as did some of Mrs. Roosevelt's friends, that the Russians would turn her visit into proof of their propaganda thesis that Truman's policy of firmness toward Russia was responsible for the breakup of the wartime alliance and was a betrayal of Roosevelt. She had dropped her plans to go to Russia, she told the press. "Just say I am going to be at Hyde Park working on my autobiography." [8]

Although Mrs. Roosevelt said she agreed with the Alsop analysis of Soviet expansionism, she carefully refrained from endorsing their further view, expressed in the same *Life* article, that Secretary of Commerce Henry Wallace was the liberal leader most guilty of an "idealized" and "otherworldly" view of the Soviet Union. And when, in September, 1947, Wallace publicly broke with the Truman administration over its "get tough with Russia" policy, her reaction was by no means unfriendly. He was the Roosevelt associate from whom she expected the most in the way of liberal leadership. On the day she moved out of the White House she had written him:

Though I hope to see you today and perhaps to talk with you more about my hopes for America and the future, I do want you to know that

I feel that you are peculiarly fitted to carry on the ideals which were close to my husband's heart and which I know you understood.[9]

She shared many of the misgivings about American policy that he voiced in his departure from the Truman cabinet. Commenting on his letter to Truman of July 23, 1946,° in which Wallace condemned the increased army budgets and the bomb tests in the Pacific and which made it look to the rest of the world as if we were only paying "lipservice to peace," Mrs. Roosevelt said, "I do not agree with it in every detail, but it's a good letter." She thought Wallace's explanation of the break with Russia, showing that the United States was not blameless, was a "fair analysis. . . . The test of any situation is to put yourself in the other man's place and we have not done that very successfully in our attitude towards Russia." She, too, had deplored the phrase "tough policy" to describe the U.S. attitude toward Russia. Wallace's highly critical stand on the increasingly military emphasis in the U.S. approach to the world, his assertion that some military men favored a "preventive war," also struck a responsive chord. In May, 1946, when President Truman had threatened to draft striking railroad workers into the Army, she had written Truman in dismay:

You will forgive me, I hope, if I say that I hope you realize that there must [not] be any slip, because of the difficulties of our peace-time situation, into a military way of thinking, which is not natural to us as a people. I have seen my husband receive such advice from his military advisers and succumb to it every now and then, but the people as a whole do not like it even in war time, and in peace time military domination goes against the grain. I hope now that your anxiety is somewhat lessened, you will not insist upon a peace-time draft into the army of strikers. That seems to me a dangerous precedent.[10]

She gave public expression to her fears about the growing influence of the military in her Armistice Day column:

Someone said to me the other day that the atmosphere in the country was changing. From having been a non-militaristic nation where the majority of the people wanted only a small army and navy, we were al-

---

° Wallace released this letter to the press on September 17, 1946.

most imperceptibly moving toward a situation where the wishes of the War and Navy departments carried more weight than did the State Department. That is more or less natural at the end of a war—particularly a war like the one we have just been through, where our men are still scattered throughout the world and where peace has been so long in the making.

Nevertheless, I believe the time is approaching when we had best take thought about where we are drifting. . . .

Whenever our fleet is particularly strong, we have a tremendous urge to send it around the world, or to some far-away point. The Mediterranean has been particularly attractive of late, and I must say it did not fill me with great joy to have the planes from the carrier Franklin D. Roosevelt writing the ship's initials in the sky over Greece at a time when many people wondered just what was going to happen in that country.

Our ships are just paying nice, friendly visits, and it surprises us when anyone thinks that some ulterior motives might lie behind these visits. This is another example of a trait no other nation seems to possess in quite the same degree that we do—namely, a feeling of almost childish injury and resentment unless the world as a whole recognizes how innocent we are of anything but the most generous and harmless intentions.

It is true that we do not have a Red Army anywhere in the world, but we do make a pretty good showing with our navy and our air force and—tucked away, out of sight of the rest of the world—a few little atomic bombs. On the whole our armed services have been doing pretty well in the way of keeping us defended, but I hope our State Department will remember that it is really the department for achieving peace. . . .[11]

Fearful of the growing influence of the military, Wallace's pressures in the other direction seemed healthy to her. But there were differences between her attitude and Wallace's which in time proved to be basic. "I have always wanted cooperation with Russia," she wrote after Tito's planes had shot down two unarmed U.S. transports that had strayed off course. "We have an obligation to meet other nations halfway in friendliness and understanding, but they have that obligation, too—and these latest developments show no realization of their responsibility." She was able to go along with Wallace's speech at New York's Madison Square Garden in September because he criticized Russia as well as the United States and Britain for the breakdown of Big Three unity. But Wallace's listeners, among whom Communists were heavily represented, had not liked that part of the speech. "Why any American audience should boo Mr. Wallace for saying what he did about Russia and the need for Russia to come halfway in her contacts with us, is beyond my understanding." [12]

Her disenchantment with Wallace began when he seemed willing to associate himself with American Communists in his attacks upon U.S. policy and his speeches fell silent about Soviet responsibility for international tensions.

She had to deal with the Russians at the United Nations. That made for realism. Her hopes that personal friendliness might pave the way for frank exchanges were proving illusory. Russian representatives, she found, despite diligent effort, were "hard to get to know as human beings" even though "more frankness between individuals would bring their governments closer together." [13]

Wallace had criticized the Baruch Plan for the international control of atomic energy. It only told the Russians, his July 23 letter said, that if "they are 'good boys,' we may eventually turn over [to them] our knowledge of atomic energy. . . ." Baruch was deeply upset. He telephoned Mrs. Roosevelt and left a message for her, saying Wallace's statement simply was not based on fact and that his effort to get Wallace to come in and talk with him so far had not succeeded. "Send Wallace a wire saying I hope he will talk to Mr. Baruch," Mrs. Roosevelt wrote on this. The two men, seconded by their advisers, eventually did talk, and Wallace, according to Baruch, agreed that Baruch's idea on "stages" was sound, and even agreed to the necessity of suspension of the veto in an international control agency. But in the end Wallace, again according to Baruch, "reneged" on issuing a statement amending his earlier criticism.

That disturbed Mrs. Roosevelt. Soviet delaying tactics in the United Nations Atomic Energy Commission seemed to her to show that it was Moscow, not Washington, that was keeping the world from moving toward disarmament. Nor did she like Molotov's attack on Baruch as "a warmonger":

On Tuesday the Russian Foreign Minister, V. M. Molotov, had impugned our motives in our plan for atomic control and development and attacked Bernard Baruch personally, and, therefore, I felt that his speech lost much of its value. People are rarely convinced by exaggerated and violent statement. So I was particularly pleased at the restraint shown by Senator [Warren] Austin.[14]

Not even Elliott's espousal of an attitude toward Russia very similar to Wallace's checked her maturing conviction that Soviet Russia was primarily responsible for the breakup of Allied unity. Elliott's book, *As He Saw It*, appeared in the autumn of 1946 and caused a world-wide sensation. It detailed Roosevelt's differences with Churchill over colonial policy and the second front. It described FDR's careful moves to make it clear to Stalin that the United States and Great Britain were not allied in a common bloc against the USSR. It gave examples of the late president's distrust of the State Department, because, among other things, he thought it too much under the influence of the British point of view.

Mrs. Roosevelt had heard her husband say many of the same things reported by Elliott, but her own experience with the Russians, the knowledge she had acquired in the thirties of how Communists exploited unwary liberals, kept her from endorsing the conclusions that Elliott drew from his father's wartime table talk—that the peace Franklin had sought to build was being lost because of the maneuvers of British imperialism and American militarism against a Soviet Russia that was portrayed in Elliott's book as largely guiltless. "Naturally every human being reports the things which he sees and hears and lives through from his own point of view," Mrs. Roosevelt wrote in the carefully phrased Foreword. "I am quite sure that many of the people who heard many of the conversations recorded herein, interpreted them differently, according to their own thoughts and beliefs. The record written by all these individuals is invaluable." [15]

She was grateful to Elliott and Faye. By settling at Hyde Park they had made it possible for her to continue to live there. He was currently the favorite whipping boy among the Roosevelt children of the Roosevelt-haters, and that only endeared him the more to her. She loyally defended him and his book against his detractors and critics, taking indignant issue, in particular, with a column by Joseph and Stewart Alsop in which they pointed up the contrast between Elliott's attitude toward Russia and that of his mother and his brothers James and Franklin Jr. She was upset that Franklin Jr. had supplied information to the Alsops. "I assure you that I can corroborate the actual things which he said in his book, and so can a good many other people because they were told many times. He may have misinterpreted but that is a matter of opinion." [16]

The differences in her own household made her acutely miserable. She knew that this author and his wife as well as Franklin Jr. felt that Elliott was being used by the Communist propaganda apparatus, and the only way that Christmas to preserve peace at Val-Kill was to stay off difficult subjects.

Despite her support of Elliott and defense of his book, her own point of view was being made clear, as the Alsops noted, by her involvement in the plans for a meeting in Washington on January 4, 1947, of American non-Communist progressive leaders to "hammer out an American non-Communist Left program with emphasis on the 'non-Communist.'" [17]

She had spent the whole day "from 9:30 in the morning till after five in the afternoon with a group of people, many of whom I have known before, who were trying to set up a liberal and progressive organization." So she wrote about the founding meeting of the Americans for Democratic Action in Washington on January 4, 1947. Looking in on the group, columnist Drew Pearson quipped, "New Deal in Exile." James Loeb, Jr., and Prof. Reinhold Niebuhr, leaders of the Americans for Democratic Action, were the moving spirits in the convening of the conference; but it was Mrs. Roosevelt's presence and, to a lesser degree, that of Franklin Jr. that immediately gave it a power of attraction for FDR's New Deal associates as strongly magnetic as Henry Wallace and the Progressive Citizens of America.

"If we fail to meet our problems here, no one else in the world will do so," Mrs. Roosevelt keynoted the meeting. "If we fail, the heart goes out of progressives throughout the world." The United

States, she said, had to pursue a course between fascist and Communist totalitarianism. She gave her blessing to the projected new liberal organization, and at the end of the day-long meeting, down-to-earth and organization-minded, she asked for the floor again. Ideas were very fine, she said, but how were they going to be put into action? She answered for herself by giving the ADA's first contribution—$100—and pledging to raise $500 more within a week. "That's all she said," recalled Loeb, "but there followed the most rapid and spontaneous and most successful fund raising in ADA's history." [18]

Wallace, who had approved the establishment of the Progressive Citizens of America, sought to minimize the break with Mrs. Roosevelt: "I am not a member or officer of the P.C.A. and Mrs. Roosevelt, to the best of my knowledge, is not a member or officer of the A.D.A. I spoke to one organization urging unity in the progressive ranks. Mrs. Roosevelt spoke to the other."

She had no wish to feud with Henry Wallace, whose integrity she believed in and whose ability she admired, "but that does not mean that you have to agree on the way in which you wish to work for your objectives." She intended "to be helpful" to the ADA, she went on, and then pointed out what basically distinguished the ADA from the PCA:

I would like to see all progressive groups work together. But since some of us prefer to have our staffs and policy-making groups completely free of any American Communist infiltration if we can possibly prevent it, while others have not quite as strong a feeling on this subject, it is natural that there should be two set-ups.[19]

Former New York mayor, Fiorello H. La Guardia, expostulated with her:

The technique and even the nomenclature of selfish, conservative, money-minded groups seem to have been adopted recently by your group. The brand of Communism is hurled indiscriminately. Do you think that is fair? What is the test of excluding any one from a progressive group? How is a sympathizer or fellow traveler of Fascists or Communists to be identified? . . . It has gotten so now that any one who has a difference of opinion or is not in agreement is charged with being a Communist or a friend of a Communist. My dear Mrs. Roosevelt, where will all this end?

She had been through all this before at the end of the thirties, when the Popular Front disintegrated and the efforts of liberals to distinguish their objectives from those of the Communists and to free their organization from Communist control were met with the cry of "red-baiter."

Of course, I do not believe in having everyone who is a liberal called a communist, or everyone who is conservative called fascist, but I think it is possible to determine whether one is one or the other and it does not take too long to do so.

She wanted to see all liberals work together,

and if PCA could remove from its leadership the communist element, I do not see any reason why ADA and PCA should not work together.[20]

She wrote even more sharply to Max Lerner (at that time, the editorial director of *PM*), who had criticized the ADA for being anti-Communist rather than non-Communist.

The American Communists seem to have succeeded very well in jeopardizing whatever the liberals work for. Therefore, to keep them out of policy-making and staff positions seems to be very essential even at the price of being called red-baiters, which I hope no member of this new group will really be.[21]

Wallace showed a further lack of sound political judgment in Mrs. Roosevelt's eyes when he undertook to barnstorm western Europe, making speeches critical of American foreign policy. Calvin B. Baldwin, the director of the PCA and a close associate of Wallace, asked her to cosign a cable to French political leaders that said, "We the undersigned Americans wish to convey our wholehearted support for the sentiments for peace expressed by Mr. Wallace. Mr. Wallace's trip to Europe is a continuation of his vigilance and constant fight for Franklin Delano Roosevelt's concept of one world." She refused:

I do not believe that it is wise for Mr. Wallace to be making the kind of speeches he is making at the present time in foreign countries.

Naturally I have no idea what my husband's attitude would be if he were alive today, and though I am convinced he would have wanted to strengthen the UN, I doubt if he would want to do it in just the way that Mr. Wallace has found necessary. I have such complete confidence in Mr. Wallace's integrity, I am sure he has taken this course because he felt he had to, but with all my heart I wish for his own sake that he had not done so.[22]

What sent Wallace abroad was President Truman's enunciation of the Truman Doctrine, a proposal to take over from Britain responsibility for giving economic and military aid to Greece and Turkey as part of a new policy of supporting "free peoples who are resisting attempted subjugation by armed minorities or by outside pressures." Wallace charged, in a series of speeches in Europe, that the Truman Doctrine meant shoring up reactionary governments. It would require the United States to "police Russia's every border." It committed the country to a policy of "ruthless imperialism" and in the end would bring the United States to war with the Soviet Union.

Although Mrs. Roosevelt was shocked that Wallace should make this kind of an attack abroad, she, too, had serious reservations about the doctrine. She demanded further information. "For instance, why must this country accept Great Britain's military responsibilities?" She doubted that a government

could be completely stable, and representative of 85 per cent of the will of the people, and still require military bolstering from the outside.

I do not question the absolute need to help both Greece and Turkey with relief and rehabilitation. They certainly are unable to cope with their economic problems alone. Without help, chaos would ensue. I think the part of the President's speech which states that Communism follows economic chaos is entirely correct. The economy of Communism is an economy which grows in an atmosphere of misery and want.

Feeling as I do that our hope for peace lies in the United Nations, I naturally grieve to see this country do anything which harms the strength of the UN. If we could have given help for relief and rehabilitation on a purely non-political basis, and then have insisted that the UN join us in deciding what should be done on any political or policing basis to keep Greece and Turkey free from all outside interference, and to allow her to settle her own difficulties in the way the majority of her people desired to have them settled, I would have felt far happier than I do now. . . .

I realize that the lack of a military set-up within the United Nations makes it very difficult to use the UN in a situation requiring force.

But if force was deemed necessary, "it might better be brought in from the individual nations at the behest of the UN until we have collective force to use." [23]

Her criticism was read with anxiety at the State Department. Dean Acheson, the acting secretary of state, promptly dispatched a top aide to New York City to explain the policy to her. She was not won over. She was troubled by the go-it-alone implications of the Truman Doctrine. What if the Russians were to follow U.S. precedent and say, "since you have acted alone without consulting the United Nations, we are free to do the same," and send their army into Greece? Russia could "go into Greece, claiming she is doing exactly what we are doing and we have given her an excuse." She was indignant over the failure of the administration to give advance notification to the United Nations and to the U.S. delegates at the UN.

I hope never again that this type of action will be taken without at least consulting with the Secretary-General and with our permanent member on the Security Council beforehand. It all seems to me a most unfortunate way to do things.[24]

Senator Vandenberg felt the same way. "The Administration made a colossal blunder in ignoring the UN," he wrote. He submitted an amendment to the aid bill which acknowledged the authority of the United Nations to modify or halt U.S. aid to Greece and Turkey at any stage. She congratulated the senator:

I am very grateful for your amendment to the Administration Bill on Greece and Turkey. I still feel that our attitude toward Russia should be less negative and more a comprehensive democratic plan for the revival of the world, since it always seems to me that a positive program has more strength than a negative one.[25]

Acheson sought to reassure her on other points that she had raised. He did not think Russia could view American aid to Greece and Turkey as a threat to her security, he wrote, nor that the USSR was "apt to send an army into Greece as a consequence of such aid from us." The United Nations, he agreed with her, had to be "the cornerstone of our foreign policy," but in the absence of a unity of purpose which would enable it to act, we should not

bind ourselves unalterably and unilaterally. The Soviet Union has made loans, has given military assistance and has delivered foodstuffs to a number of countries, including Poland, Czechoslovakia and Yugoslavia. They have not reported these matters to the UN and they would certainly refuse to permit UN supervision of them.[26]

But neither Acheson nor his representative nor Averell Harriman, with whom she also spoke, fully allayed her doubts, she wrote the president. She did not believe "that taking over Mr. Churchill's policies in the Near East, in the name of democracy, is the way to really create a barrier to communism or promote democracy." She wondered about the president's advisers:

Admiral [William D.] Leahy as always will think of this country as moving on its own power. . . . Mr. Acheson is rather more sympathetic to the British point of view than I would be and what with Mr. Lewis Douglas,* who will certainly be sympathetic to Mr. Churchill's point of view, I am afraid we are apt to lose sight of the fact that if we do not wish to fight Russia, we must be both honest and firm with her. She must understand us, but she must also trust us.[27]

The United States had to bring its economic power to bear at points that might not be exemplary as democracies, Truman said in reply, if they were of strategic importance, as the Greek-Turkish land bridge between continents was. He was not insensitive to the problems she raised. The U.S. mission to carry out the aid program would be instructed to strengthen the democratic forces in Greece, he assured her, and he agreed emphatically that the over-all American approach had to be affirmative and democratic, adding, however, that this had been his approach.[28]

While differing with the administration over the Truman Doctrine, Mrs. Roosevelt was also remonstrating with Acheson about

---

* Douglas, who had resigned from the Roosevelt administration in 1934 in protest against its spending policies, had been named ambassador to the Court of Saint James's.

emergency food aid to Yugoslavia. The United States should help, she argued, despite political differences. "Starving people are not friendly to us and will not become less communistic. . . ." On the basis of departmental studies, he replied, Yugoslavia no longer had a need for free relief. "It is clear that in any case our assistance must go where the needs are most urgent." She did not dispute this. "However, I am told that U.S. will not sell to Yugoslavia and that our attitude is part of our 'Stop Russia' policy." Not so, replied Acheson. "I assure you that immediacy of need is the primary consideration in matters of this kind. This country will never sacrifice humanity in order to carry out any policy." The American Committee for Yugoslav Relief, of which she was honorary chairman, asked her to join other notables in an appeal to President Truman to use part of the unearmarked funds in the relief appropriation to alleviate the emergency in Yugoslavia. She refused to do so, but wrote Truman privately:

In spite of anything that may have occurred, I feel very strongly that it is important that the Yugoslav people should have relief in the way of food. They did hold the Nazis at bay at a time which was crucial in the war.[29]

She was never wholly won over to the Truman Doctrine.° When General Marshall, at the end of April, returned from another fruitless session of the Council of Foreign Ministers, this one in Moscow, she wrote pointedly in her column that she awaited his report to the nation anxiously: "Has he come to a conclusion as to what a comprehensive plan for world recovery must contain or is he still groping?" [31]

There were many who were asking the same question, and a day after this column appeared General Marshall issued written in-

---

° John Foster Dulles, who had accompanied Gen. George C. Marshall to Moscow and with whom she corresponded about the inclusion of Soviet Russia in an over-all economic aid program, shared her uneasiness about the negative stress of U.S. policy. He sent her an advance copy of an address that he was to deliver at Northwestern University, "which seeks to clarify our national attitude in certain respects where it seems to be unduly aggressive and imperialistic." She was interested. "It makes me want to talk to you more than ever on certain things," she wrote back.[30]

structions to George F. Kennan, who was on the newly created policy planning staff of the State Department, to consider what could be done to aid European reconstruction. Kennan had never shared the hopes of friendly and intimate postwar collaboration among the Big Three. Nor had he thought that the United Nations could take the place of "a well-conceived and realistic foreign policy." Nonetheless, he was a critic of the Greek-Turkish aid bill. Although fated to go down in history as the father of "containment," he disapproved the sweeping nature of the bill's commitment to aid all nations threatened by Communism. The Soviet challenge to the West, he felt, was essentially political and economic, not military.* "I suspected that what was intended primarily was military aid, and that what had really happened was that the Pentagon had exploited a favorable set of circumstances in order to infiltrate a military aid program for Turkey into what was supposed to be primarily a political and economic program for Greece." The policy planning staff's recommendations to General Marshall represented a studied effort to correct the impression created by the Truman Doctrine that the American approach to world problems was a defensive reaction to Communist pressure. The American aid effort in Europe, its report stated, "should be directed not to the combating of communism as such but to restoration of the economic health and vigor of European society." This key concept emerged still further sharpened in General Marshall's speech at Harvard on June 5, broaching the Marshall Plan:

Our policy is directed not against any country or doctrine but against hunger, poverty, desperation, and chaos. Its purpose should be the revival of a working economy in the world so as to permit the emergence of political and social conditions in which free institutions can exist. Such assistance, I am convinced, must not be on a piecemeal basis as various crises develop.[33]

* This emerged more clearly in Kennan's later writings. The famous Kennan dispatch, published in *Foreign Affairs* in 1947 under the pseudonym "Mr. X," was a penetrating analysis of the springs of Soviet conduct, but it left open the question of how American power might be mobilized to cope with Soviet pressures and probings. "I read the article (I imagine somewhat abbreviated) in *Life* which was published by *Foreign Affairs*. It was interesting but not very illuminating and I don't really know just what our policy is going to be, do you?"[32]

The general invited Europe to take the initiative and draft a program of its requirements. In London, British Foreign Secretary Ernest Bevin read and reread the speech with growing excitement and, in his own words, "seized the offer with both hands" and took the initiative in organizing Europe's response.[34]

She liked the general's approach, Mrs. Roosevelt wrote, especially the invitation to Europe to come "to an over-all economic agreement in which we would try to aid. It was a very constructive suggestion. . . ." To a correspondent who feared that the aid-to-Greece-and-Turkey program had been undertaken in order to bring about war with Russia, she wrote that the administration's purpose was to prevent war with Russia, which "has inaugurated an expansionist program and somewhere it had to be stopped. I do not think it had to be stopped in just that way, and I am very much happier about Secretary Marshall's over-all plan." [35]

But Russia, she went on to point out, was "nearly always obstructionist" and was making it difficult to bring the Marshall Plan into being. "The Marshall Plan is a bona fide offer to help Europe to get back on its feet. Mr. Molotov, in refusing to join the rest of Europe, is creating the very thing he says he fears, which is division instead of cooperation." She had to say, she added a few days later, "I do not in the least understand some of the actions taken by the Russian Government." Russia's refusal to join with the rest of Europe in the Marshall Plan opened that country "to the accusation that she does not really care so much about European recovery as she does about her power to make the Europeans feel that they have to turn to her for help." [36]

Mrs. Roosevelt was concerned about the relationship of the United Nations to the program that was taking shape. The European nations were meeting in Paris to draft their reply to the Marshall initiative. "I understand that the United Nations has not been invited to the Paris Economic Conference. I should think it should be," she wrote Marshall from Campobello, where she had gone in order to work on her autobiography. It was his understanding that the participating countries were keeping the Economic Commission for Europe, a UN body, "fully informed" of the Paris proceedings, he assured her. "I would imagine that it will be through this body that the United Nations will be brought into relation with the results of the Paris Talks." But the hostility of Russia made it impossible to give the ECE any operational relationship to the developing recovery program. Watching Soviet policy from afar, it seemed to her that

The Soviets have decided that if things can be made disagreeable enough for the United States in Europe, and if complications in the Security Council can be made to seem insoluble, then perhaps they can succeed in creating a home situation in this country which will force our government to abandon all interest in Europe. Once this has been accomplished, it is easy to see that they feel sure they can, in one way or another, control the whole of Europe.

The only obstacle to that desired objective which they can see today is the interest of the United States. They count on the people of this country finally saying: "The situation over there is a headache. Let them get out of it as best they can. . . ."

Because of the things which have been said in our papers and in our Congress, the Soviets undoubtedly believe that the Marshall Plan will never get from our people the support which would be required to make it work.[37]

His opposition to the Marshall Plan was another count in her growing disenchantment with Wallace:

I think Mr. Henry Wallace is a fine person but I do not think he is very wise as a politician. He has succeeded in misleading the Russians into believing that the majority of the people of the U.S. agree with them and that, of course, leads them to do things which they would never otherwise do.[38]

The United Nations General Assembly, which opened on September 18, 1947, was the first at which the delegation was headed by General Marshall. She had never been happy about Byrnes's leadership in foreign affairs. When Truman appointed him secretary of state in June, 1945, she wrote her son, James,

I hate Jimmy Byrnes going in because with all of his ability, I think he is primarily interested in Jimmy Byrnes, but after all, Father used him and I imagine that President Truman will feel that his past association will make working together easier. . . .

She felt very different about Marshall. "My dear General," she had written him after Franklin's burial:

I want to tell you to-night how deeply I appreciate your kindness & thoughtfulness in all the arrangements made. My husband would have been grateful & I know it was all as he would have wished it. He always spoke of his trust in you & of his affection for you.[39]

In turn, that austere, incorruptible soldier warmed toward Mrs. Roosevelt, and occasionally even permitted a personal note to intrude into his correspondence with her: "I signed this morning a rather formal letter to you expressing appreciation for your splendid work during the last meeting of the Assembly of the United Nations," he wrote her in July, 1947. "In this note I merely wish to tell you that I am much relieved to know that you are willing to participate as a delegate at the coming meeting of the Assembly in September." He believed in delegation teamwork and he sent her a draft of the speech he intended to deliver in the Assembly, asking for her comments. It seemed to her "excellent in tone and admirably frank. I wish if it were possible somewhere at the start the United States might emphasize the value of the UN bringing all nations together for cooperative action." Marshall sent her comment to Charles E. ("Chip") Bohlen, who was working on the general's speech, and Eleanor was delighted with the final product:

I was deeply proud of our Secretary of State today as he welcomed the delegates to the UN General Assembly. His speech was temperate in tone, honest and forthright. No one could be with Secretary Marshall and not recognize the integrity of the man and his deep convictions. He is a good democrat in the best sense of the word, and he wants to get on with the business of creating a peaceful world in which you and I and all the people can have a chance for a better life.[40]

The next day Andrei Vishinsky mounted the high podium in Flushing Meadow to present Russia's position. The first part of his speech she considered a clever bit of obfuscation on the disarmament issue; but that was overshadowed by the second part, which was "unbelievable." Dulles was so outraged by Vishinsky's attacks that he began to splutter audibly and General Marshall had asked her to please calm him down. The general did not mind the invective because it would solidify the public behind him, which might otherwise have been confused by the sophistries on disarmament. Afterward, members of the delegation speculated about the meaning of Vishinsky's approach. Adlai Stevenson, an alternate delegate, thought it might be a prelude to a Soviet withdrawal from the UN. Chip Bohlen did not. It was obvious, as she spoke of these matters to friends, that she was pleased to be included in the discussions of high policy.[41]

"At the Cabinet luncheon today," Robert Hannegan wrote her when the 1947 Assembly was at midpoint, "General Marshall was emphatic in his praise of you—he was almost dramatic in recounting his experience in New York; he said that while his duties in New York were difficult, the most intelligent, cooperative and *effective* assistance came from Mrs. Eleanor Roosevelt." [42]

She found working with Marshall "a very rewarding experience." For the first time she was getting a real knowledge of the inner workings of the State Department, and of the various cliques in it. Byrnes had kept her on the periphery, but Marshall consulted her regularly and had her present at the small meetings. One of the first problems the delegation faced was which Slav nation to support to succeed Poland on the Security Council. The USSR had proposed the Ukrainian SSR to which the United States refused to agree. Vishinsky had then proposed Czechoslovakia, but her representatives had come privately to beg the United States not to support her, since as a member of the Council, she would have to line up with the Soviets. Mrs. Roosevelt felt, as did Marshall, that Czechoslovakia's wishes should be respected; but advisers like Chip Bohlen were all for forcing Czechoslovakia to get off the fence. Mrs. Roosevelt considered this attitude a blunder, but all of Marshall's top advisers supported the Bohlen position. And even if the secretary agreed with her, she pointed out, could he go against their recommendation? [43]

The 1947 General Assembly session did much to persuade her that Russia interpreted efforts to take account of her anxieties as weakness rather than as a desire for friendly relations. In October the Cominform, successor to the Comintern, was established. She had never believed that the Comintern had ceased to function. "There were too many signs throughout the world of activity that was well directed and unified." She thought the Cominform manifesto a warmongering document because it arbitrarily divided the world into two camps and denounced "concessions to the United States of America and the imperialist camp" as a form of Munich-like appeasement. She found it "strange" that the Wallace liberals and the Cominform parties "are condemning with one voice the Marshall proposals!" [44]

The 1947 Assembly brought a return engagement with Vishinsky, who pictured American defense of freedom of the press as a defense of warmongering. "I found myself in the absurd position of defending the *Chicago Tribune*," she wrote afterward:

I defended that paper, certainly not because I either agree with or believe most of the things which it stands for, but because I think we should defend the right of all individuals to their freedom of thought and speech.[45]

In her rebuttal of Vishinsky in Committee III she noted that the author of the pamphlet cited by the Russians in their attack upon the "monopolistic" American press was "one of our American Communists." The fact that "we allow American Communists freedom to print what they want to say in criticism of this country" demonstrated that the United States had freedom of the press. She was still reluctant to end on a polemical note. Despite a basic difference in philosophies, "we must work together; growing apart is not going to help us." [46]

She had not wholly abandoned the idea of a trip to Russia. Her *Ladies' Home Journal* publishers, Beatrice and Bruce Gould, reported to her that when they had applied for a visa at the Soviet consulate, they were told, "Now if you would get Mrs. Roosevelt to go over with you, there would be no trouble at all about visas or interviewing Stalin." The Czechs were also anxious for her to visit them, she informed Marshall. A visit to Czechoslovakia would be worthwhile, he replied, but it might acquire a different significance if she only visited Prague, and he feared that a visit to Moscow might be subject to exploitation both by Soviet and Republican propagandists. In view of his doubts, she decided not to make the trip. "In fact, I am relieved at not having to go, but I felt it my duty to make the inquiry if I could in any way be helpful." [47]

Nine days later, February 24, 1948, an armed Communist coup ended Czech democracy and independence and led to the death, either by murder or suicide, of her old friend Foreign Minister Jan Masaryk. On top of these sinister events came the chilling top-secret telegram from Gen. Lucius Clay, chief of U.S. occupation forces in Germany, in which he stated that he was no longer able to advise Washington "that war was unlikely for at least ten years. Within the last few weeks, I have felt a subtle change in Soviet attitudes which I cannot define but which now gives me a feeling that it may come with dramatic suddenness." The shock waves of the ensuing war scare in Washington reached Mrs. Roosevelt. On March 13, she wrote Marshall an alarmed letter. She was becoming "more and more worried." She urged a peace mission of a "picked group" that would sit down with Great Britain and Russia "around a table before we actually get to a point where we are in a war."

You say the situation is serious and any one can see that we can not let the USSR go on pulling coups in one country after another. It looks as though Sweden and Norway were pretty worried as to whether they will not be treated to the same kind of "invitation" that Finland has had, and certainly it will not be very difficult to pull a coup off in Italy. . . .

I am sure that we have not been blameless and probably the Russians think we have done some things against them. I am sure they believe we are trying to build up Germany again into an industrial state. I some times wonder if behind our backs, that isn't one of the things that our big business people would like to see happen in spite of two World Wars started by Germany.

If war comes and this final effort has not been made, I am afraid the people of this country are not going to feel that we have done all that we should have done to try to find a solution to the deteriorating situation between ourselves and the USSR.[48]

She sent to President Truman a copy of her letter to Marshall, saying,

I do not think I have been as alarmed before but I have become very worried and since we always have to sit down together when war comes to an end, I think before we have a third World War, we should sit down together.

You and the Secretary must feel the rest of us are a nuisance. Nevertheless, as a citizen I would not have a clear conscience if I did not tell you how I feel at the present time.[49]

Truman replied on the sixteenth, Marshall a day later. The president reviewed the record of agreements broken by the Russians. He thought Soviet aggressiveness was fed by a belief that Wallace would win the presidency in 1948 and if that did not end the U.S. policy of firmness, a depression would. The only hopes for peace rested in the European Recovery Program and in U.S. military build-up. "I am as much concerned as you are," Marshall wrote Mrs. Roosevelt, "as much troubled, and I am seeking in every way to find a solution which will avoid the great catastrophe of war. It is evident that we cannot sit quiet in this situation and also that mere words get us nowhere at this time." He was "terribly disturbed over the rapid growth of a highly emotional feeling in this country which runs to extremes, yet at the same time something must be done." He was sending Bohlen to talk with her about her suggestion of a "picked group" to sit down with the Russians. Evidently the suggestion interested the administration. It surfaced in abortive form in the 1948 election when Truman announced that he was sending Chief Justice Fred M. Vinson to Moscow, a suggestion that was dropped when Secretary Marshall opposed it and it was widely criticized as a campaign gesture. "Truman's last move on Vinson and the resulting publicity have been very bad," she wrote. Bernard Baruch, an old friend, informed her that he had known about her proposal to send a peace mission to Moscow as early as last spring. It

made good sense then. When I was told about it this time (and it was even suggested that I be on it) I said it was impossible in the present circumstances, and as far as I was concerned, I would not go for it would be by-passing and destroying the usefulness of the UN. The proper person to make the statement, or undertake any discussion now, is either the President or General Marshall.[50]

Mrs. Roosevelt received this letter in Paris, where she was attending the General Assembly. There was nothing like daily contact with the Russians to quench hopes of an easing of tension. "The Russians attack verbally in every committee," she wrote.

They seem to want to see nothing accomplished until one wonders whether they should be banned from contacts until they want them enough to try to cooperate.[51]

She took General and Mrs. Marshall to Les Porquerolles, a little restaurant she had discovered on the Left Bank:

I like him so much & he is a strong person, but I fear very tired.
Russia's attitude is discouraging & Marshall I think believes it is a case of outstaying & outbluffing your adversary but the stake of war is such a high one that this game cannot be played lightheartedly.[52]

"It is sad, dear," she wrote a friend a few weeks later,

but I think it will take a long time to get real understanding with the USSR government. It will be the result of long & patient work. Their government & its representatives think differently. They will have to reach a higher standard of living & not be afraid to let others in & their own out before we can hope for a change.[53]

She had begun her career at the United Nations bending over backward to show the Russians she was ready to meet them halfway. By 1949 she was stating publicly she would "never again" compromise, "even on words. The Soviets look on this as evidence of weakness rather than as a gesture of good will." When State Department counselor Ben Cohen expressed misgivings about statements that implied it was impossible to get along with the Russians, she replied, "But we have to win the cold war." "The only way to win the cold war," he counseled her, "is to end it." And, of course, basically she agreed with him, even though the Russians, who had begun by courting her as FDR's widow, now denounced her as a "hypocritical servant of capitalism . . . a fly darkening the Soviet sun." Vishinsky was even heard, in the heat of the 1948 debate, to characterize her as a meddling old woman, which reminded one observer of Stalin's reported threat to appoint someone else Lenin's widow "if that old woman doesn't shut up." "There is no doubt," commented author-reporter Elizabeth Janeway, after observing Mrs. Roosevelt at the United Nations, "he would like to have the power to appoint someone else Franklin D. Roosevelt's widow." [54]

In September, 1949, President Truman disclosed that "within recent weeks an atomic explosion occurred in the USSR." There was little danger of war, Mrs. Roosevelt reassured friends. She did not believe Russia had a stockpile of bombs, certainly not one as large as that of the United States. But then she added, and it was a measure of how completely Russia had alienated this woman of good will, that it would do well to be more on the alert than ever in order to avoid another Pearl Harbor, this time with atom bombs.[55]

V. The United Nations and a Jewish Homeland

Among the war's victims, those who seemed to Eleanor Roosevelt to have the strongest claim on humanity's compassion and charity were the pitiful survivors of the death trains and gas chambers.

They had been a weight upon her heart for a long time. In 1943 word had filtered out of Fortress Europe that Hitler had given orders for the extermination of all Jews. She took part in a memorial service of protest and had written afterward: "One could not help having a great pride in the achievements of the Jewish people; they are the great names in so many nations, and yet rage and pity filled one's heart for they have suffered in this war in so many nations." Louis Bromfield, author and the head of the Emergency Conference to Save the Jews of Europe, wired her: "The Nazis are rapidly carrying out the threat to annihilate the Jewish people of Europe as reprisal against approaching doom. . . ." Would she serve as a committee sponsor? "I have your telegram and cannot see what can be done until we win the war," she replied. And to another, she wrote:

[I do] not see beyond the statement which the President has made, what more emphatically could be said. I will be glad to say anything or help in any way but I do not think it wise for me to formally go on any committee.[1]

Behind the scenes she did what she could to squeeze visas out of the balky State Department for the refugees who managed to get to Spain and Portugal. She worked with the U.S. Committee for the Care of European Children to get the State Department to stretch its interpretation of the laws in the issuance of visas to children. Louis Weiss, a distinguished and selfless attorney who was working with the committee, inquired of Tommy as to whether Mrs. Roosevelt wanted to go back to the State Department—". . . the matter may have been pushed as far as she wishes to push it at this time." [2]

In January, 1944, a group of Treasury Department officials headed by the secretary, outraged over State Department apathy and stalling in regard to helping Jews to escape extermination, confronted President Roosevelt with a carefully documented "Report on the Acquiescence of This Government in the Murder of the Jews." Roosevelt heard the group sympathetically, accepted its suggestion that he establish a war refugee board to direct rescue operations, and placed at its head a young Treasury Department official, John W. Pehle, who had helped draft the report and whose energy and clarity had impressed him. Pehle soon was soliciting Mrs. Roosevelt's help.

He's worried over the war closing the Balkan & Turkey routes through which they've been getting out some people & then there will only be Spain left & our Ambassador [Carlton] Hayes is not cooperative. I spoke to Franklin & asked if perhaps a change might be advisable & Franklin said wearily "well the complaints are mounting." [3]

She was not successful. Hayes remained at his post.

She did what she could to open America's doors to the survivors of the holocaust, having little sympathy with the extreme Zionist position that Palestine was the only place where Jews might live in safety and without apology. "I fear Palestine could never support all the Jews, and the Arabs would start a constant war if all of them came," she replied to a physician who protested what he called her "assimilationist" approach. "Why can't Jews be members of a religious body but natives of the land in which they live?" she asked.[4]

But she was not assimilationist in the sense of believing that Jews should deny their identity as Jews. She once asked Judge Justine Polier, daughter of Rabbi Stephen S. Wise, why, when she sought help for people—whether unemployed miners in West Virginia, sharecroppers, or Negroes in the South—Jews were always among the first to come forward to offer aid. Yet when Jews were mistreated, she found they were most hesitant to ask her help, and when they did, seemed embarrassed in doing so. Judge Polier tried to explain to her the background of oppression and exclusion that led some Jews to believe that safety and acceptance lay in escaping their Jewishness.[5]

Having conquered the conventional attitude toward Jews instilled by the world in which she had grown up, Mrs. Roosevelt rejected the Zionist view that the Jew must always feel himself an outsider in a gentile culture because gentiles would always regard him as an alien. Author Ben Hecht sent her his *Guide for the Bedevilled,* in which he flailed away at anti-Semites and anti-Semitism with wisecrack and vitriol. "I read it half through today & find his style trying," she wrote to a young Jewish friend:

Some of the things he says remind me of what you once said to me about being "with your own people" & the main theme that people who are prejudiced racially & religiously are just manufacturing a whipping boy for their own feelings is doubtless true. I'm just no good at judging a book like this, it is distasteful & I don't feel any of the things as he describes them. I don't lump people together. I don't think of them except as individuals whom I like or dislike. I love you & I don't feel strange *ever* with you & I've never had to argue about it in my own mind.[6]

To Zionists—especially European Zionists—who argued that there was no "home" for Jews except Palestine, she replied, "The Jewish people can live in other places and the future will be open to them as to all others, I am sure." [7] But as it became evident that other lands, including her own, were not ready to receive the refugee and that the Jewish refugee did want to go to Palestine, she began to examine more closely the case for a Jewish homeland in Palestine as well as the chief argument of the opponents of Zionism, that Palestine's deserts could not support a larger population.

Mrs. Felix Frankfurter brought Dr. Chaim Weizmann to lunch with her. He told her the story of Palestine, beginning with the Balfour pledge of a Jewish homeland there. He had negotiated the original agreements with the Arabs, Dr. Weizmann went on, and they had understood clearly what the Jews envisaged by a homeland. On the basis of the British pledge, endorsed by Woodrow Wilson, and their agreements with the Arabs, the Jews had brought hundreds of thousands of settlers to Palestine and transformed the arid deserts into garden spots. "He was very convincing," Mrs. Roosevelt wrote afterward, "but I've heard many arguments on the other side." [8]

One of the chief arguments on the other side was being advanced by Dr. Isaiah Bowman, the president of Johns Hopkins University and a world famous geographer who headed the State Department's advisory group on Palestine and the Middle East. "Incidentally I understand that Isaiah Bowman has said that Palestine cannot support even its present people satisfactorily," Mrs. Roosevelt informed Louis Weiss at the time that she was trying to help him get more visas for children. "It has imported far more than it has exported in the past and they have the figures on this." This argument was to be heard everywhere, she went on, and was "one of the things that the Jewish organizations should undertake to face." Mrs. Rose Halprin, a Zionist leader, sent her a statement on "The Absorptive Capacity of Palestine." It reflected the conclusions of Dr. Walter C. Lowdermilk, an expert on agronomy and soil development, who, on the basis of an exhaustive survey of Palestine, had come to a conclusion quite different from Bowman's. Palestine could be transformed into another California, he maintained, and the full utilization of the Jordan River would make possible the absorption of four million Jewish refugees.[9]

"A very convincing statement," Mrs. Roosevelt acknowledged to Mrs. Halprin. "I will turn it over to the President and his advisers." A skeptical President Roosevelt asked her to talk to Dr. Bowman about the Lowdermilk survey. Bowman unsettled her again. He dwelt on the security rather than the economic problem. A Jewish state in Palestine could not be set up and protected from regional hostility without a U.S.-British guarantee. Would the country back up the guarantee of a state 6,000 miles away? "The Jewish problem is one of the many problems that lie upon the conscience of the world," Bowman wrote her subsequently.

Only a heart of stone would deny the Jews full and sympathetic consideration. . . . Is it in their long-term interest to create a growing problem of security in the Near East that may require for its solution the more or less immediate use of American bayonets? The answer may prove to be *yes*, if there is no other way. But in all this wide world must there be a solution by force in just this particular area of 10,000 square miles? [10]

As she indicated in a letter she wrote in January, 1944, she accepted Bowman's reasoning:

I have talked to the State Department people and I have talked to a great many British people. It would be foolish to think that Palestine by itself could stand up against the Arab world, and neither Great Britain nor the United States can be expected to constantly be prepared to fight the Arab world. So a compromise which looks both to the possibility in the future of the self-support of whatever population is in Palestine and to cooperation of the Arab world must be envisioned, and at the same time the Jewish people must find homes in many places. [11]

Felix S. Cohen, the brilliantly creative son of the philosopher Morris Raphael Cohen and assistant solicitor in the Department of Interior, sent her a "very wonderful old gentleman," Dr. Milton Steinberg, who was described to her as neither Zionist nor anti-Zionist and who brought her a plan for Jewish resettlement in Australia, which needed people and had an overabundance of land that could easily be developed. She thought enough of his plan to forward it immediately to her husband at Warm Springs. It was among the items she sent down on April 12, 1945. [12]

She knew that FDR had favored a homeland for Jews in Palestine, but she also knew that he felt it could only be established with the consent of the Arabs and that he had failed to win this consent in his meeting with Ibn Saud. When Rabbi Stephen Wise saw Roosevelt on March 16, 1945, after his return from Yalta and congratulated him on a successful mission, Roosevelt's mournful response, as Dr. Wise informed Chaim Weizmann, was:

I have had a failure. The one failure of my mission was with Ibn Saud. Everything went well, but not that, and I arranged the whole meeting with him for the sake of your cause. . . . I tried to approach the Jewish question a number of times. Every time I mentioned the Jews he would shrink and give me some such answer as this—"I am too old to understand new ideas!"

When President Roosevelt began to tell Ibn Saud of what the Jewish settlers had done for Palestine through irrigation and the planting of trees, Ibn Saud's answer was, "My people don't like trees; they are desert dwellers. And we have water enough without irrigation!" Roosevelt added, "I have never so completely failed to make an impact upon a man's mind as in this case." [13]

The immediate issue was what to do with the homeless and destitute Jews coming out of the extermination camps. When Dr. Wise stressed the horror of sending 1,200 Jewish refugees released from Bergen-Belsen to Algiers instead of to Palestine, Roosevelt said, "I have discussed that matter with Winston Churchill and he says 'don't talk about the White Paper or regulations, but we will let the Jews come in.' " [14]

Within two months, however, Roosevelt was dead, and although Truman vigorously supported the request of the Jewish Agency, spokesman for the Jewish inhabitants of Palestine, for the admission of 100,000 Jewish refugees into Palestine, Clement Attlee, who succeeded Churchill during the Potsdam Conference, was not ready to discuss the issue. As an alternative Truman dispatched Earl G. Harrison, former U.S. commissioner of immigration, to Europe to investigate the situation in the camps. Harrison's report, which Truman released, said it was "nothing short of calamitous to contemplate that the gates of Palestine should be soon closed," and urged the issuance of the 100,000 additional immigration certificates. Truman asked Attlee to go along with this recommendation, but the British leader turned him down and proposed instead a joint Anglo-American Committee of Inquiry which would associate the United States with responsibility for carrying out whatever the committee recommended.

To reassure the Arabs, the State Department obtained Truman's consent to release a letter Roosevelt had written to Ibn Saud in which he promised that no decision would be made about Palestine without full consultation with both Arabs and Jews. Rabbi Wise had known nothing about this letter, and there was a general feeling of depression and letdown in the Jewish community. "My husband meant the Jewish people no harm," Mrs. Roosevelt wrote the director of the Franklin D. Roosevelt Jewish Memorial Book Committee. "He dreaded war between them and the more numerous Arabs and felt that a more amicable agreement could be reached. He felt that he had not succeeded with Ibn Saud." [15]

She herself was a passionate advocate of immediate issuance of the 100,000 admission certificates. In August, 1945, May Craig, after five months in the European theater, had come to her Washington Square apartment. May, a flinty New England journalist, had spent three days at Dachau and her reports were more terrible than any Mrs. Roosevelt had read in the press. She was deeply upset. If the Germans, a civilized people, can sink so low, she remarked to May, so might the Americans. The Bilbos and the Rankins, she said, referring to two southern demagogues then riding high, would probably behave the same way if they had the power. [16]

Mrs. Craig was followed by Helen Waren, an actress who, in 1944, had left the Broadway hit *The Searching Wind* to go overseas for the USO in *Ten Little Indians*. She came to tell Mrs. Roosevelt of her "grimmest journey" through the Third Army Sector in Germany after V-E Day, where she had found the most appalling and deplorable conditions among the displaced Jews, who were, she said, being forced to live in camps together with their former persecutors—SS men, Gestapo, Nazis, Polish and Ukrainian collaborationists. "All over Europe I found the same heartrending plea: 'We want to go to Palestine—we want to be among Jews.' " She should write her observations out in the form of a report, Mrs. Roosevelt said. "I shall see that it gets into the proper hands." She sent copies to the president, General Marshall, Henry Morgenthau, and Adele (Mrs. David M.) Levy, the daughter of Lessing J. Rosenwald, who was then heading the women's division of the United Jewish Appeal.[17]

When Truman and Attlee on November 13, 1945, announced the establishment of an Anglo-American Committee of Inquiry, Mrs. Roosevelt, in a letter to Truman, voiced her unhappiness over the delay it represented:

> I am very much distressed that Great Britain has made us take a share in another investigation of the few Jews remaining in Europe. If they are not to be allowed to enter Palestine, then certainly they could have been apportioned among the different United Nations and we would not have to continue to have on our consciences the death of at least fifty of these poor creatures daily.
>
> The question between Palestine and the Arabs, of course, has always been complicated by the oil deposits, and I suppose it always will. I do not happen to be a Zionist and I know what a difference there is among such Jews as consider themselves nationals of other countries and not a separate nationality.
>
> Great Britain is always anxious to have some one pull her chestnuts out of the fire, and though I am very fond of the British individually and like a great many of them, I object very much to being used by them.

Truman assured her that he would do what he could to get as many Jews into Palestine as possible without waiting upon the report of the joint committee. The latter, however, might produce a report leading to a lasting settlement.[18]

In spite of her opposition to the appointment of yet another committee and her support of 100,000 visas, she still believed that a large influx of Jewish settlers would trigger an Arab uprising and that the Jewish community was not capable of defending itself. "Unless the British and the Americans are ready to protect the Jews by force from the Arabs it would seem like suicide to allow them to go back," she wrote at the beginning of 1946.[19]

Mrs. Roosevelt's visit to Germany after the London session of the United Nations confirmed for her the passionate longing of the Jews for Palestine, the despairing sorrow in the displaced persons camps, that Miss Waren had reported. She was invited by the Army, "at my own suggestion, be it said, but tactfully put so they wouldn't have me if they didn't want me, to visit our men before I go home. . . ." She wanted to take a look at the refugee camps and to see for herself how much truth there was in reports of GI "fraternization" with German *Fräulein*. Those camps were the "saddest places . . . the Jewish camps particularly are things I will never forget." In the mud of the Zilsheim camp an old Jewish woman knelt and, throwing her arms around her knees, murmured over and over, "Israel, Israel," and Mrs. Roosevelt knew "for the first time what that small land meant to so many, many people." [20]

She could not forgive the Germans for what they had done. "The weight of human misery here in Europe is something one can't get out of one's heart." In Frankfurt, Army officers at her request located her old classmate Carola von Schaeffer-Bernstein. When Mrs. Roosevelt sadly remarked on Europe's tragic situation, her friend quickly replied, "It was everybody's fault. We are all to blame. None of us has lived up to the teachings of Christ." Mrs. Roosevelt had no wish to hurt her friend but she felt duty-bound to ask how it was possible to be "so devoted to the principles of the church yet not protest the mistreatment of the Jews?"

"Sometimes," the reply came back, "it is wiser not to look over the hill."

"It was good to see you again," she wrote Carola afterward, "but there is a sadness over the whole of Europe which, I am afraid, it is hard to get away from." [21]

Not long after her return from Germany, the Anglo-American Committee of Inquiry handed in its report. It was unanimous in its recommendation of the immediate issuance of 100,000 entry certificates. It also urged that Palestine become a binational state dominated by neither Arab nor Jew. And, in view of the hostility between Arab and Jew, it favored continuance of the British mandate. Truman promptly endorsed these recommendations. The British, however, backtracked, and Ernest Bevin, the foreign secretary, who earlier had promised to implement any recommendation that was unanimous, now told a British Labor party conference that the only reason Truman wanted Palestine to take Europe's Jews was because Americans did not want any more Jews in New York City.

Mrs. Roosevelt disregarded the slurring implications of Bevin's remarks, because she felt he had a point:

It is not fair to ask of others what you are not willing to do yourself. Mr. Bevin's speech gave many of us pause. We should not so conduct ourselves that such things can be said about us by responsible statesmen.[22]

She felt the United States should relax its immigration laws. "I think we have a duty to lead in taking our share."

But she was angry with the British response to the joint commission's recommendations. "There was really no need for a commission of inquiry, but we went along with Great Britain. The obvious reason we went along was that we believed Great Britain would accept the report of such a group and try to implement it." There was no escaping the immediate point at issue—the 100,000 Jews in Europe

who must find homes immediately and they want to go to Palestine. The Arabs threaten dire things. The British talk about the impossibility of increasing the military force. But surely our allied Chiefs of Staff could work out some form of military defense for Palestine which would not mean an increase in manpower.[23]

In Palestine, the British rejection of the joint commission's recommendations turned the desperate Jewish settlers toward acts of terrorism against the British forces and illegal immigration organized by the Jewish defense force, the Haganah. Bridges were blown up and British officers kidnapped. There were pitched battles between British and Jewish troops. The British, with 50,000 troops in Palestine, decided on drastic action. The Zionist leaders were jailed. That strengthened the influences of the terrorists. The King David Hotel, headquarters of the mandatory and the British Army, was blown up with forty-three killed and forty-three injured. She was horrified:

Violence of this kind kills innocent people, and enough innocent people have already died in the world. More innocent Jews have suffered than any other people. . . . Violence can only make a fair and reasonable solution in Palestine more difficult.[24]

A few days later the British retaliated, which distressed her because she felt a great nation should have self-control and patience. She was even more revolted by the British decision to deport to Cyprus all captured "illegal" immigrants. "Dear Lady Reading," she wrote her old friend and co-worker on August 23, 1946:

I am writing you this letter which you can pass on if you think wise, to Mr. Attlee and Mr. Bevin. I do not feel I have any right to express my feelings to them officially and yet as a human being, I can not help wanting to tell them how certain actions as regards the situation in Palestine have made me feel.

In the first place, I hope and pray that they will not actually put to death the young terrorists. I do not approve of what any of these people have done in the way of violence. I understand perfectly, however, the fact that this feeling of despair on the part of the Jewish people [has] been growing for a long time and the show of force . . . Great Britain has made in Palestine has probably built up this resistance movement, since force always creates a similar attitude in the opposition.

If these young people are killed there will without any question, be a sense of martyrdom and a desire for revenge which will bring more bloodshed. A generous gesture will, I think, change the atmosphere.

In addition, I can not bear to think of the Jews of Europe who have spent so many years in concentration camps, behind wire again on Cyprus. Somehow it seems to me that the 100,000 Jews should be let into Palestine and that some real agreement should be reached with the Arabs. Willy-nilly, the feeling grows here that it is [not] just justice which Great Britain is looking for where the Arabs are concerned, but it is that she wishes the friendship in order to get more favorable consideration where oil concessions are concerned. I know this may not be true but no matter what the real reasons are, it is in such a mess that ultimately I feel it should be turned over to the United Nations. In the meantime the gestures should all be on the generous side where Great Britain is concerned. . . .

I shall be grateful for whatever you decide to do about this letter. With every good wish, I am,

Affectionately,[25]

Lady Reading passed the letter on, commenting ambiguously to Mrs. Roosevelt that there was more to the problem than appeared to the naked eye.

Mrs. Roosevelt still opposed a Jewish state. "The suggestion that the country be partitioned seems to me no answer to the problem," she wrote in midsummer. She still had questions about Palestine's absorptive capacity, and questions, too, about the number of Jews in Europe who wanted to go to Palestine. "Not all Jewish people want a nation and a national home," she wrote a Zionist critic. "The greater part of the Jews throughout the world in the past have been nationals of the lands in which they lived, and they wanted only to be different as to their religion, just as Catholics or Protestants might be different." It might be that Jewish attitudes had changed and "that like many other people, the Jews wish to establish and fight for the right to the land. I hope this isn't so. . . ." At the end of 1946 she informed the correspondent for the Palestine paper *Davar* that of the six solutions for the future status of the Jews in Palestine that he listed—British mandate, Jewish state in the whole of Palestine, Arab state in the whole of Palestine, partition, federalization of Jewish and Arab cantons, and UN trusteeship —she preferred the last.[26]

So it was with delight that she hailed the British decision in February, 1947, to turn the Palestine problem over to the United Nations, although she was appalled that Bevin, in disclosing this decision to the House of Commons, said all might have been well if President Truman for domestic political reasons had not made agreement impossible by his insistence on the 100,000. An "extraordinary outburst," Mrs. Roosevelt called it, "a fit of temper" which she hoped the president, whom she described as "a patient man," will accept "with charity." Her own sense of charity was taxed to the limit when, on the eve of the special assembly which had been convened at the request of the British government, its spokesman in the House of Lords said Britain would only carry out the decision of the assembly if it approved of it. The British attitude undermined the authority of the United Nations, she wrote. "The British Government is a Labor-Socialist government, but as far as the Empire and foreign affairs are concerned, it might as well be a Tory Government, because there is a similarity in the official pronouncements by every British government on these subjects." Though there were "comparatively few people" involved in the Palestine agony, "the horror of their situation is what makes it tragic, because those who are being kept out of Palestine are the waifs and strays of horror camps." She deplored terrorist tactics, "but I deplore even more the attitude of self-righteous governments." The British were not to blame alone. "Our own Government's position has never gone beyond pious hopes and unctuous words." [27]

She was impatient when the special assembly, under U.S. leadership, decided to postpone grappling with the substance of the Palestine problem and set up a Special Committee on Palestine (UNSCOP) to report to the regular session of the Assembly in September:

For two years now, displaced Jews have waited for the day of freedom and in many cases they are still behind barbed wires. The question of Palestine is as far from being settled as it was when the war came to an end.

Anglo-American interest in oil, she suggested, was behind the delay.

It seems to me, however, that this question cannot be settled on a commercial basis.

When we allowed the Jews to dream of a homeland and allowed many thousands of them to settle in Palestine—under the British mandate to be sure—we tacitly gave our support to this final conclusion. We are obligated today to see it through, giving every consideration, of course, to the rights of the Arabs, guarding their access to the religious shrines that are sacred to them, and seeing that from the economic standpoint whatever is fair is done.[28]

She respected General Marshall yet she wrote to him evidently complaining over the lack of firmness in the U.S. position in the Assembly. She was particularly concerned about Great Britain's remaining responsible for the maintenance of law and order in Palestine while UNSCOP was preparing its report. He regretted her critical comment, Marshall replied. "It was our view that this session had been called for the procedural purpose of constituting and instructing a special committee to prepare the Palestine question for consideration at the regular session. . . ." Only in that manner would all the member states have a chance to study "this complicated problem" and the way be prepared for "the widest possible support of world opinion" of UNSCOP's conclusions.[29]

"I think that our Government will take a firmer attitude and I hope in the right direction when their report comes before us," she wrote a correspondent. The right of the Jewish people to a homeland should have been considered and settled long ago, she continued. The United States, she felt, should support that right. She drew comfort from UNSCOP's membership, made up as it was of smaller nations and excluding the great powers which were primarily concerned with the future of the oil fields.[30]

Her misgivings about allowing Britain to administer Palestine pending UNSCOP's report were borne out when the British embarked upon a policy of interception of illegal immigrant ships, returning them to France and, when the passengers refused to disembark, ordering the ships to sail for Hamburg. It was easy to understand the refugees' sense of despair, she wrote, adding, "They feel perhaps that death is preferable." [31] She received an imploring letter from Eva Warburg, sister of Ingrid with whom she had worked in 1940–41, to save political refugees from the advancing Nazi armies. Eva Warburg had settled in Palestine in the thirties. "I am writing you on behalf of the 1700 Jewish orphans living in the camps on Cyprus. . . . They are, all of them, survivors from death camps or children who were hidden somewhere five long years." She described how they were held behind barbed wire, machine guns and searchlights trained on them. Could the women of the world not speak out against holding children as political hostages? Mrs. Roosevelt sent the letter on to President Truman, whose reply to her anguished telegram about the illegal immigrant ships called attention to the Jewish capacity to commit outrageous acts. "The British still seem to be on top and cruelty would seem to be on their side and not on the side of the Jews," Mrs. Roosevelt commented. When the three shiploads of Jewish displaced persons docked in Hamburg, she wrote sadly:

The thought of what it must mean to those poor human beings seems almost unbearable. They have gone through so much hardship and had thought themselves free forever from Germany, the country they associate with concentration camps and crematories. Now they are back there again. Somehow it is too horrible for any of us in this country to understand.[32]

Much of the world reacted as Mrs. Roosevelt did. British policy made men ashamed. It even affected viewpoints in UNSCOP.[33] Its report, issued just before the General Assembly convened in September, called for termination of the British mandate. It recommended that Palestinian independence should take the form of two separate states—Jewish and Arab—tied together in an economic union, with Jerusalem, a separate entity under the direct trusteeship of the United Nations. Although she had doubts about partition, she was even more dubious about the minority's recommendation of a vague cantonal plan. If the United Nations was to exercise any influence over events in the Near East, where the Arabs were vowing defiance of any UN resolution that upheld the right of the Jews to a homeland in Palestine, it would be along the lines of the (UNSCOP) majority recommendations or not at all. Within the U.S. delegation she became a strong supporter of those recommendations.

Most of the career men in the State Department were opposed to the majority report. Their problem was to persuade General Marshall and President Truman. For weeks the struggle raged inside the government. Sandifer, Mrs. Roosevelt's chief adviser, recalled Marshall saying at the end of all the discussion, "Here is a case where we have to do what is right. We have to do this as a matter of principle. We are obligated to support the establishment of a Jewish state." Sandifer, who shared the doubts of his State Department colleagues, felt that "the case of the Arabs in terms of U.S. interests was inadequately presented in the U.S. delegation." The presentation was made by Loy Henderson. "I'm sure General Marshall was influenced by the fact that there was not a clear simple presentation of the Arab case." Mrs. Roosevelt's firm attitude undoubtedly influenced the secretary. "She impressed me as having an open mind on every subject other than Palestine," said Sandifer. "She was not open to persuasion on that issue." All the department people were against Marshall's position in support of the UNSCOP recommendations, Mrs. Roosevelt told friends shortly after the Assembly opened. "They tell him 'no' and put it in such a way that to stand by his support of the UNSCOP recommendations is to go against the advice of all the qualified experts in the Department." But she thought Marshall would stand firm if the president did. She was fearful of the influence of Edwin W. Pauley, oil man and Truman intimate and powerful in the Democratic party. She had once cautioned Truman against Pauley:

I remember very well the pressure under which my own husband was placed and his agreement to name Mr. Pauley as Assistant Secretary of the Navy, and then we had a long discussion about it because I was very much opposed to having Mr. Pauley in any position where oil could be involved. Franklin assured me that if he put Mr. Pauley in as Assistant Secretary of the Navy, he would have nothing to do with oil because Mr. Forrestal would be over him and he would never be Secretary.°

Truman had turned aside her warning with the comment that he thought very highly of Pauley. It was now evident that Pauley had the ear of the president and, Mrs. Roosevelt feared, might tip the scale against Marshall. But Truman also came down on the side of partition and instructed the State Department to back it in the Assembly.[35]

Even after the United States announced its support of the majority report, its adoption by the General Assembly, requiring a two-thirds vote, was still doubtful and dependent in large measure on how strongly the United States campaigned. Henderson was authorized by Undersecretary of State Robert A. Lovett to assure Arab representatives that while the United States would vote for partition, it would not pressure other UN members to do so. At the same time, however, David Niles, an administrative assistant to the president, instructed Ambassador Warren Austin's deputy at the United Nations, Herschel V. Johnson, to twist arms if necessary. As

---

° Secretary James Forrestal, former president of the Wall Street firm of Dillon, Read & Company, was himself not oblivious to the Near East's oil reserves. Saudi Arabia was one of "the three great [oil] puddles left in the world," he told Secretary of State Byrnes in July, 1945, and although the United States was spending millions there, "the British and not ourselves were getting the benefit of it." [34]

the showdown vote approached, Zionist pressures became almost frenetic, antagonizing even Mrs. Roosevelt. She withdrew as co-chairman of a dinner of *The Nation* Associates when that group sent out a letter saying that "a gigantic doublecross" was in the making and that President Truman had decided to yield to the Arabs. She asked that her name be removed from the letterhead. "I do not feel I can be affiliated with a group which does such irresponsible things," she wrote Lessing J. Rosenwald, a leading anti-Zionist who had called the offending passage to her attention.[36]

U.S. support of the majority plan was announced on October 14. "Justice cannot be for one side alone, but must be for both," she wrote in her column. What about justice for the Arabs, a critic responded. The Palestine situation had to be seen in historical context, she replied:

You must remember that Great Britain and ourselves, without any protest at the time from the Arabs, agreed that the Jews were entitled to a homeland in Palestine. In the interim years, 600,000 Jews have gone there and at the cost of many lives, have developed an arid country into a garden spot. Much of it was malaria country and many Jews died so that blood and sweat has literally gone into that land.

Now the Arabs have awakened to the fact that a change is coming over the type of life that some of their own people lead as a result of this Jewish homeland and that they are not quite sure they like it. It seems to me that that decision has come a little too late and that all of us must abide by the plan which has been offered by the majority of a commission of the United Nations.

It will not hurt the Arabs, in fact they will profit by it, but we do not always like what is good for us in this world.[37]

On November 29, amid intense excitement, the General Assembly approved partition by a vote of 33 to 13 with ten nations not voting. The Soviet bloc voted for partition. If it had not, partition would not have passed. "A real miracle," commented Moshe Shertok of the Jewish Agency.

The Assembly's adoption of the partition plan transformed the problem in Mrs. Roosevelt's mind. Partition might not have been the best way to deal with the problem of a Jewish homeland, but no nation had suggested a better one, and now that it was endorsed by the United Nations it had become the first real test of the organization's capacity to take a position and make it stick. Moved by compassion for the Jewish remnant as well as by the hopes that she had invested in the United Nations, she was ready to do battle with president and secretary of state and secretary of defense to ensure that the United States stood firmly behind the United Nations as it proceeded to implement its resolution:

. . . it would be a blow to the prestige of the United Nations from which it would never recover, if they do not implement their decision, and if we do not do our share we will be responsible for sabotaging the only machinery we have for having peace today. This is, of course, neither in the interest of the Arabs or the Jews as far as I am concerned as I have never been to Palestine and have no personal feeling on the subject. But as to the preservation of the UN as machinery through which we may work for peace in the future, I have a great deal of conviction and I hope that other people will feel the same way.[38]

Troops of the Arab nations surrounding Palestine were on the move with the avowed purpose of nullifying the UN decision when the British left the country on May 15, 1948, as they had announced they would do. The Jewish Agency advised the United Nations that an international police force would be required to put the partition into effect. The UNSCOP did the same. But the United States, which had taken the leadership in the passage of the partition resolution, suddenly drew back. It did nothing to organize a UN peace-keeping force, and it imposed an embargo on the sale of arms to both Arabs and Jews, the effect of which, under the appearance of even-handedness, as in the case of the Spanish embargo, was to hamper and harass Jewish efforts to procure arms in the face of better-armed and more numerous Arab forces. And in Palestine the withdrawing British did their best to keep the Jews disarmed and defenseless.

The Palestine crisis came to a head at a moment of high tension with Soviet Russia. Because of the Communist coup in Czechoslovakia and rising Soviet pressures in Germany, Washington officials, especially those in the Defense Department, thought war might come at any moment. The military, led by Secretary Forrestal and Adm. William D. Leahy, began to get a more attentive hearing for their argument about the strategic importance of oil and air bases, and the further argument that if the United States took the leadership in enforcing the Assembly decision, Arab hostility would be turned against it.[39]

Mrs. Roosevelt sensed the administration's growing faintheartedness. She saw President Truman early in January, 1948, and told him people were worried over the increasing military influence in the government. "Now I know very well," she wrote the president a few days later,

that the defense people and probably the oil people are saying we must not offend the Arabs, that we need the oil and will need it particularly if we are going to have trouble with Russia. I feel it absolutely essential that we do not have trouble with Russia but we can only prevent it by being cleverer than Russia and keeping her out from the places where we do not wish her to be without offending her. That means we move first and we have a definite policy.

Great Britain has been arming the Arabs and has cooked up much of the trouble in that area for the very simple reason that Great Britain knows that only two people will buy Arab oil—the United States and the United Kingdom. Russia will walk in and take it when she is ready. We have to out-think Great Britain as well as Russia and I am very much afraid that some of the people in the State Department and some people in the defense group are not thinking very far ahead and if the United Nations becomes a second League and disintegrates as it well may, if it gets no support in this situation, then another war is inevitable. On top of that a Republican election is inevitable.[40]

An article by James Reston in the *New York Times* added to her uneasiness. It spoke of State Department and Defense Department moves to weaken the influence of Zionist pressure groups with the president. Reston reported Forrestal's "grave concern," as he stated it to the House Armed Services Committee, over a "strategic oil shortage vital to the European Recovery Program" arising from "hostile Moslem response to the UN partition plan." There was strong pressure from the State and Defense departments against any action by the United States that might antagonize the Arabs.[41]

On January 28, using the Reston article as a peg, Mrs. Roosevelt sent a forceful note to General Marshall. Since the United States had led in the adoption of the partition plan, it carried a responsibility to enforce it. The United Nations

can probably recruit a volunteer force among the smaller nations but they can not get the necessary modern equipment of war except from us. It would seem to me that the quicker we removed the embargo and see that the Jews and any UN police force are equipped with modern armaments, which is the only thing which will hold the Arabs in check, the better it will be for the whole situation.[42]

The next day she wrote even more vigorously to the president:

It seems to me that if the UN does not put through and enforce the partition and protection of people in general in Palestine, we are facing a very serious situation in which its position for the future is at stake.

She repeated the plea she had made to Marshall for U.S. support of an international police force. "If the U.N. is going to be an instrument for peace, now is the crucial time to strengthen it." [43]

Truman replied promptly. He and Marshall were trying to work out an implementation plan. He agreed with her about Great Britain's role in the Near East. The Labor government's policy there was little different from Disraeli's. General Marshall took longer to reply and was less acquiescent. Both Jewish and Arab elements were committing acts of terror and violence. He complained that "the political situation in this country does not help matters." It was the American policy to approach the Palestine problem through the United Nations rather than unilaterally. "A decision by the United States, for instance, to permit American arms to go to Palestine and neighboring states would facilitate acts of violence and the further shedding of blood and thus render still more difficult the task of maintaining law and order. We are continuing, therefore, to refuse to license the shipment of arms to that area." [44]

His reply did not impress her:

I am, of course, entirely in accord that we should approach the matter through the UN and not unilaterally, but in placing an embargo on arms we seem not to have interfered with the Arab's ability to get arms and the Jews seem to be getting them sub-rosa, so to speak, which isn't such a good thing. That is why the embargo seemed to me unwise at the present time.

She had learned that one of the objections to a UN police force was the fear of the military that it would have to include a Russian contingent. "I would be in complete accord," her letter to Marshall continued,

that we should do whatever the UN asks of us but I am seriously worried that Mr. Forrestal advises the President that even if the UN suggests a UN police force in which all nations have an equal quota, he would feel, should Russia go in with the rest of us that he had to mobilize the U.S. fifty per cent for war at once. That seems to me utter nonsense and I do not understand it very well.[45]

To President Truman she was even sharper in her criticism of Forrestal:

P.S.   James told me of Mr. Forrestal's feeling that no American should be allowed to volunteer in an International Police Force. I think Mr. Forrestal is entirely wrong. I was shocked at the suggestion that any American volunteering to fight in Palestine would lose his citizenship, and I could not understand why that was not invoked when Americans went to Canada and enlisted in the Canadian forces before the war.

It seems to me that if the UN calls for an International Police Force, it might very well say that the quotas should be equal from all nations, big and little, and then we should call for volunteers within our nation. To say that just because Russia might have some soldiers in Palestine on an equal basis with us and all the other nations involved, we would have to mobilize fifty percent for war seems to me complete nonsense and I think it would seem so to most of the people of the United States.[46]

How strongly she felt was made clear a few days later when she joined Sumner Welles, Herbert H. Lehman, and Sen. Elbert D. Thomas in sponsorship of a four-point plan proposed by the American Association for the United Nations to enforce the UN Palestine resolution. Mrs. Roosevelt's presence in this group was extraordinary: she was, after all, part of the U.S. representation at the United Nations, an appointee of the president. The AAUN group urged the immediate establishment of a UN force for service in Pal-

*Mrs. Roosevelt and her children in front of the White House
as the president's body arrives at the executive mansion.*

*The United States delegation departing for the First General Assembly of
the United Nations. Left to right: Sen. Tom Connally (D-Texas),
Sen. Arthur H. Vandenberg (R-Michigan), Edward R. Stettinius, Jr., U.S.
representative on the Security Council, and Mrs. Roosevelt.*

*Mrs. Roosevelt makes a point to Soviet Foreign Minister
V. M. Molotov at the United Nations. In the background Andrei Gromyko,
Soviet representative on the Security Council.*

Mrs. Roosevelt makes an observation to Secretary of State George C. Marshall at the 1947 General Assembly. In the background Francis B. Sayre, an alternate member of the delegation.
Below: *To President Truman she was the "First Lady of the World."*

She loved to come over to the Big House at Hyde Park and tell
young people some of the history that had taken place in its rooms.
The Park Service recorded her comments on tape.

*Mrs. Roosevelt accompanying Winston Churchill
to the rose garden at Hyde Park, where his old companion-at-arms
lay buried.*

Eleanor Roosevelt at Val-Kill with two of John Roosevelt's daughters, Sally at her side and Nina in the boat. Fala is on the leash and Tamas is the other Scotty.

Four generations: Mrs. Roosevelt, her daughter Anna on the left, granddaughter "Sistie" (Mrs. Seagrave) on the right, and great-granddaughter Eleanor in Mrs. Seagrave's arms.

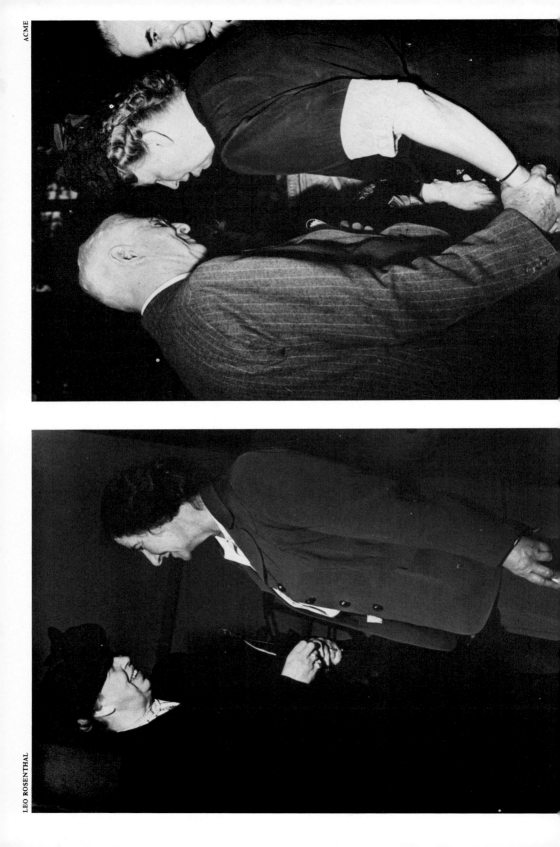

Eleanor Roosevelt with Golda Meir of Israel in 1949.

An old friend, Bernard M. Baruch, who helped Mrs. Roosevelt in many undertakings.

Below left: *He had thought her appointment as a delegate to the United Nations "terrible," John Foster Dulles confessed to Mrs. Roosevelt, but after watching her in action he was prepared to eat his words.*

Right: *At the 1951 Paris General Assembly, Mrs. Roosevelt, Warren R. Austin, chief U.S. representative at the United Nations, and Secretary of State Dean Acheson.*

LEO ROSENTHAL

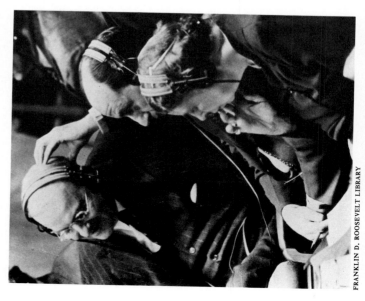

FRANKLIN D. ROOSEVELT LIBRARY

*Eleanor Roosevelt addresses a plenary session of the General
Assembly, October 20, 1949. Carlos Romulo of the Philippines is in the
president's chair.*

*For several years Mrs. Roosevelt presided over her own television
program. Her guests on this occasion were Gov. Michael
DiSalle of Ohio and James Carey, secretary of the CIO and head of the
Electrical and Radio Workers Union.*

*In April, 1948, Mrs. Roosevelt went to England for the
unveiling of Britain's memorial statue to Franklin D. Roosevelt.
At the ceremony in Grosvenor Square
(left to right): Major Hooker, Queen Elizabeth, Queen Mother Mary,
Mrs. Roosevelt, Prime Minister Clement Attlee, King George, and
Viscount Greenwood, chairman of the Memorial Committee.*

Discussing the Draft Covenant on Human Rights.
Left to right: Dr. Charles Malik of Lebanon; Prof. René Cassin of France,
who was later awarded the Nobel Peace Prize for his work in this field;
Miss Marjorie Whiteman, a State Department adviser to Mrs. Roosevelt;
Mrs. Roosevelt; and James Simsarian, another
State Department adviser.

She called the Universal Declaration of Human Rights
"a Magna Charta for mankind."

*With Dag Hammarskjöld, who
succeeded Trygve Lie as secretary-general.*

*Returning from a trip to Europe
on which she had been accompanied by her
son Elliott (standing next to her)
and two of his children, Chandler and
Tony. They are being greeted by James
Roosevelt (second from the left), the then
Democratic candidate for governor
in California, and Franklin Jr.
(far left), then a congressman from
New York City.*

Mrs. Roosevelt at a children's kibbutz in Israel in January, 1952.

Every summer the children of the Wiltwyck School for Boys picnicked at Val-Kill, and Mrs. Roosevelt would tell them stories—usually favorites from Kipling.

GRAY-O'REILLY

Mrs. Roosevelt with grandsons Franklin III and Christopher.
Fala is between them. 1950.

estine, to be activated as soon as British troops left the country, or sooner if requested. The avowed Arab determination to resist with arms a pacific settlement of the Palestine issue "poses the question of the authority of the United Nations," the signatories declared. If the UN's authority is successfully challenged by "these weak states in the Middle East, what confidence can be placed in the ability of the UN to meet and master future crises to which, perhaps, major powers may be a party?" The signatories saw Soviet support for the partition resolution as a promising development. The hopes raised by the Soviet Union and the United States finding themselves in accord "must not be shattered by inaction or timidity at the present time." [47]

She was about to go abroad to England for the unveiling of a statue of FDR in Grosvenor Square. Truman, who was in Key West, Florida, wished her a pleasant journey and said he had told Forrestal his views on an international police force, and if such a force should be organized, of course, there would be no question of loss of citizenship.[48]

But the United States, instead of moving in the United Nations to set up a police force, began to retreat from partition to the idea that a temporary trusteeship should replace the British mandate. Washington officials who were pressing the trusteeship concept, led by Forrestal and Lovett, tried to make it appear that the United Nations did not have the powers to enforce its decision. They called in everyone who had worked on the Charter, omitting Benjamin V. Cohen, to frame a statement to that effect.[49]

Mrs. Roosevelt knew of these maneuvers. She read trusteeship to be a reversal of U.S. policy, a shift that undermined the authority of the United Nations and betrayed a moral obligation the U.S. had assumed when it accepted the Balfour Declaration. She thought there would be quite a few nations who would refuse to jump to the U.S. whim. There was no perfect solution, and the one already adopted by the United Nations might as well be implemented. Trusteeship would confront the United States with exactly the same problems as it faced in its support of partition. So she wrote General Marshall, saying she would have to say these things publicly and offering her resignation. She wrote the same day to the president "a very frank and unpleasant letter," as she called it. Her disagreement with the administration over Palestine reflected a larger disagreement over the increased deference to military considerations in the formulation of American foreign policy.

I feel that even though the Secretary of State takes responsibility for the Administration's position on Palestine, you cannot escape the results of that attitude. I have written the Secretary a letter a copy of which I enclose which will explain my feelings on this particular subject.

On Trieste I feel we have also let the UN down. We are evidently discarding the UN and acting unilaterally, or setting up a balance of power by backing the European democracies and preparing for an ultimate war between the two political philosophies. I am opposed to this attitude because I feel it would be possible, with force and friendliness, to make some arrangements with the Russians, using our economic power as a bribe to obstruct their political advance.

I can not believe that war is the best solution. No one won the last war, and no one will win the next war. While I am in accord that we need force and I am in accord that we need this force to preserve the peace, I do not think that complete preparation for war is the proper approach as yet. . . .

I realize that I am an entirely unimportant cog in the wheel of our work with the UN, but I have offered my resignation to the Secretary since I can quite understand the difficulty of having some one so far down the line openly criticize the Administration policies.

I deeply regret that I must write this letter.[50]

Her letter set the alarm bells ringing at the White House. In his most vigorous language Truman expressed his conviction that the United Nations was humanity's best and perhaps only hope for peace. He knew from General Marshall that the latter was sending over Chip Bohlen to brief her on the government's policies, and, if she was able to see Dean Rusk, he would further elucidate the president's program. Her withdrawal from the United Nations would be a calamity. That organization, and the country, needed her. Addressing himself to the trusteeship controversy, the president assured her it was a stopgap measure designed to avoid further bloodshed in the Holy Land, not a substitute for partition. He implored her not to resign and invoked the Lord's blessings upon her.[51]

It was a heartfelt letter and moved her deeply, she wrote the president, adding, however, that she had talked with Bohlen and "I cannot say that even now the temporary measures that we have suggested for Palestine really makes anything simpler or safer than it was before but perhaps it will prove to be a solution and I certainly pray it will." Neither the president's letter or her talk with Bohlen kept her from publicly criticizing the trusteeship proposal in her column even as she was en route to London.[52]

A month abroad did not reconcile her to the policy. She was going to stay out of the campaign, she informed Adlai Stevenson, who had asked her to come out to Illinois where he was beginning his quest for the governorship.

I am very unhappy about going back on the Assembly decision on Palestine and I feel the handling of it up to this time has brought about much of the Arab arrogance and violence. Certainly our proposal for a change does not seem, from my point of view, to have put us in any better position. Somebody will have to implement a truce and somebody will have to implement a trusteeship. Some time the issue of serving on an equal basis with Russia under the UN will have to be faced.[53]

Although in January and February the chief arguments advanced by Forrestal and Lovett for the abandonment of partition had been the undesirability and unreadiness of the United States to provide troops to enforce it and the lack of power in the United Nations under the Charter to set up a police force to implement an Assembly resolution,° both men were ready to dispatch U.S. troops to the Near East to uphold a trusteeship proposal.[54] But, as Mrs. Roosevelt had predicted, other nations were not prepared to dance to the new U.S. tune. In the special session of the General Assembly, where the American representatives were still pushing the trusteeship proposal when she returned from London, the Soviet Union had declared its opposition to any shift away from partition and the British said there was not enough time to implement a trusteeship proposal.

° In 1956 the United States reversed itself on this, Benjamin V. Cohen has noted, when it vigorously supported the creation of a United Nations Emergency Force to supervise and police the Suez cease-fire and the withdrawal of British-French-Israeli forces, and, in connection with the Congo operation in 1960, supported Dag Hammarskjöld's concept of the United Nations as an executive agency as well as a conference one.

Truman, who all along had stoutly insisted that he did not construe the State Department's advocacy of trusteeship as abandonment of the original plan, began to back away.

She thought the people down below had tried to put one over on him. He himself later wrote in his *Memoirs* that the State Department should have known that trusteeship would be regarded by both Jews and Arabs as an abandonment of partition, and in that sense "the trusteeship idea was at odds with my attitude and the policy I had laid down." [55]

On May 11, 1948, Mrs. Roosevelt alerted Marshall:

> I have just heard from some of the Jewish organizations that they have heard that Russia will recognize the Jewish State as soon as it is declared which will be midnight on Friday, I imagine. The people who spoke to me are afraid that we will lag behind and again follow instead of lead.
>
> I have no idea what the policy of the Administration and the State Department is going to be on this, and I am only just telling you what you probably already know about the Russian position. I have no feeling that they have any principles or convictions in what they are doing, but wherever they can put us in a hole they certainly are going to do it.

Then she added a postscript in her own hand, to make sure that he understood that in her mind recognition was not simply a matter of beating the Russians to it. "I failed to say that personally I believe there is right back of the establishment of a Jewish state." Marshall and Lovett, in their first discussion with Truman on the question of recognition, were opposed to it. But then their viewpoint changed. Perhaps Mrs. Roosevelt's letter was a factor. In any event, the president had determined to extend immediate *de facto* recognition to the new state and to be the first nation to do so. He wanted to get in ahead of Soviet Russia. This was a presidential election year and he knew that such a move would be hailed with enthusiasm by American Jews. And he was not averse to surprising the State Department officials who had tried to circumvent his policy.

He moved with such secrecy that not only were friendly UN delegations unprepared, but his own UN representatives as well. In fact, Ambassador Philip C. Jessup, in the Security Council, was still pushing trusteeship when news of America's recognition came over the press wires. The procedure stirred her to new indignation because she felt the United Nations had been demeaned. She wrote General Marshall:

May 16, 1948

Dear Mr. Secretary:

Having written you before what I had heard on the subject of the recognition of Palestine, I feel I should write you again.

The way in which the recognition of Palestine came about has created complete consternation in the United Nations.

As you know, I never wanted us to change our original stand. When I wrote to the President and to you the other day what I had heard, I thought, of course, that you would weigh it against the reports which you were getting from the United Nations. Much as I wanted the Palestine State recognized, I would not have wanted it done without the knowledge of our representatives in the United Nations who had been fighting for our changed position. I would have felt that they had to know the reason and I would also have felt that there had to be a very clear understanding beforehand with such nations as we expected would follow our lead.

Several of the representatives of other governments have been to talk to me since, and have stated quite frankly that they do not see how they could ever follow the United States' lead because the United States changed so often without any consultation. There seems to be no sense of interlocking information between the United States delegate and the State Department on the policy making level. This is serious because our acts which should strengthen the United Nations only result in weakening our influence within the United Nations and in weakening the United Nations itself.

More and more the other delegates seem to believe that our whole policy is based on antagonism to Russia and that we think in terms of going it alone rather than in terms of building up a leadership within the United Nations.

This seems to me a very serious defect and I do not see how we can expect to have any real leadership if,

1. We do not consult our people in the United Nations on what we are going to do, and
2. If we do not line up our following before we do the things, rather than trusting to influencing them afterwards.

I can not imagine that major considerations on policies such as this are taken at such short notice that there is not time to think through every consequence and inform all those who should be informed.

I have seldom seen a more bitter, puzzled, discouraged group of people than some of those whom I saw on Saturday. Some of them I know are favorable to the rights of the Jews in Palestine, but they are just nonplused by the way in which we do things.

I thought I had to tell you this because I had written you before and as you know, I believe that it is the Administration's desire to strengthen the United Nations, but we do not always achieve it because, apparently, there is a lack of contact on the higher levels.

With deep concern, I am,

Very sincerely yours,

Ambassador Austin was advised, Truman and Marshall assured her, but not in time to notify other members of the delegation. Truman stressed the need of stealing a march on the Russians, who were anxious to be the first. "We were aware here of the unfortunate effect on our situation with the United Nations, which is much to be regretted," Marshall added. "More than this, I am not free to say." [56]

Recognition was a fact of the highest political importance, but one that would have been annulled had the Jewish settlements in Palestine been unable to repel the armies of the surrounding Arab states. Arab boasts that they would erase the new state in ten days were accompanied by an Arab exodus from the cities in order to facilitate the task of driving the Jews into the sea. But the Arab armies were soon in retreat.

For the moment United States policy seemed right to her.

Henry Morgenthau brought a Mrs. Meyerson [Mrs. Golda Meir] from Palestine to breakfast last Tuesday. A woman of great strength & calm & for me she symbolizes the best spirit of Palestine. Evidently at last we mean to follow through on a policy of aid to the Jewish State. The British role seems to me quite stupid, no more greedy & self interested than ours has been but at last we seem to be doing better.[57]

By summer, 1948, the Swedish Count Folke Bernadotte, appointed mediator by the United Nations, was seeking to bring about a cease-fire and a permanent settlement. His peace plan would have taken the Negeb, which was assigned to Israel under the partition resolution, and given it to Transjordan, thus providing a land bridge between that state and Egypt, both of them British controlled. Israel was to be compensated by land in the Galilee. But in September, Bernadotte was assassinated by Jewish terrorists, an act that horrified the Jewish community despite its hostility to the Bernadotte proposals. The cease-fire lines, in the absence of a permanent settlement, became the *de facto* boundaries of Israel. Again there was a struggle within the U.S. high command between the president on one side and State Department and Defense Department officials on the other over whether to go forward with the Bernadotte proposals.

"I wish you would do some work in putting pressure on Secretary Marshall so that he will consider his approval of the Bernadotte Plan was not tantamount to complete acceptance of all the recommendations contained in it, but only as being a good basis for negotiation," she wrote Bernard Baruch, who was a good friend of the secretary:

It seems highly unfair to me to turn the whole of the Negev over to the Arabs. The portion of Galilee given to the Jews is not fertile and I do not think it fair compensation because in Jewish hands the Negev would be developed and may turn out to be the only place where they can receive immigration. I have expressed these thoughts in the delegation meetings but I do not think I carry much weight. I have only one real backer and that is Ben Cohen. Neither of us was consulted before the Secretary made his announcement to the press of the acceptance of the Bernadotte report. We were simply handed a statement to read in the session after he had given it out to the press.

He had already conveyed his views to Marshall, Baruch replied. "I do not see why they ever turned any of the Negeb area over to the Arabs, nor do I yet see why, when we lobbied for the Palestine settlement, we turned our backs on it. That hurt America's position in the world more than it has been able to recover. In our fears, we are letting England put a lot of things over on us and it is not confined to Palestine." She could be tough with the British. The Palestine refugee issue was a sensitive one in the U.S. presidential election, so the American delegation sought to postpone consideration of how much it would contribute toward refugee relief until after Election Day. But British policy was oriented toward the Arabs, and its delegation pressed to have the matter come up immediately. "I have the votes," Hector McNeill, the British representative, admonished Mrs. Roosevelt. "Very well, Mr. McNeill," she replied, "but I have the money," and walked away. The British desisted.[58]

Truman finally settled the debate over the Bernadotte plan. In an election-eve speech in Madison Square Garden he came out flatly against it. "Israel," he said, "must be large enough and strong enough to make its people self-supporting and secure." [59]

"I have a feeling," Mrs. Roosevelt advised the president when she reported to him at the end of the 1948 General Assembly,

that your attitude on Palestine did a great deal to strengthen our own delegation and help the situation from the world point of view. The Arabs have to be handled with strength. One of the troubles has been that we have been so impressed that we must have a united front in Europe that it has affected our stand in the Near East. I personally feel that it is more important for the French and for the British to be united with us than for us to be united with them, and therefore when we make up our minds that something has to be done, we should be the ones to do what we think is right and we should not go through so many anxieties on the subject.[60]

She hoped that the truce negotiations being conducted by Dr. Ralph J. Bunche, who had succeeded Bernadotte, would lead to a final settlement,

since there is no question that they [the Israelis] have full control in the areas which the United Nations considered a fair partition in November, 1947. The Arabs may not like the idea of having the Jews in the Negev, for instance, but I imagine the Jews are the only people who would be energetic enough to develop it.[61]

In May, 1949, Israel was voted a member of the United Nations. The day the flag of Israel was added to all the other flags outside of the UN area at Lake Success was a memorable one:

There was a lump in almost everybody's throat, I think, at the thought of a new nation being born and one whose people had suffered greatly. . . .[62]

Ralph Bunche later said that one of the difficulties in discussing the Palestine problem with Mrs. Roosevelt was her almost "primitive" conception of the Arabs. She still saw them in the terms her husband had used when he described his encounter with Ibn Saud—as desert-dwelling sheiks who pitched their tents on the decks of cruisers and were interested neither in irrigation nor trees. If that was the case, a visit to several Arab countries and Israel in February, 1952, did not change her point of view:

The Arab countries are awakening but oh! so slowly & painfully! The refugees were a horror & it is the Arab governments who keep them stirred up to go home with a little help from the communists! It is like being in another world even in Lebanon & that is the most progressive. . . .

Israel is like a breath of fresh air after the Arab countries. Horrible problems but wonderful leaders & such able assistants. . . . I felt at home with the people of Israel.

"Israel was one of the most exciting experiences I have ever had," she wrote her aunt, Maude Gray. "The Jews in their own country are doing marvels & should, once the refugee problem is settled, help all the Arab countries." [63] °

° See Appendix B: "Mrs. Roosevelt and the Sultan of Morocco."

VI. The 1948 Campaign:
A New Party—Not a Third Party

In Albany at the beginning of September, 1946, in a smoke-filled room, the county leaders of the Democratic party had gathered for their preconvention caucus when there was a sudden hush as Mrs. Roosevelt entered. She tried to put everyone at ease but it was a little as if Saint Theresa had walked into a meeting of the Mafia and had said, "Carry on, Signori." Everyone was on his best behavior.

The state chairman, Paul Fitzpatrick of Buffalo, began his canvass of the leaders' views on a slate for the election to run against the incumbent Republicans headed by Gov. Thomas E. Dewey. Mrs. Roosevelt said little. She would have her say the next day as temporary chairman of the convention, in which capacity she was to deliver the keynote address. But when the county leader of Westchester observed that the Democrats did not need to worry about having a veteran on the ticket because the Republicans did not have one on theirs, she bristled. "We want a veteran on the ticket," she protested, "because of what the country owes the veteran." Moreover, "we want these younger men and women to come into the leadership of the Party." A little later when the leader of Rochester minimized the importance to the Democrats of the rural vote and said it would be the cities that carried the ticket, she again gestured to Fitzpatrick that she wished to speak. It was a weakness of the Democrats, she said, and of the party's program, that agricultural interests in the state were not better represented.[1]

The convention nominated a ticket headed by Sen. James M. Mead—a move that had evidently been discussed with FDR:

I remember very well talking with my husband about his hopes for the candidate, and at that time he told me that he felt if General O'Dwyer could be run for Mayor of New York City, Mr. LaGuardia could be induced to run for the Senate, as running mate for Senator Mead as Governor and that this ticket would be a winning ticket.[2]

But the top Democratic leaders did not want La Guardia and chose former Gov. Herbert H. Lehman to run for the Senate. Lehman had come to see her at Hyde Park just before the convention. She had suggested mildly that La Guardia, a political maverick, might do better in what looked like a Republican year. She was pessimistic about the ticket's chances and preferred to see La Guardia lose rather than him, she told Lehman. But the ex-governor had replied that the party wanted him to run and he could not let the party down.[3]

So many of the men who had once held public office found themselves lost when out of it, she observed. Public office as such held little attraction for her. She had firmly stopped a movement to draft her for the state ticket, partly because she preferred her work at the United Nations but also because she thought that "no woman has, as yet, been able to build up and hold sufficient leadership to carry through a program." And if you could not put through a program what was the point in holding office? She wanted to be free to speak out, a freedom that she would have to surrender in taking party office. "If I do not run for office, I am not beholden to my Party. What I give, I give freely and I am too old to want to be curtailed in any way in the expression of my own thinking." [4]

She was sixty-two. She felt a responsibility for helping young people move into the management of the world in which they lived. If she ran for public office, it would make it difficult for her sons. They all had political ambitions—James in California, Elliott and Franklin Jr. in New York. They all had lived in the shadow of their father. She did not wish to place them under a similar disability.[5]

The Republicans swept the 1946 elections, gaining control of both the House and the Senate. "The Party and the nation have been without leadership," Charl Williams, who traveled the country for the National Education Association, wrote her, "this includes the President of the United States, the chairman of the Democratic National Committee, and party leaders in Congress. Loyal rock-ribbed Democrat as I am, I could feel no sense of enthusiasm as in former days."

Mrs. Roosevelt agreed that the country lacked leadership, "but perhaps we will pull ourselves together and keep going." What she meant by leadership, she indicated a few months later when a reporter for *PM* came to talk with her on the second anniversary of Franklin's death. She met people often, she told the reporter, who said to her:

"We miss hearing his voice in our living room." You know I think he gave people a sense of security. They felt he had a pretty complete understanding of their own problems and the problems they must face in the rest of the world. Hearing his voice, they were inclined to feel they were part of what was going on.

Now, they feel left out.

Franklin had a good way of simplifying things. He made people feel that he had a real understanding of things and they felt they had about the same understanding.[6]

There was not too much that Truman at sixty-two could do about his dry, rasping voice or how he related to people. Nor did Mrs. Roosevelt look at him and think, "Franklin wouldn't do it that way," as Harry Hopkins had warned that the Roosevelt people would. She understood Truman's problems with Congress and thought he might be better off with straight-out Republican control, since the Republicans then would have to take the responsibility.* Yet his difficulties with Congress did not explain or justify his neglect of important elements of the Roosevelt coalition—the women, the cities, the liberals. That, she feared, reflected his middle-American conservatism, and many of the new men he brought in with him, including the so-called "Missouri Gang," were similarly oriented.

She was determined to do what she could to press Truman in the other direction. "I used to have to remind the gentlemen of the Party rather frequently," she had written him in mid-1946,

---

* "The luckiest thing that ever happened to me was the Eightieth Congress," Truman later said.[7]

that we Democrats did not win unless we had the liberals, labor and women largely with us. Among our best workers in all campaigns are the women. They will do the dull detail work and fill the uninteresting speaking engagements which none of the men are willing to undertake. I hope you will impress this fact on those who are now organizing for the Congressional campaigns and in preparation for 1948.[8]

By the end of 1946 some of her liberal friends were gloomily speaking of a "reversion to type" by the Democratic party now that the strong hand of FDR was removed. "That is the real meaning of the New Deal exodus from Washington. The turnover in administration personnel is fast approaching the proportions that usually accompany a change in parties," a friend wrote her. He cited the premature, pell-mell abandonment of wartime economic controls, the inept handling of labor crises, the replacement of able and talented men by political hacks, wondering whether it was not time for progressives again to think of going the road of a third party.

"I would still be opposed to a third party," she advised him, "but in the end you are right & I think we must have a *new* party, not necessarily a 3rd party." She wrote along similar lines to La Guardia:

It takes so long before a third party wields any power, I can not see much point in trying to build one up at the present time when things need to be done quickly.

She saw a role for independents, she went on, "to make the two major parties uncomfortable when they stand for something which is really wrong." She was not saying that the Democrats should be supported no matter what sort of candidates they nominated, "but I think it is the party to belong to, and we can try to improve the candidates. If we do not succeed, we do not have to vote for them." [9]

She considered Edwin W. Pauley one of the people responsible for the conservative shift of the administration and Democratic party, and politely told him so after she spoke at the California Jackson Day dinner in Los Angeles, which as Democratic National committeeman he organized in June, 1947. Irate over a statement critical of the Truman Doctrine issued by liberal Democrats with

James Roosevelt in the lead, Pauley publicly rebuked the liberals, and the press interpreted his censure to include Mrs. Roosevelt, whose questions about the Truman Doctrine were on the public record. He had meant no disrespect, he hastened to assure her, but a Jackson Day dinner was not an appropriate forum for the criticism of the administration's policies or the president.

He might be right on the issue of propriety and protocol, she replied, but the questions asked about the administration's policies in the statement of the progressives were being asked everywhere, and the mistake at the dinner was in not having an administration speaker there to answer those questions.

I was not bothered by any suggestion of disrespect. Things like that have never bothered me, but I was troubled by what I thought was stupid politically. 1948 is no walk-over for the Democratic Party or for President Truman, and he needs some really astute and liberal politicians around him.[10]

When Mrs. Roosevelt heard from Ed Flynn that Secretary of Agriculture Clinton P. Anderson would replace Robert Hannegan as national chairman, she saw it as confirmation that the party was being turned over to its most conservative elements. "I thought it only fair to tell you," she wrote Truman,

that I could never support Mr. Anderson. I consider him a conservative and I consider that the only chance the Democratic Party has for election in 1948, [is] to be the liberal party. We cannot be more conservative than the Republicans so we cannot succeed as conservatives. If the country is going conservative, it is not going to vote for any Democratic candidate.[11]

The real reason for Flynn's pique, Truman said, was a quarrel over patronage. But her protest against Anderson must have had some effect, for Sen. J. Howard McGrath of Rhode Island, a politician oriented toward urban rather than "middle" America, was appointed national chairman.

As 1948 approached, the politicians understood her political importance. There were renewed pressures in New York to have her run for senator. "Dear Mr. Mayor," she wrote William O'Dwyer:

. . . I want to tell you again that under no circumstances would I run for any office.

I am interested in the United Nations work and feel that even at sixty-three, which I will shortly be, I can do something there, but it is no time at sixty-three to start running for elective office and nothing would induce me to do it.

What she said to O'Dwyer privately, she reiterated publicly in her column to make doubly sure that the party's leaders knew she meant it.[12]

Her popularity astonished the politicians and infuriated anti-Roosevelt columnists, especially Westbrook Pegler, who had embarked on a systematic campaign to try to destroy her influence. In a popularity poll conducted by the *Woman's Home Companion* at the beginning of 1948, Mrs. Roosevelt was placed first among the nation's ten outstanding personalities, including Truman, Marshall, Dewey, Hoover, Eisenhower, and MacArthur.[13] The Gallup poll taken every year on the most admired woman in the United States regularly showed her at the head of the list.

She knew she had political influence. She knew that Truman needed her. He needed her the more because of the Wallace third-party candidacy. Wallace had announced his candidacy for president in December, declaring that a vote for him would be a vote against war with Russia. Her first comment had been a terse, motherly, "Oh dear, oh dear." Then in three columns running she assailed him, her final sally being the flat declaration, "he has never been a good politician, he has never been able to gauge public opinion, and he has never picked his advisers wisely." [14]

Yet it was by no means certain at the turn of the year that Wallace's assessment of the public mood was wrong. She hoped that Truman was "going to make a real fight," she wrote him after his State of the Union message, "for every one of the social things in your message. . . . The great trouble is that Mr. Wallace will cut in on us because he can say that we have given lip service to these things by having produced very little in the last few years."

Nettled, Truman replied that he had been making a real fight, and if he had not come to Wallace's support during the confirmation struggle in 1945 when Roosevelt was in Yalta, Wallace never would have been approved as secretary of commerce in the Senate. Truman felt that his problem with Congress was the same one FDR had had—the coalition between the southern Democrats and the Republicans.[15]

The answer was time-honored and hackneyed. It had never wholly satisfied her when offered by Franklin; it did not satisfy her now. Upset over the administration's vacillations on Palestine, worried over the increasing influence of the military, she decided she had to express her anxieties more bluntly. "Because this letter is not too pleasant, I have been putting it off," she wrote Truman. She knew how difficult it was for the people around a president "to tell him that they are troubled and of course, there are many people who tell him only what they think will serve their own interests in what they think he will want to hear." She detailed her foreign-policy worries and went on:

There is also a fear of the conservative influence that is being exerted on the economic side and I am afraid that this deposition of Mr. Eccles [Marriner S. Eccles, chairman of the Federal Reserve Board] which the *New York Times* takes as a triumph of "orthodoxy and conservatism in fiscal policy as represented by John W. Snyder, Secretary of the Treasury" is going to emphasize this feeling considerably.

Believe me, Sir, it is going to be impossible to elect a Democrat if it is done by appealing to the conservatives. The Republicans are better conservatives than we are. If the people are going to vote conservative, it is going to be Taft or Dewey and we might just as well make up our minds to it.[16]

Another portent of the inroads Wallace was making into Truman's strength came like a thunderclap out of the Bronx. In a special congressional election in mid-February, the Wallace candidate handed Ed Flynn's nominee a stunning defeat, almost reversing the landslide percentages by which the Democrats traditionally held the district.

What did she think of her Ed Flynn now, the president inquired with some trenchancy, knowing the great confidence she had placed in Flynn's political judgment. She thought the Bronx

vote had proved the point Flynn had been trying to make to the
president:

> I was not very much surprised by the results of the vote because in
> the big, urban centers, even those who are Democrats, just do not come
> out to vote because they are still radical enough to be unhappy about
> what they feel are certain tendencies they observe in our Administra-
> tion.
>
> Ed Flynn has told you this, I think, on a number of occasions. It is
> important because if the Democrats are going to win in a State like New
> York, they have to carry by a great majority, the big urban centers. I am
> sure you are well aware of this, but I feel it my duty to re-enforce what
> already has been said, disagreeable as it is. . . .
>
> . . . the two things bothering the average man most at present are
> inflation and the fear of another war. Congress is doing all it can to help
> us, I think, because certainly they are showing a complete disregard for
> the high cost of living as it affects the average human being, but you
> never know how many people realize this.
>
> I know that in order to obtain what we need in the way of military
> strength for defense, it would seem almost essential to whip up fear of
> communism and to do certain things which hurt us with the very ele-
> ment which we need in the election. How can we be firm and strong
> and yet friendly in our attitude toward Russia, and obtain from Con-
> gress what we need to keep us strong, is one of our most difficult prob-
> lems. I have often thought if you could explain the whole situation over
> the radio in a series of talks to the people of our country, it might clear
> up some of our difficulties, because I find great confusion in the minds
> of the average citizen.[17]

Truman disputed her analysis. There was always a letdown
after a war, he felt. The postwar reaction against the Democrats
that had manifested itself in the 1946 elections was still at work.
The leaders of the Democratic party were tired, having led the
country through the Depression and war. He had to do things in
his own way. Truman was right when he said that the leadership of
the party was tired, Mrs. Roosevelt replied. "Perhaps the people are
too. Unfortunately, this is a bad time to be tired." [18]

It was not only the Wallace candidacy and the southern revolt
that threatened Truman. A spreading "draft Eisenhower" movement was enlisting the support of such trade-union leaders as Wal-

ter Reuther and David Dubinsky, ADA liberals, and even northern machine politicians like Jake Arvey. Three of Mrs. Roosevelt's sons, James in California and Elliott and Franklin Jr. in New York, were part of it. They reflected the widespread feeling among Democrats that to go into the presidential campaign with Truman would result in catastrophe.

The White House made frantic efforts to stop Franklin Jr. from keynoting the "draft Eisenhower" drive. Handsome, bursting with vitality, the very image of his father, in the eyes of many he was the party's golden hope. When the White House heard that Franklin Jr. was about to urge an Eisenhower candidacy, General Marshall was called and asked to help. He made an unsuccessful effort to dissuade the young man, putting it on the basis that the move would weaken the president's hand abroad just on the eve of the Italian elections and play into the hands of the Communists. Then General Eisenhower, who had previously announced he was not a candidate, authorized Defense Secretary Forrestal to tell Franklin Jr. he would be greatly distressed by any such move. And finally Eisenhower himself called. He was primarily concerned with the dangers in Europe, Eisenhower told Roosevelt, and he did "not want to be the cause of any feeling arising in Europe that the United States was not united in helping free peoples." Roosevelt held his ground. He, General Eisenhower, was the only man capable of uniting the Democrats and the country. He alone could persuade the Russians that the aim of American foreign policy was to secure a lasting peace and at the same time lead the nation and western Europe in the preparations needed to prevent further aggression.[19]

Franklin Jr. called his mother and read her the statement he proposed to make. As a delegate to the United Nations she herself was going to stay out of preconvention politics, she told him. But she asked him several questions in order to be sure he had faced up to them. Where did General Eisenhower stand on domestic things? Suppose he reaffirmed his refusal to run? Was he prepared to be cold-shouldered by the president and his friends? Had he consulted people like Bernard Baruch and Ed Flynn?

Franklin Jr. called Baruch.

"You feel this very deeply?" his mother's old-time friend and counselor asked.

"Yes sir, I do."

"It's the first time I have known you to feel deeply," Baruch went on and ended the telephone call, "You remind me of your father. When he felt this way, there was only one thing to do, to let him have his head and go."

Ed Flynn was also reminded of Franklin's father. Unable to reach Flynn before he made his announcement, Franklin Jr. caught up with him the following day. He approved of Franklin's attack on Truman's policies, Flynn told him. He himself was going down to Washington to tell the president the score. But it was a mistake to come out for Eisenhower because he did not think the general would run. Moreover, the Democratic leaders resented Franklin Jr.'s trying to be a kingmaker. That was their job. They would accept him more readily if he did not try to grab the ball. "You're exactly like your Father. Louis [Howe] and I had to hold your Father back. Sit still now and let it simmer." [20]

But where did Mrs. Roosevelt stand, the White House anxiously wondered. She commanded a respect and affection from the American people second only to Eisenhower. Chip Bohlen was directed to find out when he went to brief her on the administration's over-all foreign policy. At the end of his visit Bohlen asked her about Franklin Jr.'s "draft Eisenhower" statement. "I want to tell you," she wrote Truman afterward,

that while Franklin told me he intended to make this statement, he did not ask me for my opinion.

There is without any question among the younger Democrats a feeling that the party as at present constituted is going down to serious defeat and may not be able to survive as the liberal party. Whether they are right or wrong, I do not know. I made up my mind long ago that working in the UN meant, as far as possible, putting aside partisan political activity and I would not presume to dictate to my children or to anyone else what their actions should be. I have not and I do not intend to have any part in pre-convention activities.[21]

She was irritated by the effort to make Franklin Jr. feel that
the move to draft Eisenhower was against the national interest. She
wrote General Marshall:

Mr. Bohlen told me that you felt this move would so jeopardize President Truman's standing that it would hurt the position of our foreign
policy in the world. I hardly think that is really true. In an election year
all countries know that the man who is at the head of the government
may not win.

It was unfortunate, she acknowledged, that the United States had

to have an election at a crucial time in the nation's history just as it was
in 1940 and 1944, but we managed to have elections in both of those
years when the rest of the countries gave up holding elections temporar-
ily. I rather think we will weather holding an election this year.

She understood the secretary's anxiety

not to have anything rock the boat at the present time, but I doubt if
the injection of any new Democratic or Republican candidate is going
to have any great effect on the actions of the rest of the world.

While she was in London, a message came to her from Marshall: "Bohlen must have confused matters a little by leading you to
think that I was approaching you regarding the Eisenhower matter.
I have no intention of expressing any view of the matter to you. I
am sorry you were troubled about it." [22]
When she returned from London and the unveiling of FDR's
statue, she went down to see Truman. Her arrival at the White
House was preceded by reports from Ambassador Lewis Douglas
on the extraordinary reception she had received from the British
people. Truman was eager to have her endorsement. But when she
came out of the president's office she turned aside reporters' questions on the subject so sharply that a surprised May Craig later cautioned her that the press had interpreted her brusqueness to mean
"we had hit you in a painful spot." She was sure reporters would
draw the conclusion they did, Mrs. Roosevelt replied, but for May's
confidential information she wanted her to know, "I haven't made
up my mind." [23]

Despite renewed indications from Eisenhower that he was not available, the draft movement continued among the Democrats. Chester Bowles went to talk to him. He came away with misgivings about Eisenhower's stand on domestic issues, Bowles informed Mrs. Roosevelt, but if Eisenhower chose liberal advisers, Bowles thought he would provide a liberal administration, and, of course, a liberal Congress would be swept in with him. So he, Helen Gahagan Douglas (the wife of actor Melvyn Douglas), and some one dozen other prominent Democrats were about to issue a call for an "open convention," and if the Eisenhower move failed, perhaps Justice William O. Douglas could be nominated. Would she join them? [24]

She turned Bowles down. "I know little about General Eisenhower and hesitate to take any part in politics, but I shall consider again in the light of the Republican nomination." A few days later the Republicans adopted a remarkably liberal platform and selected a Dewey-Warren ticket. It was thought to be invincible. Clare Boothe Luce, although a Republican, offered the Democrats some advice. Their only hope was a Harry S. Truman-Eleanor Roosevelt ticket: "She is the only person in the party qualified to tear the Roosevelt mantle from Mr. Wallace and, by sharing it with Mr. Truman, partially restore it to him." It would, in addition, raise "the woman issue. . . . To put a woman on the ticket would challenge the loyalty of women everywhere to their sex, because it would be made to seem that the defeat of the ticket meant the defeat for a hundred years of woman's chance to be truly equal with men in politics." The column was good copy and it made headlines, but among some of Mrs. Roosevelt's supporters there was doubt that benevolence toward the Democrats or Mrs. Roosevelt had inspired it. Several correspondents cautioned Mrs. Roosevelt that the Republicans wanted to have her on the Democratic ticket in order to raise the issue of Yalta and Roosevelt's appeasement of Communism. Mrs. Luce, wrote Doris Fleeson in the *Washington Star*, "is not in Mrs. Roosevelt's confidence. . . . She is not friendly with Mrs. Roosevelt and has frequently made her the victim of one of the sharpest tongues in politics." [25]

The president, predicting his own nomination on the first ballot at Philadelphia, said Mrs. Roosevelt would be acceptable to him as a running mate. What else did they expect him to say? he added, almost *sotto voce*. And less than three hours later Mrs. Roosevelt directed Tommy to tell the press she had "no intention whatsoever of running for any public office." Her swift, terse rejoinder was rightly interpreted by some newspapermen as another sign of her aloofness from the Truman candidacy. The president was not feeling kindly toward the Roosevelt clan. He was always courteous, almost deferential toward Mrs. Roosevelt, but just before the Democratic convention, while he was in California on a "nonpolitical" tour, he had backed James Roosevelt into a corner and dressed him down. "Here I am," Truman said, "trying to do everything I can to carry out your father's policies. You've got no business trying to pull the rug out from under me." Perhaps the reproof was meant to get back to the mother of the brood. If so, it would not have altered her view. Her reservations were less about the president's intentions than his capabilities and his failure to surround himself with a better circle of advisers.[26]

As it became clear that President Truman could not be denied the nomination, the liberal and labor groups that had been fighting for an open convention, began to press for Justice Douglas as the vice-presidential candidate. Truman said he would welcome the justice as a running mate, and Clark Clifford, with the president's approval, asked Mrs. Roosevelt to help persuade the justice. "I feel you are the best judge of where your services are most valuable," she wired the justice,

but you would be of great value and give some confidence in the party to liberals if you accept. My confidence in your good judgment prevents my urging you to do anything but I want you to know that your acceptance would give hope to many for the future of a liberal Democratic party.

But Douglas, not wishing to be associated with what almost everyone assumed would be a debacle, turned Truman and the liberals down.[27]

Truman's prospects could not have been bleaker. Wallace's third party, which at the beginning of the year looked as if it might draw as many as five million votes, most of them from Truman, was still going strong. But the hand of the Communists in its operations was becoming increasingly visible. "Your description of the Wallace meeting was wonderful," Mrs. Roosevelt wrote Maude Gray, "& all of them follow a similar pattern." Her work with the youth movement in the thirties had given her an understanding of Communist tactics and discipline, she wrote a Wallace backer. "Their power of control and infiltration is plainly visible in the Progressive Party's platform. I wish Mr. Wallace had had some of the same experiences." The support that the Communists gave her husband, she wrote still another aggrieved Wallaceite, "was quite different from the power they have in the third party at present. They are a hard core that does much of the organizing." However strongly she felt about Truman and the Democrats, "no matter what I question, and I question many things, I could not vote for Henry Wallace, I have completely lost faith in him." [28]

She still held back from an open endorsement of Truman. She had been nominated to serve as a member of the U.S. delegation to the 1948 General Assembly, which was to open in Paris in September. She hoped she might get out of the country without having to turn the president down. But the Truman managers had their eye on her. The Democratic National Committee advised Clark Clifford, who was managing Truman's campaign strategy, that a considerable ceremony should be made out of Truman's signing of the bill authorizing a $65,000,000 loan to the United Nations for its headquarters building and that Mrs. Roosevelt be invited because "it is felt that Mrs. Roosevelt's presence in the White House at this time would be advantageous to the President in a public relations sense."

The President wants to see me so I go down on Wed. 18th for 2 hours —a chore but not too much for him to ask! He wanted to send me to Holland for the Jubilee & coronation but I said I couldn't go. [29]

When she appeared at the White House, Truman did solicit her support. She was staying out of partisan politics, she put him off, but she would say in her column that she was a Democrat and would vote the Democratic ticket and would write what she could to help the Democratic party. She appreciated the difficulties under which he had labored, she wrote him afterward. "I wish you could have had better assistants." She hoped the Democratic National Committee would aggressively make clear to the country what the president stood for and the necessity, therefore, of the voters giving him "the kind of men in Congress who will make it possible for you to carry through a program for the benefit of the average man." [30]

By the time Mrs. Roosevelt left for Paris, the Wallace movement was fading away, but he still might draw enough Democratic votes in New York, Illinois, and California to enable Dewey to carry them. In the South the Dixiecrats, led by Strom Thurmond, were cutting into that traditional Democratic bastion. She left for France assuming, as did most Americans, that Dewey would win. She hoped not, but if there was a Republican landslide she prayed that liberals like Stevenson, running for governor in Illinois, Chester Bowles, running for governor in Connecticut, Hubert H. Humphrey, and her friend Helen Gahagan Douglas would survive it. Although she had written a column stating the case for the Democrats and, by implication, for Truman, Frances Perkins telephoned her in Paris to beg her for a letter endorsing Truman by name and to ask her to try to get Baruch to help. "I am enclosing to you a copy of a letter which I sent to the President today," was her approach to Baruch:

I am sending it to Frances Perkins because she telephoned me last night pointing out that Drew Pearson was saying that I had never come out for the President as the Democratic candidate and was supposedly in favor of Governor Dewey. That, of course, is untrue and I do agree with Frances Perkins that we should try to get as good a Democratic vote as possible. I told her there was no chance of a Democratic victory except that we might keep some of the liberals in Congress and even increase the number if we acted wisely. I hope you will approve of this letter even though I was, as you know, loath to do more than state in general my support of the Democratic Party and its policies.[31]

Her covering letter to Frances Perkins could not have given President Truman much comfort if he was shown it:

I haven't actually endorsed Mr. Truman because he has been such a weak and vacillating person and made such poor appointments in his Cabinet and entourage, such as Snyder and Vaughan, that unless we are successful in electing a very strong group of liberals in Congress, in spite of my feelings about the Republican Party and Governor Dewey, I can not have much enthusiasm for Mr. Truman. Though there are many people in the government that I would hate to feel would not be allowed to continue their work, I still find it very difficult to give any good reasons for being for Mr. Truman. . . .

Nevertheless, since you asked me to send you the enclosed letter, I am doing so because you are quite right, if we are going down to defeat, we probably should go down having done what we could for the candidate and we should try for a good vote. I have addressed my letter to the President as being the most effective way.[32]

"I am unqualifiedly for you as the Democratic candidate for the Presidency," her endorsement read. She hoped as many liberal Democrats would be elected to Congress as possible. "A Democratic administration, backed by a liberal Democratic Congress, could really achieve the policies for which you have stood." That was as much as her conscience permitted her to write. A few weeks later, on the eve of the election, she went a little further in a broadcast from Paris. Mr. Truman "has shown courage," she said, and "needs the peoples' mandate to help him if he's going to be our President. I still believe in the Democratic Party and its leadership." [33]

Truman's victory surprised and pleased her but it did not change her assessment of his leadership:

It is rather nice to be an American when the people so evidently take their democracy seriously & do their own thinking as they did in this election. I did not have enough faith in them! Dewey wasn't just big enough & I think they felt more sincerity if not ability in Truman.

I do feel, however, that those among us who want the Democratic party to stay a progressive party will have to try to remind the members of Congress that they were elected on that basis & owe labor groups & liberals some real consideration. The President is so easily fooled in spite of his good intentions. I am going through a very difficult time with the delegation on its true & future position in Palestine & am much upset by some of the things that go on. The interchange of letters between the Secretary & myself would be funny if it were not so tragic, for he as well as the President is fooled. I hope & pray Mr. Lovett goes for I think he is a dangerous person in the State Department.[34]

The election had been won in an astonishing and personal triumph for Truman, a tribute to his grit and spirit, but the struggle to transform the Democratic party into "a new party" still had to be waged. The liberal task was unending. "I hope we can keep the President & his advisers really moving on liberal lines," she wrote two weeks after the election.[35]

And when she saw the president on her return from Paris, in the memo that she left with him she set forth what she felt should be the country's major foreign-policy concern in Mr. Truman's second term:

I have a feeling that our situation in Europe will be solved in the next year without too much difficulty. Our real battlefield today is Asia and our real battle is the one between democracy and communism . . . we have to prove to the world and particularly to downtrodden areas of the world which are the natural prey to the principles of communist economy that democracy really brings about happier and better conditions for the people as a whole.

The Communist threat was not military, but political and economic. We were "really fighting ideas as well as economic conditions," another section of the memorandum noted.[36]

And from Illinois there had come a thank-you note from a man who would later articulate the challenge posed to the United States by what he would describe as "the revolution of rising expectations." "It's all your fault," Governor-elect Adlai E. Stevenson wrote her in Paris in reply to her cable of congratulation. "You told me last fall to go ahead and have a try at it, and I have profited enormously from the experience quite aside from the amazing victory." [37]

VII. Cardinal and Former First Lady

There were some in the postwar years who considered anti-Roosevelt calumny a form of patriotism and Mrs. Roosevelt's elimination from public life a public service.

Westbrook Pegler made a career of attacks upon her. The *New York World-Telegram* had dropped his column, but it had been picked up by the Hearst papers. His abuse knew no bounds. "The widow," "La Boca Grande," "the Gab," "Eleanor the Great" were some of his names for her. He described her as the daughter of "a dissolute drunkard," a coddler of Communists, accused her of living off the taxpayers' largesse, and on occasion even suggested she was a liar. Her opposition in the United Nations to the return of ambassadors to Franco Spain outraged him, as did her treatment of Joseph Cardinal Mindszenty as a political figure and not simply as a religious martyr. That was nothing but the Communist line, he maintained, "Yes, I want to know more about the whole lot of them [meaning the Roosevelts] and I want to run up the whole vile record of treachery which I know there is to be had and chisel it on rock as a memorial to Franklin D. Roosevelt." [1]

She would later explain to reporter Carl Rowan: "I always thought (and his wife, in fact, once told me) that he could never write unless he was angry and that he actually looked at my husband's picture to make him angry." That was a vicious lie, Mrs. Pegler wrote her. She considered her husband saintly, idealistic, and a patriot. "I am very sorry if I quoted you wrongly," Mrs. Roosevelt replied, "but I remember very distinctly a picnic at Mr. Bye's when you spoke to a group of us and said that Mr. Pegler wrote better when he was angry. . . . I know what a devoted husband and father Mr. Pegler has been and I have always been careful to say so."

She rarely answered Pegler publicly. Privately she thought him a "character assassin," and to answer him publicly "would please him and urge him on to further attacks." Why did her "big, strong sons . . . not 'horsewhip' him?" an outraged *Ladies' Home Journal* reader suggested. "Why should they bother," she replied, "to horsewhip a poor little creature like Westbrook Pegler? They would probably go to jail for attacking someone who was physically older and perhaps unable to defend himself. After all, he is such a little gnat on the horizon. He cannot touch my husband's memory." [2]

She was right. The public wearied of Pegler. He was dropped by the Hearst papers when William Randolph Hearst, Jr., took over their management and insisted that he stop his attacks on Mrs. Roosevelt. He transferred his fulminations to the publications of the Birch Society. As he disappeared into obscurity he was heard to express wonder at Mrs. Roosevelt's invulnerability.

Like her uncle Theodore, Mrs. Roosevelt enjoyed a good scrap. To stand up for the underdog, she knew from three decades of public activity, meant to run the chance of public attack and vilification. She rather enjoyed the fray and was resigned to the attack. "After all these years," she commented in reference to the mudslinging that was inevitable in politics, "I've learned not to let that sort of thing get me down." [3]

Yet even she was taken aback by the violence of the denunciation suddenly launched against her by Francis Joseph Cardinal Spellman in July, 1949. The issue that precipitated the controversy was federal aid to parochial schools, which Mrs. Roosevelt adamantly opposed; but the leaders of the Catholic church responsible for its political interests had long been unhappy about Mrs. Roosevelt. Her friendliness toward Loyalist Spain in the thirties, her support, even though discreet, of birth control, her sponsorship of the American Youth Congress and other organizations in which the Communists had been heavily represented had vexed the clergy to the point of public expression of its displeasure even while she was First Lady.

She, on her side, had become increasingly concerned over the growth in temporal power of an institution that she felt was aggressively conservative in social and political matters, and since she now wrote and spoke as she pleased, she did not hesitate to take positions in opposition to the church. When New York City's public schools, without a public hearing, in response to Catholic pressure, banned the *Nation* from their libraries because it had published Paul Blanshard's articles on Catholic power in America, she protested the ban. The hierarchy was furious. Just how furious it was was conveyed to Herbert Lehman, who was told that because he had signed Mrs. Roosevelt's letter asking for a public hearing on the ban, he was considered anti-Catholic; in addition, a number of monsignors warned that if he ran for the Senate in 1949 for the seat vacated by Robert Wagner, he would not get the Catholic vote. "It seems too stupid to be true," she wrote Lehman, "but the Cardinal has been doing stupid things of late." She wanted him to know that she would be grateful if he consented to run and he could count on her whole-hearted support. "In thinking over this threat of Catholic opposition, I can not take it very seriously because they have had the experience of your Governorship and no one has ever been fairer to all races and creeds." [4]

But, she felt, it was neither the issue of federal aid to parochial schools nor the controversy over the *Nation* that was exasperating the cardinal and his associates. The "real count" against her was "that they have heard I was responsible for not returning Ambassadors to Spain in the last meeting of the General Assembly." There had been a move to revoke the UN resolution that called on all member states to break relations with Franco Spain. The United States might have supported it except that Mrs. Roosevelt within the delegation firmly opposed any concessions to Franco until the generalissimo agreed to reform and liberalization at home. She was supported by Ben Cohen and John Foster Dulles. Their protest was effective.[5]

All this was in the background when Mrs. Roosevelt wrote a column courteously taking issue with the cardinal on the school-aid controversy. The nation provided public schools, she wrote, because they strengthened democracy. Others had a right to set up private schools, but they were not entitled to, and should not receive, public funds. The separation of church and state was a basic Constitutional principle, and those like herself who defended it could not be accused of religious prejudice since she firmly believed in the right of any human being to belong to whatever church he saw fit and to worship God in his own way.[6]

Cardinal Spellman's answering broadside took the form of an open letter. He charged her with misinterpreting his and the church's position on federal aid. His plan, he said, called for government provision of "auxiliary services"—nonreligious textbooks, bus transportation, and health services. He considered her column a "personal attack" upon him, accused her of conducting "an anti-Catholic campaign," and, taxing her with failure to come to the defense of imprisoned Cardinal Mindszenty, ended on an excommunicative note which stunned the country:

Now my case is closed. This letter will be released to the public tomorrow after it has been delivered to you by special delivery today. And even though you may use your columns to attack me and accuse me of starting a controversy, I shall not again publicly acknowledge you. For, whatever you may say in the future, your record of anti-Catholicism stands for all to see—a record which you yourself wrote in the pages of history which cannot be recalled—documents of discrimination unworthy of an American mother! [7]

The letter caused a world sensation. She would answer the cardinal in detail in a personal letter, Mrs. Roosevelt commented calmly in her column. She was sure the cardinal had written "in what to him seems a Christian and kindly manner and I wish to do the same." She denied "ill-feeling toward any religion," reaffirmed her belief in freedom of religious worship, and emphasized her concern not to feed the fires of bitterness and division among Catholics, Protestants, and Jews.

Her letter to the cardinal spelled out her views on federal aid. It rejected charges of anti-Catholic bias, noting that she had supported many Catholic candidates for public office. It corrected the cardinal on the subject of the defense of Cardinal Mindszenty, reminding him that she had protested his imprisonment.

I cannot, however, say that in European countries the control by the Roman Catholic Church of great areas of land has always led to happiness for the people of those countries.

She touched delicately on her fear of the church's efforts to shape public policy to its own advantage through political manipulation.

Spiritual leadership should remain spiritual leadership and the temporal power should not become too important in any Church.

She closed the letter with a sentence that an unhappy Catholic layman, who was a friend of both Mrs. Roosevelt and the cardinal, called "devastating":

I assure you that I had no sense of being "an unworthy American mother." The final judgment, my dear Cardinal Spellman, of the worthiness of all human beings is in the hands of God.[8]

If Mrs. Roosevelt was calm, feelings elsewhere ran high. Four thousand letters poured into Hyde Park, more than nine out of ten of them favorable and many from Catholics enclosing letters they had sent to the cardinal. Bernard Bishop Sheil, the auxiliary bishop of the Archdiocese of Chicago, came to her defense. But his was a maverick voice in the hierarchy. "I suppose you know that you were attacked by Catholic priests in pulpits here last Sunday," May Craig advised her from Washington, "so it is Church policy." The Spanish Falangist journal *Arriba* wrote that: "In Eleanor Roosevelt you have one of those cases which in Spain we would call mannish women or 'macherras.' " * "Is Mrs. Roosevelt a sort of Stalin in petticoats?" a Madrid radio commentator asked. "Where does her power lie? Why does Mr. Acheson obey her with so much submission?" [9]

She would not be surprised, Mrs. Roosevelt wrote a friend in mid-August, "that the Cardinal had had word from the Vatican and

---

* *Macherras* is "an ugly word which means a woman who tries to play the part of a man," a UN official who sent her the clipping translated.

that the letter was partly written there." A United Press dispatch, datelined "Vatican City, July 29," quoted a semiofficial Vatican source in support of the cardinal:

> There is no doubt here that if Cardinal Spellman deemed his intervention necessary as an expression of the Church, it was necessary and therefore approved.
> The intervention of the Cardinal is undoubtedly not directed against the person but rather against the acts of the person.
> If those acts deserved a reprimand, then the reprimand is sage.

"The whole episode with Cardinal Spellman, as far as I am concerned, is only part of a much larger situation," Mrs. Roosevelt observed. "I think they felt the time had come to form a Catholic party in this country and hoped it could be accomplished. It was a disappointment to them that it did not turn out quite the way they hoped." [10]

Whatever the motives behind the cardinal's attack on her—and one can only speculate, for the church's archives on this matter are still closed—the public outcry against the cardinal's letter showed that he had overreached himself. "It has stirred up a lot of anti-Catholic feeling that was lying just under the surface and had, I hoped, melted into tolerance," wrote May Craig. Another newspaperwoman, Doris Fleeson, raised as a Catholic, noted that the Jesuit publication *America* "did not dare to take up the cudgels for the Cardinal." "Not in a long time," said the *Raleigh News and Observer,* Josephus Daniels's newspaper in North Carolina, "has America been presented with a spectacle of a man behaving with less tolerance, less Christian humility, and more readiness to damn and malign those who disagree with him than that shown by Cardinal Spellman of New York." Although he was a Catholic, Bill Hassett, one of Truman's secretaries and formerly one of Roosevelt's, called the cardinal's letter "an appeal to prejudice." He was "outraged," wrote William Phillips, who as Roosevelt's ambassador to Italy in the mid-thirties was familiar with the workings of the Vatican. The cardinal's accusations were "absurd, but they are dangerous too, and I am a bit fearful of what our weak-kneed politicians may do in connection with the forthcoming legislation on Federal aid." The cardinal was "vindictive" and "a strikebreaker as well," wrote trade-union leader Rose Schneiderman, still a firebrand. "I shall always remember how he made the poor gravediggers crawl back on their knees and give up their union in order to get their jobs back." [11]

"Have you forgotten, Prince of Rome," wrote Archibald Mac-Leish in a poem that he entitled, quoting the cardinal, "I SHALL NOT AGAIN PUBLICLY ACKNOWLEDGE YOU":

> *Have you forgotten, Prince of Rome,*
> *Delighted with your Roman title,*
> *Have you forgotten that at home*
> *We have no princes? . . .*
>
> *Prince of the church, when you pretend*
> *By rank to silence criticism*
> *It is your country you offend,*
> *Here man's the faith and rank's the schism.*

A devil's brew of discord and division was boiling up, one result of which might be to defeat the Democrats that fall. One of the most courageous condemnations of the cardinal's letter came from Lehman. He was, at the time, vacationing in the Adirondacks. It took courage because he still planned to run that fall against Dulles for the Senate seat vacated by Wagner. "I'm going to speak out," he told his wife, "but we may as well kiss the Senatorship good-by."

The issue, said Lehman, "is not whether one agrees or disagrees with Mrs. Roosevelt on this or any other public question. The issue is whether Americans are entitled freely to express their views on public questions without being vilified or accused of religious bias." Coming on top of his protest against the banning of the *Nation*, there was every prospect that the church would use its influence to defeat him if he ran. Mayor O'Dwyer, himself a candidate for re-election in New York, was aghast upon returning to the city. The controversy "will divide our people into two camps," he warned. Privately he told Mrs. Roosevelt that "it must have been the weather," that had led the cardinal to pen such a letter. Publicly he pooh-poohed charges that her stand on federal aid might have been actuated by prejudice. He would do what he could, he announced, to bring about a reconciliation.[12]

"Do not be misled or trapped by overtures re a reconciliation," Bill Hassett begged her. "Personally, you're better off without it. The initiative must come from the Cardinal himself. He should approach you hat in hand, make public apology and beg forgiveness. . . . He knows already that Catholic opinion is divided in a controversy for which he is solely responsible." But she was not averse to a reconciliation. She thought it was very bad to have the country split "on an emotional religious issue." [13]

She told President Truman and Secretary of State Acheson that if her renomination to the United Nations would be divisive, they should not feel "the slightest embarrassment" in not naming her a member of the delegation to the 1949 General Assembly:

I realize that the attitude of Cardinal Spellman which has developed towards Governor Lehman and towards me, makes appointing me an embarrassing and difficult situation, and I would regret adding to your difficulties. I want you to feel entirely free to do what you deem best for the work of the United Nations and our government situation.[14]

He wanted her back at the General Assembly, Truman replied immediately. She was needed at the United Nations more than ever. She was right and the cardinal wrong in the controversy over federal aid to education. He wasn't backing down, the president remarked to Hassett.[15]

It was Ed Flynn in the end who wearily moved into the situation to repair the damage and bring about a truce. Tracking her down at a radio station, he asked her to have lunch with him. "I am sick of politics," he told her. He was having enough trouble with O'Dwyer over the mayoralty, but much worse was the religious division that was setting in because of the cardinal's letter. He had worked against that sort of thing all his life. He had talked with the cardinal, he went on. He had a rough draft of a clarifying statement the cardinal would like to issue but which His Eminence would first like to read to her to see if she approved.*

---

* According to Warren Moscow, Flynn made a secret flight to Rome and laid the facts of the quarrel before Pope Pius XII. "Equally secretly, Cardinal Spellman

Would Mrs. Roosevelt be willing to talk with the cardinal if he called her? "Why, Ed," replied Mrs. Roosevelt, "I'm not the one who said I would have nothing to do with the Cardinal." She would be back at Hyde Park by six that evening, if the cardinal wanted to reach her. As Flynn said good-by, he added a final word smilingly. She should not yield on Spain, if she talked with the cardinal. "Tell him the Basque priests fought and still are fighting Franco." [16]

Promptly at 6:30 P.M. the cardinal called. He was gracious and friendly, as if they had always been on the best of terms. He had re-worked the statement and would send an aide up the next morning with the revised draft, if Mrs. Roosevelt was willing.

Agnes E. Meyer, author and journalist and wife of the publisher of the *Washington Post,* was a doughty scrapper for federal aid to the public schools, whose improvement was a ruling passion in her life. She had clashed frequently with the representatives of the church and knew their arguments and stratagems well. She hastily wrote Mrs. Roosevelt that if she could not avoid the interview with the cardinal, it would be a gain for aid to education if in return for her willingness to support the principle that the parochial school child is entitled to community services "such as health, welfare and even transportation since the Supreme Court agreed to it," the cardinal would declare "categorically that the demands of the Church would never go beyond the constitutional limits." [17]

The day after the cardinal telephoned her, a monsignor appeared at Val-Kill at 9:30 A.M., "a very comfortable looking Monseigneur whose name I never did discover," she reported to Mrs. Meyer. They worked on two statements—one the cardinal's, the other Mrs. Roosevelt's—that would clarify their views and which would be issued by the chancery office. The monsignor told her as they worked away that he considered "the Quebec school system one of the best in the world. If you know the province of Quebec you may feel as I do that education there is deplorable." [18]

The two texts were agreed upon. Cardinal Spellman made it

---

was ordered to make a public gesture of friendship to Mrs. Roosevelt . . ." (*The Last of the Big-Time Bosses: The Life and Times of Carmine De Sapio and the Rise and Fall of Tammany Hall* [New York, 1971], p. 122).

clear that his proposed use of public funds for parochial schools be only for "auxiliary services," among which, however, he included textbooks. With reference to the constitutional point, the cardinal said: "We are not asking for general public support of religious schools. . . . Under the Constitution, we do not ask, nor can we expect, public funds to pay for their construction or repair of parochial school buildings, or for the support of teachers, or for other maintenance costs." His letter made no direct reference to Mrs. Roosevelt, but he noted "the great confusion and regrettable misunderstandings" that had arisen on the subject of federal aid and reaffirmed "the American right of free speech which not only permits but encourages differences of opinion." [19]

The cardinal's statement was "clarifying and fair," Mrs. Roosevelt said in her letter. She noted the cardinal's acceptance of the view that general public support of religious schools was prohibited by the Constitution. His statement on "auxiliary services," she felt, made it clear that the claim for federal support of such services was not intended to breach the fundamental prohibition against public support of religious schools.

But this was more a hope than a statement of fact. "I am more convinced than ever that they will never help us to get federal aid for education unless they think they are going to get it too for parochial schools," she wrote Agnes Meyer. The Barden bill, which would have provided federal aid, but only to the public schools, died in committee. She predicted to Cyril Clemens, editor of the *Mark Twain Quarterly,* that the church would work to get as many states and as many Supreme Court decisions as possible upholding the constitutionality of state funds for parochial schools, "and in the long run they are sure if it is constitutional for states, it may be declared constitutional for federal funds to be used not only for auxiliary services but for all services equally. Once that is done they control the schools, or at least a great part of them." [20]

At the Castel Gandolfo, Pope Pius XII put his stamp of approval on the exchange of statements between the cardinal and Mrs. Roosevelt, telling five visiting American newspapermen that the dispute had been resolved satisfactorily. In doing so, commented *Newsweek*, "the pontiff wrote finis to one of the bitterest and potentially most explosive public controversies in years." A few days later, Mrs. Roosevelt disclosed in her column, almost laconically, that the cardinal had dropped in at Hyde Park and stayed for tea.

> The other afternoon as I was signing mail, with side glances out of my window, and I am afraid my thoughts centered on how quickly I could get out for a swim, Miss Thompson came to my desk, looking somewhat breathless and said: "Mrs. Roosevelt, Cardinal Spellman is on the porch and he wants to see you!"
>
> The Cardinal had dropped in on his way to dedicate a chapel in Peekskill. We had a pleasant chat and I hope the country proved as much of a tonic for him as it always is for me.[21]

One result of that friendly forty-five minute talk was Mrs. Roosevelt's agreement that a good argument could be made for federal aid to transport children in all free schools, a modification in her position that pained some of the more militant defenders of the First Amendment. They disagreed, however, over aid for nonreligious textbooks. Before they finished, Mrs. Roosevelt brought up another subject:

"Sir, before you go, let me say something. There are rumors that you are opposed to Governor Lehman. My feeling is that if the figures show that the Catholic vote has gone appreciably against Lehman, it will make it impossible for any Catholic to get elected in this state for many years to come. Because a lot of liberals, Jews, and Protestants will be very resentful." "Oh, Mrs. Roosevelt," the cardinal assured her, "I'm not opposed to Governor Lehman! I'll get in touch with Ed Flynn as soon as he returns to town."[22]

Lehman stopped in at Val-Kill on his way down from the Adirondacks. Although earlier in the summer Democratic leaders who were Catholics had been urging him to run for the Senate, they now were saying that if he *wanted* the nomination they would support him. Mrs. Roosevelt said she would find out how they really felt and make it clear that if they opposed him she would not be able to support the Democratic ticket.[23]

He was given the nomination but Mrs. Roosevelt continued to

worry whether the party leadership was giving him all-out support. She spotted an Associated Press story from upstate New York in which a Jesuit priest was quoted as urging Catholics to vote for candidates who would not discriminate against Catholic children. She clipped it and sent it to Flynn. "This sort of story is going to do great harm in this campaign. Can't it be prevented?" [24]

In October she wrote President Truman that she feared a Catholic defection might defeat Lehman, and she asked for his help:

> I feel a little responsible for the situation here because undoubtedly Governor Lehman's statement against the Cardinal's letter to me is one of the things influencing the Catholic hierarchy and there are always some Catholics who can be influenced by a word passed down to the priests. . . .[25]

The administration did give Lehman all-out support, and Lehman defeated Dulles by some 200,000 votes.

But the episode left its scars. "I don't think the Cardinal ever forgave Herbert for supporting Mrs. Roosevelt," commented Mrs. Lehman. As for Mrs. Roosevelt, distrust of the church as a temporal institution was one of the reasons for her strenuous opposition later to John F. Kennedy's bid for the presidential nomination. She came away from her encounter with the cardinal, she wrote a young friend,

> with a horrible feeling of insincerity. In his visit he never once mentioned the fact that he had written me that letter and you would think I was one of his most cherished friends. That does not give me any explanation of the letter nor much sense of security in his sincerity. I think the Barden Bill was something through which they hoped to hurt my influence which has been exerted on the UN delegation against returning Ambassadors to Spain. That is the real crux of the attack.° [27]

° By the beginning of 1950 she was persuaded by officials in the State Department and by Gen. T. McInerny, a lobbyist for the Spanish government who had been introduced to her by her uncle, David Gray, whose military attaché he had been in Ireland, that the UN decision to withdraw ambassadors from Spain had been a mistake and might even have strengthened Franco's position at home. "I can, of course, see that it might be wise and helpful to the Spanish people if we resumed ordinary diplomatic and economic intercourse," she wrote February 12, 1950. And

As for the cardinal, when he was questioned by Irwin Ross eight years later as to why he had called on Mrs. Roosevelt, he told him: "I don't like to have any hard feelings. I want to be charitable with everybody." And in 1966 when he traveled to Hyde Park for the dedication of a Franklin D. Roosevelt postage stamp, he said a few words over Roosevelt's grave in the rose garden and was then observed to move over to Mrs. Roosevelt's grave and fold his hands in prayer.

---

when, at the end of the month, the United States decided to resume relations with Generalissimo Franco and moved to rescind the UN resolution on the withdrawal of ambassadors, she did not oppose the decision.

> I do not like the Franco government and I would much rather see Spain under a government that the people themselves had chosen. I also think that in passing the resolution in the United Nations General Assembly in 1946, we exceeded our authority in trying to interfere in internal affairs and therefore since so many nations are now returning ambassadors, willy nilly, I think it is probably better to rescind the resolution and let people resume ordinary diplomatic relationships which does not in any way imply approval of the government in power, since it is somewhat inconsistent to have Ambassadors in Moscow, Yugoslavia, etc., and in the Argentine and not have them in Spain.[26]

VIII. An American Phenomenon

The most sensational news of the day, said "the Rhamkatte Rooster," which was the way Josephus Daniels signed his column in the *Raleigh News and Observer*, came neither from Turkey nor Tibet; it was the report from Hyde Park that Eleanor Roosevelt had said, "I am tired. Let some of the youngsters carry on." She loved his column, Mrs. Roosevelt replied. "I had been walking around with pneumonia, so it was true that I was weary. I am fine, now, however . . ."; and she did not add, for it was unnecessary, that she had resumed a schedule that once had led her husband to pray, "O Lord, make Eleanor tired."

"I sometimes think of quickly finishing up all the things I have to do, and then just not doing any more, but there always seem to be so many things to do." So she told an interviewer for the *New Yorker* in mid-1948.[1]

In addition to her duties at the United Nations, she had resumed her lecture tours under the auspices of her manager, W. Colston Leigh. She did a regular radio commentary with Anna and a television show under Elliott's management. Her daily column appeared in newspapers ranging in number from seventy-five to ninety. She did a monthly question-and-answer page for *McCall's*, to which she had moved in 1949 from the *Ladies' Home Journal*. That year, too, the second volume of her autobiography, *This I Remember*, on which she had been working since 1946, appeared. She joined the boards of the American Association for the United Nations and of Brandeis University. She performed assorted chores for the Americans for Democratic Action, spoke frequently for the United Jewish Appeal, faithfully supported the work of the NAACP and the Citizens Committee for Children, and appeared frequently at the Wiltwyck School for Boys, usually with a celebrity or potential donor in tow.

These were her regular jobs; but in between the fixed points that they constituted in her schedule, a swarm of invitations, requests for her aid, for her opinion, for interviews managed to proliferate. They were reflected in the sheets of messages that Tommy had for her on her desk when she returned to her apartment:

> *Martin Lencer*, Washington, D.C. producer of documentary films called to say he is in Washington at present and Mrs. R. had said she would be interested in seeing a film of his on Juvenile Delinquency—a 30 minute film. He wonders if Mrs. R. would like him to come to meet her in New York for the purpose of showing the film or if she will be in Washington soon.

> *Mr. Koons* [lawyer for the Roosevelt estate] called. No message.

> *Mr. Zuckerman* of the Association of Private Camps called to find out what time to pick up Mrs. R. Will call again Wednesday.

> *Mr. Golden* called to ask if Mrs. R. enjoyed the ham. (Ham is in the refrigerator.)

> *Mr. Miller*, University of Chicago, called to enquire about an appointment with Mrs. R. He has a project for World Peace which he thinks will prove interesting. He was in town from 9 to 12th of Feb.[2]

Another day's messages read:

> *Pare Lorenz* would like to see Mrs. R. next week if he may. Any time would be suitable.

> *Mrs. Lucille Sullivan* called to ask for an appointment for Mrs. Alice [Nourse] Hobart, author of *Oil for the Lamps of China*. Mrs. Hobart will be in town between 15th and 25th of Oct.

> *State Department* would like to know if Mrs. R. would be good enough to interview a group of Mexicans here on Pres. Truman's Point Four program. They represent the oil industry in Mexico and are the first group of this kind to come here. They will be in N. Y. from the 17th.

Mr. Frank Beal called to ask if Mrs. R. had written the column for the St. Lawrence Seaway project. He said that now would be a good time to bring the matter up since Canada's Premier [Louis S.] St. Laurent is talking about Canada doing the project alone.

Allard Lowenstein will call for Mrs. R. at 9:00 Saturday.

Mrs. Craig McGeachy Schuller will be delighted to see Mrs. R. at the Stanhope Hotel at 1:00 or 1:15 on Wed. Mrs. Eder, President of the National Council of Women will be present and also Mrs. Barclay Parsons of Women United for U.N.[3]

Only occasionally were her iron constitution and even stronger will unequal to her schedule. For over a year William Bishop Scarlett and his wife Leah, both of whom she was very fond, had been hoping to have her come to them in St. Louis. Finally it was arranged that she would speak at the Flower Service in the cathedral. But in mid-March she came down with a bad case of grippe and lost her voice and had to cancel. "Of course we are terribly disappointed, personally, ecclesiastically and botanically!" Bishop Will, as his friends called him, wrote back. "But not for anything in the world would we have you run the slightest risk. And I am glad that your doctor seems to have control of the reins." Not everyone took disappointment as gracefully.[4]

It was an unbreakable rule that engagements must be kept, equally so that letters must be answered. Late at night, just as she had done in Washington, she went over the fifty to one hundred letters that Tommy still put aside for her daily. Often now the replies she asked Tommy to draft were ones of regret:

Thank regret will be in Geneva for a HRC meeting

ack—regret too busy to undertake any more work

Regret—plans for 1952 too uncertain

ack regret never write out speeches as always talk extemporaneously

ack regret not making any engagement which will take me away from home during summer regret already have all the engagements I can keep

regret no time

Some letters she used in her column, others she sent on to Franklin Jr. in Washington or to James in California for them to answer or, if they were related to her television program, to Elliott. Sometimes, if she knew a government official well, she sent a letter on to him or her. "Dear Anna," she wrote Mrs. Rosenberg, who had become assistant secretary of defense under General Marshall, "I am forwarding the enclosed for whatever action you think advisable." She did the same with job applicants. "I do not have any part in the selection of personnel for the UN. I will, however, send your letter to the Director of Personnel."

Occasionally she was requested to ask a favor of the president. John Ihlder, of the National Capital Housing Authority, wrote reminding her that she had asked FDR to approve the first half-million-dollar appropriation for the authority, which he had done, just as, at Ihlder's suggestion, she had asked Franklin to order an end to segregation in government cafeterias, which he also had done. Now he had a third request. He was reaching the retirement age and unless Truman signed an executive order exempting him, the services of a man who believed in public housing would be lost. Would she ask the president? She refused:

When I asked the first two things I was asking my husband and that was different from the present situation. I am terribly sorry not to be able to do what you want but since I have left Washington, I have never made a personal request of any kind of the President. I would, however, be glad to forward to him for consideration an endorsement written by someone else but I cannot myself ask for anything.[5]

There were two types of letters that she answered meticulously —questionnaires, because they challenged her to make up her mind, and inquiries from children. They were studying the lives of outstanding people, Louise Peters of Vermont wrote her in a child's labored scrawl. "Perhaps when you were in the fourth grade you started developing habits that helped to make you the successful person that you are today. . . ." "Dear Louise," she replied. "I am sending you a copy of a letter my father wrote to me when I was a little girl. I hope you will like it as much as I did." "Dear Werner," she wrote a high-school editor who wanted to do an article on the responsibilities of citizenship, "you need not be destined for a career in law or government to be policy makers. Each and every vote at every election counts as does each letter written to a Congressman or Senator or even newspaper."

In 1949 she gave up her apartment in Washington Square to move to the Park Sheraton Hotel.

We [i.e., Mrs. Roosevelt and Elliott] moved yesterday to the hotel and are nearly settled. I am entirely in order and our sitting room is in order but Tommy and the office are not yet settled. She isn't happy about it yet, but will be, I think, when she is settled and finds as I hope she will that it is less strain and less work when we are here.[6]

There were changes at Val-Kill. Having purchased 1,100 of the 1,365 acres that FDR had owned at his death, she and Elliott went into partnership "and we are going to farm the land on a commercial basis." She paid the estate $87,000 of which $50,000 came out of her own capital and $37,000 was financed through a mortgage which Elliott undertook to service as his contribution to the purchase price. "As you see," she wrote her other children,

I have made no gift to Elliott. . . . I write you this so that you may clearly see that you will get from the estate all that you would probably have received in any case, and in addition to make it clear, that Elliott is putting in all he makes so that you will not think any extra gifts have been made to him.[7]

Elliott had a 75-per-cent interest in Val-Kill Farms and Mrs. Roosevelt 25 per cent. Elliott did things on a large scale, and in the heyday of the farming operation there were 40 dairy cattle, 100 beef cattle, 30 brood sows, 2,500 laying turkey hens, and several hundred acres that had been planted by FDR to fir and spruce. "Where it seems wise, we shall continue the Christmas tree plantations which he started, and shall sell Christmas trees just as he did." [8] The trees were the only profitable crop, Elliott selling them in December at a dollar a tree. "I am doing things," she explained to a close friend, in endorsing this film [*The Roosevelt Story*] and financing the place & farm & helping Elliott with a book of his Father's letters that may cause criticism. I'm letting Jimmy go ahead on a film & with his book & will help him by not interfering though I know all will cause criticism but I surmise Elliott has to be established & encouraged to become secure. Jimmy needs to make more money to give his wife the security she demands & if I can help without doing anything I think wrong, the criticism doesn't bother me. . . . The sooner I can live in dignified obscurity at H.P. the happier I will be.[9]

Elliott lived in the top cottage. The Stone Cottage by the pool was used for guests, Mrs. Roosevelt having bought out Nancy Cook and Marion Dickerman. "I am afraid the many children we have with us in the summer were too much for their peace and quiet," she informed Henry Toombs, who had drawn up the plans for the cottage in 1925. "When Elliott came into the place, it became more difficult," was Marion Dickerman's explanation. "One day Nan and I looked up and said, 'When will we go?'" Mrs. Roosevelt bought out their interest for $17,000. "Dear Eleanor," Nancy Cook wrote, "I am leaving the keys in an envelope for you. . . . If you are home before we leave we will come over to see you and say good-bye. Affectionately." [10]

Elliott was a restless soul, much like Mrs. Roosevelt's father—in and out of a succession of ventures, often immature and reckless, and like him, too, possessing a sweetness and warmth that caused people to remark that he was "the most lovable" of the Roosevelt boys. Mrs. Roosevelt was fiercely loyal to all of her children, but Elliott had a special claim on her affections.

"If Elliott were not at Hyde Park I could not live there, in fact I would not want to." [11] That was saying a great deal about her gratitude to Elliott, for Val-Kill was home and sanctuary, the place to which she was ready to withdraw if public life became intolerable. That seemed a possibility at times in the postwar years. No nastiness or insinuation was out of bounds for columnist Westbrook Pegler. "If people want to believe that sort of thing," she said after the appearance of one such column, "there is nothing to be done." So far as she was concerned, she was perfectly content to retire from public life to the country. She did the public things, but the ones that really mattered were her personal relationships and they could not be affected by such attacks.[12]

She had always liked what Andrew Jackson had written about his much maligned wife: "A being so gentle, so virtuous, slander might wound but could not dishonor." In 1948, the wife of Earl Miller, the handsome state trooper, now a retired naval commander, who had been FDR's bodyguard in Albany and had become one of her closest friends, named her as correspondent in a suit for divorce. "Mummy," Franklin Jr. said to her, "if I am going to represent you in this action, I have to know everything." With a smile, she reassured her son: "In the sense that you mean, there was nothing." If the action went to trial it would, nevertheless, create a sensation and perhaps make it impossible for her to continue in public life. She accepted that possibility calmly, but her sons were upset, saying it would destroy them politically. That threw her into the deepest of depressions. But scandal was averted when a compromise settlement was reached between Earl and his wife and the papers were sealed.[13]

Because she viewed Val-Kill as a place of retirement, it meant a great deal to her that Elliott made his home there. There was little she would not do if he pressed her hard enough. She even agreed to sit for a portrait commissioned by Elliott from his friend Douglas Chandor. It was so good that the price jumped fivefold in the course of the painting, which so incensed her that she startled the Charles F. Palmers during a visit to Val-Kill by using the word "darn" about the bill Chandor had sent Elliott. She would not permit Elliott to pay the higher price, she announced, although he wanted to do so. She would not permit anybody to pay such a price for her picture. It remained in the painter's possession until Mrs. Lyndon B. Johnson arranged for its purchase so that it might be hung in the White House.

"Madame Roosevelt is becoming beautiful," a Frenchman in Paris was reported by *Time* to have remarked, and the magazine's explanation was the porcelain caps that had replaced the protruding front teeth that were broken in the automobile accident. That had

had something to do with her "autumnal blossoming," as *Time* described it. But the real explanation, her friends thought, was to be found in the quip that "after 50, every man is responsible for his face." [14]

There was another strong attachment to Val-Kill. Tommy and Fala were happiest there. Tommy was fading and she knew it. "Tommy is exhausted," she wrote as she was about to take off for Paris for the 1948 General Assembly. "I think this is the last time I can uproot Tommy, so I pray she will keep well and will get pleasure out of it." [15] Tommy began to break in a successor, Maureen Corr, Irish-born, Catholic, pert, and pretty, who came to them through an employment agency. Although Tommy persuaded Mrs. Roosevelt to let her accompany her to the 1951 Assembly in Paris, after the Christmas recess, it was Maureen who went, armed with much crisp advice from Tommy, including a "tipping schedule," how to get checks cashed, and how to handle Mrs. Roosevelt's funds. "I expected some kind of royalty," Maureen said of her new boss, "and here was a warm, kind, embracing person. Her total simplicity was such a revelation to me, her lack of any feeling of self-importance."

Back at Hyde Park, Fala was Tommy's only consolation. The little Scotty owed his life to her. He had once been jumped by Elliott's dog, the ill-starred Blaze, and severely mauled. Had Tommy not grabbed him up and lifted him to safety, he would not have survived. "Fala is still living, he is eleven years old but extremely frisky," Mrs. Roosevelt wrote a writer who wanted to do a story about this famous dog.

Just yesterday he ran away and was gone with his grandson [Tamas McFala] for five hours. He has lived with me since my husband's death. For a while after that he used to lie in the doorway where he could watch all the doors, just as he did when my husband used to come over to this cottage to make sure he was not left behind.

I have always made it a practice to take him over to the big house and grave when there was any ceremony. If he heard the sirens he would stand stiffly on his four, short legs, with his ears up, knowing I am sure, that this had something to do with him and his master.

Fala is still very dignified and while he is happy here with me, I do not think he has ever accepted me as the one person whom he loved as he did my husband.

He "has a special way of greeting Mrs. Roosevelt," Tommy would add. "We call it his smile." [16]

With the Big House turned over to the government, the center of gravity of the Roosevelt clan shifted to Val-Kill. It was a large family, numbering in 1952 in addition to her five children, eighteen grandchildren, two great-grandchildren, as well as assorted cousins of various degrees, nine daughters-in-law and ex-daughters-in-law to most of whom she was confidante, referee, and oracle and whose Roosevelt offspring often stayed with her at Hyde Park. Her brother Hall's second wife, Dorothy K. Roosevelt, and her three daughters Amy, Janet, and Diana also made Val-Kill a stopping-off place whenever they came East. "She's the best thing besides the girls that Hall left me," Dorothy wrote her sister about Eleanor. Her children called her "Mummy," her grandchildren called her "Grand'mère," and her friends "Mrs. Roosevelt," although a few who had known her before the White House years—such as Henry Morgenthau and Esther Lape—used "Eleanor" and Harry Hooker and Maude Gray called her "Totty."

All of her sons, except John, were active in politics. All of them realized the value of their mother's support. She was proud of Franklin Jr.'s successful entry into Congress in May, 1949, when he succeeded to the seat of Rep. Sol Bloom on Manhattan's West Side. The day after he scored his spectacular victory against the Tammany candidate in a district that traditionally had been controlled by Tammany, she responded to congratulations at Lake Success from her fellow delegates with a radiant, "Wasn't it a wonderful success?" It was "a fine beginning," and she was glad "he didn't have anything to do with Tammany. After all, he won despite Tammany, didn't he?" [17]

There already was talk of his running for governor in 1950, and when he was introduced at political meetings in and around New York it was as a future president. He was not the only Roosevelt son thinking and being talked of in those terms. In California,

James, who had been chairman of the state organization, was preparing to run for the governorship against Earl Warren, and *Look* magazine published an article by the chief of its Washington bureau, Richard L. Wilson, which it headlined:

TWO YOUNG ROOSEVELTS
RACE FOR THE WHITE HOUSE
★ Both Have FDR's Political Charm
★ Both May Become Governors in 1950
★ Together They May Upset Dewey and Warren

"It begins to look as if the Roosevelts can fill both places on the Presidential ticket!" Wilson reported a California politician as saying. "Yes," his colleague answered, "but who can get a Roosevelt to take second place?"

"That's easy," the politician replied, "Mother will decide." [18]

The timetables of aspiring young politicians, including her sons, amused Mrs. Roosevelt. A fatalist, she never considered a race for office won until the votes were counted. Within the family she could be cool, objective, and bluntly, if lovingly, realistic about her sons' political aspirations. "You are better off out of politics," she told Elliott in 1950. "You will only get into a jam." In the winter of 1949–50 she smilingly tempered her sons' ambitious blueprints with reminders that it was they, not she, who had loudly wanted for president in 1948 a general with whom they were now disenchanted as it had become clear that his sympathies were Republican. It was Mother whom James enlisted to try to gain Truman's remission for his 1948 apostasy. She saw Truman. He was in a mellow mood. She came away with the impression that he would not oppose James in the primary—perhaps even support him.[19]

It was she, also, who told Franklin Jr. that it was too early for him to think of the governorship. When there had been such talk at the time of his election to Congress, her reaction had been a spontaneous "Gracious, let him start being a good Congressman first," and that continued to be her advice to him in 1950. The politicians also advised him not to be in too much of a hurry, but for their own reasons. They wanted to tame him first. They wanted to be the ones who decided when he made his next move upward. In 1950 the organization nominated Walter A. Lynch, a Catholic, to run for governor together with Lehman, who ran for re-election as senator. Franklin Jr. ran for re-election to the House.

James, however, did get his chance at the governorship in California. Truman, although he did not support him in the primary, kept hands off, and James won. But the race against Warren was tougher. So unconditional was her support of her children that Mrs. Roosevelt even campaigned for James. It was only natural that a mother should speak in behalf of her son, Gov. Earl Warren, James's opponent, gallantly replied. She returned from California persuaded that "much of the attitude that he isn't going to win comes from the Pauley crowd who have not been willing to give any money and spread the word that he has no chance." When Truman, as the race drew to an end, issued a statement endorsing James's running mate, Helen Gahagan Douglas, who was in a close contest with Richard M. Nixon for the Senate, and failed to make a simultaneous endorsement of James, she almost resigned from the United Nations, even though James's race by that time was viewed as hopeless. She resented also that Truman, in his speech to the UN General Assembly, had not mentioned FDR. She would not accept reappointment, she said. Edith Sampson, her alternate, was perfectly capable of handling her job. Her friends were startled by the depth of her feeling. "Why punish the UN because of what the President did in California?" one of them protested, and another came away from the encounter distressed at her failure to separate her loyalty to her children from her role as a public servant.[20]

It was an old vulnerability. One of the threatening letters she had received at the height of the Cardinal Spellman controversy was from a New Hampshire Democrat, a state employee, and vice-commander of the Catholic War Veterans. He hoped some day to have the honor to vote for Franklin Jr. for president, he wrote her, but she had lost him many Democratic votes by her opposition to federal aid to parochial schools. Her reply had been firm, almost indignant:

whether it defeated my son for office at any level, I would stand for the things in which I believe. It would be unworthy of an American citizen to do otherwise. I shall in the course of his career take stands whether they help him to be elected to office or whether they defeat him.[21]

That was how she felt. Yet she also tried her best not to make life difficult for her politically minded sons by too intransigent a stand. Her willingness to have public funds used for the transportation of parochial school children could be justified on the merits of the argument that she advanced for this modification in her position, but it also coincided with a compromise federal school-aid bill that Franklin Jr. and Rep. John F. Kennedy drew up together.

"Jimmy is staying in California," she wrote after the 1950 elections, when friends wondered whether he would now defer to Franklin Jr.'s political aspirations,

but he hasn't said a word about whether he means to stay in politics or not. Franklin, junior, was re-elected easily and I hope he is going to make a good record for himself.[22]

She usually presided over the ingatherings of her family at Val-Kill with a benign, matriarchal calm, writing out the menus, making the table order, serving the food herself from a hot plate or a side table. The larger the family party—and in the Roosevelt household the line between family and friends was always blurry— the better she liked it. While children and friends milled in and out of the various rooms of the cottage, having drinks, exchanging political gossip, disputing loudly, she was always an oasis of calm. Strangers present at an argument among the Roosevelt children often thought they were about to commit mayhem on each other. "Plenty of variety but basically a great deal of unity," Mrs. Roosevelt would reassure her guests and herself.

There was much teasing back and forth. Maude Gray, still a striking woman whose tinted red hair reminded one small child of "a witch," was a great jollier. "Totty" should marry Mr. Baruch, Maude said; one week of coping with Eleanor's energy would kill him off and then Eleanor would have his money to pay off Anna's debts (which were much on her mind at that time) and for all her good works. Harry Hooker, whose birthday was being celebrated at Val-Kill that week end, spoke of how often he had wept upon Mrs. Roosevelt's bosom, although he being her lawyer was supposed to be the one to give the advice and comfort. "Isn't it nice Totty that you have a bosom to weep upon?" She would smile, enjoying her friends' enjoyment of such sallies, but only occasionally contributing herself. Elliott and Franklin Jr. remonstrated with her for having appeared to give official approval to an article about her by John Reddy, an associate of Anna's. She should not do that again, they sternly admonished her. "I need the publicity," she said with a look of sweet innocence. "Yes," someone was heard to remark above the guffaws, "two eskimos at the North Pole haven't heard about you." [23]

One evening, all of her sons were at Hyde Park, "all of us arguing passionately on ideas, all of us trying to talk at once, even the wives becoming so interested that they could not help but join in!" Instead of talk about a new car or a new fur coat they argued about socialized medicine and inheritance taxes, and while she joined in she also observed the development, the changes in point of view, the growth in intellectual powers of her children. "We separated after 11 o'clock so stimulated by each other's company that I doubt if any of us went to sleep for hours." [24]

Sometimes, however, the banter and argument among her children became angry and sarcastic. She would try to stop it, but if unsuccessful, withdrew into herself. Her children were able to hurt her in the way few other people now could. Their quarrels and divorces plunged her into the deepest of depressions. She turned silent and remote—a vestige of her old "Griselda mood." ° She had made self-discipline a ruling principle in her life. "I have a great objection to seeing anyone, particularly anyone whom I care about, lose his self-control," she wrote, explaining that she had seen what lack of it had done to her father, her brother, and her Hall uncles (those on her mother's side). The Roosevelt children had inherited from their father as well as mother enormous vitality, but they

---

° When Mrs. Roosevelt was hurt or disappointed by someone she loved, she withdrew into heavy silence, like Patient Griselda in Chaucer's "The Clerk's Tale."

never achieved the self-mastery of their parents. She had always subordinated immediate gratification to duty and long-range purposes, while the discipline of the years when he was winning his victory over polio gave FDR, she believed, the patience and determination that played such a great part in his later achievements. Her children lacked self-discipline. That seemed to her to be at the heart of their difficulties. And they seemed to be endless. "All of us made life hard for her," Elliott later said. "All of us failed her." [25]

There was a special sadness over the breakup of Anna's marriage. Mrs. Roosevelt was very fond of John Boettiger, but after the war and FDR's death he seemed lost. She had encouraged Anna and John to buy a shopping weekly in Phoenix and to try to build it up into a daily newspaper, and had helped them to raise the money for the venture from some of her friends. When it failed, John withdrew from Anna. "Something has happened to John, he seems like a shell . . . ," Mrs. Roosevelt wrote Maude, adding that he was off on a ranch, alone, writing articles. Separation led to divorce. John remarried, but a few months later committed suicide.[26]

Mrs. Roosevelt was terribly shaken. At a Belle (Mrs. Kermit) Roosevelt musicale she encountered Dr. Lawrence S. Kubie, a distinguished psychiatrist, and, agitated by what was happening to her children and almost oblivious to the crowd about them, she began to query him about psychiatry and analysis. Then she apologized for interrogating him so determinedly at a social occasion and invited him to spend a week end at Hyde Park:

That Sunday we drove alone around the country after church and she brought up very frankly her sense of guilt over John Boettiger's suicide, that he had written to her out of his depression and she had brushed it aside with hearty impatience and now felt that this had been insensitive and ruthless etc. She then turned to her concern over Elliott who was just then moving towards his divorce from Faye Emerson. This led Mrs. FDR to talk of all the children, of her role as the disciplinarian, and of the President's role as the comforter, and of what it had done to each of them to have him disappear into illness, into the governorship, into the presidency, into the war; until they had to make appointments in order to see him. She talked of how this had hit each in turn, and especially of how it had destroyed Elliott, which was why she felt such concern for him and did so much more for him than for the others.

Dr. Kubie was deeply moved and impressed with the subtlety of her insights, but she had a bias against psychiatry and, despite many discussions with Kubie, never quite overcame it.

She would catch glimpses of what I meant, understand it, and then lose it again. She never completely freed herself from the feeling that if one had courage enough, guts enough, and worked hard enough, one could hoist oneself up by one's own emotional bootstraps. . . . I do not think the arguments left a trace of anything except perplexity, and on my part at least, a warm and affectionate admiration.[27]

Another person with whom she talked freely about her problems with her children was Dr. David Gurewitsch. One evening two of her sons nearly came to blows at her dinner table. When she tried to restrain them, both turned their accusations against her. The next day, when she encountered David, she was in a deep depression, wishing, in fact, that she were dead. "My children would be much better off if I were not alive," she said. "I'm overshadowing them." They walked up and down the street for a long time.

Her ability to talk about these matters with David Gurewitsch was a measure of the extent to which this new friend had established himself in her affections. When she had left Washington in 1945 and no longer had the government's medical facilities available to her, Trude Lash, the author's wife, had recommended David, who was her doctor. They had known each other from student days in Freiburg, Germany, where David, a slim, elegant figure, had arrived to study medicine. He was the son of Russian *émigrés*. His mother was a remarkable healer, and from her he inherited gifts of empathy and sympathy, which, when combined with blue eyes and continental gallantry, had a magnetic effect upon both men and women. He was a stimulating conversationalist, a worldly, cultivated man, and a physician who cared about his patients.

In 1947, David came down with tuberculosis and was ordered to Davos, Switzerland. He could not get a plane reservation, and Trude went to Mrs. Roosevelt for help, the latter getting him on the plane that was taking her to Geneva for the meeting of the Human Rights Commission. The plane developed engine trouble and was

fogged in at Shannon Airport, Ireland, for two days. She took care
of the ailing David, brought him milk and read to him. And when
he was settled at Davos, she telephoned him frequently from Geneva. His precarious health, his responsiveness to her solicitude
subdued her. Like George Eliot, there always had to be someone
who was "the one and only." "Don't ever worry about being a nuisance," she wrote him from Geneva as the session of the Human
Rights Commission was drawing to an end:

I've always liked you & was drawn to you since we first met & the trip
just made me sure that we could be friends. I never want to burden my
young friends & with all my outward assurance I still have some of my
old shyness & insecurity & that is probably what makes you feel shy.
I've really taken you to my heart however, so there need never be a
question of bother again. You can know that anything I can do will always be a pleasure for me & being with you is a joy.

A few weeks later she was explaining to David the relationship
of the public to the private in her life.

The people I love mean more to me than all the public things even if
you do think that public affairs should be my chief vocation. I only do
the public things because there are a few close people whom I love
dearly & who matter to me above everything else. There are not so
many of them & you are now one of them and I shall just have to try
not to bother you too much!

Thus began a relationship that was to be one of the closest in the
final years of Mrs. Roosevelt's life. There was little she did that
was not shared with David and, later on, with Edna, his wife.[28]

Deeply involved as she was in the lives of those close to her,
she did not slacken her public preoccupations, but she was most
content when she was able to help her children and her friends
through her public interests and activities.

She joined Anna in a daytime radio discussion program over
the facilities of the American Broadcasting Company, during the
1948–49 season. "It will be an afternoon programme 5 days a week
& I'll record my part twice a week from wherever I may be! She'll
get *all* the pay & it will help her pay her debts." The "Eleanor and
Anna" show was carried by two hundred stations. "Mrs. R. ranks

with the standout commentators on the air," commented *Variety*. "She displays more courage and is more positive than most of the others put together." Nevertheless, ABC dropped it because of lack of a sponsor. "We were very proud to present the comments of you and Anna," Robert E. Kintner, ABC's chief executive, wrote her. "I am only sorry that we were unable to obtain commercial sponsorship for you—a failure which I feel was our fault, not yours. . . ." "Tell him," she wrote on this, "I am happy it is ending! but sorry for Anna's sake we could not succeed." [29]

It was for Anna's sake, she told friends, as well as Elliott's, that she had agreed to let Elliott package a show, which he sold to NBC-TV on the basis that few celebrities would turn down an invitation from Mrs. Roosevelt to appear on her television program. She was not sure at first that she wanted to do it, since Elliott had assured NBC that she would have as guests such world-famous personalities as Churchill, Vishinsky, and Acheson, and she doubted she could get these busy men to come on the program or would know what to do with them when they appeared. She was "scared," she told friends, and would have backed out except that her share of the proceeds were to go to Anna.[30]

The format of the Sunday afternoon program was that of tea with Mrs. Roosevelt. She presided over a silver urn, sitting on a couch with her guest, as if in her living room. It was a gracious, almost old-world setting, and Mrs. Roosevelt was an old hand at placing people at their ease. And while both Churchill and Vishinsky declined her invitation to appear, Albert Einstein, who intransigently avoided radio and television appearances, made an exception for Mrs. Roosevelt.

The invitations were drafted by Elliott but went out over her signature. To John Golden, the producer and old friend, she wrote reassuringly that they would sit as "if we were here in my apartment" and reminisce; to the Duke and Duchess of Windsor that "Elsa Maxwell is coming as a guest and I think we could have fun on this program if all four of us were there besides the solemn people who do the serious discussing." But there was also serious debate, sometimes on the touchiest subjects, such as the recognition of

Red China. One invitation upset her. "Dear Miss Tucker," she wrote Elliott's assistant:

I was appalled to find that a telegram in my name was sent to Mrs. Truman asking her to appear on my program. If I had known of this beforehand I would not have sent it because I know that she does not do anything of this kind and that I should not have asked her. When Elliott does not feel that he can sign himself, I am quite willing to sign but I must know to whom messages are going in my name.[31]

The program was a lively discussion show, the predecessor to such programs as the "Today Show," the "Dick Cavett Show," and the like. Mrs. Roosevelt's guests were variegated, the presentation of controversial political issues balanced, Mrs. Roosevelt herself a gracious impresario. But the program was unable to get a sponsor. Mrs. Roosevelt was controversial, and even though she agreed to NBC's request to drop Paul Robeson as an invited guest, when the protests poured in, the networks were skittish and commercial sponsors even more so.

In 1950, Elliott, in addition to the television show, signed a contract with WNBC on behalf of his mother and himself for a daily forty-five-minute radio program at noon on which he would be the announcer and handle the commercials. Listeners were stunned and her friends nonplused to hear Elliott reminding the audience that "Mother uses" this kind of soap or that kind of brush. "The show proves," wrote *Billboard*, "that a boy's best friend is his mother."

She brushed aside the criticism. Although she said she did the television and radio shows to help Anna and Elliott, she enjoyed them, too. They gave her access to a large audience, and she wanted that. When Lawrence Spivak invited her to appear on "Meet the Press," she accepted with alacrity. They had had "a wonderful reaction," he wrote her afterward, and she was often invited back. After Elliott moved away from Hyde Park, Henry Morgenthau III became her television producer and Thomas L. Stix her agent.[32]

There was an element of showmanship in her. She accepted Sergei Koussevitzky's invitation to come to Tanglewood and appear as narrator in Serge Prokofieff's musical fairy tale, *Peter and the Wolf*. "Republican dowagers have been refreshing their souls ever since," wrote *Time*, "by putting on the records, leaning back with smiles of dreamy malice, and listening to Mrs. Roosevelt and the wild, shrill piccolos, excitedly warning a little bird that the cat is creeping (Look out!) towards its perch." Howard Taubman's evaluation of her performance with the Boston Symphony Orchestra was more generous:

Mrs. Roosevelt spoke her part simply and charmingly. She did not have the professional polish of an actor, but her unaffected approach had a special quality all its own. She sounded like a grandmother reading a pleasant little story to her grandchildren. She seemed to take a personal relish in the fable, and she was as alert to all her musical cues as though she had always done this kind of thing.[33]

She read well. Eileen and Richard Harrity, theatrical agent and writer respectively, were friends of Elliott who had bought a little farmhouse near Val-Kill. One week end the Harritys invited her and her house guests over to eat a dinner cooked by James Beard and to listen to Colin Keith Johnston, the star of *Journey's End*, read some poetry. Johnston invited Mrs. Roosevelt to read one of her favorite poems, and without demurral she proceeded to recite "The Calf Path," and did it with such gusto, expressiveness, and elegance of diction that Johnston spent the remainder of the evening reciting poetry to her, until a disgusted Tommy said later, "He was practically in your lap." But she had enjoyed the evening. She did not get up to leave until midnight; usually she took her leave at ten so that she could get at her mail.[34]

Mrs. Roosevelt's taste in poetry was far from avant garde. Her preferences were for writers like Benét, Emily Dickinson, MacLeish, Robinson, and Sandburg, writers whose rhythms were compelling and whose meanings were clear. "Much of the modern poetry of today seems to be both obscene and senseless but I do not think that my opinion would count for much with any of those who are considered good judges," she replied to a request that she join a poetry competition jury.[35]

In 1949 she finished her book on the White House years. It had not written itself easily and fluently as had *This Is My Story*. At times it was sheer agony. "The book moves slowly, but it moves," she wrote Maude, adding, although not as an explanation, "we only have seven children here now & it seems very quiet!" Campobello, to which she retreated in order to escape the telephone and visitors, had other impediments to concentration. "There are good & bad memories there," she wrote a friend as she was about to leave for the island, "but the bad get the better of me when I'm there alone. I'll read a lot & practice typing & the lamps aren't too good for night reading & there the night has a thousand eyes."

Returning to Hyde Park, she enlisted the help of Lorena Hickok. Hick needed the money, and her life was built around Mrs. Roosevelt. She came to Hyde Park and went through Mrs. Roosevelt's files, making notes of stories and anecdotes and listing questions with which Mrs. Roosevelt might wish to deal. Bruce Gould, the editor of the *Ladies' Home Journal*, which had the right of first refusal of the manuscript, was impatient. The appearance of Robert E. Sherwood's *Roosevelt and Hopkins: An Intimate History* "makes me all the more wishful that you would actually get down to the business of writing your book as quickly and as definitively as you can," but to do so she would have to "give up" some of her other activities. "Tell him I have been doing the best I can," she directed Tommy, "but I'm no Sherwood. He'll have the whole thing in a few days now." [36]

"At last," she wrote Maude a few days later, "the book is finished. . . . Of course I suppose I'll have to do some revising as they (the publishers & those who buy the serial rights) suggest, but the real job is done & it is an immense relief." But Gould did not like the manuscript. "You have written this too hastily—as though you were composing it on a bicycle while pedaling your way to a fire." Except for "a few good passages," the book despite the changes she had made in response to his earlier suggestions remained "very dull." [37]

The negotiations over how to proceed became unpleasant. "I've had a disagreeable time with George Bye [her agent] and Bruce Gould & had to leave it to Tommy & Elliott to settle. . . ."

Tommy was involved because she was to receive half of the proceeds from the serial rights. Gould's proposal at the meeting with Elliott and Tommy was "three months solid work—day after day with a collaborator and then Mr. Gould only hoped that it would suit him," she explained to Martha Strayer, a Washington newspaperwoman. "In the first place I would have felt the book wasn't mine and in the second place I wouldn't have the time." Gould not only conditioned his price on the acceptability of the manuscript but he brusquely warned Elliott and Tommy that if she offered the manuscript to anyone else he would withdraw his offer and reduce his price, and if the manuscript were accepted by a competitor, he would immediately drop her monthly question-and-answer page.

Mrs. Roosevelt refused to accept his conditions. "So we told her," wrote Gould, "to sell her book elsewhere if she wouldn't improve it, and her column, too." [38]

Although George Bye was her agent she felt that he was not representing her with sufficient vigor. She permitted Elliott to approach Otis Wiese, the publisher of *McCall's*. He offered $150,000 for the manuscript sight unseen. He also took the monthly question-and-answer page, paying her $3,000 a month for it, which was $500 more than Gould had been paying her, and giving her a five-year contract where Gould had insisted on a month-to-month contract. [39]

Wiese was enthusiastic about the book when he read it. So was Cass Canfield, the chairman of Harper & Brothers who had contracted for the hardcover rights and who had considered an earlier version "very badly written." She had a long conference with him and Marguerite Hoyle, whom he had assigned as her editor. Afterward she summed up his comments, "In general, book gives wonderful pictures of FDR—very vivid. Ms on the whole fresh and unusual.—Main criticism—needs some rephrasing." Soon there were other indications that Gould's harsh, arrogantly expressed editorial judgment had been wide of the mark. Wiese sent the proofs of the first installment, which was to appear in June, 1949, to Jonathan Daniels. "I have written a letter saying I think it almost the most important memoir of our times in America." Bruce Gould ate humble pie: "When Beatrice and I returned from England, we found *McCall's* selling like hot cakes on the newsstands. . . . It is quite possible that in this instance we were wrong." [40]

All summer she worked with Marguerite Hoyle, who, in addition to copy-editing the manuscript, compiled lists of questions designed to jog her memory, fill out a portrait, delete an irrelevancy, heighten a climax. By the end of August she was reading galleys, and in November the *New York Times* and the *New York Herald Tribune* book-review sections carried enthusiastic lead reviews of *This I Remember*. In an age of ghosted memoirs, wrote author Elizabeth Janeway, "it is almost shockingly delightful to read a book which could have been written by absolutely no one else in the world than the great and important figure whose name is signed to it. . . ." She is no stylist, commented Vincent Sheean, but in this book words, structure, and style are subordinate "to the character of the author, and therefore it is from the character of the author that the pervading sense of great beauty arises." [41]

There was one dissenting note in the chorus of praise that greeted *This I Remember*. "Pegler is just writing as much nastiness as he can on it," she informed the Grays, "& is now trying to dig up the Lucy Mercer story & chides me for not telling it." She should not allow Pegler to bother her, David Gray replied. "It would probably have been better for you to have mentioned Mrs. Rutherfurd as being at Warm Springs but it is not very important one way or another. I certainly wouldn't let it worry me." [42]

But she did worry over what her obligations as a writer were as was clear from a letter to John Gunther, whose *Roosevelt in Retrospect* appeared in 1950. She thought it "extraordinary" that he had achieved so much understanding of FDR with so little personal knowledge of him:

I know you wrote with admiration and a desire to be completely fair. There are certain things you did not entirely understand and of course, certain things that neither you nor anyone else knows anything about outside of the few people concerned. Whether it is essential they should ever know is something on which I have not made up my mind since they are personal and they do not touch on public service.[43]

But the Lucy Mercer affair had affected the public as well as private lives of Eleanor and Franklin Roosevelt. As Elizabeth Janeway perceptively noted in her review of *This I Remember:* "Unable to dedicate herself to her husband—why, we shall never be sure— she ended by dedicating herself to his work. . . . On the basis of an unusual if not unsatisfactory marriage was built an edifice of co-operation, of mutual aid and respect which was of immeasurable influence."

Her book was her final service of love to her husband's work. By the time it appeared, however, it was becoming increasingly clear, that her own greatness had not depended on his. Readers read *This I Remember* as much for the light that it shed on her as on him. Her standing as the woman most admired by Americans, columnist Elmo Roper noted, had survived her husband's death and now seemed to be based upon her activities as an individual.

"Only a great woman could have written it," Arthur Schlesinger, Jr., wrote of *This I Remember*. "Mrs. Roosevelt has long since tired of hearing herself described as 'the first lady of the world.' *This I Remember* establishes her all the more firmly in that place." [44]

She was "an American phenomenon comparable to the Niagara Falls," said Sir Benegal Rau, the representative of India at the United Nations. [45]

IX. *America's Best Ambassador*

Ithink that her visit to England improved greatly the relations be-
velt the United States had a remarkable national asset in its relations with the rest of the world. She was truly an ambassador-extraordinary. "Everywhere she went large crowds greeted her
enthusiastically," Ambassador Lewis Douglas reported from London, where she had gone for the unveiling of the statue of FDR. "I
think that her visit to England improved greatly the relations between the American people and the people of this island." At the
1948 General Assembly, when Russia's blockade of Berlin made Europeans jittery, her presence in Paris reassured people and helped
to counteract the systematic Communist effort to portray the
United States as a money-grubbing, atom-bomb-brandishing, imperialistic nation bent on preventive war. Large crowds followed
wherever she went. When the delegates to the General Assembly
traveled on a Sunday to Amiens to a celebration in honor of the
United Nations, it was Mrs. Roosevelt whom the crowds that lined
the roads wanted to see.°

In 1950 the Norwegian government invited her to come to
Oslo for the unveiling of a statue of Franklin. "Having gone to England, I think it would look unappreciative on my part if I did not
accept their invitation," she wrote Elliott's former wife, Mrs. H.
Eidson, asking that Elliott's children Chandler and Tony be permitted to accompany their father and her. The State Department persuaded her to extend her trip to include all the Scandinavian and

---

° This so annoyed the Australian president of the Assembly, Dr. Herbert V.
Evatt, that his speech in Amiens said practically nothing about the UN and dealt
almost exclusively with Australia's role in the First World War.[1]

Benelux countries. "We are all delighted that you are going to Europe this year because we consider you our finest ambassador abroad," Dean Rusk wrote her. The leader of the labor movement in Norway felt that Mrs. Roosevelt's visit would help expose "the phoniness of the Communist 'Peace' Congresses and would help recapture the peace slogan and to identify the Western powers with the positive concept of peace rather than the negative one of containment." [2] Other labor and socialistic parties that were in power in northern Europe felt the same way.

She was received at royal palaces and trade-union headquarters. She visited industrial and agricultural cooperatives as well as housing and health projects, addressed large meetings of women, held press conferences, and spoke over national radios. "Eleanor Roosevelt has come to Stockholm," wrote the conservative *Svenska Dagbladet*. "She came and lived up to every expectation. . . . Her great warm smile filled the door of the plane when it opened at Bromme, it shone over the entire illustrious assembly at the airfield, and it was still just as alive when she later talked seriously to the press, met the King and spoke at the City Hall banquet." "She did not try to impress us," commented the liberal *Dagens Nyheter*, "she did impress us." [3]

"All goes well & the Embassy too seems happy about the visit," Mrs. Roosevelt reported from Stockholm.

The one unanimous feeling is fear & small wonder. . . . Finnland [*sic*] is most ticklish so pray for me—From Holland on I'll relax.[4]

The Finns, sitting up against the Soviet border and balanced precariously between their western sympathies and rude Soviet pressures, seemed to her

very gallant. I went to two resettled farm families this p.m. & wondered at their courage . . . to-morrow I speak to audiences which won't understand me! I dread it & yet so far it has gone well everywhere.[5]

In Copenhagen she found the same mood of apprehension:

My feeling everywhere so far that people were valiantly living with fear is keener here but they have talked more openly here to me in high places. . . . Of course there is no complete unanimity here on what

course should be followed any more than at home but fear is unanimous! I have to spend my time explaining that I hold no position in our
government & have no influence![6]

In Holland people seemed less afraid. There, in talks with Princess Wilhelmina, the title the old queen had assumed after turning
over the throne to her daughter, and with Queen Juliana, she
learned that

at least in high places they seem less worried here & very pleased over
the progress of integrating European interests.[7]

The fear in northern Europe was primarily of the Russians; but
it was fed also by uncertainty about the United States. Could the
United States be counted on in a showdown with Russia? At the
same time there was anxiety as to whether or not the United States
might not be preparing for a preventive war. "Now I must report
something that troubles me," Mrs. Roosevelt wrote Acheson in the
course of her journey, sending a copy to Truman:

namely, some of our industrialists and some of the members of Congress
seem to have left the impression that we are not averse to going to war
on the theory that we will have to go to war in the end and we might as
well do it while the balance of power is on our side. I do not know that
they have actually said it but that is the impression they left and it
frightens most of the people very much indeed.[8]

When she reached Brussels, she talked to Ambassador Robert
Murphy about the need to counteract this feeling. He misunder-
stood her, and wrote afterward that he was disturbed that at the
end of her stay she had spoken of the urgent necessity for the
United States to make an early effort to arrive at an understanding
with Russia and that if Russia evaded or refused the offer this
would then be the United States' ace in the hole with world opinion. "I indicated scepticism but the time was brief," he wrote her.

I wanted you to know that after four years of dealing with the Russians
in Berlin plus conferences during the war and since, I am convinced
that your thought, unless I misunderstand it, is not adapted to the type
of mentality or the aims of the group dictating Soviet policy. There is so
much evidence that these men do not want agreement with us except on

their terms. They are avowed enemies, determined on the liquidation of the social order for which our Government and people stand.

Any offer by the United States will be seen by "the hard men who direct matters for the USSR . . . as evidence of weakness and fear."

She had not made herself clear, Mrs. Roosevelt wrote Murphy in July after the North Korean attack on South Korea,

I was not thinking of any gesture that would impress Russia because I long since decided that nothing but force would impress that particular country. What I had on my mind after visiting the Scandinavian countries was the fact most of them required at that time some gesture from us, some gesture that would make them feel that we were counteracting the Russian words constantly repeated in favor of peace, by something more tangible and which stood out to them as a real gesture.

Since the Korean episode the whole picture has changed. . . .[9]

Just as she was a reassuring symbol to the labor and social-democratic movements of western Europe of the basic sanity, decency, and idealism of the United States, so also was she the country's most effective ambassador to the emerging Third World. The Voice of America asked the Indonesian embassy who would be the best person to comment on the prospective signing of a Point Four agreement with that country. "The answer was Mrs. Roosevelt." [10]

The 1950 General Assembly was a grueling affair, its major preoccupation being Korea, since it was during that Assembly that General MacArthur advanced to the Yalu River and the Chinese intervened to send MacArthur's forces reeling back. But that essentially was the business of Secretary Acheson, Ambassador Austin, and their advisers in the Assembly's First (political) Committee. Her responsibility was Committee III, and there were momentous developments there:

I have never seen such bitterness as I have in Committee #3 this year on the race problem and on the "haves" against the "have nots," and small nations against big nations.[11]

That was the burden of her report to the president at the end of the Assembly.

My own feeling is that the Near East, India and many of the Asiatic people have a profound distrust of white people. This is understandable since the white people they have known intimately in the past, have been the colonial nations and in the case of the United States, our businessmen. . . .

The result is that in Committee #3 at least, there has been a constant attitude among a great block of these countries to oppose everything the United States has suggested. The mere fact that we spoke for something would be enough to make them suspicious. I have completely changed my way of presentation and made it as conciliatory and reasonable as I could, but even then I know they are not believing me, they are thinking (if they are kindly disposed toward me personally) that I am duped or else they feel I am changing my point of view on humanity. They are joined by the whole Soviet block and while I am not always sure they are fooled by the Soviets, they are very glad to have their votes. They feel the Soviet attitude on race, at least, is better than ours and that is point one in the Soviets' favor. They also feel that the Soviet economy may be the only possible economy for them, and that is point two in the Soviets' favor. . . .

They are dissatisfied with the amount of help that we give them. They feel we have overemphasized help to Europe as against help in either Latin America or Asia. In fact, Mr. Bokhari of India told me we were willing to try to save the children of Europe but we did not care whether the children of India died or lived.

She was so troubled by the antagonism she had encountered that she suggested to President Truman that it might be better if the United States were represented on these questions

by Mrs. Sampson, or some other person chosen because he or she could not be accused of siding with the white race against the colored races of the world.

Another suggestion she made to Truman was that he send Dr. Frank Graham, at the time UN commissioner for India and Pakistan, as a "roving ambassador" to the Near East and Asia "to talk philosophy and get a line on attitudes and reasons for those attitudes that we really do not understand too well. . . ." [12]

Truman did not send Graham, but Eleanor Roosevelt. The administration encouraged her to accept the invitation to visit India that Nehru had extended to her during his stay in the United States in 1949. She arranged to visit India and the Middle East in early 1952, flying directly to Beirut from Paris after the adjournment of the sixth General Assembly, which was held there. She thought she might do some articles, perhaps even a book, based on the trip and her experiences in the United Nations. "The State Department asked me to make this trip," she wrote Ambassador Avra M. Warren in Karachi,

but I am entirely unofficial and on my own and coming as a writer and I need no extra protection and no particular attention. I would be grateful if you would make whatever hotel reservations you think I need. I do not want to be extravagant. I will have one secretary with me.[13]

She left Paris with a sense of achievement. Ambassador Austin had fallen ill, and in the final weeks of the Assembly she served as the delegation's chairman as well as its representative in Committee III. She had provided "wise and tactful" leadership, Acheson thanked her. Her speeches and appearances outside the Assembly in which she had presented "the American viewpoint most successfully to the European people, were a major contribution to our general effort," he added. At the request of the "Voice of America" she had done a weekly fifteen-minute broadcast in French all during the Assembly. "I am speaking to you today from the Palais de Chaillot where the sixth session of the United Nations General Assembly is taking place," she began her first broadcast.

I have been asked to tell you, from time to time, what I think of the work we are doing here and why we, of the United States delegation, believe that these meetings are so very important. . . .

I think that what you want to know—especially you the women of post-war Europe—is whether you shall be able, tomorrow, to tell your children that peace is, at long last, a reality. For it isn't enough to talk about peace. One must believe in it. And it isn't enough to believe in it. One must work at it.[14]

Her talks were carried over the French, Belgian, and Swiss networks at the peak listening hour, right after the main news program. She talked simply as a woman to women, but the men listened, too, for she was "Madame Roosevelt," a beloved name in Europe, with a reputation in her own right as a fighter for social justice. And like her husband, she had a gift for stating problems simply and concretely. She even managed to state the differences with Russia over disarmament in a way that was easy to grasp, wrote Richard N. Gardner in an admiring article in the *New York Times*. By the time the Assembly was over, the Communist press was attacking her savagely, and she had added talks in German, Spanish, and Italian to her regular French broadcast.

"I am sure," Acheson's note to her at the end of the Assembly added, "that your present trip will be a means of bringing the American views effectively to some of the Far Eastern peoples." [15]

It was a journey filled with many hazards. She canceled a stopover in Cairo. "I think it will relieve your mind and my family's," she advised Ambassador Jefferson Caffery, "to hear that we have thought it best not to stop in Cairo," but fly directly to Beirut.

Even western-minded Beirut presented problems. David Gurewitsch and Maureen Corr were to accompany her:

I hope David enjoys his trip; being with me won't add to his joys but it may give him opportunities to see some of the things he wants to see. I rather imagine I'll have to do some women's affairs & speeches & I'm sure they will plan for him to see medical things for I wrote that was his interest.

But David was Jewish. "As Mr Malik (Lebanese Ambassador in Washington and a colleague on the Human Rights Commission) has doubtless intimated to you," Harold B. Minor, the American ambassador in Lebanon, advised her, "in case [the] physician [is] Jewish it would be politically most unwise if not impossible for him to enter Lebanon or other Arab countries." So David arranged to join them in Israel. The American ambassador in Pakistan, Avra Warren, invited Mrs. Roosevelt and Maureen to stay with him. "We will make suitable arrangements for Dr. Gurewitsch to stay elsewhere." It would be better if the "three of us stayed at a hotel," she replied. The governor general and the begum "are most anxious that you and your party should find it convenient to stay at the Governor-

General's residence," the ambassador's next message read. "We will be delighted to accept for us all but do not want anyone to put themselves out," she wrote back.[16]

From the moment that she arrived in Beirut she sensed that behind the official courtesy and kindness there was hostility. She was guarded at the beginning by a carload of soldiers and security officers. She finally got rid of this escort and was able to go among the people. She was determined to get the Arab point of view, and drinking endless tiny cups of black and bitter coffee, heard many presentations of it—from Americans stationed in Lebanon, Syria, and Jordan, from educated Arabs who had managed to build new lives for themselves but still hoped to return to their former homes, and from the refugees in the camps. She came away saddened that the Arabs still talked hopefully of wiping out the people of Israel. "I have a feeling that this would not be easy." [17]

"This country teems with life and purpose," she wrote of Israel, which she entered through the Mandelbaum Gate in divided Jerusalem. She spent six days there, dismayed at the schedule the Israeli government had arranged. "The program here is simply appalling. . . ." she wrote Ambassador Chester Bowles in New Delhi. "While I will gladly visit anything you feel is necessary and important, I don't want to do it at this breakneck speed." Could the official things be crowded into the first two days? "After that I would be delighted if they would furnish us with transportation facilities to go wherever we really wanted to go." [18]

Vain hope. As the plane made its approach to Karachi, David suddenly leaned over and touched her arm. "Look!" he said, pointing in astonishment at the huge crowd gathered at the airport. "That's not for us," she said firmly. "That's for someone of importance who is arriving." But the "sea of women" was there for her, and throughout her stay in the subcontinent she was to be attended by crowds the denseness of which she had never before encountered. They knelt in the streets when she passed. "I hadn't realized how they cared about Franklin" was her comment when she spoke of this later.[19]

In Pakistan she met with all of the dignitaries, female as well as male, lectured veiled Moslem women about the League of Woman Voters, taught the Virginia Reel to some emancipated Pakistani youngsters, visited Peshawar and Lahore, and made "a sentimental journey" to the Khyber Pass which her father had visited seventy-two years earlier.

"I have come here to learn," she declared upon her arrival in New Delhi. "Eleanor Roosevelt zindabad!" (Long live Eleanor Roosevelt!) the crowd chanted, and Mme. Pandit, Nehru's sister, garlanded her with a chain of cloves and fragrant beads. Her thirty-day tour took her to almost all the important cities in India. She received an honorary degree from Aligarh University in northern India and spoke to a large civic audience in Trivandrum, in southwest India. In New Delhi she addressed Parliament. That was the most challenging and touchy of the many speeches she made while in India. What were the points she should be careful about? she asked Ambassador Bowles before her appearance. He gave her a list several pages long. She looked it over thoughtfully and remarked, "What is there left to talk about?" Talk, however, she did, and without notes. The president and prime minister were in attendance as well as the deputies. The latter, however, were cool toward her, almost impatient, as if to say: Why do we waste our time with this woman? She ignored the lectern, advanced to the edge of the rostrum, and stood there, pocketbook in hand, wearing a flowered hat and sturdy shoes, her tummy slightly visible—an American presence—her warm smile perceptibly thawing out her audience. Instead of singing America's praises, she suggested that India might well benefit from the mistakes that the United States had made during its developmental period. "Your problems are more difficult, but you are meeting them in the way our people met theirs." She showed understanding of India's desire for nonalignment. "Hear! Hear!" the deputies murmured as she said, "India's neutrality is akin to that of United States' foreign policy as far back as the thirties." Bowles already had a splendid relationship with Nehru and most of India's leaders, but the climate for his mission palpably improved after her speech.

Mrs. Roosevelt was equally effective with the left-leaning,

anti-American students, drawing heavily on her own experience with the youth movement in the United States in the thirties. Having heard from Nehru that too many of India's students preferred the traditional law and humanities training to engineering and technical studies, she recalled that students with technical degrees had come through the Depression in better style than the others. "Technical training, I imagine, is the best way by which you can help solve the problems in your country." [20]

Her experience in the thirties was particularly helpful in Allahabad, Nehru's home district in northern India, where she went, accompanied by Mme. Pandit, to receive a degree from the university and to address the student body. In anticipation of her appearance, left-wing students published an open letter stating that Allahabad students were not interested in hearing her apologies for American imperialism. Nehru, to whom this was reported, angered at this rudeness to a guest of the country, ordered that the meeting be canceled. Timid university officials, fearful the meeting would turn into an unruly anti-American demonstration, overruled Mrs. Roosevelt's plea that she be allowed to handle the situation. At least, she suggested, let the signatories of the open letter come to the house and she would answer their questions. Mme. Pandit was furious that the students should undertake to cross-examine Mrs. Roosevelt. "Don't worry about it," Mrs. Roosevelt sought to reassure her. "I have been booed for 15 minutes at a time—it doesn't bother me. And their questions are things I have been through before; it sounds just like the Youth Congress back home."

The signatories of the letter were ushered in, except for one student whom Mme. Pandit would not have in the house because he had been particularly rude. That was a mistake. As Mrs. Roosevelt began to answer the questions of those who had filed in, the outcast assembled his followers, 3,000 of them, outside of the high fence topped with spikes that surrounded the Nehru compound, to protest the "insult" to their leader. Their shouts and chants could not be ignored. Mme. Pandit went out to speak to them. She climbed on a table and then on a chair on top of the table in order to be able to speak over the fence. She made no impact on the

thousands of milling students. Finally, Mrs. Roosevelt insisted on
going outside. She mounted the table and chair and proceeded to
talk to the crowd. They did not like to receive their guest across a
gate, one of the leaders shouted. Why did she not come to the students' hall? She would if they went back, she called out to them.
Mme. Pandit wanted guards to accompany her, but she would not
hear of it. She would not even permit David to accompany her. She
was willing to take the risk, but no one else was to be endangered.
The hall was jammed when she reached it. She spoke briefly and
then answered questions, sixteen in all, about American treatment
of Negroes, America's policy toward Red China, its attitude toward
Indian nonalignment, and the like. The meeting ended in amiabil-
ity and good will.[21]

Another sentimental journey was to see the Taj Mahal in the
moonlight. "At last I know why my father felt it was the one unforgettable thing he had seen in India. He always said it was the one
thing he wanted us to see together." Like her father, too, she dined
with maharajahs and lunched at the palace of the Nizam of Hyder-
abad, and was furious that she allowed herself to be kept from riding an elephant. She inspected newly built industrial complexes and
the American-aided Etawah rural development project. She placed a
wreath at Rajghat, where Gandhi had been cremated, worked an
ancient spinning wheel as Gandhi had done, crept into native mud
huts. Everywhere, in packed city streets and along dusty village
roads, the people met her, garlanded her, and the children cried,
"Matajki Jai, Jai Hind!" (Victory to our revered Mother, victory to
India!), and she responded with the Hindu gesture of *namaste*,
folded hands and bowed head.[22]

She had many talks with Nehru. He is "a remarkable person,"
she wrote her Dutchess County neighbor Dorothy Bourne. "He
bears the burdens, which are almost overwhelming, in a calm and
courageous manner." Nehru placed his guest house at her disposal.
The first night they were there David Gurewitsch came into Maureen's room. "Do you know there are snakes in Nehru's garden and
they may come in through the window?" An alarmed Maureen
went to Mrs. Roosevelt. "Don't you worry about that, dear," she

said with a lightheartedness that in no way reassured Maureen. "We'll think about that in the morning." [23]

She came to know U.S. ambassador Chester Bowles and his wife Stebbins very well and was enormously impressed with the job they were doing. They lived in a modest house, sent their children to an Indian public school, and, instead of confining themselves to the diplomatic colony in New Delhi, tirelessly toured the countryside. "In one way I think perhaps Providence did something for us when he [Bowles] was defeated in the last election so that he could be available for his present post," she wrote Truman.

Everyone without exception, and I think I have met every government official thus far, tells me what a change there has been in the feeling towards the United States since Mr. Bowles' arrival. They feel now that we understand them, that we are more understanding of their isolationism and that we are beginning to realize that they do not want to become communistic but their problems are so great they feel they cannot take sides.

Bowles had done everything possible for her, her letter went on, "but I am afraid I can never accomplish what the Indians want as a result of my visit." The Indians hoped she would be able to persuade public and congressional opinion to see India's nonalignment as she had come to understand it, and thus pave the way for greater U.S. economic aid to India and less military assistance to Pakistan.[24]

The great Indian expectations worried her. One evening there was another large dinner. David informed her he was sick of receptions and would take his dinner elsewhere. That to her was a rebuff, and, coming on top of her concern that India expected things of her she could not deliver, triggered one of her deep depressions. The next morning she told David that she had written out telegrams to Nehru, Acheson, Cass Canfield at Harper & Brothers, canceling her trip. "I represent the United States and they expect all these things from the United States and think that I have the power to deliver for them what they need," she said in explanation. That was what she told him, recalled David. "But the real thing was that she was hurt and had fallen into one of her 'what am I living for' moods. . . . The whole day was impossible. You couldn't get a word out of her." But she recovered. "I do not know how many more official welcomes, lunches and dinners I can stand," she wrote Acheson, "but I will do as much as I can." [25]

"Mrs. R. sounds very cheerful and she has had a good press on this trip," Tommy reported to Maude Gray. "A man from India who works in the UN called me today, he had just returned from India and wanted me to know that Mrs. R. made the greatest impression of anyone who has ever visited India." "The problems here are enormous," Mrs. Roosevelt wrote as her India itinerary drew to an end,

but the resources are great. At the moment I think this is the most critical area in the world. If India becomes communist, the situation for the rest of us is desperate but if it becomes a leader India may succeed, not in preventing China from being communist, but in encouraging them to have a different type of communism. The government is becoming more outspoken in its belief in democracy and opposition to communism but it is trying to keep relations with China on an agreeable footing and even with Russia it is much less outspoken than many other countries.[26]

The U.S. embassy in Taipei transmitted an invitation to Mrs. Roosevelt from Mme. Chiang Kai-shek to visit Formosa and be her houseguest. Mrs. Roosevelt sent her regrets saying, "Must get home for Human Rights Commission meeting, so return direct from Djakarta." The government of Burma wanted her to visit Rangoon. "Burmese regard Mrs. Roosevelt as most popular living American," Acheson cabled her.[27] Again she wrote "regret," but subsequently relented. From India she went to Indonesia for a brief stay in Djakarta, where she dined with Achmed Sukarno and he showed her his collection of modern paintings. Then she flew home by way of Rangoon and Manila.

On her return she promptly went down to Washington to report to Truman and to do what she could to deepen official understanding of the countries she had visited. Acheson sent the president a memo briefing him on Mrs. Roosevelt's trip:

She was received everywhere with great cordiality except in the Arab states. . . . Her trip to India and Pakistan was a great success, and she appears to have done much to increase understanding of the United States foreign policy objectives. . . . Ambassador Bowles has described her visit to India as a tremendous success and as having made a deep impression, particularly among students and the press.

Although it was undertaken in a purely unofficial capacity, Mrs. Roosevelt's journey has served the public interest exceedingly well. . . .[28]

Word spread around official Washington that she had interesting things to report. Franklin Jr. arranged a meeting with Republicans and Democrats on the House Foreign Affairs Committee. Sen. Herbert H. Lehman assembled a group of his colleagues at his apartment to hear her. She wrote to tell her friend Anna Rosenberg that she was coming to Washington again in May. Anna showed the note to her chief, Secretary of Defense Robert Lovett, and he asked Mrs. Roosevelt to lunch with him and some of his "principal people." Everywhere she argued that economic aid was essential if India and Pakistan were expected to develop strong and stable governments and that in the long run money spent on economic development would return greater dividends than money spent on military aid. Then an unexpected invitation. "I would be ever so grateful," Gen. Walter Bedell Smith, head of the CIA, wrote her, "if you would be good enough to set aside some time when you are next in Washington in order that my people in the CIA may have the benefit of your observations on your recent trip through Southeast Asia. We are particularly interested in the thoughts and reactions of the people themselves, and I think you can help us understand them better." He was very kind to ask her, she replied. "Would sometime in June be convenient?" [29]

In the closing days of the Truman administration, she performed one final mission as ambassador-extraordinary. At the request of Claude G. Bowers, the United States ambassador in Chile, Truman sent her as head of the U.S. delegation to the inauguration of President Carlos Ibáñez. He had campaigned on an anti-American platform and had hinted that if elected he might follow the anti-American line of his friend Juan Perón of Argentina. Plans were being made to turn his inauguration into "an anti-Yankee festival." In the six days that she was in Chile she completely overshadowed all the other delegations, including the four South American vice presidents and Perón's delegation of thirty headed by his foreign minister. While Argentinians and others vying for Ibáñez's favor spent their time at social functions and military receptions, she visited housing projects and health and hospital centers, toured slum areas, held a free-swinging press conference, and so won the hearts of press and people that not even the Communists dared to criticize her. And President Ibáñez paid tribute to her by appearing at her official reception and chatting cordially with her. She boosted the American stock, wrote the *Christian Science Monitor,* "from a low ebb of the past six months." And it cited the remark of an American executive, "If the President himself had come down, he couldn't have done more to boost pro-United States feeling." [30]

X. Resignation Accepted

It will be a sad day for him & in a way for the country, if he runs for President. He will run, but as a hero he will be tarnished & it will get worse & worse. We need our heroes & we need him here & I doubt if we need him more as President.

I'd rather see Truman back if he'll really clean house!

So Mrs. Roosevelt wrote about General Eisenhower on January 21, 1952, from the Paris General Assembly.[1]

Her candidate was Adlai Stevenson, who, she thought, "would make a good President but I doubt if he can get the nomination." This was before she left for India. By the time she returned Truman had announced his decision not to run again, thus clearing the way for other candidates. But Stevenson was proving equally reluctant to run. He told Truman early in March that he had made a commitment to the people of Illinois to run for re-election as governor, and he did not feel he could go back on that pledge. Several people came to ask her to urge Stevenson to run. "I will be for him if he runs," she told them, "but he has to make the decision himself whether or not to run." She could understand his feeling that if Eisenhower was the Republican candidate he would be in a better position to lead the Democratic party after 1952 as the successful governor of Illinois than as the defeated candidate for president. "Governor Stevenson has bowed himself out which I deeply regret," she wrote Chester Bowles in April, 1952, "and New York is making

Averell Harriman its favorite son. Franklin, Jr. is going to run the citizens' committee. . . . Kefauver appeals to me less and less." [2]

One candidacy she promptly squashed—her own. India Edwards, vice-chairman of the Democratic National Committee, director of the women's division, and a Truman loyalist, reported that a Long Island housewife wanted advice on how to start a draft movement for Eleanor Roosevelt. "We think Eleanor Roosevelt is the only Democrat who could surely defeat General Eisenhower." The more she thought of this suggestion, India Edwards went on, "the more I agreed with her so I am writing to ask you if there is any chance that you could be persuaded to accept the nomination if it should be offered to you. We have some good younger men—I personally think Adlai Stevenson is the outstanding one although in my position I cannot have a candidate—but I agree with my young Long Islander that you are the outstanding Democrat in the country." [3]

Mrs. Edwards sincerely admired Mrs. Roosevelt, but an Eleanor Roosevelt draft movement also had the advantage from the viewpoint of the Democratic managers, for whom Mrs. Edwards spoke, of tying up support that might otherwise go to Estes Kefauver. The Tennesseean was bidding for the nomination via the primary route, and, with his coonskin hat and relaxed manner, was already showing formidable vote-getting powers. The Truman loyalists wanted to slow him down. A draft movement for Eleanor Roosevelt was one way of doing so. But she would not play. She was as firmly opposed as ever to running for elective office, and she certainly had no wish to be a stalking horse for the establishment politicians. "I most certainly would not accept the nomination if it were offered to me," she replied to Mrs. Edwards. "I doubt there is any chance for any woman at present. Governor Stevenson is the one I would favor." [4]

With Stevenson appearing to have removed himself from consideration, she became unsure as to whom to support. James was campaigning for Kefauver, Franklin, Jr. for Harriman. And between the two she seemed to lean toward Harriman. He was the speaker at the Hyde Park Memorial Day services for FDR in the rose garden. Did that mean she was supporting him for the presidency, Cyril Clemens inquired:

I have not come out for any candidate, either Republican or Democratic. I have known Averell Harriman since he was a little boy. He came to Hyde Park to speak at the Memorial Day ceremonies for my husband but it was not a political speech.

It was not a political speech, but she was keenly aware of the value to any candidate of identification with the Roosevelt heritage.[5]

She had little time for politics in the spring of 1952 as the Human Rights Commission was in session, still trying to reach agreement on the two covenants, one covering civil and political rights and the other economic, social, and cultural rights. She doggedly kept at it, even though Republican support for the Bricker amendment, which would make it impossible for the United States to adhere to the covenants, made it unlikely that the Senate would ever approve the covenants. What was to turn out to be her last day with the Human Rights Commission proved to be the longest, and she remained to the bitter end. The Commission's parent body had directed the eighteen-member group to terminate in mid-June the session that had begun early in April. All that remained to be done on the final Friday was to adopt a routine report on the Commission's progress. At eight thirty, Friday evening, the Commission settled down for what they thought would at most be a three-hour session. But they had not reckoned with the Russians, who felt they had to get in the last word—even, as one delegate remarked, if no one were listening. Earlier in the day Mrs. Roosevelt had circulated among the delegates a mimeographed document answering some of the accusations against the United States during the Commission's debates. In order to expedite the Commission's business, Mrs. Roosevelt chose this method of reply rather than a speech. But the Soviet group, instead of being grateful for one speech less, called this procedure unfair and unprecedented, and at four in the morning, using the pretext of explaining his vote on the Commission's report, the Soviet delegate launched a lengthy attack upon the United States and Mrs. Roosevelt. It was close to 6:00 A.M. when she left the UN headquarters building and gratefully sank back into the cushions of a passing taxi. "What are you doing up at this hour?" the incredulous taxi driver asked her.

Having been away from Hyde Park so much, she decided not to attend the Democratic convention in Chicago in July and turned down India Edwards's invitation to speak to it about the United Nations. Then Truman urged her to come. She was reluctant because "a political convention audience would not want to listen." But Truman pressed her. "If you really meant that you want me to make a speech at the Democratic Convention, will you please have someone let me know what day and what hour as soon as possible?" He certainly did mean it. He wanted someone to tell the country just what the United Nations meant to peace in the world, and she was the best person to do so. "I will do my best to make a speech to which the delegates will listen," she wrote Frank E. McKinney, chairman of the Democratic National Committee, and then added a few crisp thoughts on the conduct of conventions in the new day of television:

I watched the Republican Convention and I think TV has completely revolutionized what should go on at a convention. I was bored to death by the parades and floor demonstrations. If we can possibly prevent any such goings on at our convention it would gain in dignity and in interest and in educational value to the TV audience.

Also I think the length of speeches could with profit be materially cut down. Nearly everyone in the room with me went to sleep before General MacArthur and ex-President Hoover had finished and yet I have heard people say General MacArthur's speech had real oratorical appeal, but it did not keep people awake.[6]

The day before she flew out to Chicago she told reporters she hoped the Democrats "will adopt a really courageous civil rights plank," but refused to indicate her preference among the candidates for the presidential nomination. When the reporters persisted, she laughingly called attention to the division among her sons and maintained that as a mother she could not take sides. Not only was James for Kefauver and Franklin Jr. Harriman's campaign manager, but Elliott and John had come out for General Eisenhower.[7]

"MRS. F.D.R. STOPS THE SHOW," the *New York Post* headline described her reception by the convention. The crowd rose to its feet as it spotted her coming down the runway to the speaker's platform. A roar welled up. The band began to play "Happy Days Are Here Again." The state standard bearers, except for a few southern holdouts, massed in front of the platform. Mrs. Roosevelt sought to begin but the tumult continued until the temporary chairman banged his gavel and said, "Will the delegates please take their seats. Several million people are waiting to hear the First Lady of the World." [8]

She spoke first of her husband. "This demonstration was not for me," she said. "It was for the memory of my husband." Then she launched into her speech about the United Nations, criticizing the "small articulate minority" that advocated U.S. withdrawal from the United Nations, an attitude she characterized as "a selfish, destructive approach which leads not to peace but to chaos and might eventually lead to World War III." She compared the cost of the United Nations—seventy-seven cents per person each year—with the cost in dollars of World War II—"$1,708 for every person alive" —and concluded her speech with another reference to her husband (was it an unspoken rebuke to Truman for having failed to mention Franklin in his speech to the United Nations?). She read to the delegates from the speech on international cooperation that FDR had planned to deliver at the Jefferson Day dinner on April 13, 1945, "If civilization is to survive, we must cultivate the science of human relationships—the ability of all people of all kinds, to live together and work together in the same world, at peace."

Lily Polk, whose friendship with Eleanor Roosevelt dated back to the early days of their marriages and who knew the Lucy Mercer story, wrote her in admiration: "What a wonderful thing it is to be able to pay a tribute to one's husband as you did to-night and how very fortunate he was to have a wife who could so wonderfully carry on his work." The Roosevelt mystique was still alive and potent, a State Department official watching the convention concluded. He sent her a paragraph from a letter of a colleague, a lifelong Republican.

For a long time now it has been unfashionable even to mention Roosevelt. . . . Her appearance on the platform set off the most spontaneous and gigantic demonstration of either convention. There could be no doubt that it was something each individual delegate wanted to do and was doing only because he wanted to do it. The whole sense I got out of it was that in a strange kind of way Roosevelt and everything he stood for, represented the conscience of America and she stood there as the symbol of that conscience. It was a deeply moving hour. . . .

Herbert Beaser, one of her advisers in the Human Rights Commission, felt that her speech "contained just those things which I think must be said and said repeatedly about the UN and our stake in its work." And Agnes E. Meyer, of whom she had become quite fond in the course of their battle together for federal aid to the public schools, struck a militantly feminist note:

You really saved the day for political women because the Republican women were if anything even more vulgar in their speeches and in their appearance than the Democratic women. It certainly must have been a relief for the women of the country to realize that one could be a woman and a lady and yet be thoroughly political.

I realized once more how important it is the way women dress when they appear before the public. You were the only one who was suitably garbed.[9]

She did not stay for the balloting, but when Stevenson was nominated she wired him congratulations, eliciting a graceful response from the candidate, about her "splendid speech" and the strength that her expression of good will gave him. Thus encouraged, she was soon sending him a "few" suggestions:

The papers state that you are coming to New York City late in August. Will you forgive me if I make a suggestion to you? I have a feeling that Mr. Baruch would be very much flattered if you ask, as soon as possible, whether you could see him while you are in New York. . . .

Unfortunately President Truman is so annoyed because Mr. Baruch would not give up his old rule of not coming out openly for a candidate and heading a financial committee for him that they exchanged unfortunate letters and President Truman felt that his information could be of no use to him.

You may feel exactly the same way but I have always found that while it took a little tact and some flattery to get on with the old gentleman I got enough information with valuable experience back of it to make it worth while. He is not always a liberal and you will not always agree with him but fundamentally he is sound and I think it is valuable to have some contacts with him, particularly unofficial ones.

He had written Baruch, Stevenson promptly replied. He knew Baruch was a mine of sound advice. "You have never added a 'headache' and you never will. I hope you will give me any suggestions [you have] as the campaign progresses." [10]

She was for Stevenson, but she was also looking him over. A note of vexation crept into a reference to him in mid-August:

Eisenhower does not seem to me to be saying much. I'm anxious to see Stevenson develop his theories. He told Averell he was critical of FDR in his handling of Congress & his inability to get along. It isn't really possible under our system I fear, for the Executive and Legislative to get along well.[11]

Stevenson called on Baruch at the end of August. The elder statesman was not taken with him, or perhaps he had already decided he was going to support Eisenhower, an old friend. In any case when Eisenhower, hard on the heels of Stevenson, came to see him, he showed how his mind was running when he eagerly posed for a picture with the general, something he had not done with the governor. "I do not like the gang around Stevenson one bit," he informed Mrs. Roosevelt.[12]

While Stevenson's first campaign speeches displeased Baruch, they exhilarated her. Indeed, a shiver of delight was felt throughout the liberal community as this new voice spoke out with a clarity and wit that were as rare in politics as was the courage that compelled him to criticize patrioteering before the American Legion convention and the filibuster when speaking in the South.

I grow more enthusiastic about the governor day by day. Even General Eisenhower and Senator Nixon and Senator McCarthy, all of whom have wept over the amount of humor that Governor Stevenson has been able to put into his speeches and who have remarked that such things as the Korean War, taxes and inflation had nothing humorous about them —even these gentlemen's tears haven't dampened my ardor.[13]

Unlike 1948, she was ready to campaign this time and disappointed she was not asked. Whose fault it was is not clear. She blamed the Democratic National Committee. "I could not have taken an active part in the campaign," she wrote India Edwards,

> but I have not been asked to do anything and now when I am going back in the General Assembly the most I could do would be two or three radio or TV programs in New York City but if what I have been asked to do is a sample of what others have been asked not much can be going on.

The Volunteers for Stevenson were short of money, she added, and the New York organization, although inactive itself, was keeping the Volunteers from operating upstate.[14]

She thought the regular organization, from Washington down, was sulking. Stevenson had fired McKinney and had installed his own man as national chairman and had shifted campaign headquarters from Washington to Springfield. The Truman people felt that he had done this in order to dissociate himself from the Truman administration. Their resentment was accentuated by Stevenson's failure to ask the president "until too late" to get into the campaign. "The President can do a great deal for Stevenson," Mrs. Roosevelt's letter to India Edwards ended, "but it is Stevenson who is running and certainly most of the work must be done by him." [15]

The growth of her confidence in Stevenson was matched by her disenchantment with Eisenhower. Despite her "many ties" to the Democratic party, Mrs. Roosevelt told a campaign rally in Harlem, she was "willing to listen" when the general was nominated.

> I felt that a victory had been won because we were going to have two good people. As the campaign has progressed I have never been sadder in my whole life. I had great respect for Eisenhower. I knew him as a general. I did not know him as a candidate. As a candidate I have never felt so sorry for anyone before.
>
> I know that it must have been terrible to face yourself—to realize that you have been persuaded that you must go out and stand beside men who had said things about someone who had been your best friend, someone who had really given you the opportunity to rise to great position.
>
> Yet he [Eisenhower] stood by the side of [Sen. William E.] Jenner, who said that General Marshall's life was a living lie.
>
> How General Eisenhower could do that I cannot understand. I

cannot understand how he could give a mark of approval to Senator McCarthy. I consider that Senator McCarthy in fighting communism has injured the people of the country because he fought it in the wrong way. . . .[16]

Of Governor Stevenson, Mrs. Roosevelt said that "he knows more about the world than almost any other man in this country," and that as governor of Illinois, in working with the legislature, he had received good training for working with Congress. The August annoyance with Stevenson for having spoken disparagingly of FDR was wiped out. She arranged for Stevenson to come to Hyde Park to lay a wreath at Franklin's grave and to breakfast with her. "I have heard no one in the campaign who could make the people understand the complicated situations before us so well and in such simple and beautiful prose, as Governor Stevenson," she wrote in her column.[17]

The western alliance was building up its armed strength, but for Mrs. Roosevelt this was strength needed in order to bring about a settlement with Soviet Russia. Her report to Truman after the 1951 General Assembly had returned to the subject, Ambassador Murphy's admonition notwithstanding, of the need to make some dramatic bid for a settlement with Moscow:

We need something dramatic to prove to our allies that we are not planning war when we have attained equal strength with the Russians or what we feel is equal power, but we must show that we are going to use NATO to bring about peace.

I think it can easily be proved that nothing can be done with the Russians except when we have power but with SHAPE doing a military organization job something dramatic must emphasize what our ultimate objectives are.

Stevenson understood the interrelationship between power and peace, she thought, and would know how to handle the Russians. "Mr. Stalin, I think, will find a better match in Governor Stevenson than in General Eisenhower," she wrote privately.[18]

But Election Day produced a Republican landslide. Eisenhower received the largest vote ever given a presidential candidate up to that time in American history. There was, nevertheless, some comfort for Stevensonians like Mrs. Roosevelt. More than 27 million Americans voted for Stevenson, which was the largest vote ever given any Democratic candidate.

"The campaign was well worth while," she wrote Mrs. Ives, Stevenson's sister, "in that it started a process of education which I hope will continue for the next four years." She saw Stevenson leading the Democratic party in opposition; and to the tender, solicitous note that she wrote him after his defeat, he replied that he had no regrets except the disappointment of his friends, and she was at the front of the list of those to whom he was grateful.[19]

She would help Stevenson, but she also had to face the problem of her own role under a Republican administration. In 1948, after Truman's surprise victory, she had told reporters that she planned to devote the rest of her active life to the United Nations as "the best hope we have for peace." By the end of 1952 as the Republicans prepared to take command, she had come to symbolize humanity's search for common ground more than any other UN personality, except the secretary-general. While FDR was alive there had been an internal monitor that kept her from statements and actions she thought might embarrass him. In her service to the United Nations since his death, it was as if the brakes had been taken off. As a public personality she was freer, more self-assured, a powerful voice for world peace and respect for human dignity.[20]

She seemed a natural choice for President-elect Eisenhower to continue at the United Nations, especially in the light of the principle of bipartisanship that had governed U.S. representation at the United Nations since its inception. She wanted to stay on, but she also wanted Eisenhower to feel free to designate whomever he wished. Her appointment as a delegate to the General Assembly automatically ceased with its adjournment in December. Her appointment as the U.S. representative on the Human Rights Commission was for a five-year term, but, she informed the State Department the day after the election,

even though I was appointed for a full term on the Human Rights Commission I would prefer to resign so that the incoming President and Secretary of State may feel free to appoint a Republican woman.[21]

There were press reports that she would refuse a UN appointment from President-elect Eisenhower. They upset Baruch. "May I ask that you do not resign or take any step before we have a talk," he asked her. "You have learned much and are the recipient of as much experience as anyone in dealing with the Russians." Her reply indicated not only the reasons why Eisenhower might not wish to reappoint her but the terms under which she would be willing to serve in a Republican administration:

November 18, 1952

My dear Friend:

Thank you for your kind letter.

It isn't within my hands to resign or not to resign. Each of us does that automatically and I think it would be highly unfair not to resign from the Human Rights Commission.

I want you to think over the problem in the following way. I have been able, because the President has always been willing to see me, to discuss with him at the end of every meeting or of any mission which I undertook, everything that had occurred. The State Department, which always received my report first, was glad to have me do this because they felt that frequently reports sent from the State Department go to secretaries and never reach the President. Therefore I was able to get to the President what I thought the non-government organizations and the women of this country generally felt on a great many subjects, as well as the routine report of what had occurred and my opinion of what other nations felt.

This would be impossible with General Eisenhower, since I hardly know him and since I do not belong to the party that will be in power. If there were a number of American women being given important positions on the policy-making level in the United Nations, then I think it would be right to have representatives from both parties. But since the number of women is very limited, I think it is important that it be a woman who can reach the President with the point of view of the women and who also has the interests of the United Nations at heart. . . .

. . . I have spent many years of my life in opposition and I rather like the role.[22]

Despite this letter, she did not forbid Baruch to talk to the president-elect. His report back was most surprising. The general, he said, had been angered by some personal remarks about Mrs. Eisenhower that Mrs. Roosevelt was alleged to have made at a dinner party in Europe and which had been passed on to him by Perle Mesta. Gossip was so out of character for Mrs. Roosevelt—she could not recall ever having made the remarks ascribed to her—that her friends concluded that the general, perhaps because of her stinging attack on him for having turned his back on General Marshall, perhaps out of deference to the McCarthy wing of his party, was glad to accept the resignation of someone who, although esteemed throughout the world, was execrated by the extreme right.[23]

She made her last speech in the United Nations. Appropriately it was on the political rights of women in the course of a discussion of a draft convention on the subject. Her theme—when it came to the "great decisions" in politics and government, men still made them, while the women were left to cool their heels outside. The draft convention, she said, went far deeper than encouraging equal political rights for women in all countries. It reached to the "real issue of whether in fact women are recognized fully in setting the policies of our governments." She doubted this was the case. She conceded that women in forty-five countries voted on the same basis as men, but added, "Too often the great decisions are originated and given form in bodies made up wholly of men, or so completely dominated by them that whatever of special value women have to offer is shunted aside without expression."

"Too few women" were serving in positions of real leadership, even in countries where women's suffrage and eligibility for public office were of long standing. "I am not talking now in terms of paper parliaments and honorary appointments." The Soviet delegate had boasted that thirty-seven women were members of the National Assembly in Bulgaria, thirty-one in Romania. Neither was she talking about

any such artificial balance as would be implied in a 50-50, or a 40-60 division of public offices.

What I am talking about is whether women are sharing in the direction of the policy-making in their countries; whether they have the opportunities to serve as chairmen of important committees, and as cabinet members and delegates to the UN.

Thus Eleanor Roosevelt, whom the *New York Times* termed the "most popular delegate," whom even the blasé members of the Secretariat always stopped to look at when she went whisking down the corridors or lined up in a cafeteria queue, ended her tour of duty.[24]

On December 22, Sandifer, who was now deputy assistant secretary for UN affairs, wrote her that "It really makes me sad to see your signed letter of resignation from the Human Rights Commission. I certainly hope that it is not accepted. . . . We are registering a strong recommendation that you be continued on the Human Rights Commission." On December 30, she received an impersonal, lukewarm note from Eisenhower, formally thanking her for her services and accepting her resignation as a delegate to the United Nations. She replied immediately.

December 31, 1952

My dear General:

I am very grateful to you for your extremely kind letter.

You will receive, when the State Department thinks it proper to present it, my resignation from the Human Rights Commission as a Presidential appointee. This would naturally have to wait until you became President.

I do not have to resign formally from the Delegation since any Delegation to the General Assembly is only appointed for the term of that General Assembly. Therefore, at the end of each Assembly we automatically cease our services. As only that part of this Session which is concerned with the political questions will reconvene in February, I have, of course, terminated the services for which I was appointed.

I appreciate your saying that you feel I have rendered good service and I want to thank you for your letter.

Very sincerely yours,
Eleanor Roosevelt [25]

"From top to bottom in this Mission," Richard S. Winslow, its secretary-general, wrote her, "you will stand as the finest symbol of all that is best in the United Nations and, in a personal way to each of us, as the finest type of civic leader, public servant and working colleague." [26]

"There seems to be a jinx on my getting to Washington!" she advised President Truman as inauguration day approached.

I have completely lost my voice and decided the weather was not propitious for going down to Washington today. This means I will not see you and Mrs. Truman before the 20th, I am afraid, and so I want to send you this line to tell you how grateful I am for all you have given me in the way of opportunity for service in the UN in the last few years and to wish you relief from the burdens of state which I know have been overwhelming and an interesting and happy life from now on with many satisfactions.[27]

Years later, at Mrs. Roosevelt's burial service in Hyde Park which was attended by the three presidents who had succeeded FDR, David Gurewitsch went up to General Eisenhower and asked him, "How could it happen that you did not make use of this lady? We had no better ambassador." Eisenhower shrugged and moved on.

"I made use of her," commented Truman, who was standing nearby. "I told her she was the First Lady of the World." [28]

XI. Private Citizen Again

The Eisenhower administration took office just as the "know-nothing" campaign against U.S. support of the United Nations was reaching its shrillest crescendo. Senators McCarthy and McCarran regularly portrayed the organization and the Secretariat as a nesting place of Communist spies. Sen. John W. Bricker's amendment, which would seriously hobble the treaty-negotiating powers of the president, seemed assured of the two-thirds vote it needed for adoption in the Senate. The neoisolationist slogan "take the United States out of the UN and the UN out of the United States" was no longer considered a jesting matter. A counterattack at the grass roots was sorely needed.

One day, shortly before Eisenhower's inauguration, Clark Eichelberger, director of the American Association for the United Nations (AAUN), was surprised to see Mrs. Roosevelt walk into his office.

"Do you think you could use me in your Association as an educational volunteer?" she asked. Eichelberger, who had been fighting the collective security battle for thirty years, was rendered speechless by the windfall her offer represented and, even more, by the modesty with which she presented it. "I practically fell on the floor," he recalled. A firm believer in organization, she told Eichelberger that she wanted to devote herself to building chapters around the country and spreading the message of the United Nations, and when not traveling, she would spend two days a week at the AAUN's headquarters.

In January she moved into the small, austerely furnished cubicle that she insisted would suffice. "She walked into it as if it were the Gold Room at the White House," reported A. M. Rosenthal of the *New York Times*, "and after a moment it did seem quite grand."[1]

Although Mrs. Roosevelt expressed herself forcefully on the broad issues of policy that came up at AAUN staff and board meetings, her stress was on organization and grass-roots education, finding the right person to serve as state chairman, the establishment of chapters, the raising of the budget. "Everyone here is very keenly aware of the wonderful contributions you have made," Henry Cabot Lodge, Jr., Eisenhower's representative at the United Nations, wrote her, "and are making!" he added in his own hand. By November she was barnstorming the nation for the AAUN as systematically as she had New York State for the women's division of the Democratic State Committee in the 1920s.

I am not having any holiday but am working as hard as I know how on the organizing of the American Association for the United Nations and have just come back from a trip covering the whole western part of our country. It was unbelievably strenuous but successful and as I have always told you I thrive on work.[2]

A few months after Dulles assumed command of the country's foreign relations it became clear to her she could never have served as Eisenhower's representative on the Commission on Human Rights. Sandifer informed her that the new administration had decided "not to continue to support the completion of the Human Rights Covenants." She was not surprised. She had already heard that Dulles was prepared to back away from all human rights treaties if that was the price of defeating the Bricker amendment. She disagreed with the order to retreat. Although she knew that there was not "the slightest chance" to draft the Economic and Social Rights Covenant in a way that might make it acceptable to the Senate,

I did hope it might continue under discussion for a number of years and eventually become more palatable, but the one on Civil and Political Rights I still feel we ought to be able to ratify. My real feeling for this, of course, is that just as the Supreme Court decision which said that educational facilities must be equal for all citizens has made it possible for a fight to be made which is gradually removing segregation in higher education in the South, so having a Convention on Civil and Political Rights would not mean that every nation would live up to those rights immediately, but it would be invaluable as a legal background for those people wishing to make the fight to promote human rights and freedom in this area. The United States is going backwards and taking the same stand that Great Britain has taken. . . . I am very glad I was not asked to stay on the Human Rights Commission. I could not possibly have accepted the Department's stand and I am very sorry for Mrs. [Oswald] Lord. Anything emptier than to go to Geneva with these positions, I can not imagine. I would certainly feel it was a terrible waste of time.[3]

In April, Dulles informed the Senate that the United States would no longer press for adoption of the two covenants on human rights or ask for ratification of the completed genocide convention or go ahead with the treaty on the rights of women. His stand permitted the Soviet Union, which did not wish to sign a human rights covenant, to get off the hook, an indignant Doris Fleeson wrote. It undermined the world-leadership position in the field of the promotion of human rights that Mrs. Roosevelt had gained for her country. He had abandoned this high ground, Miss Fleeson went on, although the Democratic leadership in the Senate was confident it had the votes to defeat the Bricker amendment.

"Good luck to you in Switzerland!" Mrs. Roosevelt wrote her successor:

I can't say I envy you your time in Geneva. . . . It will be hard for you to get along with the other representatives and to do any worthwhile work, I am sure.[4]

Sandifer sent her the three resolutions the United States introduced at Geneva. One called for an annual report by member governments on what they were doing about human rights. The second proposed a series of studies on a world-wide basis of specific aspects of human rights such as slavery. The third would set up a United Nations Advisory Service for the countries that requested it and fund fellowships in human rights. "You will excuse me if I think these three resolutions are really comic," she wrote the hapless Sandifer. The national commissions on human rights were what the Russians had wanted all along and she considered them window dressing. "You know that in this country this year, the Commission set up for that purpose is not being given any appropriation by Congress, so it does not look as though we would do so well on that subject." Nor did she feel that anything useful would come out of the studies or the advisory services. "Dear Irene," she wrote Sandifer's wife, "I have just written a rather nasty note on the work of the Human Rights Commission to Sandy, so I am glad to have a chance to write you both a personal note." [5]

She had told Dr. Eichelberger when she began her work with the AAUN that in June and July she would take a round-the-world trip, beginning with a six-week visit to Japan. The latter had originated in the spring of 1952 when the U.S. Committee on Intellectual Interchange with Japan submitted a list of Americans to the Japanese committee and asked it to indicate its preference. "Mrs. Roosevelt," the word came back. "Your presence in Japan at this time when Japanese womenkind are in the midst of a veritable social revolution would be of inestimable value to them," wrote Harry J. Carman, dean of Columbia University, which acted as host in the United States for the program. The State Department told her to go ahead. But after the Eisenhower victory she decided it might be better to send a Republican woman who would be able to interpret the Republican point of view. Carman, however, considered her a national not a party figure and begged her to inquire of the incoming secretary of state whether he objected to her going. Dulles's reply was very guarded. He felt insecure about his own status with Eisenhower, and the McCarthy wing of the party viewed him suspiciously. Mrs. Roosevelt represented danger. He wrote her a lawyerlike letter. Since she was going as a private person, at the request of a private U.S. foundation, in response to the desire of a nonofficial Japanese committee, he saw no reason why the incoming administration should "recast" the project, "unless it carries some implications affecting national policy which I do not see now." He left himself an out. If the situation should change by the time she was ready to leave, "I suppose we might both feel differently."

She sent this on to Carman saying she still thought it was wiser not to go, but if he decided otherwise, she was prepared to abide by his judgment. Carman renewed the invitation. The Japanese would be disappointed, since they had asked especially for her. Finally she agreed, and he happily put her in touch with Miss Fusae Ichikawa, "who through the years has been the spearhead of the women's rights movement in Japan and who is now here for three months on the Interchange Program." [6]

So, late in May, together with her newest daughter-in-law, Elliott's wife Minnewa, who wanted to get to know her extraordinary mother-in-law, and Maureen Corr, she flew to Japan with the message of democracy and women's liberation.

After being briefed by her Japanese hosts and some Americans long resident in the Orient and by her old friend Father George B. Ford, who had preceded her on the exchange program, she went to her first meeting at the Ministry of Labor, which brought together the handful of women in government to discuss women's status. A minor incident occurred as she left the ministry. A group of Communist women, headed by an American woman married to a Japanese, with the implausible name of Mrs. Anna Rosenberg Fujikawa, shouted at her, "Go home Yankee! We know war and don't want it." "I stopped long enough to say we didn't either, then got in the car & drove away." But the Japanese press exaggerated the story. It was "not true" that the Communists had dragged her from her car, she reassured David Gray. "They just called out to me but did not touch me." Her friends at home continued to be anxious. Finally she laid down the law to John Golden, who importuned "Dearest First," as he addressed her, to take greater precautions for her safety:

It is quite unnecessary to ask the Consul, Ambassador or anyone else to get the Japanese government to watch over me. Nobody has made a gesture that was anything but kind since the Communist ladies made themselves unpopular.

My main trouble is having petitions handed to me. I have to tell everyone there is nothing I can do but that I will send their letters to the Ambassador, which I suppose is not very satisfactory. [7]

By the time she sent this letter she had addressed innumerable audiences of women, of students, had toured textile factories, visited farm areas, dined with Prime Minister Shigeru Yoshida and other Japanese notables, and that very day was in Hiroshima, the Japanese encounter that she had most dreaded. In fact, the committee initially had excluded it from her itinerary, wishing to spare her spiritual anguish, and instead had urged a day's cruise down the Inland Sea from Osaka to Beppu, but Mrs. Roosevelt asked to go to Hiroshima and to meet with some of the victims.

Hiroshima was a moving experience. . . . I walked on eggs while there. I know we were justified in dropping the bomb but you can't help feeling sorry when you see suffering.

The papers here are somewhat unreliable. They color stories and sometimes make them up when they can. I did not weep in Hiroshima, as some of them said I did, at the sight of some girls who suffered bad burns, but the little Japanese girl with me was in tears. It is always hard to tell people that it is the causes of war which bring about such things as Hiroshima, and that we must try to eliminate these causes because if there is another Pearl Harbor, there will be undoubtedly another Hiroshima. Somehow I have tried to get this point across.[8]

At least one Japanese observer appreciated the "calm but uncompromising manner" in which Mrs. Roosevelt answered questions in the A-bombed city. Tatsuo Morito, the president of Hiroshima University, felt she brought into the discussion of these sensitive problems a healthy sense of "concrete and harsh reality." "I felt nowhere any personal antagonism, not even in Hiroshima," she reported to Dean Carman at the end of her trip, not even, she might have added, from those who had been leaders in Japan before Pearl Harbor. A touching note in longhand had come to her from Adm. Kichisaburo Nomura. He was the Japanese ambassador in Washington at the time of Pearl Harbor, although he had been superseded by special envoy Saburo Kurusu. "I never spoke to the President Roosevelt and Secretary of State Cordell Hull any lie or played to them any double play," he wrote Mrs. Roosevelt. "My conscience does not allow such dirty acts. I did not know, of course, Pearl Harbor attack, in advance. . . . I wish earnestly to make crystal-clear to the soul of the late President Roosevelt and Mr. Cordell Hull my true mind, just before the outbreak of the war." "Dear Admiral Nomura," she hastened to reply,

I know my husband always felt you had been honest with him. I remember his saying so. There were others he was not quite so sure about but I never heard him express a doubt about you and I have always had the friendliest of feelings toward you, and I hope we will have an opportunity to discuss how best we can improve relationships between our two countries.[9]

She had felt a lack of candor at her first meeting with Prime Minister Yoshida, but subsequently they did talk freely at a luncheon on a Sunday when few others were present. She was not happy with what she learned:

To my astonishment the Prime Minister said that of course Japan was going to rearm, though he would not say so openly for political reasons. There is a contradiction in this whole political situation here because the reactionaries are actually in power but they accepted and uphold the very liberal constitution which we forced upon them. They really do not believe in most of the measures which are actually accepted but the people do believe in them and they do not dare repudiate them, though I think they will try to whittle them away. . . . Mr. Yoshida was a charming host, easy and talkative, but I do not think he is a progressive in our sense of the word.[10]

She was chiefly concerned with the status of women: the MacArthur constitution was western and modern in its conception, but the underlying Japanese thought patterns and family structure were still almost feudal:

It is always amusing to me that only a few of the men bring their wives to these parties and when the wives do come, they are usually very silent and they gather together afterwards and stay quite apart from the men. But the women who are working in different fields have appeared at nearly all the entertainments for me and I think it gives them a little lift to feel that the gentlemen are being so attentive to a woman.

In Kyoto at a formal tea ceremony in a "very grand house," for the first time "I really had to sit on a cushion on the floor and I am not very good at it, I am sorry to say. I wish I had preserved the Japanese women's ability to flop down on their knees and sit on their heels and on their knees for an endless length of time." [11]

The women, except for the Japanese mother-in-law, served the men, too deferentially for Mrs. Roosevelt's taste. She discovered that the Japanese mother-in-law was the key to the subjugation of the women, more perhaps than the men. The mother-in-law tyrannized the women in the household, especially her daughters-in-law. She ran everyone except her husband and her oldest son. All the family's earnings went into the mother-in-law's leather pouch and it was she who doled out the money, even to married sons and their wives. The daughter-in-law was practically a slave taking her bath last, arising early, preparing the food, and serving everyone else "before she kneels a step below her husband and his mother to eat her own meal."

"In the United States," a young village woman asked her, "what do you do with your mother-in-law?" There was no single answer, she replied, and then turned to Minnewa, "Perhaps my daughter-in-law can answer your questions better than I can." But Minnewa only blushed, shook her head, and refused to speak up.[12]

Mrs. Roosevelt did not note the similarities between the dominating position of the mother-in-law in Japan and her own mother-in-law's long years of matriarchal control. The need to fight Sara had long since abated. When Irene Sandifer mentioned that a book by H. A. Overstreet, *The Mature Mind*, cited Mrs. Roosevelt as an example, she protested, "I matured late in life; if I had matured earlier I might have been more tolerant of my mother-in-law." [13]

"On the level of women," she wrote in her final report to Dean Carman,

it is difficult to see, with the family system still untouched in rural areas and in the poorer areas, how great changes are going to happen quickly. . . . I can not help but feel there is a great lack in Japan of leadership from the upper class groups. The students need someone to look up to and to listen to. There just seems to be no one whom they feel is their friend. The women need some woman who will sit down and discuss their problems and try to find solutions even though they do not happen themselves to work in a factory or work on a farm. . . . Everywhere the women were willing to talk. . . . I think my being here has given the women quite a lift and added to their sense of confidence and importance. . . .[14]

She had met many beautiful and charming princesses, ladies of good breeding, but they were not at the meetings of the women

who were concerned with women's rights. Except for Princess Chi-
chibu (Setsuko Matsudaira), the widow of the emperor's brother,
they were not concerned with the conditions of the women workers
in the factories or on the farms. "More and more I wanted to ask
the Empress about this problem," and her chance came on the final
day of her stay when she was granted an audience by Emperor Hi-
rohito and Empress Nagako.

She drove into the moat-surrounded, high-walled palace with
American Ambassador John M. Allison. He was in cutaway coat
and striped pants, and she wore a dress with three-quarter sleeves,
which, she had been told, was acceptable court costume provided
she wore long gloves that met the sleeves. Inside the palace they
were ushered through a series of rooms filled with furniture covered
in pink damask, priceless carved objects, and lovely hangings, with
attendants in each room bowing low. Finally they came into the audience chamber where they were seated with care. Their Majesties
then entered and they all bowed to each other, and the empress, in
a flowered kimono, seated herself on the sofa beside Mrs. Roosevelt.
The emperor began the discussion, telling her of the great efforts he
had made to prevent the war. It was an important avowal, and she
thought the emperor was sincere and saw his statement as evidence
that he would help the United States build up friendly relations in
Asia. But she was impatient to draw the empress into the discussion. She turned to her and reported what she had seen in Pakistan
and India of efforts to emancipate women. "We need more education," the empress commented. Then she thought for a moment and
agreed that there were great changes coming about in the life of
Japanese women. But she was anxious. "We have always been
trained in the past to a life of service and I am afraid that as these
new changes come about there may be a loss of real values." What
was Mrs. Roosevelt's impression? That was her chance. There was
less danger of old values being lost in a period of change, Mrs. Roosevelt replied, "when the intelligent and broadminded women who
have had an opportunity to become educated take the lead to bring
about the necessary changes." She mentioned the emancipation
work with women that the Begum Liaquat Ali Khan was doing in
Pakistan.

Here the emperor broke in: "Our customs are different, Mrs. Roosevelt. We have government bureaus to lead in our reforms. We serve as an example to our people in the way we live and it is our lives that have influence over them." Mrs. Roosevelt did not feel she could press the matter further. But in writing about the audience, she presented as historical prophecy what she hoped would happen. She could not help believing that "the future may see greater leadership exerted by the women of high social status, including members of the entourage of the Imperial family." After some talk of other matters, economic conditions, overpopulation, and the crown prince, Their Majesties arose, wished Mrs. Roosevelt a safe journey, and "left us, bowing again as they went out and, of course, we returned their bows."

When the embassy submitted the article that she wrote on the audience to court officials, they took exception to matters of style and substance. They preferred Mrs. Roosevelt to use the expression "cutaway" rather than "frock coat" in describing the men's dress. She made too much of the regulations governing court dress for ladies, they felt, and there were too many references to the etiquette of bowing. They objected to her juxtaposition of the description of the empress's lovely obi (a broad sash worn with a kimono) and the information that women who wove these intricate sashes often developed eye trouble. It might suggest the empress was callous. They did not take exception to the main burden of her article, that women's emancipation in Japan might well start in the palace. She made the changes the court suggested in the manuscript that she submitted for magazine publication, but not in her book, *On My Own*. However, the latter appeared in 1958, and she probably had forgotten the embassy's memorandum. That occasionally happened, by then.[15]

Minnewa flew from Japan to Honolulu to meet Elliott, but Mrs. Roosevelt and Maureen Corr headed for Hong Kong, their ultimate destination being Yugoslavia, where she would have a chance to observe how a governmental system that called itself communistic actually operated and where she had been promised an interview with the archrebel against Stalinism, Marshal Tito. In Hong Kong she was feted and shown the sights. She was briefed on the Chinese refugee problem and given "the English point of view" on the Far Eastern question "with a heavy hand," she wrote her son John, who was asked to circulate her letters among other members of the family and close friends. She also met Mr. Keswick, "a British merchant whose firm, Jardine & Co., owns practically everything in Hong Kong" and who knew a good deal about Russell & Company, "Grandad Delano's old firm." She asked him about the stories assiduously circulated by Pegler and other anti-New Deal columnists that the Delanos had made money in the opium trade in the days of the clipper ships. All foreign merchants, Mr. Keswick told her, were obliged to take a small amount of opium in their cargos if they wanted to trade in tea.[16]

There was a stopover in New Delhi for refueling and repair because the plane had been buffeted by hurricane winds in Calcutta. Mme. Pandit was waiting for her. They talked for twenty minutes and, informed the plane would be delayed another twenty minutes, Mrs. Roosevelt persuaded Mme. Pandit to go home. But the twenty minutes stretched into hours, and the passengers were finally taken into the city to a hotel. Mrs. Roosevelt decided to have her hair done.

This was a waste of time because my permanent has come out completely because of the heat and climatic conditions, and the next day it was as straight as it could be and a perfect nuisance. I wish I had never tried to let it grow and yet I can't bring myself to get it cut now that it is half grown.[17]

It was a torrid July day in New Delhi, but Mrs. Roosevelt had had a hot Indian curry before boarding the plane. She loved it, she insisted to Maureen.

The next fueling stop was in Istanbul where the consul general, Mr. Macatee, was waiting for her although it was five in the morning. He was "a rather wispy, wan-looking" gentleman who wanted to take her and Maureen to a nearby hotel to bathe and rest. But Mrs. Roosevelt was determined to see Istanbul and, although the shops were closed, managed to visit three mosques and the walls of the city and then breakfast with Mr. Macatee's wife and daughter on a balcony that overlooked the Golden Horn.

Her plane arrived in Athens ahead of schedule. "This caused much consternation because all of the American Embassy could not come to meet us. There were quite enough of them, however." David Gurewitsch joined Mrs. Roosevelt and Maureen here, and the three toured archeological diggings, visited the Acropolis at sunset, and she lunched with the king and queen. "I wished they had asked David because I hated going alone, but there were only a few members of their family there and both the King and Queen were charming." She evidently did a little missionary work in the palace of the Hellenes, for she asked her son to send Her Majesty information about Berea and Antioch colleges, where work was a part of the curriculum, as well as material on the Henry Street Settlement and the Alfred E. Smith low-cost houses.[18]

She landed in Belgrade in a drenching downpour. This was the first time she had been in a Communist country, and she felt a curiosity not unmixed with tension. Deposited in her hotel by welcoming officials, Mrs. Roosevelt looked out on the empty streets and, consulting with Maureen and David, decided that this was the moment to get a glimpse of Belgrade without official guides, interpreters, and hosts. So the three of them slipped out through a rear door onto the rain-darkened street and went into one shop after the other asking what wares they had to sell and their prices. "We thought we had stolen a march on them," commented David, "but the next morning every question that we had asked in the shops was in the papers. That's how secret we were."

She was briefed by the embassy, and saw the sights, and lunched with Vladimir Dedijer, the biographer of Tito, even though he was out of favor with the Communist party and Tito. Leaving Belgrade, she toured five of the six Yugoslavian republics, visited agricultural cooperatives, talked with Yugoslavian officials of every degree from Vice President Kardelj down:

Everyone agrees that great changes have taken place in the last years, but that does not mean they are not communists. They are and what is more they are proud of being communists—but not Soviet Communists.

In her next letter, she corrected herself:

. . . I have now had a long interview over two days with the President and I have discovered that he looks on Communism as an ideal stage in which everybody receives according to his needs, the selfishness of human nature has been wiped out, nobody is greedy, everybody is satisfied with receiving what he needs and interested in the well being of others. He keeps telling me that it is socialism, which is only the first step toward Communism, which actually exists in this country. He calls himself a "social democrat" and says that he became a Russian Communist because of his term in prison and the belief that the Soviet Union alone cared about the wellbeing of all the people. When he found that the Russians are as selfish and imperialistic as imperialist nations, he decided that his nation must develop in its own way and he did not want what existed in Yugoslavia to be called Titoism because he felt it might hinder the development of each nation according to its own way. Pretty interesting as a statement, isn't it, but don't spread it about because it is part of my article.[19]

President Tito and his wife entertained Mrs. Roosevelt on Brioni, his vacation island in the Adriatic. There were several handsome speedboats about, and the president piloted one himself, insisting that Mrs. Roosevelt be his passenger. He was not without vanity, Mrs. Roosevelt observed to herself, and clearly loved power. But she was also impressed with him. "You cannot meet this man without recognizing that he was a real mind. He is a doer and a practical person." She was interested in the relationship between Tito and his young, beautiful wife, who also had been a Partisan. She had just taken her examinations in Belgrade, she told Mrs. Roosevelt. "Examinations?" a puzzled Mrs. Roosevelt inquired. Yes, she had gone back to the university to complete her education. The president, Mrs. Roosevelt was pleased to observe, was proud of his wife's determination to complete her education and encouraged her to do so.

When she returned to Belgrade she had tea at the home of Elie Abel, the *New York Times* reporter, with some U.S. correspondents who gave her "a pretty good idea of their observations since they have been here." She, in turn, told the reporters how she had asked Tito whether his officials respected the rights of the individual citizen under the law, and Tito had replied with a story. In a village pub people were arguing about Tito and in loud voices expressing their hostility to him, to the annoyance of some good Communists who were at the next table. Finally one of the Communists had had enough and punched one of the most offensive critics on the jaw. For his loyalty, said Tito, the good Communist had gotten a month in jail. He had heard the story, Tito explained, from his police chief, Vice President Aleksandar Rankovic. "The only thing I believe in that story," commented Elie Abel with a chuckle, "is that Mr. Rankovic knew what was going on in that village pub." [20]

On the way home there were stops in Zagreb and Ljubljana, where they had dinner with Mrs. Roosevelt's novelist-friend Martha Gellhorn, and in Vienna and Paris. Maureen Corr flew to Ireland, while Mrs. Roosevelt, joined in London by her granddaughter Sisty and Sisty's husband, Van Seagrave, both of whom were with the Mutual Security Administration, drove down to Lady Reading's "and had a delightful weekend." She would get in on a Sunday, she informed John, but she did not want him to leave Hyde Park in order to meet her. She wanted to go to her new apartment on East Sixty-second Street, a small duplex which Esther Lape had located for her and which she had rented sight unseen. It had a garden where her little dog Duffy might be let out to run, and provided easier access to her office at the AAUN than the Park Sheraton Hotel. "I will call you just as soon as I reach the apartment on Sunday," she advised John. "It will be wonderful to hear your voices." But John and Anne were at the airport, and she could not have been more pleased. There was the usual press conference, and the reporters asked her about Senator McCarthy. [21]

Everywhere on her trip she had been asked about McCarthyism, she told them. "Things are certainly edgy and touchy," she had written Sandifer from Tokyo, "and the extraordinary thing is how much attention is paid to Senator McCarthy. He really has done us a great deal of harm over here." The first question asked of her during a visit to a winegrowers' cooperative in Yugoslavia, she had written her Republican son John,

was on Senator McCarthy. He has certainly made an impression. The question was phrased like this: "What about Senator McCarthy? Are the American people losing their freedom?"

She was unable to understand why Eisenhower was not firmer with the Wisconsin senator. "I hope you are right that Ike has things in hand and that his technique will win out," she wrote David Gray. Mischievously she had disclosed in her column before her departure that she had been visited by the FBI, whose agents with solemn faces were checking on the loyalty and competence of John Foster Dulles.[22]

The spread of fear in the United States dismayed her. She was appalled that young people were frightened to attend a meeting because it might have unforeseen consequences. It would never have occurred to her in her youth that she should not go to a meeting if it interested her. "We must preserve our right to think and differ," she found it necessary to say in a speech to the ADA. Americans should be able to disagree and to consider new ideas.

The day I'm afraid to sit down with people I do not know because five years from now someone will say five of those people were Communists and therefore you are a Communist—that will be a bad day.

I want to be able to sit down with anyone who may have a new idea and not be afraid of contamination by association. In a democracy you must be able to meet with people and argue your point of view— people whom you have not screened beforehand. That must be part of the freedom of people in the United States.[23]

There was a problem of Communist espionage and penetration of U.S. government agencies, she acknowledged. But it should be handled by the FBI. She knew from firsthand experience how the Communists operated as "secret battalions" within trade unions and progressive organizations. That was why she supported the ADA and such non-Communist trade-union leaders as Reuther, Carey, and Dubinsky. But the right wing of the Republican and Democratic parties, in exploiting the public's fear of Communism, were after larger game. They wanted to impose thought control, rendering the discussion of certain subjects—such as recognition of Red China—taboo. They wanted to demoralize and divide the New Deal wing of the Democratic party. In that connection she knew they would have dearly loved to bring her down.

"The time has come," wrote Pegler of Mrs. Roosevelt at the

height of McCarthy's power, "to snatch this wily old conspirator before Joe McCarthy's committee and chew her out. . . . Joe McCarthy or Bill Jenner could tear her to tatters if either of them should ever drag her to the stand. She deserves far less respect than any conventional woman." She was quite prepared for such a call.

Actually some of the gentlemen in the Committee are a little annoyed with me because I have expressed my disapproval of some of Mr. McCarthy's methods, but they have never asked me to appear before the Committee. I would be very glad to do so. . . .[24]

The committees gave her a wide berth. Even Senator McCarthy realized this was a battle he might not win. And she, far from being intimidated, went out of her way to defend the victims of the McCarthyite madness. Mary McLeod Bethune and Dr. Channing Tobias, the head of the NAACP, came to tell her that the next target of the witch hunters was to be the Negro leaders. "I said we must fight back, not in an organization, but by standing together wherever we are sure of anyone." When the *Nation* came under attack, she changed her mind about not attending its dinner:

I thought that I could not be with you tonight because I had so many things that I had set out to do today. But I decided that it would be wise to come since I understood that there had been some attacks made. I believe that it is a great mistake not to stand up for people, even when you differ with them, if you feel that they are trying to do things that will help in our country.[25]

"I hear Jimmy Wechsler & Joe [Joseph Lash] are to be dissected by the *Journal-American* in Sept. or Oct.," she alerted this author and his wife. "I'm a bit suspicious that it is aimed at me too & if so I will be glad to take any part possible, short of answering Pegler!" Eugene Lyons, author of *The Red Decade*, challenged her assertion that many persons "label anything they don't like as Communist" and her implication that this was happening on an alarming scale. The cry of "hysteria," Lyons insisted, "is largely bogus. I find that the American people have remained remarkably calm and sensible, considering what they have learned recently about the Soviet conspiracy in our midst. . . ." He thought that liberals in shouting "hysteria" were "attributing to the public their own inflamed and guilt-ridden state of mind, which is of course a familiar psychotic type of behavior." She dictated a brief answer to Lyons:

I have plenty of material to back up what I said but I think your letter is sufficient proof that hysteria exists.

Lyons sent her a long list of quotations that he said supported his contention that the hysteria was self-generated "among self-styled liberals, native and imported." But to this letter she made no reply.[26]

On the eve of her trip to Japan she had met with some troubled ADA leaders. McCarthyism was a national peril, and the ADA was looking for someone who was not afraid to take him on. She would be the ideal chairman, they said. She could not do it, she told them. She had committed herself to the AAUN. Grave as the danger of McCarthyism was, America's relationship to the United Nations also was in jeopardy because of right-wing attacks. But she was moved by the plea of James A. Wechsler, having great admiration for the way he had stood up to the Wisconsin senator. Until he had done so, "nobody else dared to challenge McCarthy before his own Committee," she said. "People were inclined to be intimidated." She agreed to serve as the ADA's honorary chairman.[27]

She had faith in the "common sense" of the American people, she had said in Hong Kong, when asked about McCarthyism. The senator would "cease to be a headline when the people realize their safety lies in knowledge and not in fear." Until that time arrived, there was nothing to do but stand together and fight back. "Go down and answer up if you can," she advised the Volunteers in Politics, a Stevensonian organization, but added, "it's not easy." [28]

"I am appalled to see that the Un-American Activities Committee is going to investigate Ralph Bunche," she wrote Clark Eichelberger. "Will you tell him if there is anything whatever I can do, I will gladly do it." When the Americanism Commission of the American Legion attacked the Encampment for Citizenship, sponsored by the Ethical Culture Societies, citing the appearance of Roger Baldwin as one of the encampment's speakers and the showing of a film of Julien Bryan (a producer of film documentaries with a social theme), she commiserated with the encampment's chief patron, Alice ("Nanny") Pollitzer, eighty-four years old and still battling for good causes. "I am so very sorry, but all are suspect today and I think we must fight." A few months later she accepted the honorary chairmanship of the encampment's tenth-anniversary celebration.[29]

In October, 1954, Mrs. Roosevelt celebrated her seventieth birthday. Her hair had grayed and her tall figure thickened. She no longer rode horseback, although she still walked a great deal in the Hyde Park woods accompanied by her two Scottish terriers, Tamas, the grandson of Fala, and Duffy, a puppy given to her after Fala's death. The range of her interests was reflected in her taxable income from professional activities which, in 1954, was almost $90,000: $36,000 from *McCall's*, $28,000 from her column, and $25,000 from Colston Leigh for lectures.

"No, I have not slackened my pace," she told Emma Bugbee. "At least, not yet. I probably shall. Everybody does." Old friends were vanishing. In 1949, Elinor Morgenthau had died, and at the service she had moved Elinor's family to tears with her remarks about how greatly she had admired Elinor's devotion to her family, a devotion that she always managed to render while sustaining an active interest in what was happening in the world. Cousin Susie, in whose house Mrs. Roosevelt had been married, died in 1950, and two years later Aunt Maude, a last link with her childhood. And then in 1953, Tommy, who had served her for nearly thirty years, who not only made her life easier "but gave me a reason for living," died. "My boss is a very big person," Tommy once told Lorena Hickok, "just about the biggest person in the world. Anything I can do to help her—no matter what—justifies my existence. It's enough for me." In her column, Mrs. Roosevelt wrote, "Her standards were high for me, as well as for herself, and she could be a real critic." When Tommy died, "I learned for the first time what being alone was like." In her bedroom desk at Val-Kill she kept two letters, one from Tommy on her birthday renewing her "yearly pledge of my devotion to you & all that you do," on the back of which Mrs. Roosevelt wrote, "a pledge always kept." It was clipped to a Christmas letter from George Marvin, the Groton tutor whom she had often gotten out of scrapes, promising better behavior, on which she had written, "a pledge broken within a month." [30]

Summing up her general attitude toward life at seventy, she declared. "Life has got to be lived—that's all there is to it. At 70, I would say the advantage is that you take life more calmly. You know that 'this, too, shall pass!' "

There were, however, joys—among them nineteen grandchildren and four great-grandchildren. In 1952, Anna had remarried. Mrs. Roosevelt and Tommy flew out to Los Angeles for the ceremony. She liked Dr. James A. Halsted:

I am very happy about Anna's marriage because I feel that she will be happy. He is a fine person . . . on the staff of the Veterans Hospital and also a teaching professor at the University of Southern California. Her life will be simple.[31]

In June, 1954, she went to Cambridge to attend the fiftieth reunion of the Harvard Class of 1904—her husband's. Once again her husband's stand-in, she marched with the class and even attended the Harvard-Yale baseball game. She enjoyed seeing her husband's classmates relive their college years and, in doing so, become young again. "Father would have loved it," she told her family afterward.[32]

What achievements had given her the greatest satisfaction, the press wanted to know on her seventieth birthday?

As for accomplishments, I just did what I had to do as things came along. I got the most satisfaction from my work in the UN. There I was part of the second great experiment to bring countries together and to get them to work for a peaceful atmosphere in the world, and I still feel it important to strengthen this organization in every way.[33]

She did not like to have people make a fuss over her birthday. This time she made an exception. "You are a dear to want to do something for my birthday," she wrote Edith Helm, who had served as her social secretary during the White House years:

The American Association for the UN is really commercializing it and I have permitted them to do so because I would like to see them clear themselves of debt. Until they can do that the work will not really be well done because they will always be living from hand to mouth. So, if you want to do something, will you send a check to the AAUN? [34]

Not a single member of the Eisenhower-appointed American delegation attended the AAUN's birthday party for her, Doris Fleeson noted. But Dag Hammarskjöld and Ralph Bunche came, as did an unexpected guest—Andrei Vishinsky—who had wanted, in this way, to apologize for his rudeness in 1948. He understood, he told the AAUN, that he would not be seated with Mrs. Roosevelt's friends on the dais. He would be "very glad to sit anywhere." [35]

"I would like," she said in her remarks which closed the party, "to see us take hold of ourselves, look at ourselves and cease being afraid." Her final words were for her family. More than achievement, "I treasure the love of my children, the respect of my children, and I would never want my children or my grandchildren to feel that I had failed them." [36]

XII. "Madly for Adlai"

At dinner in Mrs. Roosevelt's East Sixty-second Street apartment in late 1953, after the folding tables had been put away and the party had reassembled around the fireplace in the living room, the hostess brought up the subject of the mediocrity of leadership in the present time. Where were statesmen of the calibre of FDR, Churchill, and Stalin? Mrs. Roosevelt asked. Perhaps Marshal Tito, she went on. Perhaps Adlai Stevenson. At this, Judge Samuel Rosenman demurred. Stevenson lacked political instinct, FDR's old counselor insisted. To prove his point, he told a story involving Cardinal Spellman. The cardinal had asked him to urge Stevenson to speak at the annual Alfred E. Smith dinner. It was a forum coveted by most politicians, since it indicated their acceptability to the cardinal, yet Stevenson the year before had turned it down. To the renewed invitation conveyed by Judge Rosenman, Stevenson replied that he had two invitations for the evening in question—one to address the Smith dinner, the other the Woodrow Wilson Foundation —and he was not sure which he should accept. Stevenson had to make up his mind, commented the judge, as to whether he wanted to be a statesman or a politician.

Mrs. Roosevelt defended Stevenson. She thought he was a world statesman with the potentiality of the wartime leaders—if only he would develop greater self-confidence.[1]

The Democratic defeat in 1952 had one compensation—her discovery of Adlai. Exhilarated by his wit, eloquence, and integrity, held by the grace and glow with which he illuminated a problem, she came out of the campaign believing he should have another chance:

DR. DAVID A. GUREWITSCH

*Mrs. Roosevelt dining with Marshall Tito on Brioni in
the Adriatic. Mrs. Tito at the left.*

A palm reader in Hong Kong, who did not know who Mrs. Roosevelt was,
said that she had the hand of a very forceful woman
who had in the past done extraordinary things. "You see," she commented,
"everything he says concerns the past, not the future."

Eleanor Roosevelt being greeted in New Delhi by Prime Minister Nehru and
Nehru's daughter, Mrs. Indira Gandhi. March, 1952.

In Bali.

*"My soul stood erect," Helen Keller wrote Eleanor
Roosevelt after the Universal Declaration of Human Rights was approved
by the United Nations Assembly.*

*A couple of seasoned politicians put on
their best party smiles. Mrs. Roosevelt and Thomas E. Dewey meet at
a diplomatic reception.*

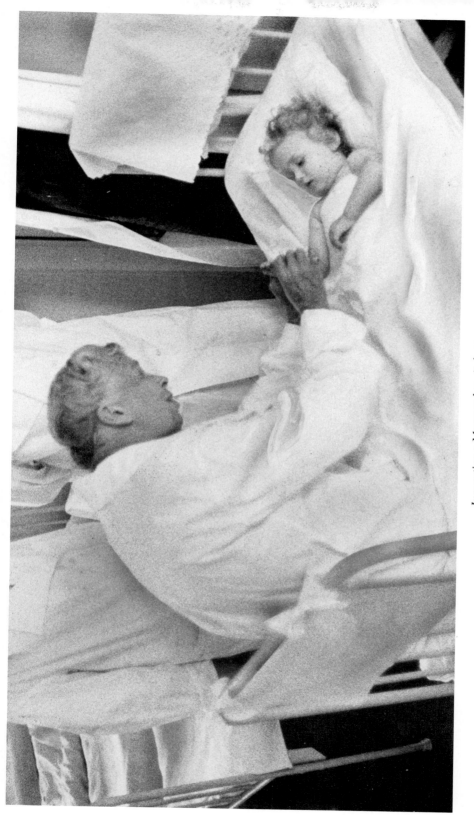

Inspecting a Moscow hospital, 1957.

At the side of her pool in Val-Kill. With Mrs. Roosevelt is Mrs. Walter Reuther (at right).

July 4 at Val-Kill. On the terrace of the Stone Cottage, which then was lived in by the John Roosevelts, John in bathing trunks. James is reading the Declaration of Independence.

Fourth of July parade in Hyde Park. Tubby Curnan, Mrs. Roosevelt's three-hundred-pound chauffeur, could barely squeeze into the Fiat roadster provided by Franklin Jr., who owned the Fiat agency in the United States.

Christmas Day dinner at Val-Kill. Mrs. Roosevelt's grandson Curtis is pouring the wine.

*Nikita Khrushchev and his wife Nina came to
Val-Kill but did not have time to eat the picnic lunch that
Mrs. Roosevelt had prepared for them. The Soviet leader took a roll,
calling out to the reporters, "One for the road."*

Mrs. Roosevelt with Edna and David Gurewitsch.

"I am not a candidate," Adlai E. Stevenson insisted in 1960,
but Mrs. Roosevelt would not take "no" for an answer.

At the 1960 Democratic Convention in Los Angeles.
Mrs. Roosevelt had just been introduced by Chairman Leroy Collins
to second the nomination of Adlai Stevenson.
John F. Kennedy was nominated.

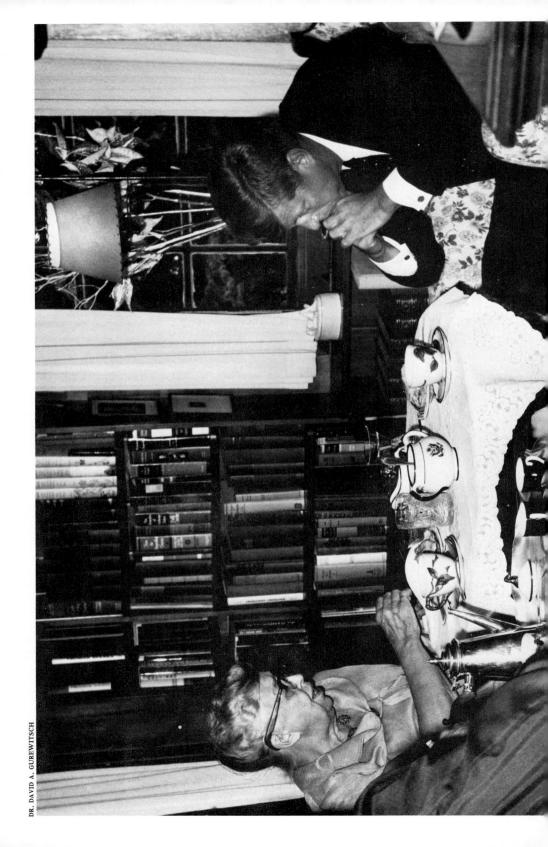

"I had my talk with Senator Kennedy yesterday," Eleanor Roosevelt reported to her closest friends. Kennedy left Val-Kill "absolutely smitten by this woman," William Walton, the artist who accompanied Kennedy to this meeting, later wrote.

Eleanor Roosevelt and her four sons in 1958. Left to right: John, James, Elliott, and Franklin Jr.

I.N.S.

Left: *Three battlers for peace—Alfred M. Landon, Eleanor Roosevelt, and Norman Thomas in New York.*

Below left: *At a Polo Grounds "Salute to Israel" meeting. To Mrs. Roosevelt's left are Gen. Moshe Dayan and Abba Eban of Israel and George Meany, president of the AFL. Directly behind Mrs. Roosevelt is Ralph Bellamy, who portrayed FDR in Sunrise at Campobello.*

Arriving in Washington on one of her many journeys there.

Mrs. Roosevelt is buried in the rose garden at Hyde Park.

Left to right: Mrs. Lyndon B. Johnson, Mrs. John F. Kennedy, President Kennedy,
Vice-President Johnson, former President Harry S. Truman and Mrs. Truman,
and former President Dwight D. Eisenhower.

I am really worried about this new administration, but I hope Governor Stevenson will really take the leadership of the Democratic party and keep doing a constructive job of criticism.[2]

The more widely she traveled abroad after leaving the United Nations and sensed the extent to which the United States of the McCarthy period was on trial before the world, the more strongly she felt that it was Stevenson who most clearly understood the dimensions of the problem and, being held in the highest esteem in foreign capitals, was best equipped to deal with it. Somehow he always had an apt word to meet every situation, she reported while trailing him around Europe in 1953 and hearing of the enthusiasm he had aroused.

Stevenson was reluctant to criticize American policy while abroad, and she agreed with him on that. Henry Wallace's willingness to do so had shocked her. But she also felt Stevenson had to speak up—forcefully—at home.

I think Stevenson has a difficult position. He must not give the impression that we are a divided country on most issues but he must disagree enough with the Administration to have some points of difference in the campaign. I don't think he is in full swing as the leader of the party and I hope he gets there soon.[3]

She encouraged him to accept speaking engagements. He was a great orator, but she felt he did not know how to communicate with the man in the street. She had hinted at this in her column during the 1952 campaign. At the time she thought it was Arthur Schlesinger, Jr., who was giving Stevenson's speeches "too much of the academic touch." She felt they were "not simple enough." She came to realize later that this was Stevenson's, not Schlesinger's, doing. She thought he fussed too much over his speeches, wanting to make each a polished gem. "I wish I had mastered the speech preparation problem like you have," he once remarked to her, confessing that he was already quaking with anxiety at the prospect of having to address the Columbia Bicentennial Conference. It was, at that time, more than six months away.[4]

Stevenson came to ask Mrs. Roosevelt for advice on whether to run again. Did she not feel there were others better able to lead the party? She did not. There was something else on his mind, she learned. He came from a patrician background very much like hers and President Roosevelt's, he said, yet they both were always "much more at home in talking with people" than he was. She liked his modesty and his ability to view himself with critical detachment. She explained some of the circumstances that had given FDR his ability to "feel" his way into how people felt and thought, an explanation that, of course, said little about her own contribution to her husband's education.

She urged Stevenson to don an old suit, get into a jalopy, and travel about the country talking to farmers, gas station attendants, housewives, and not leave an area "until you can 'feel' what they are feeling." Stevenson did not take her advice, and this troubled her. But whatever her reservations, she considered him the ablest man in Democratic ranks. "I don't agree with you that Averell [Harriman] is going to be our next President," she cautioned David Gray, "because I believe Stevenson is by far best equipped and so far ahead in the nation." "You might like to know," she informed Al Lowenstein who was with the Second Armored Division in Europe, "that I saw Adlai Stevenson recently. He is announcing his candidacy and he is prepared to fight." [5]

Her relationship to the 1952 campaign had been peripheral; in 1956 it was central. Stevenson consulted her on the setting up of his Stevenson for President Committee. She helped raise funds for his preconvention drive. As she traveled about the country on paid lecture trips, she sent back the names of contacts and political intelligence to Barry Bingham and Thomas K. Finletter, heads, respectively, of the national and New York Stevenson committees. At Hobcaw, she spent a night with Baruch, who seemed more interested in Stevenson than he had been before.

In devious ways Mr. Baruch will give you money when you want it in cash for specific things. If you sigh a little and say you haven't enough to meet a specific need, I think you will find it forthcoming.

"Among these women," she reported from Dallas, after having addressed a Democratic women's group, were at least two who were admirers of Kefauver but who would be satisfied with Kefauver as Vice President and were somewhat impressed with my reasons for Stevenson's being President.[6]

To her old friend Lord Elibank, who kept her advised on British politics, Mrs. Roosevelt confided:

I don't know what is going to happen in the next nine months but I am doing what I can to get Mr. Stevenson the nomination. Many of my friends tell me there is no question but that Eisenhower will be nominated and Nixon will be Vice-President. If that is the case the Democrats will have to work harder than ever because I doubt if Eisenhower can stand a second term and I doubt if the country can stand Nixon as President.[7]

It was a period when Dulles was speaking of the "art of brinkmanship," an added reason to change pilots as quickly as possible:

Mr. Dulles has just frightened most of our allies to death with a statement that there is an art in actually threatening war and coming to the brink but retreating from the brink. He certainly is a strange Secretary of State and I shall feel relieved if we can elect a Democrat in the next election and change the State Department attitude.[8]

Eleanor Roosevelt's greatest contribution to Stevenson's preconvention drive was the fact that she, who continued to be the woman most admired by Americans, favored his candidacy and campaigned for him in the primaries. Although ahead in the polls, Stevenson decided he had to go into the primaries because most of the party's politicians, including that key figure, Harry S. Truman, were not for him. Minnesota was the first important primary, and she agreed to go out to Minneapolis and the Iron Range. Mrs. Roosevelt was the best campaigner she had seen, Jane (Mrs. Edison) Dick, national cochairman of the Stevenson committee, testified afterward, but except for the two congressional districts in which Mrs. Roosevelt campaigned, Kefauver carried the Minnesota primary. It was a serious setback for the Stevenson forces.[9]

"You are often in my thoughts," she wrote Stevenson on April 2, in an effort to buoy up his spirits, "and I know you are going through the hardest part of your struggle just now. Once the primaries and the Convention are over, the campaign will seem very easy in comparison!" Yet Minnesota showed that "it is going to be hard to get him elected," and the more she thought of the significance of Stevenson's defeat there, the more strongly she felt it was not enough to bolster Stevenson's morale—he had to change his approach. "Dear Adlai," she wrote him a week later,

I am really worried about one or two things that I think I should say at the present time. It seems to me that it is unwise to be attacking Mr. Kefauver as much as you have been doing. The things that need to be attacked are the issues that need to be made clear to the man in the street in the simplest possible terms. The people need to feel that you have done all the agonizing over how to meet situations, that you are sure of what you would do if you were starting in today. . . .

The problems of today are serious enough. Nobody knows the answers but the people must feel that the man who is their candidate knows where he is going to begin, that he is not so tortured by his own search that he can't give them reassurance and security. . . .

This is not meant to be a discouraging letter but an encouraging one. If I did not think you could win, it would not be worth doing a good job.[10]

She admired doers, men of action who carefully considered the options open to them, chose one, and if it did not work, tried another. That had been Franklin's way, she often said. It was also her own. "I don't really have more energy than many, many people," she had once explained to novelist Edna Ferber, "but I never use up any energy in indecision or regret. If I make a speech and know it isn't very good, I get on the plane and say I'll do a better job next time. But I am never undecided about anything and never have time for remorse or regret about the decisions I make." [11]

Yet Stevenson's weaknesses may have added to his attractiveness. She could help him. He needed her. Women stuck to Adlai, Dorothy (Mrs. Samuel I.) Rosenman would later tease her. They either wanted to marry or protect him. Nonsense, Mrs. Roosevelt would reply. Adlai did not interest her as a man. It was the thrust and sparkle of his mind that appealed to her. But her interest in Stevenson was not simply political. It rarely was when she worked as hard for a man as she did for him. There was a personal involvement with Stevenson of the kind there had been with Harry Hopkins before he had moved into the White House and, in Tommy's words, had "dropped" her. She was his protectress, and if, at times, he seemed to rely too much on her, that, too, was not unflattering. The worst thing was not to be needed.[12]

She had reason to be concerned over the Minnesota defeat. The professionals were gloating. William Benton, former senator and publisher of the *Encyclopaedia Britannica,* had chatted with Truman while in Kansas City and reported to her that the former president thought Stevenson was going downhill and by the time of the convention will be finished as a presidential possibility unless he did well in the California primary. Truman was strongly opposed to Kefauver, but Benton was unable to find out whether his candidate was Harriman or Stuart Symington of Missouri.[13]

The next primary was in the District of Columbia on April 30. Few convention votes were at stake, but a delegate slate pledged to Kefauver was entered and a poor showing by Stevenson might be fatal. The Stevenson Club begged Mrs. Roosevelt to come down. Afterward, its head, Nancy Davis, wrote her: "I realize that Saturday was an awful day for you—hectic and exhausting—and I hated to put pressure on you to fly down here. Nevertheless it was necessary and your strong endorsement of Governor Stevenson was the strongest single factor in the area. Senator Kefauver told the press that your appearance turned the tide in Adlai's favor." Stevenson, campaigning in Portland, Oregon, sent her his thanks. "Wait till it is over and we can sit down quietly and rejoice," she replied.[14]

The California primary in June proved to be a 2 to 1 triumph for Stevenson. "Thanks for the good wishes on Mother's Day," she wrote Al Lowenstein:

I have been running around so madly speaking for Adlai that I had forgotten that I was a grandmother, and a great-grandmother at that!—but the victory in California is certainly satisfactory and I have more hope than I have had in a long time.

Again her contribution was central: "The local leaders were all in agreement that your stay there was the most helpful thing that happened during the campaign," Finletter reported.[15]

She had been particularly helpful in the Negro precincts,

which Stevenson had carried by the surprising margins of 4.5 to 10 to 1 in spite of NAACP opposition. The Negro vote elated Stevenson because Harriman's bid for the nomination—and he was emerging as Stevenson's real rival—was based on the argument that only an aggressive champion of New and Fair Deal principles could win in November. This, in his view, ruled out Stevenson, whom he charged with "moderation," especially on civil rights. Mrs. Roosevelt did not question Harriman's liberalism, but having known him since he was a little boy, tidings that she always managed to convey in a motherly tone of voice that suggested he was still in pantaloons, she doubted that there was any real difference between Stevenson and Harriman on civil rights. She saw his militancy as a tactical maneuver, the purpose of which was to divide Stevenson's support in the North or, if he was forced into a more militant position, to lose Stevenson the support of the South.

He had heard from responsible newspapermen, Stevenson informed her, that the Republican press, having failed to dispose of him in the primaries through Kefauver, would play in with the Harriman strategy. "Your analysis of the Republican attitude is, of course, correct both on what they did for Kefauver and what they will undoubtedly do for Averell," she replied. The civil rights issue was the key. "They," the Republicans,

would like to see the party completely divided and I don't know that there is any way one can hold it together and live up to one's convictions, but somehow I think understanding and sympathy for the white people in the South is as important as understanding and sympathy and support for the colored people. We don't want another war between the states and so the only possible solution is to get the leaders on both sides together and try to work first steps out.

I have been asked by Mr. [Paul] Butler [Democratic National chairman] to come down to Washington in an effort to get a Civil Rights plank developed for the Convention which will not mean the South will walk out of the Convention. I don't look forward to it because I have spent endless hours in the UN discussing over the value of words and I think that is what we will have to do in this case.

It is essential for the Democratic party to keep the colored vote in line, so you can't take away the feeling that you want to live up to the Supreme Court decision and go forward, and that this can't be done in one fell swoop. Desegregation of schools in the South must follow a number of steps. Even in the North we have to desegregate housing be-fore we can desegregate schools. . . .

You have not in any [way] aggravated my burdens. I chose myself to do this because I felt it was important that we have a nominee in the Democratic party who had not only a chance of winning but a chance of giving us a good administration.[16]

During the White House years, Mrs. Roosevelt had always been on guard against the wiles and stratagems that her husband had employed in pushing for his goals lest the objectives be com-promised. That had especially been the case in regard to Negro rights. When she saw a thing to be done, she had charged ahead asking, "Why not?" FDR, being the politician, approached his objectives with a circumspection and care that often shaded into deviousness, biding his time, looking for cracks in the wall or ways around it before he went driving into it frontally.[17]

But having committed herself to seeing Stevenson elected pres-ident, she showed that she, too, could be a fox as well as a lion—to invoke the distinction drawn by James M. Burns in his biography of FDR. In her approach to the civil rights issue, she displayed Frank-lin's toughness and maneuverability in balancing the political ne-cessity of not alienating the South against the moral imperatives of the Negro cause.[18]

Civil rights groups, especially the NAACP, were beginning to make life hard for Democratic politicians, even the liberals among them. They were demanding that the federal government enforce the landmark Supreme Court decision of 1954 on school desegrega-tion even if it meant the withholding of federal funds and the send-ing in of troops. In Congress, Rep. Adam Clayton Powell had intro-duced a rider to the school construction bill that would deny federal funds to the states that refused to comply with the Supreme Court's decision—at that time, almost the whole South. Rep. Rich-ard Bolling, former head of the American Veterans Committee and a liberal congressman from Kansas City, wrote Mrs. Roosevelt that "despite the fact that I have supported all civil rights measures in the House during my term of service, I have concluded that I must

oppose this rider in the interest of enactment into law of the bill itself." He had heard that she had taken the same position. Was that
the case, and could he say so? When the school construction bill
had been discussed by the NAACP board in the spring of 1955, she
replied,

Walter Reuther and I asked the Board to allow it to be brought out of
committee without an amendment, stating that the Federal aid should
only go to school construction in unsegregated areas. We had the promise of Senators Lehman and Hubert Humphrey that as soon as it
reached the floor of the Senate they would amend it. They asked that
this be done in order that there would be an open debate on the floor so
the whole country would know what the argument was about and who
the people were who were taking sides. Otherwise it would be killed in
the Rules Committee and never reach the floor and no one in the country would know anything about it.
       The NAACP did not agree with our position at that time and there-
fore insisted that the rider should be attached in the Rules Committee.

She saw the dangers of a rider, she went on. It would invite a filibuster in the Senate and enable the Republicans to characterize the
Congress, which was controlled by the Democrats, as a "do
nothing" Congress.

So I think if I were a member of Congress, I would feel obliged to vote
for the bill and prevent the amendment from being introduced if possible. I am, however, not a member of Congress nor a candidate for office.
I have, therefore, an obligation, I think, to live up to the principles in
which I believe. I believe that it is essential to our leadership in the
world and to the development of true democracy in our country to have
no discrimination in our country whatsoever. This is most important in
the schools of our country. Therefore I feel personally that I could not
ask to have this bill passed without an amendment since unless the situation becomes so bad that the people are worried about all education, I
fear nothing will be done in the area of discrimination.[19]

     This answer was not wholly satisfactory. Although she was not
a candidate for office, she was a principal backer of the Stevenson
candidacy. He had to take a position on the Supreme Court decision and the Powell rider. What should it be, and, if he did not satisfy the Negro leaders, where should she stand? Would she still re-

fuse to accommodate principle to political realities? The problem soon confronted her. Stevenson, campaigning on the West Coast in early February, emphasized conciliation and gradualism. He did not believe that deeply rooted racial attitudes could be changed by "a stroke of the pen," and he opposed "punitive (or coercive) action by the Federal Government." [20]

Roy Wilkins, who had succeeded Walter White as chief executive of the NAACP and top strategist of the civil rights movement, was outraged by Stevenson's emphasis on "moderation." "To Negro Americans 'gradual' means either no progress at all, or progress so slow as to be barely perceptible," he wrote Stevenson, sending a copy of his letter to Mrs. Roosevelt.[21]

She did not like his statement as reported in the press, she wrote Wilkins. She had had a long talk with Stevenson, had made a careful study of his record in the Navy and as governor of Illinois, and had satisfied herself that "his stand on civil rights is the correct one in every way. . . . We will need great wisdom and patience in the next few months, not hotheaded bursting into print." To Walter White's widow, who protested that liberal Democrats like Stevenson might be expected to express views as strong, at least, as those of the Republicans, Mrs. Roosevelt replied, "Yes, but Stevenson is our best friend and we should not run him down."

Ralph Bunche was the Negro leader in whom she had the greatest confidence. "I had a long talk with Ralph Bunche yesterday," she wrote a protesting Pauli Murray, whose youthful militance she had treated so understandingly in the thirties and who was now a successful lawyer and writer,

and I don't think that fundamentally there is any cleavage between my point of view and that of Mr. Stevenson and that of the really wise Negro leaders. I did not like Roy Wilkins' hot-headed statement which I thought poorly thought out, nor did I like the garbled reporting of what Mr. Stevenson said in Los Angeles. Unwittingly Mr. Stevenson used the word "gradual" and this means one thing to the Negroes but to him it was entirely different. However, Mr. Stevenson's record remains remarkably good and he certainly was courageous in the statements he made in the last campaign. I think so far he has made no really deeply felt statement on the situation but I don't think that is because of any political reactions that might come. I simply think that he is waiting for the time when he thinks it will be of most value. However, the more he seems to be under attack by the Negroes, the less possible it is for him to make such a speech because he will be accused of doing so in order to get the Negro vote.

The only thing on which Stevenson and I differ with some of the Negro leaders is in support of the Powell amendment. His feeling is that aid should not be withheld from the states that need education most in order to improve. . . .

I think it is a mistake for the Negro leaders to be tearing down Stevenson who is after all the only real hope they have, the President having told Mr. [Adam Clayton] Powell that he would make no statement on whether the Executive would refrain from allocating funds where schools were segregated. Yet the papers and the Negro leaders have not attacked the President. Why this discrimination? [22]

Her differences with Wilkins came to a head in April when, in a speech under NAACP auspices in Chicago, he suggested that Negroes were not wedded to the Democratic party. "Up here we can strike a blow in defense of our brothers in the South, if necessary by swapping the known devil for the suspected witch." Some Negro papers interpreted this as a call to Negroes to desert the Democratic party if that was the only way to get around Sen. James O. Eastland of Mississippi, who, as chairman of the Senate Judiciary Committee, kept all civil rights legislation effectively bottled up in committee.

"I think you are being most unwise," Mrs. Roosevelt wrote Wilkins.

You are losing the people who have done the most for you in the past few years. I agree that the teaming up of the reactionary Democrats with the reactionary Republicans is a very bad thing but if the Republicans win it is not going to change that and you will certainly have as much inaction with either President Eisenhower or Nixon or any other Republican candidate as you have had in the past four years.

She did not see how having Sen. William E. Jenner, the ranking Republican on the Senate Judiciary Committee, become chairman would improve the prospect for civil rights legislation. She was angry. "I am unable to come to many meetings or spend the time to be [an NAACP] Board member," her letter ended, "and so I am herewith tendering my resignation. I am telling you this because I am forwarding my resignation to Dr. Tobias." Channing H. Tobias, a Negro leader with a long view, implored her not to resign, at least not before she had talked with Wilkins, who was out of town. "I am a registered Democrat and have voted for the party candidate consistently beginning with Alfred E. Smith," Wilkins wrote her in a letter that was a model of dignity and firmness. But his concern was "first and last for civil rights. . . . My view is that the political parties have not hesitated to use the civil rights issue advantageously for themselves, and I see nothing wrong with our trying to use political developments in either party advantageously for our cause." He asked her to reconsider her resignation. "I would consider it as a great personal loss, as well as an official one, if you should insist upon resigning." [23]

She had her talk with Wilkins and was satisfied that in the future he would not make statements that seemed to be anti-Democratic and anti-Stevenson in their thrust. "He assures me that he will remember to make very clear his meaning in what he says and writes," Mrs. Roosevelt notified Dr. Tobias, withdrawing her resignation.

In addition, he will try not to be tempted by the picturesque phrase into saying something that might excite the emotions and actually might also be harmful. I feel, therefore, that with your help and close cooperation the Association will be nonpartisan and a little wiser in its approach to certain questions.[24]

After the California primary, in which he had scored so heavily in the Negro precincts, Stevenson asked Mrs. Roosevelt to embody her sensible and understanding views on civil rights in an article for *Colliers* or *Look*. Negroes, high and low, esteemed her, and he thought it would have an effect. She declined. She did better "talking to the Negro leaders. I am doing this at every opportunity, and I told Mr. Butler I will go down for a meeting and try to work on getting an agreed plank for the platform. Though I confess I think it very difficult!" [25]

She returned from Paul Butler's meeting in Washington quite

buoyed up. Although the draft plank would not meet all the demands of the Negro leadership, the two southerners on the committee had been quite reasonable. She was surprised by their acceptance of what she considered was

pretty good wording on both the planks on education and civil rights. It won't be strong enough for Harriman, but I think it actually says all that needs to be said & would allow for any action one could take & still I think it won't divide the party.[26]

Joseph L. Rauh, Jr., of the ADA got wind of what was going on and, as a militant advocate of pushing the Democratic party hard on the civil rights issue, suggested to Mrs. Roosevelt that the best formula for the plank would be to reaffirm the 1952 position "with the additional statement that the Supreme Court's decision on school segregation is morally right and must be implemented with all deliberate speed by the executive and legislative branches of Government."

She did not usually disagree with the ADA, of which she was honorary chairman, but now she did. "Dear Mr. Rauh":

I have been working quite *sub rosa* and informally with some people on what might be acceptable to the South as well as the North. Neither one can have everything they want but if we can get the backing we want without mentioning the Supreme Court decision, we will be able to hold the South and hope for the backing we need to work with. I have worked out wording for the beginning of an education plank and the civil rights [plank] which is, of course, not all one would want but it is, on the whole, sufficiently good to give us the backing we want. Then, if we can get a candidate in the Democratic party who really is willing to use the powers of the Presidency to do something, I think we will be all right.

I have no idea what Governor Stevenson would be willing to do but whatever he has said he will do, I know he will stick by. I am more interested in what we can present to him as ways in which we can get the law implemented.[27]

Her letter did not persuade Rauh. The ADA felt that the Democratic civil rights plank "must contain a provision endorsing the Supreme Court's desegregation decisions as ones which are morally right and deserving of implementation by all branches of Government," he replied. But in pressing for a strong plank, the organization wanted to be sure it would not embarrass her. There would be no embarrassment for her, she wrote on this letter. Mr. Stevenson would agree with the proposal on the Supreme Court, "but you won't get it & the co-operation of the Southerners." But Stevenson now veered toward the ADA position:

Mr. Stevenson came here for a couple of hours Thursday to discuss Civil Rights & he wants much more specifically said in the platform which I would love to see done but doubt if he can get by the Southerners.[28]

He wanted a "firm and clear statement of what we know is right," Stevenson advised Butler, and enclosed a draft of what he thought should be said on civil rights, including the Supreme Court:

Words are no substitute for deeds. What is required is cooperative effort on the part of individual citizens as well as action by local, state and Federal governments. . . . In this spirit, the Democratic party stands firmly in support of the Supreme Court decisions regarding desegregation in the public schools and in other public facilities, including transportation, as we stand firmly in support of all Supreme Court decisions.

Stevenson sent her a copy of this draft, asking her to notice how it spoke of "support" rather than "approval" of the court's decision, although he cautioned her that in talking to an interviewer, he had said that "the platform should express unequivocal approval of the Court's decision. . . ."[29] It was not the finest hour of either of these normally staunch supporters of civil rights.

The convention was at hand, and Mrs. Roosevelt performed one final service for Stevenson. "We raised $75,000 at the Stevenson dinner last Wednesday night with 135 people present." She did not say, although the Stevenson people did, that her speech was the high point of the evening. They wished they had a recording to play for the undecided delegates. She gave the credit to Kefauver's announcement releasing his delegates. "It sparked the optimism everyone felt." She sent her thanks to Kefauver!

I am sure that your move will strengthen the Democratic Party, and bring the nomination to a quicker conclusion, and make it possible for a unified Party to win in November.[30]

Having done what she could for Stevenson in the primaries and in the drafting of a civil rights plank that she felt would hold the party together, she informed Butler that although she had agreed to speak at the convention on the sixteenth, she was bowing out. "I don't think it the least important and it would make it very difficult to make my overseas flight on the afternoon of the 17th." She was going to Europe with two of her grandsons and David's daughter, young Grania Gurewitsch, and did not want to start out tired.

If I can go to Chicago at all, I would do so on August 13th or 15th in the hope that I might be able to do something for Mr. Stevenson. However I am not sure I will go unless they feel there is something really helpful that I can do.[31]

Anna Rosenberg, Mary Lasker, and Tom Finletter, with whom she had been working closely, blanched when they heard the news. They had been equally nonplused a few days earlier when they discovered that she had booked herself solid for the fall with lectures for the AAUN and Colston Leigh. She could not see why people were so agitated, Mrs. Roosevelt said a little wearily. She would not be of much help. Younger people should be taking over. All the world, it seemed to her, including her sons, remonstrated with her. Stevenson begged her to make at least an appearance at the convention and to keep every possible date open in the fall. "Let me know," he wrote her, "but I should like to have you available *all* the time." [32] She yielded to Stevenson. Whatever he asked, she would try to do. She canceled all her speaking dates except those for which contracts had actually been signed, and with Stevenson, Jane (Mrs. Edison) Dick, Elliott, and the Finletters, she flew out to Chicago for the convention.

By all accounts, her appearance there, although brief, was largely responsible for stopping dead in its tracks Harry Truman's blitz for Harriman. He had come to Chicago determined to destroy the Stevenson candidacy, and the day before she arrived he let loose his blockbuster, saying that the party needed a "fighting" candidate, which Stevenson was not, nor was the Illinois governor well enough prepared to take over the presidency.

Instead of taking her to her hotel from the airport, Stevenson's managers drove her about Chicago while they filled her in on what Truman had said. Then they escorted her directly to a press conference at which she would answer the former president. She entered the room and faced "more reporters and more cameramen than I had ever seen before."

Graciously, in her best patrician style, Mrs. Roosevelt in forty-five minutes disposed of Mr. Truman. She could not take seriously his preference for a "fighting" candidate, she said, noting that while Stevenson fought it out in the primaries "there was a conspicuous lack of that kind of fighting" by Harriman. Was Stevenson any less prepared to take over the presidency than Truman was on April 12, 1945? she wanted to know. She thought Stevenson was perhaps "better equipped" in the field of foreign affairs than Truman had been. She then answered the attacks upon Stevenson's "moderation." Being a moderate did not mean you believed in standing still. FDR's policies were those of moderation, she asserted; he did the new things that had to be done, but did not destroy what his background and beliefs told him were valuable in the old.

To the Negro leaders and the ADA, who were pressing for a stronger civil rights plank, she said:

You can't move so fast that you try to change the mores faster than people can accept it. That doesn't mean you do nothing, but it means that you do the things that need to be done according to priority.

If the Negro leaders "knew Mr. Stevenson at all," she argued, "they must know that he believes you have to uphold the law of the land." The civil rights plank did not say everything she would like it to say but she felt southern members of the platform committee had come a long way.[33]

Columnists wrote that it was doubtful any other northern Democratic leader could say the things she did and survive politically. Resolved on getting the nomination for Stevenson, she demonstrated she could be a politician of "a formidable toughness." Her most deadly thrusts against Truman were her gentle reminders that they were both old—they were seventy-two—and that it was time to permit a younger generation of leaders to take hold of the party reins. She did not think Mr. Truman would change many votes, she told the reporters. People were fond of him, but he belonged "to the old tradition when the professional politicians had more influence than they should have."

"It was an adroit and ruthless performance," commented Arthur Schlesinger, Jr., one of Stevenson's top aides at Chicago. After her press conference, she and Truman lunched together. There was only one reference to the convention.

"I hope you will understand that whatever action I take is because I think I am doing the right thing," Truman said.

"Of course," she replied. "I know you will act as you believe is right and I know you will realize that I must do the same."

Truman nodded and grinned. "What I want to do is make this convention do some real thinking about issues." [34]

Although this was Truman's wish, it was Mrs. Roosevelt who forced the intellectual pace at the convention with her powerful speech to the convention sounding the theme that it was a time for new beginnings. After Franklin Roosevelt's death, his memory and the historic work he had accomplished had no more loyal a custodian than Mrs. Roosevelt. The politicians and leaders with whom she had dealt in the postwar years were admirable men with forceful qualities, but FDR by contrast seemed to tower over them. She jealously defended her husband's place in history, but she was also the one to insist that history had not come to an end with the New Deal. Her convention speech now took the form of a moving and powerful plea that the Democrats go beyond the New Deal and the Fair Deal and launch a campaign to end poverty in America.

At Mary Lasker's country place in Amenia, just before the convention, Mary had showed Mrs. Roosevelt a book she (Mary) had compiled documenting the extent of poverty in the United States. It was a popularization of the data turned up in the hearings on low-income families held by the Joint Congressional Committee on the Economic Report. Mrs. Roosevelt borrowed the book, and, taking it with her to Chicago, made it the heart of a speech that Edward R. Murrow called "the greatest convention speech I ever heard."

She believed in a Democratic victory, she started out, but she did not believe "that victory in itself is enough."

I want victory, and I believe we will have it in November, but I want even more that each and every one of you, as you go back to your communities, take the message of what you want that victory to mean.

The party had had great leaders, "but we could not have had great leaders unless they had had a great people to follow. You cannot be a great leader unless the people are great," she said, commenting on the movie depicting the history of the Democratic party that had been shown.

The world was again looking to the United States for leadership, for

the meaning of democracy and we must think of that very seriously. There are new problems. They must be met in new ways. . . . It is a foolish thing to say that you pledge yourself to live up to the traditions of the New Deal and the Fair Deal—of course, you are proud of those traditions; of course, you are proud to have the advice of the elders in our party, but our party is young and vigorous. Our party may be the oldest democratic party, but our party must live as a young party, and it must have young leadership. It must have young people, and they must be allowed to lead. They must not lean on their tradition. They must be proud of it. They must take into account the advice of the elders, but they must have the courage to look ahead, to face new problems with new solutions.

The party needed a "vision," and she wanted to suggest a thought:

You will remember that my husband said in one of his speeches that our job was not finished, because we still had a third of our people who were ill-housed, ill-clothed, and ill-fed.

We have lessened that group in our country that are ill-housed, ill-clothed, ill-fed, but we still have a job to do.

Twenty per cent today is the figure they give us.

Could we have the vision of doing away in this great country with poverty? It would be a marvelous achievement, and I think it might be done if you and I, each one of us, as individuals, would really pledge ourselves and our party to think imaginatively, of what can be done at home, what can make us not only the nation that has some of the richest people in the world, but the nation where there are no people that have to live at a substandard level. That would be one of the very best arguments against Communism that we could possibly have.

It was absolutely imperative that the Democrats come back to power, she had said earlier in her speech, "but they must come back with the right leaders." Party custom forbade her mentioning her candidate, she stated smiling broadly. She did not need to name the man who she thought could again lead the party to greatness. On her dress was pinned a large ADLAI button.[35]

Mrs. Roosevelt stayed in Chicago's steaming environs less than two days, but while she was there, wherever there was a cluster of delegates, like as not, at the center would be this tall, smiling lady in a gay flowered hat, boosting the virtues of her candidate. Before she left for New York, there was one final matter she had to face. Eugenie Anderson of Minnesota, former ambassador to Denmark, sent her a copy of a lengthy letter that she had addressed to Stevenson, arguing the advantages of selecting Humphrey as his running mate. Mrs. Roosevelt's friend, Abba Schwartz, and his law partner, James M. Landis, pleaded the case for Sen. John F. Kennedy. "Thanks," she had noted on the margin of the Landis letter. "I am troubled about Sen. K's evasive attitude on McCarthy." A session with the young senator at the convention did not change her mind. She declined to help him, and in the end Stevenson left the designation up to the free choice of the convention and Kefauver emerged from the balloting as the winner.[36]

She arrived in New York in time to dine with the Nottingham Roosevelt scholars—recipients of scholarships established by the town of Nottingham in honor of FDR—but she spent a good part of the evening taking calls from Chicago, which was in the midst of the fight over the civil rights plank. The minority report, representing the viewpoint of the Civil Rights Coalition, was defeated. "I may have been very wrong in my stand on the platform," she confided to a friend. Her position was opportunistic and unmilitant. A few months later she herself would describe President Eisenhower's stand on civil rights as being "about as aggressive as a meek little rabbit," and in the Little Rock crisis, when Arkansas governor,

Orval E. Faubus, defied a federal court integration order, she would say that President Eisenhower should have gone down and personally led the nine Negro children into the school. But that was in the future. At the 1956 convention, she was instrumental in defeating the minority plank. There was no southern bolt; and Stevenson was nominated. He would have preferred a "specific endorsement" of the court's decision, he told the press afterward.

She took off for Europe knowing she had done a first-rate job, for her press conference and speech continued to reverberate politically. An old Washington hand, the talented writer Helen Hill Miller, sounded a note that many felt strongly. "It isn't very often that a person who has been at the very center of one period in the life of a political party has the forward-lookingness and the resilience to note the transition to a new time, much less to bring it forcefully to the attention of the current members of the party. That's exactly what you did." In New York David E. Lilienthal made an entry in his *Journals:* "Up last night until long after midnight for the happy business of seeing Stevenson nominated overwhelmingly. . . . Mrs. Roosevelt said so well, and with such authority, the very thing I was trying to say to Stevenson, in December, 1955. I felt good that I had tried to give Stevenson the feeling, thus early, that there were those who wanted him to strike out into new ground, not try to live on the glories of the New Deal past, great as they were." "I doubt whether any leadership was more potent than yours in advancing Adlai's nomination at the convention in Chicago last week," William Benton, Connecticut's ex-senator, congratulated her.[37]

Although busy in Europe at a task she loved—introducing young people to her favorite museums, sights, and restaurants—for once she was bored. Her thoughts were with Stevenson:

I read in the papers of your trip with Estes Kefauver to see the leaders in different parts of the country which seems to me a good idea. At this distance Chicago and San Francisco seem a long way off and ten days over here make me feel I am in another world, so I hesitate to pass on certain observations but I do so in the belief that you will pay no attention to anything which you don't feel is valid.

Everyone I talked to feels that the crucial point in the election is to show that prosperity will not come to an end if the Republicans are defeated. . . . I saw the Queen of Holland and she talked to me about New Guinea and Indonesia, but there is time for that after I get home as it is tied up with our whole position on the colonial question. . . . The Suez situation does not look very happy to me. The Soviets have a knack for standing back and being enigmatic and letting us wonder what they will do while they shove somebody else to the fore, usually a weaker nation that would never dare stand up on its own. . . . I was much impressed in Denmark with the tiny garden holdings for factory workers outside the cities. The government and the city buys the land and sells it to a group (usually about 300) of factory workers. . . . It might be helpful in combating juvenile delinquency.

Now we are in Paris, having a busy but, on the whole, pleasant time. I think the boys are enjoying it much more since Grania Gurewitsch joined us. . . . I will be (D.V.) at home in New York on September 9th and I hope to go to Hyde Park from the 10th to the 12th. I think I saw you were going to be in New York about that time to speak. If you let me know, I would love to have a chance to talk with you and hear something of your plans and campaign preparations.

Tell Mr. [James A.] Finnegan [Stevenson's campaign manager] I will be glad if he will send me any dates he has lined up that he wants me to fill and also any suggestions of what he would particularly like me to cover in speaking. Since the Republican convention I feel more certain than ever that you can win. They seem to me empty and void of imagination or content. . . .[38]

The campaign was in high gear when she returned. "I think Adlai has begun to rise," she wrote David Gray, but she was frightened at the way the Stevenson people seemed to be counting on her to perform miracles and the impossible schedules they handed her. "You have to be in Harlem with Adlai on the 4th," they told her, and she agreed even though it meant flying back from Michigan in the afternoon and out to Wisconsin the next morning. The pressures were remorseless but she loved it all, and for a time it looked as if she might perform the miracle that the Stevenson workers were expecting of her. She appeared on "Meet the Press" on September 16, and her answers to questions about Nixon and Eisenhower showed again her deadly capacity for setting off dynamite charges while looking and sounding her most grandmotherly.

QUESTION: Mrs. Roosevelt, the Democrats have said that "A vote for Eisenhower is a vote for Nixon." Do you think this should be made an issue with the American people?

MRS. R.: I think it is an issue you have to face because at no time do any of us know what may happen to us, therefore when we elect a president and a vice-president, we must be prepared to face the facts that the vice-president may become president. That may happen to anybody at any time, and I think all of us should face that issue and know whether we are prepared to elect on that basis.

QUESTION: We have heard some criticism from both Democratic candidates about Mr. Nixon. Could you tell us how you feel about Mr. Nixon running for vice-president?

MRS. R.: Yes, I know how I feel personally but I know that what I feel personally is probably a feeling that might not be shared by other people. I am told that Mr. Nixon is a very fine young man by many Republican people whom I know, particularly young people, and that he has matured and grown in many ways. I happen to remember very clearly his campaign for the Senatorship. I have no respect for the way in which he accused Helen Gahagan Douglas of being a Communist because he knew that was how he would be elected, and I have no respect for the kind of character that takes advantage and does something they know is not true. He knew that she might be a Liberal but he knew quite well, having known her and worked with her, that she was not a Communist. I have always felt that anyone who wanted an election so much that they would use those means did not have the character that I really admired in public life.

QUESTION: Mrs. Roosevelt, do you really think the present administration, and particularly President Eisenhower himself, wants prosperity only for big business and that he doesn't care about the little guy?

MRS. R.: Oh, no! The President is a good man and he would want always to do the right thing as he saw it, but he has a great admiration for the achievement of the successful business man because he has never been a successful business man and you always admire what you really don't understand.

"That was the wisest, most gracious and convincing performance in my recollection," Stevenson wired her. "I thank you, I congratulate you and I bless you." The professional politicians were equally pleased. "I have been watching this program for many years," Paul Butler wrote her. "Never has a person done a more magnificent job than you did." Katie S. Louchheim, director of women's activities for the Democratic National Committee, said that Mrs. Roosevelt had been "an inspiration. . . . My husband and I spent the entire half hour assuring each other you are the very ablest spokesman the Democratic party has." "I think you are Adlai's one greatest asset," wrote author-journalist Agnes Meyer.[39]

Mrs. Roosevelt was brimful of ideas on campaign policy and strategy. She sent on to Stevenson Esther Lape's proposal on medical care:

> I will try this out in speeches and if I find it is not well received you can stay clear of it. But I think something constructive as a Democratic program of action has to come before the people. Criticism is not enough.[40]

"From Bernard M. Baruch via Eleanor Roosevelt" another memorandum to Stevenson began:

> Just at present the South is so annoyed with Mr. Eisenhower that they are all for Mr. Stevenson. It would seem to be wiser not to go there and to let them pull against Mr. Eisenhower and not run the danger of antagonizing any of them. If you have to go, be very careful what you say.

But when, at Stevenson headquarters, the state treasurer of New York, Archibald Alexander, asked her to talk to the old gentleman about coming out for Stevenson, she advised against it. It was not the way he did things. Baruch had told her he was indebted to Eisenhower, and she did not think he would want to jeopardize this relationship. A few weeks later even his private help was imperiled because of Stevenson's brave advocacy of an end of H-bomb tests. He was "completely in disagreement," Baruch informed her. "My dear Friend," she replied,

> I was very sorry to get your letter and also sorry to see your statement in the paper. I feel it was a mistake for Mr. Stevenson or Mr. Finletter not to have explained to you long ago what they were actually proposing, as you have evidently accepted the Republican interpretation of Mr. Stevenson's suggestion. I grant you his first speech was not suffi-

ciently explanatory but since then he has made very clear what he is trying to do and more than 270 scientists have agreed with his position. . . .[41]

She favored ending nuclear tests and replacing the draft with a voluntary system of better-paid, better-trained technicians. Audiences responded well to her discussion of these ideas, she reported:

I find that an explanation of what Mr. Stevenson meant in reference to the draft and H-bomb can all be pulled together into a pretty appealing topic which the women find of real interest. . . . I think if Mr. Stevenson can speak directly to women in this way, giving them a feeling that he really cares about what they feel and about the problems of their young people, it will make a difference in the women's vote.[42]

She was deeply troubled over Stevenson's inability to get across to his audiences:

I am not hearing any objection any more to your humor, so don't worry about that! Just let it come naturally.

If you can speak to the mass of people as though you were talking to any one individual in your living room at Libertyville, you will reach their hearts and that is all that you have to bother about.[43]

Once she went in with Anna Rosenberg and Tom Finletter to counsel him about his speeches. They had learned that he was staying up until the early hours of the morning worrying over the turn of a phrase. "Not every speech has to be a Gettysburg address," she admonished him gently. There were other kinds of promptings. Take a rest whenever you can, she begged him, as the campaign began to exact a physical toll from all of them. She had some very remarkable cold tablets given to her by David Gurewitsch. Stevenson should take them the minute he felt "achey," and they would head off the cold. She made a contribution of $1,000. She accompanied him to a rally in Harlem. "Mrs. Roosevelt, what shall I say?" he asked her in the car on the way uptown. "Adlai, you know what to say." [44]

"I have never worked as hard as I have this autumn in our national campaign," she wrote her old school friend "Bennett" (Mrs. Philip Vaughn) at the end of October, "but I have enjoyed it very much." [45]

When the defeat came, she was sad. "Wasn't it a strange election?" she wrote David Gray. "To carry the House and Senate in spite of Ike's tremendous vote seemed unbelievable." But she knew how hurt Stevenson was by the vote. "As for me, let there be no tears," Stevenson's concession statement gallantly ended. "I lost an election but won a grandchild."

"No one could have done more," she wrote the defeated candidate,

but the love affair between President Eisenhower and the American people is too acute at present for any changes evidently to occur. I think in spite of the responsibility you felt, it is probably a relief to be relieved of it. Now you can enjoy your grandson and the boys and devote yourself to your own interests and feel at least that the weight of the world is not exclusively on your shoulders. None of us can, I fear, escape some sense of responsibility but we will all of us be able to do less. . . . If you are in these parts, please come and see your very devoted friend and admirer.[46]

For herself, she would go back to her column, to her lectures, and to her work for the American Association for the United Nations, hoping, she told her friends, she would not again have a candidate she wanted so badly to win that she felt she had to campaign for him day and night.*

Her husband's achievement seemed greater than ever now that she had had to face the problem of tempering principle to the need to be elected. "I never was ahead of Franklin in social reform or any of those things," Mrs. Roosevelt insisted to reporter Carl Rowan. "I wanted things to happen faster, but Franklin always knew what he wanted." She had often found his pragmatism, his concern with timing, his skill—almost pleasure—in manipulation and maneuver exasperating, she told Lorena Hickok in 1954, when they collaborated on *Ladies of Courage;* but those techniques were necessary in politics, she acknowledged, and in the 1956 campaign she demonstrated an astute mastery of the tools of the trade. Yet there

---

* Stevenson's 89 electoral votes came from the South, but Eisenhower carried Tennessee, Texas, and Virginia. At the same time, in most Negro precincts, there was a perceptible increase over 1952 in the Eisenhower vote.

was a price. "If your husband had believed you advocated 'moderation,'" Judge Samuel I. Rosenman, a supporter of the Harriman candidacy, had reproached her, "we'd have little on the statute books." [47] And, indeed, because she had been so heavily committed to the success of the Stevenson candidacy, she had failed to do justice to the urgency of the civil rights issue.

XIII. Two Bosses—Khrushchev
and De Sapio

Mrs. Roosevelt paid for her intense involvement in the Stevenson campaign. The number of newspapers subscribing to her column was cut almost in half—from eighty to about forty.

The Scripps-Howard people have cancelled my column since the election in all of their papers, which leaves me with a reduced number of papers. Perhaps, if you and others who really miss the column would write in, individual papers might take it again but they will not do so without pressure. This is the result of my political activity but I am glad I did it just the same.[1]

The cancellation meant a substantial diminution in income from the column—from $28,000 in 1956 to $9,630 in 1957. For a moment she thought that perhaps the time had come to give it up, but United Features Syndicate asked her not to, saying it would make an effort to pick up other papers. Although she was seventy-two, she was willing to cooperate. She liked the platform the column gave her. When Paul Butler, the chairman of the Democratic National Committee, asked her to join the advisory committee of party notables that he was establishing, she declined formal membership:

They [the United Features Syndicate] fear that the feeling would spread that whatever I said on political subjects would not represent my own thinking but the thinking of a political party group. . . . I think the column people are right in feeling that my influence will be greater, as I write a daily column, if I am not a full-fledged member of the Committee.[2]

In New York City the loss of the Scripps-Howard paper there, the *New York World-Telegram,* was more than offset by the acquisition of the *New York Post.* The latter's liberal publisher, Dorothy Schiff, had tried, since 1939 when she acquired the paper, to persuade Mrs. Roosevelt to come over to it, and she quickly renewed the invitation when the *World-Telegram* dropped the column. It was a more satisfactory arrangement for Mrs. Roosevelt. The *World-Telegram* had taken to editing her copy mercilessly, shifting it from page to page, sometimes omitting it altogether. The *Post* was honored to have her as one of its columnists, published all that she wrote, gave it prominent display in the paper, and suggested assignments that would take her into newsworthy situations. "How would you like to go to Red China for us?" Mrs. Schiff inquired not long after Mrs. Roosevelt had joined the paper. She was ready, but the State Department was not. It declined to modify its embargo on travel to Red China even—or, perhaps, especially—for her, maintaining that it had no way to protect U.S. travelers in that sealed-off country. Mrs. Schiff wanted to test the travel ban in the courts, but Mrs. Roosevelt did not wish to make herself a *cause célèbre.* It might be wiser to have the case brought to court by someone more exclusively the representative of the newspaper fraternity. Would she go to Russia instead? Mrs. Schiff asked.[3]

That was a journey she had been wanting to make since wartime. She had been all set to go in 1954 for *Look* magazine—indeed, had had her bags packed—but had reluctantly abandoned her plans when the Russians declined to issue a visa to a Russian-speaking reporter whom she had wanted to accompany her.

No visa came through for [William] Atwood or the other man *Look* offered tho' I warned twice, so this morning at 10 I had a press conference in *Look's* office & explained why reluctantly I had to give up the trip. At 3:25 the Soviet Embassy phoned the second man could have a visa & if he could not get it in Washington he could in Paris! Everything was cancelled & we decided not to go later.[4]

In 1957 she still feared that the Russians might not want to have her accompanied by someone who spoke the language (i.e., David Gurewitsch, who, in addition to being her doctor, was an accomplished amateur photographer and spoke Russian fluently). But this was the Khrushchev era, and in time the visas came through.

On her arrival in Moscow she learned that Mrs. Anna Lavrova, who had helped interpret for FDR at Yalta, had been assigned to her as an interpreter. She realized that a special effort was being made for her, and even though she did not receive red-carpet treatment, she found "the welcome in spots almost embarrassing." But she had come as a correspondent, and the Russians evidently were happy to respect her wish that she be treated as such. She had the foreigner's usual difficulties in making appointments with top officials, and discovered that in order to get the interviews she wanted she had to insist and in the end go to the "head man" at Intourist.

Getting appointments to see "services" and not just museums is very difficult. No one does anything till you arrive & then Intourist is a reluctant agent.

On her arrival she immediately asked to meet with Nikita Khrushchev, who had survived the brutal succession struggle after Stalin's death to emerge as premier and party leader. She was requested to submit the questions she intended to ask and then was informed that in time she would learn their decision. "They love to keep you waiting," she wrote friends, "but they hate you to deviate from a plan you once make!" [5]

So she began her tour of inspection, not knowing whether she would see Khrushchev or any other important Soviet leader. After a few days in Moscow, attending the ballet and the circus, touring the museums, and negotiating with Intourist, she was taken to a state farm twenty miles outside of the city. Despite her long training at breaking away from the officially guided tour in order to see the things she wanted to see, Soviet bureaucracy bested her. At the state farm she asked to see a worker's home. They would arrange it, she was told, and later was escorted down a village street to a house that looked to her like the newest in the group. Spotting some older ones on the other side of the street, she asked whether she could not look into one of them. Her guide would not hear of it and firmly steered her into the demonstration house. Even that, she noted, lacked running water and an inside toilet, although it did have a television set.[6]

At the suggestion of Justice William O. Douglas, she had asked to visit Tashkent and Samarkand in central Asia. Tamerlane became "quite real" to her in Samarkand, but the hospital and health institutions that she visited there, although primitive in facilities by U.S. standards, provided modern treatment with good results. She traveled to Zagorsk, where there were

really lovely 15th Century Churches & a most amusing midday meal at the Greek Orthodox divinity school! They are stout these gentlemen & eat & drink well. We were plied with champagne & I was glad of my agreement to drink only water. Maureen found her limitation of one glass looked upon with incredulity & not accepted!

There were jaunts to Sochi and Leningrad. "What a lovely city this is!" she wrote of the latter:

Far lovelier than Moscow but they tell me cheerfully that it rains every day except in summer & summer is over & even then it rains now & then! They were badly bombed by the Germans but rebuilding has gone on fast & the scars are almost hidden but 900 days of siege are still much on the minds of the people.

Everywhere she tried to get figures, and though "reliable statistics are hard to get at," it seemed to her that

security exists materially. The lower paid workers find life hard but shelter & food are available. Clothes are poor. Glamorous women, well dressed & groomed, do not exist & yet the older women dye their hair! [7]

She tried to understand what was happening in Soviet Russia by looking at the country through the eyes of its people. The most important thing she learned about the Soviet Union she summed up in the formula—Lenin and Pavlov. As she watched thousands of Soviet citizens patiently queue up outside of the tomb of Lenin—and, at that time, the tomb of Stalin as well—she realized that it was through the teachings of these two men—and chiefly that of Lenin —that the Soviet citizen saw his society and the world, and that this vision embodied relentless hostility to the West. And in a visit to a pediatrics institute in Leningrad, it dawned on her that the Pavlovian system of conditioning children embodied the methods by which the Russians as a whole were turned into a "completely disciplined and amenable people." [8]

It frightened her that this vast apparatus of discipline and power was dedicated to the triumph of Communism, and it frightened her even more that her own people misread the danger as primarily military. She thought the immediate arena of challenge was in the Third World, where the Soviet model of forced industrialization seemed more relevant than the American model of free enterprise to the leaders of the developing nations. The abstract talk of democracy, to which America's leaders were so addicted, seemed to her meaningless. The freedom that primarily interested the peoples of Asia and Africa was the freedom to eat, she wrote after her return. [9]

As her trip drew to an end, she still had no answer to her request to see Khrushchev. She had just returned from Sochi, on the Black Sea, and was saying her good-bys to various government officials preparatory to departure, when Mrs. Lavrova informed her abruptly: "I forgot to tell you, but we go to Yalta early tomorrow morning." That meant a thousand-mile trip back to the Black Sea. Mrs. Roosevelt was so irritated with this rude way of doing things that she was scarcely able to reply. "Well," she said, "I'm glad you finally remembered!" [10]

Early the following morning, she flew to Yalta with David and Mrs. Lavrova, spent the night in a Yalta hotel, and managed, in the hour before Khrushchev's car came to fetch them the next morning, to visit the palace where the Yalta conference took place. Khrushchev's villa on the outskirts of Yalta was comfortable but not ostentatious. The Soviet leader, bareheaded, in a white, handsomely bordered peasant's blouse, came to greet her. He was relaxed and friendly and first insisted on showing her about the grounds. Then the group settled itself on the porch, and David placed the portable tape recorder that they had brought from the United States just for this occasion on the table. Khrushchev made a little speech about FDR and then the interview began. It soon turned into a debate about which nation was responsible for the cold war, the arms race, the violation of the Yalta agreements, the tensions in the Middle East, with Khrushchev's hearty peasant vehemence sometimes shading into red-faced anger and with Mrs. Roosevelt upholding her viewpoint graciously, but with equal firmness. It was inconclusive, as all such debates, inside the UN and out, had been since the end of World War II. The discussion took on the flavor of practicality only when Mrs. Roosevelt challenged Khrushchev on the subject of Soviet treatment of the Jews. When, in answer, he cited the many Jews of high rank in the Soviet Army and elsewhere, she was not satisfied. "That may be but it is very difficult for any Jew to leave the Soviet Union to settle or even visit Israel."

"I know," Khrushchev answered defensively, "but the time will come when everyone who wants to go will be able to go." [11]

It was a long two-and-a-half-hour interview. The visit ended on a family note—a table laden with delicacies and Khrushchev's whole family joining them.

"Can I tell our papers that we have had a friendly conversation?" Khrushchev asked as he bid her good-by.

"You can say," she replied, "that we had a friendly conversation but that we differ."

He laughed. "At least we didn't shoot each other."

She departed from Moscow the next day. "I was oh! so happy when our airplane, flying out of Moscow, touched down at Copenhagen." It was only after she was in the Danish capital "and heard laughter and gay talk and saw faces that were unafraid that I realized how different were our two worlds. Suddenly, I could breathe again!" [12]

She arrived back in the United States as the world was reverberating to the news of the first Soviet sputnik, a spectacular development in science and technology that Soviet propagandists were exploiting to suggest that the balance of power was moving in favor of the Soviets. There was that possibility, Mrs. Roosevelt thought. Khrushchev was "honest" when he told her that war was unthinkable, she told interviewers, because he and other Soviet leaders "have made up their minds they can win what they want without war." Khrushchev was committed to coexistence but it was "competitive coexistence," and the West, especially the United States, could not afford to be complacent. The need was to turn it into "cooperative coexistence." "It seems to me," she wrote Queen Juliana of the Netherlands, who hoped for a long talk with Mrs. Roosevelt about her Russian trip, "we have reached a place where it is not a question of 'can we live in the same world and cooperate' but 'we must live in the same world and learn to cooperate.' " [13]

She never gave up trying to establish on a personal basis points of communication and cooperation with the Russians. Many of the Soviet delegations that visited the United States were her guests. She visited the Soviet Union again in 1958. And a year later, when Khrushchev toured the United States as a guest of President Eisenhower, he accepted her invitation to visit Hyde Park even though in the interim, at the suggestion of the Russian-born novelist Vladimir Nabakov and Arthur Schlesinger, Jr., she had written him to protest Russia's refusal to permit Boris Pasternak to accept the Nobel Prize.[14]

The visit to Hyde Park was a hectic expedition, as were most of Khrushchev's travels in the United States. There was, however, a moment of the deepest solemnity and ceremony when Khrushchev, preceded by two aides carrying a large floral wreath and followed by Mrs. Roosevelt and Mrs. Khrushchev, walked to FDR's grave in the rose garden and placed the wreath at the graveside. It bore the inscription:

To the outstanding statesman of the United States of America
—the great champion of progress and peace among peoples.

Chief of the Council of Ministers of the
Union of Soviet Socialist Republics
N. S. Khrushchev.

Khrushchev stood for a moment in silence, his head bowed, and then Mrs. Roosevelt led him to the Big House and library for hurried inspections and finally to her cottage at Val-Kill where she offered him tea, coffee, and cake. But there was little time. It was all "very rush-rush," she said later. "He enjoyed nothing. A man behind him all the time kept whispering, 'seven minutes . . . seven minutes.' " As he came out of her cottage, he held up a seed roll for the photographers and said in Russian, "one for the road." Back in New York, Khrushchev sent her a handsome shawl. "Tell your wife and daughter," she wrote, "if they are here and in need of any help in shopping, I can easily arrange to give them guidance." [15]

In 1960 Khrushchev returned to the United States, this time uninvited. He came for the UN General Assembly, to make anti-Western demonstrations. He was in the midst of his quarrel with the Chinese. In her opinion, he "behaved outrageously." He savagely attacked Hammarskjöld. He interrupted speakers. He banged his shoe on the desk. It was a hooligan performance. Nevertheless, she invited him to tea, and he accepted. When people criticized her for having done a "dreadful thing," she coolly replied that it was just politeness, that he had gotten nothing to eat when he had last been to Hyde Park and so she had to make it up to him. She was greatly relieved that he did not bring up the United Nations during his visit, for "I would have had to have been rude." Instead, they argued economics—he boasting about the Soviet economic progress and she asking whether the Soviet consumer would be the beneficiary, he replying that the Soviet goal was the four-hour day and she innocently asking whether he had begun to educate his people on how to use their leisure time. Khrushchev was not indifferent to her arguments. The next morning a stack of books arrived from him, all in English and with little paper slips in them marking the pages on which he had underlined passages bolstering his case. To those who attacked her for having talked with the Soviet premier, she said:

We have to face the fact that either all of us are going to die together or we are going to learn to live together and if we are to live together we have to talk.[16]

At Hyde Park in September, 1959, just before Khrushchev's arrival, she was asked whether she expected to have extensive talks with the Soviet premier. "He has no interest in me whatsoever," she replied. "I have no power. That gentleman likes power." The lady-like denial that she had any power or any acquaintance with the uses thereof was characteristic. Often when she was asked her opinion on a political matter and did not wish to commit herself, she mildly insisted, "I know nothing of politics," a bit of guile that was part of her feminine stock in trade. When a young man proposed to do a thesis on her political influence, she brought him to Dr. Elizabeth Drewry, director of the Franklin D. Roosevelt Library. "Please tell him that I have no influence and that he will be wasting his time." [17]

She was, of course, an astute politician and at times could be as implacable and unforgetting as FDR and Louis Howe in avenging a treachery. That was the case with Franklin Jr.'s defeat for statewide office in 1954. Tammany Hall, which Franklin Jr. had bested in 1949 when he defeated its candidate for Congress, retaliated five years later when the county heads, led by Carmine De Sapio, leader of Tammany and Democratic National committeeman, turned down his bid for the gubernatorial nomination, giving it to Averell Harriman. His mother had warned him, "Don't ever trust him," referring to De Sapio, when Franklin told her that De Sapio had advised him to come to the convention as the upstate candidate in order to avoid the "big city boss" stigma. Denial of the gubernatorial nomination was a setback to Franklin's political hopes, but since he was nominated for attorney general it was also an opportunity, especially if he were to run ahead of the ticket in November. Mrs. Roosevelt, who had been sitting with Franklin Jr. and his wife in a little room at the back of the armory, was the only one to suggest he might lose, adding, however, "They may never forgive you if you don't run." Disaster came on Election Day when Franklin was the only state-wide loser—to Jacob K. Javits—in a Democratic sweep. "F jr. was defeated because they put a *very good* Jew against him," she wrote Uncle David. "Ordinarily he has the Jewish vote but much of it had to vote for a good Jew. Then De Sapio & Buckley in Manhattan & the Bronx cut him in the Italian & Irish votes." [18]

Deeply unhappy for her son, Mrs. Roosevelt, although she was aware of Franklin's shortcomings, in time came to hold De Sapio primarily responsible for his defeat. Franklin's political team disbanded. He moved to Washington to concentrate on his law and business interests. Mrs. Roosevelt, however, did not forget. If the chance came, she would even the score.

This was not the only reason for the relentless duel with De Sapio that now began. In 1956 he again ran afoul of her when he not only politically masterminded Harriman's bid for the presidential nomination against Stevenson but kept Stevenson supporters off the New York delegation, despite Stevenson's popularity in the state, and gave him only listless support in the campaign.

In 1958, at the Buffalo state convention, De Sapio publicly affronted Mrs. Roosevelt, Herbert Lehman, and Governor Harriman by hand-picking New York District Attorney Frank Hogan for the senatorial nomination over Thomas K. Finletter and Thomas E. Murray. Normally a good soldier in Democratic ranks, she was by now so indignant with De Sapio that it overflowed against Hogan. The Democrats could have had a nominee "who knew more about foreign policy" was her "Meet the Press" comment on Hogan's candidacy, a damaging statement that was only partially offset by an election eve clarification that she intended to vote for him.

Her distrust of De Sapio was so great that she voiced the theory as the campaign drew to a close that he would arrange matters in such a way that Harriman lost while Hogan won.[19]

Not exactly the most popular figure at Democratic headquarters at the Biltmore Hotel that election night, she sensed the hostility in the room and, pleading that she could not stand the photographers, left a few minutes after putting in an appearance. When it became clear Harriman and Hogan both had lost, she crisply voiced the hope that the defeat would mean the downfall of Tammany. De Sapio's domination of the Buffalo convention was the basic reason for the rout. "When the Tammany Hall boss bossed the convention it meant the defeat of the democratic process." [20]

She now joined Lehman, who had been equally incensed by De Sapio's ham-handedness at Buffalo, and Finletter in setting up the New York Committee for Democratic Voters, dedicated to the reform of the Democratic party, including the unseating of De Sapio. "No campaign in which I have participated," she said, "has meant more to me than this present struggle to bring real democracy into the party in this state."

It took three years and endless campaigning on hot summer nights. "Short speeches, climbing up a ladder onto a sound truck, I often wonder how much sense one really makes," she asked but stuck to it doggedly. Finally on September 7, 1961, with the assistance of New York's Mayor Wagner, who also had broken with De Sapio, he was overthrown.

Was she opposed to De Sapio personally, she had been asked. No, she was opposed "to the kind of boss rule he represents" was her reply.[21]

On New Year's Eve, 1961, friends and family were gathered at Hyde Park. Mrs. Roosevelt was in gay spirits. Someone remarked he had heard De Sapio might be made ambassador to Tanganyika. Why not Somaliland? another voice was heard to say, where his knowledge of Italian would come in handy.

"But he doesn't know Italian," protested Mrs. Roosevelt from the head of the table. She had campaigned in Italian over station WOV, but he was unable to, she remarked. She had been told, she went on, that Mr. De Sapio was very bitter toward her. She could not understand why, she said, putting on her most grandmotherly look. Justin Feldman, who had been Franklin's administrative assistant, broke in to remark that all of them had dispersed after the 1954 defeat to attend to their private affairs, "But not Mrs. Roosevelt. She evened the score with Carmine for having knifed Franklin."

Louis Howe, she commented, had always said that in politics you never forget a double cross. She hadn't done anything. Governor Lehman had done all the work. She had just awaited her opportunity.[22]

XIV. A New Generation Takes Over

In the summer of 1959 Mrs. Roosevelt received a gay card from Adlai Stevenson postmarked Corsica. He was cruising in the Mediterranean with Adlai Jr., his wife, Bill Benton and his family, and some friends, "and all we've missed is you!" It was exciting to get a postcard from him, she replied:

I don't think I would be the perfect addition because I have never had Franklin's success in really enjoying the ocean even when it is fairly calm. I would have loved to have been with all of you, however, and I hope that the rest of the summer will be as pleasant as these past weeks.

Her letter went on to give news of other Stevenson friends. She had seen Mary Lasker, "and poor Anna Rosenberg has had to go into the hospital." The Stevenson "loyalists" were keeping in touch with each other.[1]

After the 1956 defeat she assumed that Stevenson would not run again but felt that the forward-looking elements in the Democratic party should continue to look to him for leadership while younger men in the party were encouraged to come forward to establish their claim to the 1960 nomination. Asked in 1957 who would make a good candidate in 1960, she named Wayne Morse, G. Mennen Williams, Joseph Clark, Edmund Muskie,* and Chester Bowles.[2]

The handling of the nation's foreign affairs loomed uppermost

---

* "I wish he were better known throughout the country," she wrote of Governor Muskie when he was running for the Senate in 1958, "for I think he has the qualities of greatness which might even lead him to be considered for the Presidency some day" ("My Day," August 29, 1958).

in her mind, especially after her visit to Russia, as she wrote Bowles:

I think we are in a real emergency and the Democratic party must have someone who will look at the world as it is and begin to meet its problems in new ways. The only two people I can really feel happy about negotiating with Khrushchev would be you or Walter Reuther. . . . Our Democratic leadership seems to me impoverished in the Senate and House and even Adlai can do little about it.[3]

Paul Butler sent Mrs. Roosevelt a report prepared by the Democrats on the Senate Armed Service Preparedness Subcommittee, headed by Lyndon B. Johnson. It deplored the nation's lack of military preparedness. "A truly patriotic service," Butler said of the document. Military preparedness was most important, she agreed, "but I hope he [Johnson] will not forget that a military speedup alone will not meet the Soviet challenge." [4] Of all the men in public life, Stevenson best recognized the many-dimensioned complexity of the Soviet challenge, but the practical politicians, she knew, felt strongly that a twice-unsuccessful presidential candidate could not win on a third try. Although Stevenson seemed unavailable, she declined to commit herself to any one candidate. At a dinner in Kansas, in October, 1958, the national committeeman began to boost G. Mennen Williams, the youthful governor of Michigan. He is one of the good younger men, Mrs. Roosevelt said agreeably. That did not quite satisfy the committeeman. Adlai Stevenson just did not get across to people, he pressed on, assuming her loyalties were still hitched to the Stevenson standard. In judging 1960 aspirants she would be insistent on only one commitment, she commented, that whoever the Democratic candidate was, he would pledge to make Stevenson secretary of state.

Her trip out to Kansas was a reminder to her that she was slowing down. Although she had flown out Saturday afternoon, and back to New York late that night, arriving at dawn in an impressive display of energy and will for a woman of seventy-four, she had only remembered why she had agreed to go when she heard one of her hosts at the dinner say: "We are so happy and honored that you should come to our first FDR dinner." It was time for her sons' generation to take over, she felt.[5]

One of the younger Democratic leaders upon whom she looked favorably was Senator Humphrey. At the end of 1958 she gave his candidacy considerable impetus, greater perhaps than she had intended, when she told questioning newsmen that of the names being mentioned he came closest to having "the spark of greatness" the next president would need.[6]

For a time she said she was inclined to support Justice William O. Douglas if for no other reason than his willingness to speak frankly to the American people about relations with Red China. Mrs. Roosevelt was one of the first to sense the growing rift between Russia and China, advancing the theory after her second visit to the USSR in 1958, that perhaps the Chinese Communist tail was trying to wag the Soviet dog and that might make the Russians more disposed to deal with the West. But China, as well as Russia, was here to stay, and the United States should not make the mistake with China that it had with Russia and ignore its existence for fifteen years. The American people were living in "a dream world," and she wanted a candidate who would take them out of it.[7]

Mrs. Roosevelt was distinctly cool toward Senate Democratic Majority Leader Lyndon Johnson. He was "one of the ablest people at maneuvering that we have in the party," she said on "Meet the Press," but she did not know what his basic convictions were. "You're crazy," was her comment when Mary Lasker described him as a "secret liberal."[8] And when her son James invited him to speak at the Memorial Day exercises in the rose garden in 1959 she was unenthusiastic and, after his arrival, kept herself out of sight, leaving him and Lady Bird to her friends to entertain. But he took it in his stride and, if he was aware of her absence, gave no sign of it, plying her friends with stories calculated, when they reached Mrs. Roosevelt, to evoke a favorable impression (how he had told "Aubrey" [Williams], who had appointed him first director of the National Youth Administration in Texas, to bring his delegation of southern Negro bishops over to his office—he would sit for a photograph with them, even if they were in Washington to lobby for civil rights; how he had picked up "Hubert" [Humphrey], and together they had gone over to talk to Chancellor Adenauer, who was in Washington, on the need for disarmament). He managed also to get in a few digs at Richard Nixon for his treatment of Helen Douglas in the 1950 senatorial campaign in California. It was a virtuoso performance, the famous Johnson treatment, which, combined with the "genuineness of his feeling for FDR," did cause her to unbend before the day was over, although it did not reconcile her to his candidacy.[9]

She gave the hardest time to front-runner John F. Kennedy. She had not always been so hostile. In 1952 she backed him against incumbent Sen. Henry Cabot Lodge. "It is important, I think, that these young courageous representatives who have had experience in the House, move into the Senate and bring into that body some of the influence of youth." [10] But in the Senate Kennedy had been "evasive" on McCarthy—so she wrote in a magazine article in early 1958. The senator's father, getting wind of the article, got James Landis to talk to Mrs. Roosevelt, which he did, but without success. Joseph Kennedy then asked that the matter be dropped, since Mrs. Roosevelt was obviously anti-Catholic. His son disagreed. That could not be the case since she had supported Al Smith. A few months later, in December, 1958, on ABC-TV, she thrust at the senator more harshly. She conceded that John Kennedy was a young man with an enormous amount of charm. Although he had written a book, *Profiles in Courage*, she

would hesitate to place the difficult decisions that the next President will have to make with someone who understands what courage is and admires it but has not quite the independence to have it.

She suggested that he was too much under the influence of his father, Joseph P. Kennedy, who had been "spending oodles of money all over the country" in his son's behalf and who "probably has paid representatives in every state by now." This would be "perfectly permissible," if the senator had done it for himself.[11]

The charges stung, but Kennedy declined to be provoked. She was a victim of misinformation, he asserted coolly. He asked Mrs. Roosevelt to name one such paid representative or give one example of spending by his father on his behalf. "If my comment is not true, I will gladly so state," she replied:

I was told that your father said openly he would spend any money to make his son the first Catholic President of this country, and many people as I travel about tell me of money spent by him in your behalf. This seems commonly accepted as a fact.[12]

He was disappointed, Kennedy answered, that she now seemed to accept the view "that simply because a rumor or allegation is repeated it becomes 'commonly accepted as a fact.' It is particularly inexplicable to me inasmuch as, as I indicated in my last letter, my father has not spent any money around the country, and had *no* 'paid representatives' for this purpose in *any* state of the union—nor has my father *ever* made the statement you attributed to him—and I am certain no evidence to the contrary has ever been presented to you." "Dear Senator Kennedy," she replied to this,

I am enclosing a copy of my column for tomorrow and as you will note I have given your statement as the fairest way to answer what are generally believed and stated beliefs in this country. People will, of course, never give names as that would open them to liability.[13]

This did not satisfy Kennedy. He appreciated her courtesy in printing his denial, but "since the charges could not be substantiated to even a limited extent, it seemed to me that the fairest course of action would be for you to state that you had been unable to find evidence to justify the rumors." She retreated slightly:

In reply to your letter of the 10th, my informants were just casual people in casual conversation. It would be impossible to get their names because for the most part I don't even know them.

Maybe, like in the case of my family, you suffer from the mere fact that many people know your father and also know that there is money in your family. We have always found somewhat similar things occur, and except for a few names I could not name the people in the case of my family.

I am quite willing to state what you decide but it does not seem to me as strong as your categorical denial. I have never said that my opposition to you was based on these rumors or that I believed them, but I could not deny what I knew nothing about. From now on I will say, when asked, that I have your assurance that the rumors are not true.

If you want another column, I will write it—just tell me.[14]

Kennedy was out to make friends, not score debating points. He thanked her for her "gracious" letter. "I appreciate your assurance that you do not believe in these rumors and you understand how such matters arise. I would not want to ask you to write another column on this and I believe we can let it stand for the present." He hoped there might be a chance to get together and talk about other matters.[15]

Somewhere deep in her subconscious was an anti-Catholicism which was a part of her Protestant heritage. In her Great-grandmother Ludlow's Sunday school exercise books, there were lessons on the dangers of popery. Enlightened Protestantism had long since outgrown such primitive prejudice—she had ardently supported Al Smith in the 1920s—but her fear of the church as a temporal institution was reawakened from time to time by its political operations. The clash with Cardinal Spellman had left its scars.

Although Maureen Corr, Mrs. Roosevelt's Irish-born secretary, whom, significantly, she employed after the Spellman episode, considered her boss one of the least prejudiced human beings she ever knew, she sensed Mrs. Roosevelt's deep fear of the church in politics in her opposition to Kennedy. It was opposition that was all the more striking to her friends as her sons James, Franklin, and Elliott began to work for the senator and sought to overcome her distrust of him. They had no more success than did Abba Schwartz, who had worked with her on refugee matters and had carefully cultivated her and her friends in Kennedy's interest.

Her resistance to Kennedy matched, perhaps even fed, a reviving hope that Stevenson might again win the nomination, although she freely conceded that to have twice lost the race for the presidency was a greater liability than being a Roman Catholic in such a competition. Mary Lasker sent her a Gallup poll showing that 20 per cent of the voters would not vote for a Catholic for president, which, Mrs. Lasker argued, would be a great handicap for any presidential candidate. Mrs. Roosevelt, studying the same figures, was impressed by the increase over the years in the number of people who would vote for a Catholic.[16]

By the end of 1959 the drift of her thinking on the presidency was indicated when she mentioned that Stevenson was "the only person in the Democratic Party who might be appealed to" in the event of a stalemated convention. "The Democrats have a lot of good Vice Presidential material" was her dry comment on the names most frequently mentioned.[17]

Noting that a good many professional politicians were talking about the "favorite son" of Texas, Lyndon B. Johnson, she commented mildly that she was listening to "everybody's arguments" and still enjoying her above-the-battle posture. But the professionals should not count on her staying out of the fray. She had "a little nagging feeling," she warned in her column, that somewhere along the way to the convention she would have to decide which of the candidates was best qualified to meet the problems of the day. "I shall resist this little nagging thought as long as I possibly can." [18]

She did not know who that other elder statesman of the party, Harry Truman, would be for in 1960—Stuart Symington or Lyndon Johnson—but she was sure he would not be for Stevenson. The former president made that abundantly clear at a glittering fund-raising dinner at the Waldorf in December, 1959, staged by the Democratic Advisory Committee in her honor. It was graced by most of the presidential hopefuls except Senator Johnson, who, as leader of the congressional wing of the party, was feuding with the Advisory Committee, which was representative of its presidential wing.

Truman startled everyone by his introductory remarks, which assailed "the self-appointed guardians of liberal thinking." The price of not going along "with these hothouse liberals" was to be abused as "a reactionary." Often, "these self-styled liberals," he went on, "hurt the cause of liberalism" and "paved the way for reaction."

There was a buzz and murmur throughout the large dining room. What was Truman after—the *New York Post?* The ADA? Mrs. Roosevelt thought he was after bigger game and that this was a replay of the Chicago effort of the party professionals massed behind Truman to control the choice of a candidate and the direction of party policy. She was going "to differ with him a little bit to-night," Mrs. Roosevelt began, directing a smile at the former president who grinned back prepared for the spanking he knew would follow this disarming opening.

She welcomed "every kind of a liberal" who came into the party willing to learn "what it is to work on being a liberal." But older people—both she and the president were now seventy-five—also had "something to learn from liberals that are younger . . . because they may be conscious of new things we have to learn." Changes were coming in the world. "We cannot exist as a little island of well-being in a world where two-thirds of the people go to bed hungry every night." She hoped the Democrats would help the nation meet the challenges confronting it. "I want unity but above everything else, I want a party that will fight for the things that we know to be right at home and abroad."

Stevenson drew the greatest round of applause that evening. He managed with a witty, graceful anecdote to draw a line between himself as the leader who had twice been honored with the party's nomination and the bevy of young hopefuls who were on the stage with him—and at the same time, without seeming to grasp for the prize of a 1960 nomination, to suggest he was available.

He recalled that in 1952 he had come to a similar rally in New York. Since he was insisting at that time that he was candidate only for re-election as governor of Illinois and not for the Democratic presidential nomination, he had ducked the issue by proposing marriage to Mrs. FDR. Although she had not accepted him, he remained, he went on, "a patient man and still available." [19]

Early in 1960, Mrs. Roosevelt had some kind words for Lyndon Johnson. He had kept his promise to civil rights groups, she reported, and she was grateful to him for getting the civil rights bill to the floor. A short time later the bill passed and she said publicly that the party owed Senator Johnson a vote of thanks, adding that "we are fortunate to have had a parliamentary leader with the skill of Senator Johnson." There was a softening toward Kennedy, who appeared on her television program in January, an invitation that had been engineered by J. Kenneth Galbraith as part of a strategy to make Kennedy more acceptable to the liberals. [20]

But her preference continued to be for Stevenson. He called at her office at the AAUN after a spell in the Caribbean sun, and she noted in her column that the reporters who saw him afterward had commented, "But this is a new Stevenson. It is the Stevenson of 1952." She presented the ADA citation to him at the ADA Roosevelt Day Dinner, and in her remarks reminded her audience that in 1956, when Stevenson had called for a nuclear test ban, which the Eisenhower administration was now actively seeking, Vice President Nixon, the man slated to run for president, had called it "treasonable nonsense." [21]

Her friends thought she would be happy to see Stevenson run, but Mrs. Roosevelt felt even more strongly that he should be free to make up his own mind. She definitely did not wish at that time to share the responsibility for his decision. In February, just before he departed on a two-month tour of Latin America, Stevenson asked to see her alone. She summoned David Gurewitsch and his wife Edna to be present to preclude his asking her to tell him what to do. Although the organizers of the unofficial draft-Stevenson movement were in touch with her she was not sure whether a fight should be made to get him the nomination, whether Stevenson wanted a fight made, or how much she should become involved. She was certain of one thing, however, as she confided to her friend Lord Elibank, Stevenson was "the only mature person among the lot." Stevenson himself, on his return from Latin America, reiterated that he was not a candidate, and when pressed as to whether he would turn down a draft, parried with the quip that he was not a "draft evader." [22]

The Rosenmans and Averell Harriman were at Hyde Park on April 12 and tried to smoke her out, she reported to friends with a smile, thus suggesting that they had been unsuccessful. Harriman had taken the lead. He and the Rosenmans had come to the conclusion on the drive up to Hyde Park, he said, that Humphrey came closest to what they wanted a candidate to be and should be supported. What did she think? She refused to rise to the bait. She was equally noncommittal when they sought to elicit whether her heart still belonged to Adlai. [23]

Walter Reuther came to see Mrs. Roosevelt at the end of April. It was getting better every day for Stevenson, he reported. But he was worried that the Humphrey-Kennedy battle in the primaries, especially in West Virginia, might pave the way for a conservative nominee and even endanger Democratic chances in November. He asked her to communicate with the two candidates and urge them to avoid sanguinary charges that might be long in healing. "I called Hubert Humphrey the other day," she wrote Reuther, "but had absolutely no effect upon him. He and Kennedy both seem to feel that they have no chance in the nomination unless they go on with these primaries." [24]

In May, right after the West Virginia primary, where Kennedy, with the aid of Franklin Jr., gained the victory that was a turning point in his bid for the nomination, she reported, still from "the sidelines" and as "a neutral," that she had found in going around the country "an underlying groundswell" for Stevenson among rank-and-file Democrats that professional politicians had better not ignore. She thought it reflected the country's anxiety over the deterioration in U.S.-Soviet relations that followed the U-2 fiasco and the angry breakup of the Paris summit meeting.

Stevenson's chance would only come if the convention deadlocked, meaning that the front-runner Kennedy had to be kept from getting a majority on the first or second ballot. By the end of May her views had crystallized sufficiently that she agreed to the request of the draft-Stevenson people to write "please wait" letters to Reuther and Gov. G. Mennen Williams of Michigan:

Someone has told me that you plan to come out shortly for Senator Kennedy for President. I have a feeling, judging from the mail which comes in each day, that there is a greater and greater demand for Adlai Stevenson—the feeling being that we need a more mature man with more knowledge of the world in the next four years.

I wonder if you would not consider waiting until the Convention to find out what Stevenson's chances are before making your decision.

I know this is perhaps difficult for you to do but I thought I might suggest it since it seems to me that a Stevenson-Kennedy ticket is probably the strongest ticket we can have in the fight against Nixon, or, if the situation should change in the Republican Party, against Rockefeller.[25]

Mrs. Roosevelt was becoming more involved in the draft-Stevenson movement than she had intended. The dangerous state of the world after the collapse of the summit conference moved her to do so, but an equally powerful motivation was the apprehension with which she viewed Kennedy's winning the nomination. That feeling came out on Memorial Day in a conversation with Rep. Richard Bolling, an outstanding House liberal and Kennedy supporter. He came to Hyde Park to speak in the rose garden. She knew the sins of the father should not be visited on the sons, she explained apologetically to Bolling, but she had to admit she was strongly affected by her feeling about Joe Kennedy. Just as she found it difficult to forgive the son for his equivocation on McCarthyism, so she had not forgiven the father for his prewar defeatism. She recalled how the ambassador had come to Hyde Park and had angered her husband with his defeatist talk about the overwhelming German air force. FDR had called her, and his tone was glacial as he told her to take Ambassador Kennedy and feed him lunch at her cottage and then see him to the train. She had not known what was up until Ambassador Kennedy began to talk with her. Then she had understood FDR's fury.[26]

Yet a few days later a Stevenson breakthrough still seemed so unlikely that she decided not to go to the convention in Los Angeles. "If there is a chance that Adlai might be nominated," she wrote Mary Lasker, who was pressing her to come, "and that I could help on that, I will certainly come at once." An additional factor in her reluctance to go to Los Angeles was a desire not to be ranged against her sons, who were all going to Los Angeles to work for Kennedy. Perhaps she sensed the inconsistency in a position that, since 1945, had urged the younger generation to take over but was so strongly opposed to a representative of that generation.[27]

Anna Rosenberg refused to accept Mrs. Roosevelt's decision not to go to Los Angeles as final:

Today Anna Rosenberg called me & reasoned with me! She said I couldn't interfere with the boys if I didn't come till Wednesday. Paul Butler wanted me to speak towards the end if we had trouble on the platform & I could help on that, I cd leave Friday p.m. so this I will do.

I don't know whether Stevenson *or* Kennedy can be elected. S. &
K. can I believe but Paul Hoffman [former administrator of the Marshall Plan and a Republican] said to-night "the Democrats have a ge-
nius for defeating themselves"! He thinks it will be Nixon & Rockefeller.[28]

That was on June 7. The same day in a column datelined
Pittsfield, Massachusetts, she said flatly, "I am not coming out for
any candidate until the national convention. This is the stand I
have taken from the very beginning and it would take some very
compelling reasons to make me change this." The "compelling rea-
sons" became evident the next day when she picked up the *New
York Times*, whose front page carried a story that such long-time
Stevenson supporters as Schlesinger, Commager, Galbraith, and
Rauh were planning a formal endorsement of Kennedy. He would
have supported Stevenson, Commager was quoted as saying, but
Stevenson was not a candidate. This indication that the traditional
Stevenson bastions were crumbling came hard on the heels of
Michigan's endorsement of Kennedy. If the lines were not bol-
stered, Kennedy would have the nomination clinched even before
the Democrats assembled in Los Angeles. The draft movement
would have to be invigorated; Stevenson would have to indicate his
availability. The organizers of the draft felt that this was a job for
Mrs. Roosevelt, and she agreed to do it.

"I am about to exercise the prerogative of a woman and
change my mind," her statement issued on June 10 began:

Up to this time I have been firmly saying I would come out for no one
as the Democratic nominee for the presidency until the convention and
now I am going to join some of my friends in a plea to the convention
delegates to nominate as the standard bearer of the Democratic party
Adlai E. Stevenson. . . . So far he has been unwilling to become a candidate and I can well understand how a proud and sensitive man
would be unwilling to offer himself as a candidate for a third time
when he has been twice defeated.

Without any question the leading candidate for the nomination is
Senator Kennedy who has worked hard and I admire him for the way in
which he has worked and campaigned. Up to the time of the Summit

conference my political mail hardly mentioned any of the other candidates. I was either being berated for not coming out for Kennedy or I was being berated for fear I would come out for Kennedy. As a matter of fact, I had made up my mind that the time had come for a woman of my age to leave the active effort to nominate a particular candidate to the younger members of the party. Since the Summit conference, however, I have not had a letter in my political mail mentioning anybody but Governor Stevenson and in my many personal contacts more and more people talk of him. The reasons given are that the position in the world now requires maturity, it requires experience, and that the only man meeting these requirements since the failure of the summit is Adlai E. Stevenson. . . .

It was not going to be an easy campaign to win, her statement continued. "If Mr. Nixon is nominated on the Republican ticket you can look for a tough and unscrupulous campaign." The Democrats had to nominate "the strongest possible ticket and there is no question in my mind that this ticket is a Stevenson-Kennedy ticket." It was asking "a great deal of Mr. Kennedy" to be willing to take second place. But it would give him "the opportunity to grow and learn and he is young enough yet to look forward to many more years of public service."

Stevenson, who had been informed by Mary Lasker that Mrs. Roosevelt did not plan to go to the convention, heard about her statement while he was writing her that as a Democrat he considered her presence in Los Angeles most important, although he doubted very much that he would become involved out there. Her statement, he added, had left him shaken.[29]

The next day she followed up her call for a Stevenson-Kennedy ticket with an announcement that she was asking Mr. Stevenson "to clarify his position on being a candidate" in view of the declaration by Schlesinger, Commager, and Rauh that they were coming out for Kennedy because of Stevenson's nonavailability. His reply and Mrs. Roosevelt's reaction to it were issued in the form of a release by the draft-Stevenson office in Washington. He had taken no part in presidential politics during the past three years, Stevenson noted. He would not engage in any stop movement against any candidate.

He would not lift a finger for the nomination. But his letter ended, "I think I have made it clear in my public life, however, that I will serve my country and my party whenever called upon."

That was enough for Mrs. Roosevelt's purposes. "From this statement I think you will find it clear that Mr. Stevenson is a candidate," she said.[30] Reporters called Stevenson at Libertyville, Illinois, and read him Mrs. Roosevelt's interpretation of his statement. Was he a candidate? they wanted to know. "My message to Mrs. Roosevelt speaks for itself. I reiterated the position I have taken for several years that I will not seek the nomination for President at the Democratic convention. Therefore, I am not a candidate."

When the reporter for the *New York Times* read this statement back to Stevenson for confirmation, the governor murmured as though to himself: "Oh, dear, I suppose this will get me into it with Eleanor, won't it?" She would stand on her statement, Mrs. Roosevelt said when apprised of Stevenson's renewed affirmation of noncandidacy. "That's how I interpret Mr. Stevenson's statement, regardless of how anyone else—including Mr. Stevenson himself—may interpret it." [31]

Privately, Stevenson wrote her that he had not meant to appear ungracious in declaring he was not a candidate but he could not say anything else and remain true to his position of the previous three and a half years. The confusion arose because there was a difference between seeking and availability if drafted.[32]

But the veteran analyst Arthur Krock, as astute an observer as any of the ambiguous ways of politicians, wrote that Mrs. Roosevelt was right in her classification of Stevenson as "a candidate." Krock cited *Webster's Dictionary*, which says that a "candidate is one who offers himself, or is put forward by others . . ." for an office. Stevenson's statement, "I will not seek the nomination for President at the 1960 Democratic Convention—therefore I am not a candidate," added Krock, represented a challenge to "the highest authority in etymology as well as Mrs. Roosevelt, a combination against which mere intrepidity cannot possibly prevail." [33] Stevenson clipped the Krock column, underlined the sentence about "intrepidity," and attached a note:

> My dear Mrs. R—
> I surrender! !
> With love—
> Adlai

Reuther had spent the week end of the eleventh with Mrs. Roosevelt at Hyde Park:

Walter feels we are lost unless Stevenson & Kennedy agree before the convention that whichever one can't win will throw his votes to the other, which means if Kennedy starts a band wagon he'll win. Walter's argument is that unless they are agreed, they will elect the Republicans as Johnson will swing his disciplined votes & Symington's to Adlai & a Rep. victory. Petitions are being circulated now in every state for Adlai. Finally I've agreed to go out Monday a.m. July 11th & if I have to I'll stay till Friday.[34]

A great many of Mrs. Roosevelt's friends were Stevenson loyalists—Lehman, Benton, Finletter, Agnes Meyer, the *New York Post* people, Ruth Field, Mary Lasker, Anna Rosenberg, Robert Benjamin. Senators like A. S. Mike Monroney and Eugene McCarthy were in the developing Stevenson drive. Some, like Mrs. Roosevelt, favored Kennedy in the event Stevenson could not make it; some, like Mrs. Lasker and Mrs. Rosenberg, had Johnson as their fallback candidate.

Overnight, as in 1956, she became a pivotal figure in the Stevenson camp. She wrote Governor Edmund Brown of California, "I know that in California there is a good deal of support for Governor Stevenson and therefore I thought you might like to see what I had written." "Dear Governor DiSalle," she wrote the Ohio executive,

I know that your state is bound in the first ballot for Jack Kennedy but if by chance he is not nominated on the first few ballots I hope that you may decide to join some of the rest of us who believe that Stevenson is our best nominee, and hope for a Stevenson-Kennedy ticket.[35]

Key questions of convention strategy were submitted to her— whether Stevenson's name should be presented before the first ballot at the convention. "Dear Agnes," she wrote Mrs. Eugene Meyer:

In thinking over my conversation with you and Mike Monroney, I think it would be better if Adlai's name was not put before the Convention until it is clear that the votes are beginning to change. I did not realize that the galleries would be so controlled, as the Senator told me last night, by Mr. Butler's having carefully issued tickets to the big subscribers. This will certainly make a complication and it is better that the first few ballots should go by. There is, of course, a chance that Kennedy will be nominated, but if that is a really good chance it is going to happen in any case, I think, and it would be a mistake to put Stevenson's name in nomination and then have a very poor showing even from those who are not delegates, and as this is going to be so carefully controlled we had better not take any chances. This is going to be a convention where one is going to have to work by ear all the way through and I hope that wiser heads than mine will be directing it! [36]

As the convention neared, Mrs. Roosevelt spoke at several local Stevenson rallies. "We do talk to ourselves I fear," she commented on one such meeting, "but perhaps some wobblers come!" She grasped at straws. Joe Alsop came to see her at Hyde Park, "which made me wonder if Adlai had more of a chance than I thought." [37]

The Johnson people were trying frantically to stop the Kennedy band wagon:

We all listened to Truman's press conference in which he charged the convention was rigged for Kennedy & resigned as a delegate. I got a feeling he wouldn't mind having it rigged for Lyndon Johnson & he listed 10 possible candidates & never mentioned Adlai! Yesterday Kennedy answered in a press conference. He did very well. Firm about not giving up but most courteous to Pres. T. I have a feeling he did himself good but H.S.T. did himself harm. [38]

The night before she flew out to the convention, accompanied by David Gurewitsch, she wrote her young friend Gus Ranis:

I doubt very much whether I can do anything and I am not too hopeful of Stevenson's nomination, but certainly we will not give up, and we will try hard to persuade Mr. Kennedy that his future will be benefited if he will run with Stevenson and run later in first place himself. [39]

She arrived in Los Angeles on a Sunday—"swooped" was the way one columnist described her descent upon the convention city —made her first speech for Stevenson within an hour after leaving the plane, attended the party dinner where she was cheered lustily, and then prepared for a Monday press conference during which her associates hoped she might be able to repeat her devastating 1956 performance when she had stopped the Harriman bandwagon dead in its tracks. But circumstances were considerably different. Kennedy—not Stevenson—was the front runner and, in fact, was almost sure of first-ballot nomination. The politicians did not want a two-time loser, and Stevenson himself was a reluctant candidate, whose emissaries, according to Franklin Jr., were bringing word to the Kennedy people that he was embarrassed by the whole movement in his behalf, but that he could not let down his most devoted followers.

Stevenson escorted Mrs. Roosevelt to her press conference. "For an articulate man, Stevenson seemed embarrassed in introducing her," commented N. R. Howard, contributing editor to the *Cleveland Plain Dealer*. He spoke of her as "Ambassador to the world. . . . I saw people in London take off their hats as she rode by . . . ," and ended, almost precipitately, "Sorry I cannot remain, another engagement takes me instantly away."

She arose and embraced the crowd of reporters in the smile that suggested there was no other place she would rather be. At that smile, wrote Howard, "the applause became a roar of welcome."

"Now, the first question," she began. Three about Kennedy were immediately shouted at her, "and she set forth to plunge the tomahawk which for so many years she has wielded so prettily." She admired and respected Kennedy. She had said all along the perfect Democratic ticket for a great Democratic year would be Stevenson and Kennedy. It would combine age and youth, wisdom and heroism. But—as a candidate for president, well, she was doubtful Kennedy could command Negro support, and without the Negro vote could the Democrats win? The doubts really troubled her.

Then she answered the question about the impact of the Catholic issue on Kennedy's candidacy. So far it had not worked to Kennedy's disadvantage, she began in an allusion to the strong organizational support that had rallied to him just because of his Catholicism. But she could not say what would happen when the opposition, with its well-known ruthlessness, began to exploit it in the rural areas and in the South. "Just six sentences," commented columnist Howard, "spoken almost like a grandmother, and Senator Kennedy had been hatcheted twice."

She was asked about her Kennedy-supporting sons. Her answer, wrote Howard, suggested "the plight of a mother who knows best but who like all mothers must sigh and sit back at the idiocies of youth." She had asked James and Franklin Jr., "Isn't this really too much of a jump even for a brilliant young man like John Kennedy?" They had refused to argue with her, she went on, although she was unable, however, to suppress a flash of pride over Franklin's foray into West Virginia. "He did a very good job for Senator Kennedy there."

"President Truman? I am sorry Mr. Truman isn't here. A Democratic convention each four years is a religious thing and he should be at it. . . ."

After she had exhausted the reporters' questions, she thanked them, took off the heavy spectacles that contained her hearing aid, shook some hands and left. "Eleanor Roosevelt, 75," wrote Howard, who as a "kid reporter" had covered Franklin and Eleanor Roosevelt on their arrival in Cleveland in the 1920 campaign, "might not see another Democratic convention. . . . She was a tall pillar of some quality no one else in our time has produced. . . ." [40]

The Stevenson movement had few delegates but it put on a great show. Delegates were inundated with telegrams. There were wild pro-Stevenson demonstrations in the streets outside the convention hall and pandemonium within when Stevenson entered. Eugene McCarthy made a memorable speech placing Stevenson in nomination. The Kennedy camp was nervous. Reuther came to Mrs. Roosevelt and said if Stevenson came out for Kennedy it would cinch his appointment as secretary of state and keep Johnson from slipping in. He made a plausible case, she told him, but it was up to Stevenson, not her. She would continue to fight until Stevenson himself asked her to desist. Reuther went to Stevenson, as she had urged him to do, but she heard nothing further from him, from which she concluded that he had not persuaded Stevenson to withdraw.[41]

The night before the balloting she went to eleven state caucuses, ending up at the makeshift Stevenson headquarters, where a rip-snorting, enthusiastic rally led by Bill Benton was under way. "There was Eleanor Roosevelt, fine, precise, hard-worked like ivory," reported Norman Mailer. "Her voice was almost attractive as she explained in the firm, sad tones of the first lady in this small town why she could not admit Mr. Kennedy, who was no doubt a gentleman, into her political house." The Stevenson candidacy alone was stirring delegates' emotions, but demonstrations were not indicative of the delegate count. The smoothly functioning Kennedy organization had the nomination locked up. She was as popular and beloved as ever. When she came into the convention hall, all heads turned, people stood up and there was an ovation. She quickly took her seat and began fiddling with her purse. David nudged her. "It's for you. You have to get up." Under protest she did, but sat down quickly. It was rude to interrupt the speaker on the platform, she said, and later wrote him an apology.[42]

The steam roller could not be stopped. Unlike 1956, this time her prestige and authority, the reverence in which the party held her, did not change votes. When Nannine Joseph congratulated her on her convention performance, she commented, "Didn't do much good, did it?" As soon as Kennedy scored his first-ballot victory, she decided there was nothing more for her to do in Los Angeles. She called her old friend Tiny (Mrs. Hershey Martin), with whom she had left her bags, and asked her to bring them out to the airport. She was cross and resentful. David Lilienthal thought she had left the convention hall "almost in tears." Rank-and-file Democratic sentiment, she felt, had not been accurately reflected by the delegates. In the New York caucus Lehman and Finletter were able to muster only 4.5 votes for Stevenson. She was sure that a much larger proportion of New York Democrats preferred him, but De Sapio had held the other delegates "captive." But there was more to her discontent than that. She was exasperated with Stevenson's indecisiveness in neither telling her to stop nor ever saying clearly to go ahead. She had not wished to be in opposition to her sons. She was also upset with herself. Perhaps in her distrust of Kennedy she had pushed Adlai into a position he did not wish to occupy and hurt his chances of becoming secretary of state. Moreover, just as she had observed that Truman had done himself harm with his press conference, so she knew that she had weakened her influence by her Los Angeles performance, and she cared about her influence.[43]

Abba Schwartz, learning of her hasty departure, got word to Kennedy and, sensing her angry mood, urged him to call her quickly. When she reached the airport, the manager was waiting. There was an urgent call for her from Senator Kennedy. She refused to take it. But her plane was not scheduled to leave for an hour, Kennedy persisted, and finally she relented. She went to the phone. He did not have to bother about her, she told him. He had more important matters to worry about. They did not have to talk together. Any messages he wanted to get to her, he could send through Franklin and she the same with him.[44]

If the draft movement did embarrass Stevenson, he gave no sign of it in the affectionate letter he sent her from Ruth Field's place in Maine after the convention. He spoke gratefully of the outpouring of loyalty and love that had manifested itself in Los Angeles and even referred to it as his "finest hour." He had gone to Hyannis Port, he reported, for a long and often interrupted talk with Kennedy, who asked him to campaign for him and asked his advice on various organizational problems, but there was little discussion of issues. Kennedy had said nothing about the State Department, and neither had he.[45]

Some of Stevenson's most ardent backers had not been happy with his response to the draft movement. "Herbert [Lehman] was fighting for Stevenson at a time when Stevenson was not fighting for himself," Mrs. Lehman observed. "Stevenson wanted it in 1960, but I don't think he enjoyed a fight. My husband always felt it was hard for Stevenson to make up his mind." Mrs. Roosevelt shared some of Governor Lehman's feeling that a lack of decisiveness had been behind Stevenson's ambiguous performance before and at Los

Angeles—holding back personally, yet permitting friends like herself and Lehman to carry the ball. She was not overjoyed when she later heard that he had not wanted the draft movement, but could not tell Mrs. Roosevelt to desist.[46]

She may have been disappointed with Adlai but she declined to join Herbert Lehman as honorary chairman of Kennedy's committee in New York until she had a chance to talk with Kennedy and ascertain how closely he intended to work with Stevenson and Bowles, especially in the foreign-affairs field. "Dear Adlai," she advised him on receiving his letter:

I'm seeing Kennedy on Tuesday & I hope he'll not talk only about getting the vote in Nov. but also about what he hopes to achieve if elected. He's got a hard fight here & in California & I wish people who meet him didn't feel he is such a cold & calculating person.[47]

Kennedy was elated when Mrs. Roosevelt agreed to receive him, and also apprehensive. "Will, you've got to go with me," he said to William Walton, the artist, who was his New York coordinator. Walton demurred, "This is just a meeting between you two." "It's the raft at Tilsit," Kennedy replied, referring to the meeting between the czar and Napoleon that resulted in the Treaty of Tilsit, "and I want an ally with me."

They went up to Hyde Park on a Sunday. On Saturday, John Roosevelt's daughter Sally had been killed falling off a horse and Kennedy offered to cancel the meeting, but she said to come ahead. Kennedy and Walton arrived at the cottage "thinking that she had a price for her support, and that it was the Secretaryship of State for Adlai Stevenson. Not at all. She quickly made a little speech saying that she thought all Presidents should be totally free to choose their own Cabinets, that no one should be committed in advance to any office of any kind. She said, 'And I believe that very sincerely.' "

Kennedy left Val-Kill "absolutely smitten by this woman," Walton reported. "She really wove her web around him . . . from then on she did everything for us she possibly could." [48]

She sent a lengthy report on the visit to some of Stevenson's closest friends and hers:

I had my talk with Senator Kennedy yesterday—an hour alone during lunch, and at the very end he called in Mr. (William) Walton for a few minutes before going over to address the Golden Ring Clubs. . . .

I did not ask the Senator for any definite promise as I felt that this would be almost impossible. But I told him that he needed the Stevenson votes in New York and California and that he had to carry these two states or he would be in trouble because he probably could not hold the Solid South. . . .

I gather that his understanding of the difficulties of the campaign that face him have matured him in a short time. He told me that he had phoned Adlai this past week and asked him to set up a small group to do research in the area of foreign policy. I told him that this was not enough, that he would have to give the people who were for Adlai the assurance that they were working together. All of us know that unless Adlai felt their philosophies were similar he would not accept the Secretary of State post. Therefore, I felt that he had to prove by working in the campaign and appearing on the same platforms, and perhaps by references and quotation, that there was close cooperation. Bringing both Chester Bowles and Adlai in whenever he could would mean that these were the men he was counting on for advice. He agreed and said he would try to do this. . . .

Now, I have no promises from the Senator, but I have the distinct feeling that he is planning on working closely with Adlai. I also had the feeling that here was a man who could learn. I liked him better than I ever had before because he seemed so little cocksure, and I think he has a mind that is open to new ideas.

I agreed that I would go on the citizens committee here as honorary chairman, and that I would do what I could here. Whether I would take any trips or become more involved would depend on whether or not I was happy with the way he progresses as a person in the campaign.

My final judgment now is that here is a man who wants to leave a record (perhaps for ambitious personal reasons as people say) but I rather think because he really is interested in helping the people of his own country and mankind in general. I will be surer of this as time goes on, but I think I am not mistaken in feeling that he would make a good President if elected.[49]

She sent a copy of this letter to Kennedy, saying it had gone to Mary Lasker and Ruth Field and that she had reported verbally to Agnes Meyer, Anna Rosenberg, and Robert Benjamin. She would hear from Franklin Jr. about Kennedy's feelings on his visit to Hyde

Park and if there was anything outside New York Kennedy wanted her to do. Meanwhile, she was speaking at a press conference of the New York Citizens Committee for Kennedy and for the citizens' committee in the Bronx which was headed by Robert Morgenthau. She advised Kennedy to call Anna Rosenberg. "She will be twice as anxious to work for you if she feels that you personally have contacted her and consider her help important."

Kennedy thanked her. He had talked with Anna Rosenberg as she had suggested. He had some thoughts for the campaign, which Franklin would be able to pass on to her. He looked forward to another meeting with her,

when we can discuss further some of the important issues. Again, let me assure you that I intend to work in close association with Adlai and Chester Bowles and I am delighted that you are willing to take an active part in the campaign. . . .[50]

Mrs. Roosevelt spoke for him and worked for him, always careful to note his stand on separation of church and state. She also sent him suggestions from time to time. It would be useful for one of his people to see Bernard Baruch. Kennedy sent Galbraith. After his first debate with Nixon she advised him of a few simple oratorical rules, the observance of which would give his audience a stronger sense of being included. She was so prejudiced against Nixon she did not trust her own reactions, but she thought the debates, "judging by this first one, are definitely an advantage to you." [51] Kennedy's statements on Cuba worried her:

I thought I understood you to say during the last debate that you did not intend to act unilaterally but with the other American states. Since this is not fully understood, I pass the letter along to you because I think it would be unwise for people to have the impression that you did expect separately to interfere in the internal affairs of Cuba.

She thought the campaign was going well.

I cannot, of course, ever feel safe till the last week is over because with Mr. Nixon I always have the feeling that he will pull some trick at the last minute. On the whole, however, things look pretty good. In the meantime, good luck! [52]

She became increasingly confident as the campaign progressed that he would make a good president:

As you know, I wanted Mr. Stevenson as our nominee but I have grown, as I watch Mr. Kennedy and talk with him, to have a great respect for his mind and ability and his truthfulness of purpose in wanting to be a good public servant. I don't think it is a choice of the least of two evils. I think we will have a good President in Mr. Kennedy who will take the advice of the best people around him and who will be honest with the people. To say he would not make mistakes would be silly. Anyone would make mistakes with the problems that lie ahead of us.[53]

Mrs. Roosevelt was unhappy, after Kennedy's victory, that he did not appoint Stevenson as secretary of state. His failure to do so, may have been a factor, as well as her aversion to Joe Kennedy, in her insistence on sitting with a few friends in the stand below the inaugural platform instead of coming to the presidential box, as he had invited her to do. He wanted her at his side, Kennedy had written. She preferred to sit where she could see better, she replied. So she came early and sat in the twenty-degree cold wrapped in a mink coat and an army blanket.

It was a sky-blue, frosty day with the new snow crisp on the boughs of trees and the ledges of the Capitol. The vast crowd of people, their breath filling the air with vapor, clung to each other for warmth and chafed their hands impatiently as the red-hatted cardinal intoned his blessings, the wispy-haired poet recited his prophecies, and the chief justice solemnly administered the oath of office. Then the youthful voice, blend of Irish lilt and Boston flatness, rang out: "Let the word go forth from this time and place, to friend and foe alike, that the torch has been passed to a new generation of Americans—born in this century, tempered by war, disciplined by a hard and bitter peace, proud of our ancient heritage." Her stooped shoulders straightened. She looked at her friends with pleasure in her eyes as she heard the sound of youth and fearlessness again filling the land. "Let us begin anew. . . . Let us never negotiate out of fear. But let us never fear to negotiate. . . . And so, my fellow Americans—ask not what your country can do for you— ask what you can do for your country."

She left the stands with the vivid phrases ringing in her ears and her heart sang with new hope for America and mankind.

On the eve of the inauguration she had spoken in her column of the qualities a strong and successful president must have—confidence in himself, buoyancy and optimism, joy in the meeting of responsibilities, and a mind "flexible enough to be willing to try new approaches. . . ." She left Washington feeling that perhaps this young man had the making of a strong president.[54]

XV. To the End, Courage

After Franklin Roosevelt's death, admirers as well as detractors had assumed—as she had herself—that Eleanor Roosevelt would gradually fade from public sight into "a private and inconspicuous existence." Yet of all of Roosevelt's associates, she had become more rather than less of a public eminence. Henry Morgenthau came to her upset because he had gone to the White House and had not been recognized. "Don't you know that if you are out of the limelight three days they will forget you?" she comforted him, adding, "they will forget me too." They did not. The leading woman in the Roosevelt administration, Frances Perkins, was given refuge in her final years at the Cornell School of Industrial Relations. Miss Perkins was never wholly reconciled to the contrast between herself, almost forgotten after President Roosevelt's death, and Mrs. Roosevelt, who had moved onto a world stage and was functioning as a world figure. Why Eleanor Roosevelt did not even have an intellectually tidy mind, she confided to her Cornell associates.[1]

Tidy mind or not, Eleanor Roosevelt had a right to feel, as she did, that she had made a success of her professional career and had done so on her own. Sixteen years after her husband's death she continued to be America's "Most Admired Woman," more popular than Jacqueline Kennedy, Queen Elizabeth, Mrs. Dwight Eisenhower, Clare Luce, and Mme. Chiang Kai-shek. Her professional income in 1961 totaled more than $100,000, of which lecture fees accounted for $33,500, her writing close to $60,000, her column $7,794, and Brandeis University paid her $6,500.[2]

"When you cease to make a contribution you begin to die," she wrote in her seventy-fifth year. "Therefore, I think it a necessity to be doing something which you feel is helpful in order to grow old gracefully and contentedly." [3] Occasionally she resurrected the image of herself contentedly sitting by the fire in lace cap and shawl. Her friends and children never took it seriously. Perhaps it was her way of indicating a readiness to retire to Hyde Park and a life of "dignified obscurity" rather than yielding to her critics or to the president on a point of principle. Or perhaps it was a reaction to a calendar that suddenly became overcrowded with things she did not wish to do, places she did not wish to be, away from the people of whom she was really fond. Sometimes, especially after she was seventy-five, she even reached the point of telling Maureen Corr to send off wires canceling everything. But in a few weeks the fat little engagement book filled up again.

"I suppose I should slow down," she acknowledged when children and friends remonstrated with her, but to reporters on her seventy-seventh birthday she said, "I think I have a good deal of my Uncle Theodore in me, because I could not, at any age, be content to take my place in a corner by the fireside and simply look on. Life was meant to be lived. Curiosity must be kept alive. The fatal thing is the rejection. One must never, for whatever reason, turn his back on life." [4]

At seventy-five Mrs. Roosevelt launched a new career as visiting lecturer at Brandeis University, declining, however, to be called "professor." She did not deserve the title, she said. She met her class faithfully. One week end she finished at Brandeis late in the evening. The airport was fogged in when she arrived there. She went to the railroad station only to find the sleeper would get her in too late to make a plane at Idlewild the next morning for the Midwest. So she took a coach and sat up the entire night all the way to New York. She was then seventy-six. When she was seventy-seven, Brandeis offered to send a car to the airport for her, but she refused. She did not want to be treated either as Mrs. Franklin D. Roosevelt or as an old woman, she said. Once as she set out she looked so weary that a worried Maureen called the office of Dr. Abram Sachar, the president. "She will kill me if she finds out I called, but please have someone meet her." They did. When she returned to New York, she marched straight into Maureen's office and told her, "Don't ever do that again." [5]

She still had a regular television show, now called "Prospects of Mankind," which was produced by Elinor (Mrs. Henry) Morgenthau's oldest son, Henry. She lent herself willingly to the stratagems of her agent, Thomas L. Stix, to get her a sponsored program and a wider audience. He found she was "a very difficult person to get a job for" because she was "controversial." Finally an advertising agency asked whether she would be willing to do a commercial for margarine. It was a chore for which she would be well paid, but Stix was hesitant. She would come in for a lot of criticism on the grounds that it was undignified, he cautioned her, but if it were successful she would no longer be "poison" to sponsors. She thought it over and the next day told him, "I'll do it. For that amount of money I can save 6,000 lives," thinking of the number of CARE packages the approximately $35,000 fee would purchase. She did the commercial, and the protests poured in. "The mail was evenly divided," she said. "One half was sad because I had damaged my reputation. The other half was happy because I had damaged my reputation." Tom Stix was right. Advertisers lost their fear of her. "In a few weeks Frank Sinatra asked her to appear on a 'spectacular.' There was no argument about the high price I named," wrote Stix.[6]

She continued to be an indefatigable writer, doing her brisk monthly question-and-answer page for *McCall's* and a variety of books and articles, many of them suggested by Nannine Joseph, who had succeeded George Bye as her literary agent after Elliott bowed out of the picture. *You Learn by Living*, a reflective distillation of her life experience, appeared in 1960. It originated during a Hyde Park drive in her tiny Fiat roadster the objective of which was to find a roadside stand from which to buy apples. She was at the wheel, Nannine beside her. "You have more energy than any person I have ever known," Miss Joseph said. "People always ask me where I get it," she replied. "Why don't you write it?" Miss Joseph urged, and Cass Canfield of Harper & Brothers, with whom she discussed it, immediately agreed. Miss Joseph got Elinore Denniston, who had written over two hundred books under other peoples' signatures, to help, and Mrs. Roosevelt found her a congenial collaborator. She still filed her column regularly, although now only three times a week, the number of papers taking it about forty.[7]

She had become pretty good at saying "No," she assured friends: requests that she wanted to get out of, if they related to articles she sent to Nannine Joseph; speeches to Colston Leigh; radio or television appearances to Thomas Stix. "Yes or no?" she wrote on the letter. They tried to save her from engagements they considered unimportant, but then, as often as not, her sense of duty would bother her, and she would call them to say a little apologetically that she wanted to make an exception.

Although over seventy-five, she retained a freshness of vision that was always on the lookout for excellence, a spirit of compassion that inevitably made her the ally of the victim, and an unspoiled goodness of heart that was especially responsive to integrity and courage. A Negro poet seeking a publisher suddenly discovered that he had Mrs. Roosevelt acting as his literary agent; a mimeographed petition reaching her through the mails on behalf of some Communists who had been jailed too long was returned with her signature; a vituperative racist received a courteous and reasoned reply in the hope of touching some chord of humanity in him. One day on her way to a charity meeting in Greenwich Village at her hairdresser François', a Negro youth carelessly backed a station wagon into her and knocked her down as she was crossing Eighth Street. She told him to leave quickly, before people gathered and he got into trouble, limped to François', and although in considerable pain, made her speech. Later David Gurewitsch taped up her leg, but despite torn ligaments, she insisted on going through with the rest of her engagements for the day, ending up at 10:00 P.M. at the Waldorf-Astoria, where she apologized to her audience for making her speech seated on a high pillow. "People saw that I was in pain and we raised more money," she later told David, who had not wanted her to go.

Anna Halsted, who was in Shiraz, Iran, with her husband and had seen a news item about her mother being knocked down, wrote

anxiously to David Gurewitsch. Mother was doing "far too much.
. . . If there was something specific about her health on which you
could base the essentiality of her cutting down on her activities,
then I think she will cooperate—particularly if she realizes that cutting down now will prolong her total years of activity—activity
which is so much needed in today's world."

Mrs. Roosevelt was now living in a house on East Seventy-
fourth Street. She had liked her small duplex on East Sixty-second,
with its garden and easy access to her AAUN office, but then the
landlord had demanded a large rent increase, so back she moved to
the Park Sheraton. Later, she and the David Gurewitsches were
able to locate the East Seventy-fourth Street house, which they divided and occupied together.

But "home" continued to be her cottage at Val-Kill. She enjoyed her drives through the countryside, with glimpses of the
Berkshires on one side and the Catskills on the other, and with the
farms fat and prosperous, a result, she felt, of New Deal programs.
She looked forward to the flowering of the dogwood beneath her
bedroom window and to the first June week end when the swim-
ming pool could be used and luncheon served on its fringes. When
she went off on a trip, it was to her cottage and her dogs that she
said good-by. "It is always a wrench to leave home and try to explain to wistful little Scotties that I am not deserting them for
good."

After Tommy's death she had taken over her part of the cottage, converting Tommy's living room into her workroom and the
two bedrooms into additional guest rooms. When the telephone
rang, she often answered herself, and then, remembering that it
might expose her to some wild petition, said, "Mrs. Roosevelt's secretary." She insisted, however, that she was the world's "most reluctant telephone user." She definitely disassociated herself from the
people for whom telephoning was a way of life. "When I have to take
a call, I say what needs to be said and hang up." Writing a letter was
a much more satisfactory form of communication, especially with
family and friends, she maintained. She was a faithful and tireless

correspondent when away from home and the first to telephone when she returned. She often lent the Val-Kill grounds, fronting down to the pond, for picnics to groups in which she was interested, provided them with refreshments, and, sitting on a log by the outdoor fireplace, answered questions. Filed away under the Wiltwyck School for troubled boys, a card read, "400 hot dogs, 200 rolls, 200 cup cakes, 50 quarts milk, 25 quarts ice cream, 100 comic books, 100 bars candy, potato salad, mustard." As she had helped her father serve the newsboys at Thanksgiving, so she was delighted to have John and her favorite niece Ellie and their children help her at these picnics. Afterward, everyone, grownups as well as young, fell silent and listened to her reading of Kipling's *Just So Stories*, especially the Wiltwyck boys' favorites—"How the Elephant Got His Trunk" and "The Butterfly that Stamped."

Once as she was greeting the boys one of them stopped in front of her and said: "Mrs. Roosevelt, do you remember me?"

"Yes," she answered, "I remember all of you. I have seen you at school and many of you were here last year. Of course, I remember you."

That did not satisfy the little boy. "Mrs. Roosevelt, what's my name?" he persisted. There were one hundred boys, she explained, and she could not possibly remember all their names. She was an old lady and her memory was not as good as it once was, she added.

The boy then told her his name. But he was so anxious to be identified by someone, Mrs. Roosevelt noted, that within five minutes he was back again: "Mrs. Roosevelt, what's my name?"

"To have a friend who knows you by name gives you a sense that you are not alone in the world," she commented. To the end of her life, her own "very miserable childhood," her wanting to be loved, especially by her father, gave her a profound sense of kinship with all lonely, deprived, and excluded youngsters. Whether they were the Wiltwyck boys or the children about whom the Citizens Committee for Children was concerned, the youths in the Encampment for Citizenship or the students of the Hudson Shore Labor

School, the girls at the Women's House of Detention or those in the Junior League, young people were always a special object of her solicitude.

Her lack of pretense remained a continuing source of wonderment to those around her. She entertained two raw-boned young Mormon "elders" who had knocked at her door as readily as she did the queen of Nepal, who listened one night at Hyde Park, her eyes widening in amazement, as Mrs. Roosevelt and her son John lustily debated the merits of the right-to-work laws.

She campaigned on street corners and in living rooms and spoke to audiences of fifteen with the same intensity as to those of 1500. "She never asked how many people were going to be present," said Richard Brown, director of the Committee of Democratic Voters. "Herbert Lehman might." She was as solicitous of her neighbors and friends in Hyde Park as of the diplomats and statesmen who thronged the United Nations, as content to work with her neighbor Dorothy Bourne on a project to improve the health of the children of Dutchess County as with Maurice Pate of UNICEF to improve the health of the children of the world. She appeared before the New York City Planning Commission to argue against tampering with Washington Square and before the Senate Foreign Relations Committee to warn against tampering with the UN Charter. "She did everything because it was worth doing," said Adlai Stevenson. "She did nothing because it would help to enhance her own role. Of that she seemed simply to be unconscious."

Why do you bother with the small groups? she was sometimes asked. "But nobody else will go," she replied. "It's important they should know someone cares."

Occasionally "Tubby" Curnan came down from Hyde Park to chauffeur Mrs. Roosevelt around town in the small Jaguar she had acquired from Franklin Jr. At other times, especially when she was going to the theater or the airport, she rented a limousine driven by Roosevelt Zanders, the head of an auto rental agency. Sometimes she went by subway, but mostly in her final years she used taxis. Once she told a cabbie with sixty cents on his meter to wait for her while she stopped for a minute to shop. But when she came out, he was gone. "I cheated that driver out of sixty cents, plus a tip, and I feel guilty," she advertised in her column.

So, I would be grateful if, on the chance that particular driver sees this item of confession, he would send me a note telling me where I could reimburse him.

Gentlemen, seeing her on the curb looking for a taxi, would stop and offer to turn over theirs. If she accepted, she insisted they both make use of it.

She was a little late with her Christmas shopping, she confessed to a reporter when she was seventy-seven. "I have a long list —such a long list." She smiled. "I have 20 grandchildren now, and 13 great-grandchildren." [8] A large black loose-leaf Christmas book listed what she had given people from 1935 on. The last entries were in a wavering hand. She sent royalty maple sugar, her newspaper friends cheeses, her ex-daughters-in-law perfume. She sent out innumerable checks.

Each friend, especially those about whom she really cared, answered some deep need in her, but she was the one who gave the most. During her White House years she made a special Christmas for the friends who were almost family—Tommy, Hick, Earl, and a few others. For each of them she filled a stocking to open Christmas morning, got together beforehand for a little dinner or celebration, and then called them on Christmas Day. After her White House years she tried to combine family and friends into one sparkling Christmas celebration at Hyde Park.

She loved to celebrate the birthdays, wedding anniversaries, and other special occasions of those close to her. She listed these anniversaries in a little black birthday book. Until Grace (Mrs. Louis) Howe's death in 1955, she always sent her flowers on Louis's birthday. No relationship was ever terminated because of her neglect or thoughtlessness. If the other person was forgetful, she was careful, in reminding him, not to make him feel guilty. She carried on and remembered where others had long left off. She arranged her travel itineraries so that during the year she saw not only the children and grandchildren, who were scattered throughout the country, but Tiny (Mrs. Hershey) Martin in California, Esther Lape in Westbrook, her old newspaper friends in Washington, and June Rhodes and Earl Miller in Florida.

The other person's interests took precedence over her own. She asked a friend what play she would like to see on her birthday. *How to Succeed in Business without Really Trying* was the answer. Mrs. Roosevelt promised to get the tickets. Later the friend learned that Mrs. Roosevelt had already seen that play and suggested they go to something else. Knowing her friend wanted to see *How to Succeed . . .* , Mrs. Roosevelt would not countenance any change in plans, but to make her feel less uncomfortable, said, "I have forgotten it anyway, so it will be like a new play."

But if she enjoyed celebrating her friends' birthdays, she discouraged them from making a fuss about her own. One day would be ruled out for a party because she could not have the people she wanted, another because there would be people present she did not want. In the face of outraged protests, she finally settled on her seventy-seventh birthday for a quiet dinner with the Gurewitsches, a luncheon with her children, an exchange of toasts with the Lashes, and some little ceremony with Maureen and Hick.

To the very end she entertained extensively. Old friends came to dinner regularly—Harry Hooker, soft-spoken Belle (Mrs. Kermit) Roosevelt, Dutchess County neighbors like Mrs. Olin Dows, Mrs. Gerald Morgan, and Laura Delano.

Most of the "river" people admired her, even if a little resignedly, when it came to her public activities. "Once Eleanor invited Helen [Mrs. Theodore Douglas Robinson] and myself over to Val-Kill for lunch," recalled Mrs. Gerald Morgan, who, as Mary Newbold, had once canoed on the Hudson with Franklin. "We thought it would be a nice small intimate party and give us a chance to talk with Eleanor. Before we knew it, a delegation of two hundred ladies arrived—colored. That was the way it usually was in the last years." But Mrs. Morgan also remembered "a very pleasant evening. My younger boy was interested in the Clarion Concert Society and we asked her to dine and hear about it. It was like old times. We had no great discussion about the Peace Corps or anything like that. We discussed old friends. Helen Robinson was there, and she was most kind about the concerts, taking subscriptions." 9

One river lady was unreconciled to Eleanor Roosevelt, the social reformer. Mrs. John Henry Livingston, who occupied Clermont, considered herself the "Lady of the Manor," and even her neighbors called her "Lady Alice." Once she spotted Mrs. Roosevelt picnicking with some friends on her grounds. They were asked to leave. "Why, I was wiped off the face of the earth," Mrs. Roosevelt later said in talking about the incident.10

A former Dutchess County neighbor whom Mrs. Roosevelt saw frequently was Geraldine (Mrs. Lewis) Thompson. One of the Morgan sisters of Staatsburgh, she was now a New Jersey Republican of such determination that even though she was in her eighties, when she decided Mrs. Roosevelt had to help her on some welfare or prison reform project, it was difficult to say no. Mrs. Roosevelt rarely turned her down and was happy to go to a dinner in her honor given by the New Jersey Board of Control of Social Institutions. In the midst of the toastmaster's introductory remarks, his voice began to thicken, and he was led away from the table, suffering, it was later learned, from a stroke. There was a great buzz at the tables. Mrs. Roosevelt calmly took charge of the proceedings and went on to introduce Roger Baldwin, "who will tell us of Mrs. Thompson's lifelong interest in birds." 11

Old friends like Baruch dropped in, as did new friends like Charles Purcell, a young actor who never quite made it on Broadway but who made her laugh; Allard Lowenstein, a crusading young liberal whose projects she assisted; the Reverend William Turner Levy, whose talk about religion and poetry interested her as did his fervent solicitude for his mother; and Ray West, a lonely Arkansas boy trying to make good in the big city.

She was indulgent toward her young friends, more so, often, than toward her own children. Al Lowenstein was frequently late and sometimes turned up with acquaintances whom he had not asked whether he could bring. She had a double standard, Maureen gently complained—stern in these matters with her children, easy-going with people like Al. "By now, Maureen," she said, twinkling, "you ought to know me well enough to know that I like young men." [12]

Associates of New Deal days dined with her—David Lilienthal, Anna Hoffman, William Benton, Chester Bowles, Frank Graham, Aubrey Williams—as well as the younger generation of reform politicians. Father Ford, "the priest maverick" and premature ecumenicist, whose courage and sparkle she admired, came as did vivid Nila Magidoff and Justine Polier, a woman of luminous intelligence, business tycoons like C. R. Smith and Lansdell Christie, and artistic people like Harry Belafonte and Leonard Bernstein. Once or twice a year she had lunch for "the cousins," children of her Hall aunts and uncle (those on her mother's side).

Her relationships to people about whom she cared followed a pattern. At first there was a kind of rosy glow as she saw them as she wanted them to be, but as time went on, she knew them for what they really were. When Maureen remarked that someone who had asked to see her did not want anything, she replied, "Everybody wants something." She did not hold it against them. That was her vocation—to be helpful. "What other single human being," Adlai Stevenson said later, "has touched and transformed the existence of so many others? What better measure is there of the impact of anyone's life?" [13]

There was a special place for ailing Henry Morgenthau, whom she often visited at his Fishkill farm, and for his children. On the anniversary of Elinor Morgenthau's death she sent roses to Morgenthau's eldest son Henry, and one of her last political acts was to use her influence with the reform movement on behalf of the gubernatorial candidacy of Robert Morgenthau. She also sent him messages from her sickbed on how to "humanize" his campaign as well as a $500 contribution.

She had a vivid sense of American history and the Roosevelt contribution to it and a strong feeling for tradition which she enjoyed passing on to her grandchildren. At her last Thanksgiving dinner, before Franklin Jr. and John began their competition as to who could carve the two turkeys as elegantly as their father, she read FDR's 1933 Thanksgiving Day proclamation. Memorial Day, 1961, when the Roosevelt Home Club conducted its annual ceremony in the rose garden, she arranged for Mayor Robert Wagner to speak, entertained him, and had her cottage bursting at the seam with New Dealers, family, and friends.

On New Year's Eve, 1961, at midnight, as on every preceding New Year's Eve, she proposed a toast "to the United States of America" as the president had done in the White House, and followed it with a toast "to absent family and friends." And then the company toasted her.

She was in gay spirits, that last New Year's Day, taking a long walk through the snow with Trude and Maureen out to the Harritys'. On the way back she stopped to watch John teach his new retriever his duties. At dinner there was much banter and uproarious Roosevelt laughter.

On July 4, there was the usual picnic lunch at the pool outside the stone cottage that she, Nancy Cook, and Marion Dickerman had built in 1925 and that now was occupied by the John Roosevelts. Afterward, she read aloud the Declaration of Independence and the Bill of Rights. On that last July 4 before she died, beside sundry children belonging to Franklin and John and to her niece Ellie, the company that grouped itself around her included the Soviet cultural attaché and his young wife and ninety-two-year-old Uncle David. When Mrs. Roosevelt had finished her reading, noting for the benefit of the younger ones the signatories who were among their ancestors, Uncle David's voice was heard accusing her of "trying to indoctrinate" her Russian guests.

"You should have put fingers in your ears," he said, turning to the somewhat embarrassed Soviet couple.

"No, no, David," she interrupted. "I was only trying to indoctrinate my grandchildren." [14]

David Gray stayed with her most of the summer. He was a man of elegance, wit, and good manners, who still wore country tweeds made for him before World War I. He was sharp-tongued and a favorite of the old Hudson River families. "I am her wicked uncle," he had introduced himself to Khrushchev during his visit to

Hyde Park. At his age he had a right to say what he thought, Mrs. Roosevelt maintained, but she, too, gasped at one of Uncle David's sallies during a Soviet medical group's visit to Hyde Park. The group's leader had just finished a little speech to "dear Mrs. Roosevelt" about how much they appreciated her hospitality and how highly regarded she was by the Soviet people, when suddenly Uncle David's voice was heard: "And when you get ready to drop that atom bomb on us, I hope you will think of dear Mrs. Roosevelt." There was a moment of shocked silence. Fortunately the Russians understood that they were being teased.[15]

She was full of stories in her final years about her childhood in New York City. She loved telling them when there were grandchildren around. She had run into a contemporary of her Aunt Maude's, she said, who blamed all of Eleanor's unorthodoxies on the fact that she had been brought up by her young aunts, Maude and Pussie. At the turn of the century those two were regarded as wild: they had even driven in hansom cabs alone, without a maid. When her grandfather, the first Theodore Roosevelt, built his house at Fifty-seventh Street, she said, beginning another story, Freddy Weekes, who lived on Washington Square, was invited to the housewarming. That is an overnight trip, his mother warned him. When he said he planned to be back the same night, she refused to believe him. She remembered Mrs. Weekes as a gentle, charming old lady, who, she added, "once danced with Lafayette."

When Mrs. Roosevelt regaled the company with these recollections, young eyes gleamed as all American history seemed to materialize in the person of their grandmother.

It was especially pleasurable for her when her own grandchildren gave signs of sharing her interests and values. One of her stories was of how she had been a volunteer for the Consumers League when she was eighteen and, at a rally in Union Square, had heard the labor song "Joe Hill" for the first time. Nothing delighted her more than the lively and intelligent way in which Nina, John's child, entered into their trip together to Israel and Iran in 1959, or Nina's brother Haven's spending a year teaching in the Tanganyika bush, or Anna's son Curtis's involvement in the New York reform movement, or Franklin III's quiet assistance to the freedom movement in the South, or her grandson Johnny Boettiger's heading up the college clubs for the AAUN.

Her grandchildren paid her the most satisfying compliment of all—wanting to learn from her. Her grandson Frank counted her his most important teacher in trying to find a meaningful purpose in his life. He sent her a review he had written for his own edification of William F. Buckley's *Up from Liberalism*. She liked it very much and would try, if he wished, to get it published.

I have only one comment on what you say about Social Security on page four. You seem to think that everyone can save money if they have the character to do it. As a matter of fact, there are innumerable people who have a wide choice between saving and giving their children the best possible opportunities. The decision is usually in favor of the children. Social Security has meant they could obtain insurance for future life at a much lower rate than they could possibly get it in any other way and stand by the employers.[16]

Advanced in her views about the acceptance of social responsibility, she was curiously strait-laced in her views about social behavior. In Iran, where she and Nina visited Anna and Jim Halsted, the U.S. ambassador arranged some parties for Nina with young people in the diplomatic colony.

"Grand'mère says I have to be in at twelve," Nina complained to her aunt. "Suppose I can't get home by twelve?"

"Oh, she will be asleep," Anna assured her, to which Nina replied that her grandmother had told her to come in and kiss her good night when she got home. The young lady got in at 2:00 A.M., and, of course, her grandmother, who was sleeping, woke up.

"But Nina, it's two o'clock," she chided.

The next morning Anna went to her mother. "Mummy, dear. Please realize times have changed. . . . She shouldn't be under restrictions and have to check in with you. She is with people selected by the Ambassador. Nothing will happen to her."

Mrs. Roosevelt was visibly annoyed. "Oh, very well. If that's the way it has to be, I'll tell her." [17]

If there was sickness or a family crisis, she was the one the children turned to for counsel and comfort. In their many divorces and marriages, the "moment of truth" with their mother was the one they found hardest to face. By her middle seventies, however, she had survived so many family crises and witnessed so much history that nothing surprised her any longer. Even what appeared to be disaster, she took with philosophical detachment.

At dinner in 1959, David Lilienthal, as he helped her serve the plates that she filled, mentioned how deeply impressed he had been by her article in *Harper's* on "Where Do I Get My Energy?," particularly by the part "about not getting too self-absorbed. She looked at me in the most earnest way and said: 'And this becomes more important as one gets older. Inevitably there are aches and pains, more and more; and if you pay much attention to them, the first thing you know you're an invalid.' " [18]

These "aches and pains" were coming with increasing frequency. On Adlai Stevenson's recommendation, Kennedy appointed her a member of the U.S. delegation to the Special Session of the General Assembly that convened in March, 1961. She paid a visit to the Human Rights Commission. There was applause as she entered the chamber, accompanying the U.S. delegate Mrs. Ronald Tree, the granddaughter of Endicott Peabody, FDR's old rector at Groton. The chairman, Chandra S. Jha of India, asked her to say a few words. She hoped to see the day when the principles enunciated in the Declaration would be accepted as law, she said. "Then we will have made real steps forward in human rights." [19]

There was nothing to do, Stevenson had assured her, except attend the plenaries. Yet illness kept her from fulfilling even that limited role to her own satisfaction. She was not a good assistant, she apologized.

To all intents and purposes I am marooned at Hyde Park till Wednesday afternoon with the 'flu. Actually, I don't have the 'flu but phlebitis! I didn't want to talk about it and thought the 'flu a good excuse.

If there is a delegation meeting Tuesday or Friday, I will try to come but I think I should probably be at home with my two old legs in the air!

To the president she wrote, as the session drew to an end, "I don't think I have been very useful but I think I accomplished what Adlai wanted in just appearing at the UN." [20]

Although her strength had begun to ebb, she took on a variety of assignments for President Kennedy. She served on the "Tractors for Freedom" Committee after the failure of the Bay of Pigs invasion (an enterprise to which she euphemistically referred as "this unfortunate raid"). She accepted a place on the Advisory Council of the Peace Corps. Of Kennedy's first 240 appointments, only nine were women, so in March she called at the White House to turn over to him a three-page list of women she considered eligible for high positions in his administration. At its head was Dr. Leona Baumgartner, whom he subsequently appointed as deputy chief of the AID. Law, custom, and the forgetfulness of men, Mrs. Roosevelt told members of the Lucy Stone League, were keeping women from equal opportunities in government and other jobs. She abandoned her forty-year opposition to the Equal Rights Amendment. "Many of us opposed the amendment because we felt it would do away with protection in the labor field. Now with unionization, there is no reason why you shouldn't have it if you want it." Having reminded the president that women, too, were qualified for top government jobs, she agreed to preside over the Commission on the Status of Women that he appointed at the end of 1961 and faithfully chaired its meetings until illness made attendance impossible. "You are very much in our thoughts today," the members of the commission wrote her as they realized no ordinary illness was keeping her away.[21]

She followed avidly all the news from Washington brought to her by her sons Franklin and James and by Abba Schwartz, whose efforts to become assistant secretary of state for immigration and refugee affairs she backed. "I have tried not to speak for anyone in connection with positions," she wrote the president in February, 1961, "but . . ."[22]

Since Kennedy encouraged her to stay in touch with him, there were letters of advice. He should jog the Veterans Administration, she suggested. He did, and asked her never to hesitate to call such matters to his personal attention. A month later she was writing him that she feared because of his preoccupation with Cuba he might not be paying much attention to legislation affecting the migratory farm worker. Migrants were receiving short shrift from the House Agricultural Committee, he replied, but he was in close touch with the situation.[23]

She hoped he would forgive her presumption, she began a long letter to him on the subject of the president as educator,

but I am concerned because I feel that there is not as yet established a real feeling among the people that you are consulting them and that they must react and carry on a dialogue with you on such subjects as you choose to bring before them.

I listened during a rather long drive which I took, to your last press conference and decided that it did not take the place of fireside chats. The questions asked were asked by men and women of good background and were much too sophisticated for the average person to understand. I think the people are anxious to have you talk to them on one question at a time and explain it fully and ask for their reactions and understand that their answers will be analyzed and considered.

I wish you could get someone like my old teacher (probably her daughter) to help you deepen and strengthen your voice on radio and TV. It would give you more warmth and personality in your voice. It can be learned, and I think it would make a tremendous difference. . . .

The problem with his voice was an old one, the president answered. He had tried voice instruction during the campaign and would try again. "It is difficult to change nature, but I will attempt to nudge it." [24]

She went to the White House as a member of a delegation that also included Benjamin V. Cohen, Norman Cousins, and Clark Eichelberger, to urge that the United States, instead of involving itself in the fighting in Vietnam as the Taylor-Rostow Report had recommended, take the question to the United Nations. The White House referred the delegation to the State Department. There the delegates were told that the department had considered going to the United Nations but, after talking with Dag Hammarskjöld, had concluded that it could not get the action there that it wanted. "They decided they could handle the situation better alone," Ben Cohen commented. "Had they gone to the United Nations I am sure they would not have gotten what they wanted. But the American people might have had time and opportunity to learn into what a tragic pit they were being asked to leap." °

In the face of highly provocative actions by Khrushchev—the building of the infamous Berlin Wall and unilateral abrogation of the nuclear test ban moratorium—she urged Kennedy not to abandon the effort to negotiate with the Soviet Union. She had just signed a "Declaration of Conscience and Responsibility" circulated by the American Friends Service Committee, "and one of the things I had to promise to do was to write to you." She urged him to resist "the usual pressures being put on the government by certain scientists, by the Pentagon," and by others opposed to a treaty to end nuclear tests.† She pleaded for give and take on Berlin. She understood East Europe's fear of the revival of German power.

> I would think it might well be considered of mutual interest to obtain withdrawal of troops on either side for a demilitarized central Europe. I realize that it would be considered that we were weakening NATO by not having Germany in, and therefore weakening our western defense, but if we get equal concessions on the other side, is this perhaps not a good way to beginning disarmament? Negotiations must go on, and that means give and take, and we had better be preparing our people not to look upon anything which pleases both sides as appeasement on our part.

° Remarks of Benjamin V. Cohen on the occasion of his being presented the Isaiah Award of the American Jewish Committee. Reprinted in the *Congressional Record*, CVX/187, November 13, 1969.

† As late as August, 1959, she did not consider the use of the atom bomb against Japan a mistake. At that time (August 12, 1959) she wrote ex-president Truman:

> As you know, I have always said that you had no choice but to use the atomic bomb to bring the war to an end. For a time I was disturbed at our having used it in Nagasaki but after being in Japan and seeing the defenses and talking with one of our representatives who had been a prisoner of the Japanese and who explained that unless there had been a second demonstration the Japanese would have felt they could defend themselves which would have resulted in the destruction of the whole of Japan and the loss of millions of our own men, I realized that you had this knowledge and that you could make no other decision than the one you made. I have since written this publicly a number of times. I would give a great deal, however, now if we could come to an agreement for stopping the whole use of atomic energy for military purposes.

He was giving the problem of nuclear testing his close personal attention, the president assured her, and, as she could tell from his speeches, he had little use for those who equated negotiation with appeasement.[25]

Mrs. Roosevelt's last letter to President Kennedy, written from Campobello, suggested that the Roosevelt home there, which was then owned by Victor Hammer, be acquired by the government in connection with U.S.-Canadian plans to convert the island into an international Franklin D. Roosevelt memorial.

It would be nice to feel that the house might be an F.D.R. Memorial Conference site because he was interested in friendship between Canada and the United States and made considerable efforts to promote it.[26]

She was in touch, too, with Robert Kennedy, the attorney general, mostly about civil rights in the South. The government was trying to do what it could, he wrote her, after his aides had persuaded local officials in Albany, Georgia, to drop charges against the Reverend Martin Luther King, Jr., and other civil rights protesters, but the federal government's powers were extremely limited. "You are doing very well and the results are gratifying," she wrote on the margin of this letter.[27]

She liked to see the White House inhabited again by a young family that was obviously enjoying itself. Before the Kennedys had moved in, Mrs. Roosevelt wrote a warm and understanding letter to Mrs. Kennedy:

I know that there will be difficulties in store for you in the White House life but perhaps also you will find some compensations. Most things are made easier, though I think on the whole life is rather difficult for both the children and their parents in the "fish bowl" that lies before you.[28]

A tender correspondence developed between the two. Mrs. Kennedy thanked her for her wise words of advice and enclosed a drawing made by Caroline, to whom she had read a book about Fala. She had begun to learn what Mrs. Roosevelt meant about the difficulty of making new friends while in the White House.

It was wonderful to have "so young, intelligent, and attractive" a First Lady, Mrs. Roosevelt observed, and the changes Mrs. Kennedy was making in the White House showed a sense of art and history, she thought.

Jacqueline Kennedy had served her country well when she accompanied her husband to his meetings with de Gaulle and Khrushchev:

> To smile no matter how weary one is, to look well-dressed and interested at all times is a remarkable feat, especially when it is considered that we do not have the long training given to royalty to meet these situations.

Then in a postscript that, as a First Lady who had faced the exacting test and more than met it, she alone could write, she added:

> I think back to the days of my husband's Presidency and realize that the problems of that time—first of the depression and then of the war—required a background and understanding of social justice and social needs. That is still needed by the woman in the White House, but much more is required.
>
> Both the President and his wife can never give way to apprehension even though they are probably more aware than most citizens of the dangers which may surround us. If the country is to be confident, they must be confident. They cannot afford to harbor resentment, or to have enemies where it is possible to turn these enemies into friends. This demands from both the President and his wife a high order of intelligence, of self-discipline and a dedication to the public good. We are extremely fortunate to find these qualifications in the White House at the present time.[29]

To the world Mrs. Roosevelt still seemed a marvel of energy, but she was slowing down. "I know you think she never tires," Nina said in London during her trip with her grandmother. "Well, one of the reasons is that she's got the knack of falling off to sleep wherever she is, even on her feet. It can be awkward if she's in company. I keep a very close watch. If I can catch her just as her head is nodding, one tap of the ankle is enough. But once her head reaches her chest, it takes a good old-fashioned shake." [30]

But it was not only age that was causing her to doze off and reach gratefully for a chair. In early 1960 an anguished David Gurewitsch diagnosed the flare-up of a blood disease as aplastic anemia.

"You have to realize," Jim Halsted told his wife Anna when they heard the news on their return from Iran, "this will shorten her life. You will get to broken down veins and transfusions." [31]

Mrs. Roosevelt knew. She had called on Israeli Prime Minister David Ben-Gurion during his 1960 visit to the United States. A friend mentioned Ben-Gurion's well-known interest in longevity. She had no such interest, she said firmly. There were a few things she still wanted to do, such as taking some of her grandchildren to her favorite places in Europe. She would take them that summer. Otherwise, it was interesting to do things, saying to yourself, "This is the last time you will do them." It was an excuse to do a great many things you might not otherwise feel free to do. She had left a memorandum on her funeral and burial. She wanted a plain wooden coffin, covered with pine boughs from her woods, no embalming, and her veins cut (because she had an irrational fear of waking up with piles of earth on top of her).[32]

The illness would flicker and subside—infections, fevers, chills, and aches. She dealt with them by ignoring them. Doctor, children, friends told her repeatedly that by any standard she was overdoing things, but she had her own firm ideas on how she wished to live—and die.

In February, 1962, she went to Europe to meet Henry Morgenthau III and to do some recordings for her "Prospects of Mankind" series on "Europe: Rival or Partners?" In London she stayed, as always, at Claridge's and dined with Lord Elibank one night and the next with Lady Reading, who brought along six ladies in policy-making positions in government. She lunched with Hilda Fitzwilliams, an Allenswood schoolmate, and Louise Morley Cochrane and her children came to tea. In Paris she checked in at the Crillon and took her "crew," as she called them, to "different good, little French restaurants." There was a quick trip to Israel ("They are still dreamers, but they make their dreams come true") and a stay at St. Moritz with the Gurewitsches and Maureen Corr, whom she entertained with reminiscences of her honeymoon stay there in 1905.[33]

She had a sense that her time on earth was drawing to a close. She sent out checks six months early—to godchildren whose school tuition she was paying, to friends who had come on hard times, to favorite organizations. A Tacoma housewife received a birthday check for $10 after Mrs. Roosevelt died. She was the daughter of Al Kresse, a hitchhiker whom Mrs. Roosevelt had picked up in the depths of the Depression and had sent to her Sixty-fifth Street house with a note that he should be fed and helped to find a job. He named his daughter after her, and Mrs. Roosevelt asked to be her godmother, sending her a $10 check on each birthday. She used a bequest of $25,000 from Mrs. Parish ("Cousin Susie") to purchase Liberian mining stock, which Lansdell Christie assured her would pay fantastic dividends, and left the stock in her will to Maureen Corr and a few others to whom she felt especially grateful.

She was still going strong in late spring, 1962, lending a hand and her apartment to a group of liberals whom James Wechsler, editor of the *New York Post,* brought together to purchase that newspaper when, for a brief moment, Dorothy Schiff thought she wished to sell it; joining two other lifelong champions of the underdog, Norman Thomas and Roger Baldwin, to hold hearings in Washington on police and judicial harassment of the Negro protest movement in the South—"horrifying," she called it; spending a day in Hartford speaking for Mrs. Beatrice Fox Auerbach; organizing a birthday party for Faye Emerson's son Scoop; bantering on a plane flight up from Georgia with Governor Rockefeller, who wanted her to tell him who the Democratic candidate for governor was going to be; asking Tom Stix to investigate the possibilities of a fall TV program about books, "as I am afraid I must reluctantly admit that I am not quite as young as I was . . . [and] I think I shall have to give up lecture trips," adding, however, that she would not want to compete with Faye Emerson's anticipated book program.[34] Her strength was flowing out, but in the moments that it returned she was back at the old schedule, touring the borough of Queens for the Committee for Democratic Voters. "My head is heavy and if I go, you'll have to steady me when I get out of the car," she told the young man who came to get her. "You see I had to come," she remarked when a little Negro girl gave her an armful of flowers at one of their speech stops. "I was expected."

David had been giving her antibiotics to combat her recurring aches and fevers but thought she was well enough, and she insisted that he go through with his commitment to spend a month on the hospital ship *Hope* in Peru. He placed her in the charge of another doctor. A few months earlier, when Jim Halsted suggested that an internist be brought in to take charge, she had rebuffed David, who had transmitted the message to her, with a terse "Very well, then, I'll have no doctor." He remained the only physician whose advice she would follow, but would not hear of his not going off on an assignment where he might do good for others. "To me all goodbyes are poignant now," she wrote him as he left for Peru. "I like less & less to be long separated from those few whom I deeply love."

Although she began to feel really unwell in the middle of July, it was an effort to get in touch with a doctor whom she really did not know, and she tried, as she had so often in the past, to shake off her illness by sheer will power. But the pain rarely left her now, and she was always so weary that if she saw a chair she was unable not to sit down.

All summer she had been working with Elinore Denniston on a new book, *Tomorrow Is Now*. One day she got as far as the desk and lifted a shaking hand for Miss Denniston to see. "I can't work. I don't understand it," she said and added apologetically, "and you have come so far." [35]

Finally, since she had to go to New York City for the meeting of a committee that was advising the Board of Education on the selection of a new school superintendent, she went to see the doctor.

"You go right home and go to bed," he ordered.

She was happy to receive the order. She got into bed, relieved that she would not have to get up again and dress. The next day the doctor insisted on a blood transfusion. She tried to put him off. Could it not be postponed until Sunday when David was returning? The doctor insisted. The transfusion was a disaster. Her fever, instead of abating, shot up, and by the time David returned it had reached 105.5 degrees. She felt like "a fiery furnace," she said later. And when David ordered an ambulance to take her to the hospital, she was scarcely able to recognize her son James, who had flown up from Washington to be with her.

Her first days in the hospital were unmitigated torture. There were injections in order to take samples of her blood and injections to fill her with medication. Every half hour nurses recorded her blood pressure, pulse, and temperature, and hospital attendants came with questionnaires. She complained to David about the endless tests. If it were not for the tests, why would they want her in the hospital, David replied. "Eureka!" was her answer to this. "They have you there! You get well but is it really worth it?" [36]

There were days of the deepest depression triggered by new anxieties over Elliott as well as her illness. One dream left her shaken and emotionally spent. Her brother Hall and her son Elliott somehow seemed combined into one figure, like a Picasso drawing, and were smothering her. She no longer wished to go on living, she told the few friends whom she allowed to visit her.[37]

But then her spirits began to revive. She was permitted to get out of bed for a half hour. She found herself interested again in the newspapers. Why had not Maureen brought the mail, she wanted to know one day. Maureen produced two fat brown envelopes. "Oh, you are efficient," she beamed. Among the letters was one from Thomas Stix, reporting that he had lined up a sponsor for a new television show along the lines of her "Prospects of Mankind" series, for which she would receive $1,000 an appearance. "Oh, dear. Tell Tom Stix I can't see him till I feel better. Tell him I'm in the hospital." [38]

As soon as she was allowed to sit up, Mrs. Roosevelt began to plan again a trip to Campobello for the dedication of an FDR Memorial Bridge, linking the United States with this Canadian island. She overruled David's protests; she conceded that her constitution no longer could take the punishment she meted out to it, but she insisted on going. She wanted David and his wife to fly up with her, and the author's wife Trude would drive down with her.

Trude, who had joined her in Campobello on the last day of her stay there, wrote of their trip back:

For the first time that morning she walked up and down in front of the Campo house "so that I can manage the steps of the Scarlett house," she said. She was terribly frail and complained that she had forgotten how to take a deep breath and had to learn again. She said that she learned that Friday night (when she had 105.6 temperature) how easy it was to die. She was just slipping away without regret or pain, and she was pleading with David to let her go.

We drove down the Maine coast to do once more the things she always loved to do. We visited Bishop Scarlett and his wife, Leah. We met an old friend, Molly Dewson. . . . Then we went to a place called Perry's Nuthouse where Mrs. R., Joe and I used to stop to buy wild-strawberry preserves. She was too weak to get out of the car, and when we came back, having purchased what she wanted us to get, was only vaguely aware of what was going on.

On the long drive to Boston she hardly spoke and when she did it was so faint we could hardly understand her. In Boston Henry [Morgenthau] III came in. From Boston on the way to Hyde Park she stopped for a last visit with Esther Lape, one of her oldest friends, and then she went on to Val-Kill, where she had a few days when she even worked—but after Labor Day the fevers and the chills and the blood transfusions and endless injections took over and the lonely descent began.[39]

After her first spell in the hospital, she informed her housekeeper at Hyde Park, Marge Entrup, she would be glad to know there would be no more big parties. In the next breath she casually told her there would be fourteen for breakfast. As a friend explained to Marge the next day, "In Mrs. Roosevelt's book, that isn't a big party."[40]

She had spent the Friday before the Labor Day week end in New York City, meeting with Nannine Joseph, trying to help her niece Ellie get a contract to do drawings for a children's book, conferring with Tom Stix about her television show. Friday night on her return she seemed in good shape, asked for her usual drink of Dubonnet, and although her cheeks were disturbingly flushed, at Johnny and Anne's where everyone went for dinner, she entered into an animated discussion of the impending Rockefeller-Morgenthau gubernatorial race. But the next morning when she came down and took her place at the head of the table, she was unable to ring the old Mother Hubbard silver bell to summon Marge. She breathed with difficulty and trembled violently. While her friends made conversation, pretending not to notice, she leaned over to sip her cup of hot tea. She blamed her trembling on the sleeping porch —it had been a cold night. Someone brought a shawl, and finally she was persuaded to go into Tommy's living room and sit by the fire. As soon as she revived she insisted on going to work with Miss Denniston. David came, but she would not permit him to take her temperature.

"This I know," she dictated to Miss Denniston, in a voice that was almost a whisper. "This I believe with all my heart. If we want a free and peaceful world, if we want to make the deserts bloom and man grow to greater dignity as a human being—*we can do it!*" When Miss Denniston discreetly managed to leave a half hour early, Mrs. Roosevelt finally agreed to allow her temperature to be taken. It registered 101. She would not sleep on her porch again, she announced, and her listeners had the feeling that she was saying good-by to another of the things she loved to do.[41]

After lunch she went upstairs for a nap, and when she insisted on coming down at four for Charley Curnan's surprise party—he had worked for the Roosevelts for twenty-five years—her temperature was down. After the party she sat at her desk trying to balance her checkbooks. There was a telephone call from Rep. Emanuel Celler's secretary. He wanted to notify her that the congressman was going on television the next day to propose her as Democratic candidate for the Senate. "Under no circumstances," she said emphatically. "I don't believe in old people running."

Walter and May Reuther arrived, on their way to New York City from Putney School in Vermont, where they had left their daughter. She had always found Walter stimulating. The after-dinner discussion went on until eleven. She would like to borrow an idea of his, she told him, that economic, not military, aid was the way to stiffen the borderlands against the Communists. She described her illness to Reuther in considerable detail so that he might explain to Jim Carey why she was unable to come to his convention, where he was in a fight for control of the electrical workers' union.

Breakfast on Sunday was a sad repetition of the previous morning, and the Reuthers saw for themselves how ill she was. She took little part in the conversation, except to ask Reuther, when he went to Japan, to get in touch with her grandson Franklin, whose ship was based there. Again, she refused to allow David to take her temperature. She knew it was high, she told Reuther, but she was going to have Tubby Curnan drive her to church. She was, to the end, one of the Reverend Gordon Kidd's most faithful parishioners, attending services, paying her pew rent of seventy-five dollars, subscribing an additional $425, and each Sunday handing in an envelope containing two dollars.

September was a month in which she tried not to give up and take to her bed. She insisted that Lady Reading stay with her. Geraldine Thompson arrived with a bagful of projects and, finding Mrs. Roosevelt strangely resistant, asked in some desperation, "and what do you do for the Audubon Society?" She went out with Tubby to buy some sturdy chairs for the dining room. It was too painful to get in and out of the station wagon, so she had chairs brought out to the sidewalk to her to inspect. She attended the AAUN's reception for the U.S. delegation to the 1962 General Assembly, sitting on the dais for two hours, and conferred with Robert Benjamin and her grandson Curtis on how to merge the AAUN with the U.S. Committee for the United Nations. Doggedly she kept on doing things she had always done, for fear that if she stopped it would be difficult to do them again afterward. But her mouth bled and her throat was sore. She was feverish and often listless, and it took her an hour and a half to dress in the morning. Instead of saying good night to friends and children she now said good-by.[42]

Her children, whom David had kept in touch with the progress of her illness, were in and out. Other doctors were brought in, and when her temperature, instead of going up and down as it had been doing, stayed up, she was taken on September 26 to the hospital again. Elliott and his wife flew in from Minneapolis. Anna and Jim Halsted, who had been in and out all through August and early September, came from Detroit to consult with David and remained,

staying at her apartment, Anna taking charge of the household.
Mrs. Roosevelt had told David that if her illness flared up again,
she did not wish to linger on a helpless invalid, and expected him
to save her from a dragged-out, agonizing death. But Dr. Gurewitsch was unable to comply with her wishes. And when the time
came, his duty as a doctor prevented him.

There was only suffering for Mrs. Roosevelt [Trude Lash wrote Paul
Tillich] from the first day in July when she was taken to the hospital
for the first time. There was no moment of serenity. There was only
anger, helpless anger at the doctors and nurses and the world who
tried to keep her alive. The doctors had her where they wanted her.
  "They can do with me what they want, not what I want," she said
bitterly.
  I don't think there was anything to comfort her. She was completely alone and felt betrayed and persecuted by all of us.
  She was not afraid of death at all. She welcomed it. She was so
weary and so infinitely exhausted, it seemed as though she had to suffer
every human indignity, every weakness, every failure that she had re-
sisted and conquered so daringly during her whole life—as though she
were being punished for being too strong and powerful and disciplined
and almost immune to human frailty.[43]

There were so few people she really cared about, so few, Mrs.
Roosevelt whispered to a friend in the hospital. She did not want
visitors. She did not want to be seen in her invalid condition. Adlai
Stevenson came to the hospital. David, believing it reflected her
wishes, sent him away. "Dearest Eleanor," he wrote her tenderly. "I
have been getting regular bulletins from Maureen and *pray* it won't
be long before I can come to see you—and what a long deferred
visit it will be! . . . I love you dearly—and so does the whole
world! But they can't *all* come to see you and perhaps I can when
David gives me permission. Devotedly—Adlai." [44]
  For her seventy-eighth birthday, she gave orders from the hospital that she wanted a party at her Seventy-fourth Street
apartment—of little children. So on October 11, John's daughter
Joan, Edna Gurewitsch's Maria, and Trude's grandchildren Christopher and Annie Pratt came for ice cream, games, favors, and a

birthday cake on which glowed a single candle. Curtis Roosevelt (Buzzy) and John Boettiger and their wives joined the sad group of grownups who came with the children for birthday toasts.

She hated the hospital and implored the doctors to let her go home and "rejoin the human race," but the specialists who had been brought in insisted that she remain until another series of tests were completed. She was allowed to return home on October 18. Someone tipped off the photographers, and she, who had such dignity and pride of bearing, was shown to the world stretcher-borne, her face puffy, her white hair straggly, her head sagging.

Yet, so happy was she to be at home in her own room, amid familiar surroundings, that her will to live seemed momentarily to revive. "Maureen, I forgot to thank the stretcher-bearers," were her first words when she was installed in her own bed. "Will you please tell them that I think they did a magnificent job." She ordered a small table set in her bedroom and invited Edna and David down to dine while she tried to manage a small meal on a bed tray. She asked for her checkbook and, with unsteady hand, wrote checks in advance. Anna and David did their best to nurture the spark. The Cuban missile crisis, which Stevenson at the United Nations was calling the gravest challenge to world peace since 1945, was at flashpoint.

"We are almost at war," David said to her, almost shouting the words because her eyes were closed, as if she wanted to be withdrawn from those around her. "We will read the papers to you." "I don't want them read," she replied. "Joe will read them," he suggested. When she did not renew her protests, Anna and David decided that this author was the man to try.

"Hello, Joe," she said, but then, as the latest developments in the tense confrontation were described to her, appeared to become confused. "It'll never come together," she said, "nobody makes sense." Was she talking about her head and the difficulty she had in focusing on what was being said to her, or about the state of the world? She stirred restlessly. "All I want," she began again, and her visitor thought she was going to say "is for them to get together," but instead she said, "is to be turned over."

On October 25 her disease, which had been thought to be aplastic anemia, was positively diagnosed as a rare bone-marrow tuberculosis. That was "cheering news," David told the press. "It shows we're on the right track." But Anna, fearful that Mrs. Roosevelt's friends might be led to believe she was on the road to recovery, told the newspapers that her condition was "very much the same" and that she "was not responding to treatment." *

One day, when she told Nurse Waldron that she wished to die, the nurse said that the Lord who had put her into this world would take her from it when she had finished the job for which she was here. "Utter nonsense," Mrs. Roosevelt said, looking at the intravenous tube in her arm, the oxygen tank, and the needle punctures in her skin. Confused and incoherent, often in a semicoma, her determination to die alone was steady and iron-willed.

She rejected pills, clenched her teeth to keep her nurse from administering them, spat them out if the nurse was successful, and, becoming more wily, secreted them in the recesses of her mouth. "There really is no change in her condition," Anna sadly reported to Uncle David. "There are so many indignities to being sick and helpless. . . . I find myself praying that whatever is the very best for her happens and happens quickly." [46]

---

* "Nothing could have been done to save her," David Gurewitsch wrote after the autopsy. "The pathological findings show without any question that Mrs. Roosevelt had a primary disease of the bone marrow, in which the bone marrow, to a very high extent, lost the capacity to form blood. Therefore the anemia. We know no treatment for this condition." At the end of his letter, David added that the men who examined her brain said she had the brain of a young person.

"As you know," Dr. James Halsted wrote to James Roosevelt, "the diagnostic problem confronting her physicians during the last two years of her life were extremely difficult. . . . She had aplastic anemia (also known as bone-marrow failure) which was diagnosed in 1960. The cause of aplastic anemia is usually unknown and this was the case with your Mother. Approximately six months before her death she was given steroids because the course of the anemia indicated that she might begin to develop internal bleeding and steroids are an effective remedy for that in aplastic anemia. Unfortunately she had an old tuberculosis lesion dating back to 1919, the scars of which were shown in the x-rays of her chest. Steroid treatment of many illnesses sometimes 'light up' inactive and healed tuberculosis if carried out over several weeks or more. That is what happened in your Mother's case. The tuberculosis which was activated by steroid treatment spread rapidly and widely throughout her body and was resistant to all kinds of anti-tuberculosis treatment. This was the cause of her death." [45]

The children decided that Stevenson, who had been deeply hurt by David's rebuff, should be allowed to make a last visit to his old friend, if only to stand at the door and wave to her. "Come, if you would like," Anna said to him, "but I don't think she will recognize you." He dropped everything and came.

"I am a tough old bird," she had written David Gray in 1956. On November 7 her strong heart finally ceased to beat.

"I don't know whether I believe in a future life," she had said on Edward R. Murrow's program "This I Believe."

I believe that all that you go through here must have some value, therefore there must be some *reason*. And there must be some "going on." How exactly that happens I've never been able to decide. There is a future—that I'm sure of. But how, that I don't know. And I came to feel that it didn't really matter very much because whatever the future held you'd have to face it when you came to it, just as whatever life holds you have to face it in exactly the same way. And the important thing was that you never let down doing the best that you were able to do—it might be poor because you might not have much within you to give, or to help other people with, or to live your life with. But as long as you did the very best that you were able to do, then that was what you were put here to do and that was what you were accomplishing by being here.

And so I have tried to follow that out—and not to worry about the future or what was going to happen. I think I am pretty much of a fatalist. You have to accept whatever comes and the only important thing is that you meet it with courage and with the best that you have to give.[47]

APPENDICES
REFERENCES
INDEX

Appendix A: Eleanor Roosevelt and the Nobel Peace Prize

Several efforts were made to have the Nobel Peace Prize awarded to Mrs. Roosevelt. In 1961 Adlai E. Stevenson, at that time United States representative at the United Nations, nominated her, not only because of the contribution that she had made to the drafting and approval of the Universal Declaration of Human Rights, but because "in this tragic generation [she] has become a world symbol of the unity of mankind and the hope of peace." [1]

A year later, when he renewed his request for consideration of Mrs. Roosevelt's nomination, he was seconded by President Kennedy, who wrote the Nobel Committee that she was "a living symbol of world understanding and peace," and that her "untiring efforts" on its behalf had become "a vital part of the historical fabric of this century." An award to this remarkable lady, Kennedy added, "in itself would contribute to understanding and peace in this troubled world." [2]

This was nine months before Mrs. Roosevelt's death. Death did not stop the efforts on her behalf. Ralph J. Bunche, himself a recipient of the prize, proposed that it be awarded to her posthumously. "I can think of no one in our times who has so broadly served the objectives of the Nobel Peace Award," he wrote Gunnar Jahn, chairman of the Nobel Committee of the Norwegian Parliament which made the award. [3] The prize went to Linus Pauling in 1962 and to the International Red Cross in 1963.

In the summer of 1964 a new effort got under way to obtain the prize for Mrs. Roosevelt posthumously. Lester B. Pearson, prime minister of Canada and a winner of the prize for his work in establishing the first United Nations peace force, wrote Gunnar Jahn urging a posthumous award. "She certainly was an outstanding woman and I believe that the world does owe her a special debt of gratitude for her magnificent work for peace, and for the freedom and human rights on which peace must be based." Nobel officials replied that the statutes of the Nobel Foundation prohibited the submission of the names of deceased persons. But Mrs. Roosevelt's friends thought the committee, if it wished, could interpret the statutes to make the award. Andrew W. Cordier, Dag Hammarskjöld's closest collaborator in the United Nations Secretariat, wrote Jahn pointing out that Mrs. Roosevelt had been nominated prior to her death, and in his view, therefore, she "technically qualifies under the rules of your Committee." [4]

At Adlai Stevenson's request, the Norwegian ambassador to the United Nations, Sivert A. Nielsen, inquired whether Mrs. Roosevelt could not be awarded the prize since she had been nominated while alive. "My attention has been drawn to the fact," Ambassador Nielsen added, "that the late Secretary-General [Dag Hammarskjöld] was awarded the prize post-mortem." The director of the Nobel Committee did not find the parallel persuasive. "It is not possible to award the Nobel Peace Prize to Mrs. Roosevelt post-mortem," he informed Nielsen. "The last time she was recommended was in 1962." Nielsen took up the matter with Nils Langhelle, president of the Norwegian Storting and a member of the Nobel Committee. The rules of the Nobel Foundation concerning post-mortem awards, Langhelle replied, were interpreted to mean: "Deceased persons cannot be proposed whereas one who has been proposed and subsequently died can be awarded the prize post mortem for that year." [5]

Mrs. Roosevelt's friends were not to be deterred. Since the 1964 prize had been awarded to the Reverend Martin Luther King, Jr., an organizing committee, consisting of the Dowager Marchioness of Reading, former publisher of the New York *Herald-Tribune* Mrs. Ogden Reid, and Esther Lape, undertook to secure consideration of Eleanor Roosevelt for the 1965 award. Twenty-eight distinguished citizens from all over the world sent supporting letters.[6]

Former President Truman, with characteristic bluntness, wrote Gunnar Jahn:

I understand that there are regulations in your committee that rule out an award of the Peace Prize to Mrs. Franklin D. Roosevelt because she has passed away.

The award without the financial prize that goes with it can be made. You should make it. If she didn't earn it, then no one else has.

It's an award for peace in the world. I hope you'll make it.[7]

Clement Attlee, former British prime minister, wrote from the House of Lords with equal brevity and bluntness:

Eleanor Roosevelt did a great work in the world, not only for her fellow citizens of the United States, but for all people, and there is no doubt at all that if posthumous awards are given then the name of Eleanor Roosevelt should be among the recipients, and this nomination has my full support.[8]

"If there is anyone who serves the posthumous award of the Nobel Prize it is she," wrote Jean Monnet, father of the Common Market:

Fundamentally, I think her great contribution was her persistence in carrying into practice her deep belief in liberty and equality. She would not accept that anyone should suffer—because they were women, or children, or foreign, or poor, or stateless refugees. To her, the world was truly one world, and all its inhabitants members of one family.[9]

Letters of support came from United States cabinet members and senators as well as from foreign statesmen.* Two former presidents of the United Nations Commission on Human Rights, Charles Malik of Lebanon and René Cassin of France, endorsed the nomination. One letter came from a Harvard professor of international relations in whose class Eleanor Roosevelt had regularly lectured and who later would become better known. "As someone who knows Mrs. Roosevelt for many years," wrote Henry A. Kissinger,

and admired her work all his adult life, I can say that she was no ordinary person, not even an ordinary Nobel laureate. Mrs. Roosevelt was one of the great human beings of our time. She stood for peace and international understanding not only as intellectual propositions but as a way of life. She was a symbol of compassion in a world of increasing righteousness. She brought warmth rather than abstract principles. I am convinced that recognition of her quality would move people all over the world. . . .[10]

"We have no illusions about the flexibility of the Nobel Committee," Esther Lape wrote David Gurewitsch. "Its statements reflect a rigidity *extraordinaire*. But that the views of these distinguished persons in the United States, United Kingdom, Japan, and France will have an impact on the Committee, I cannot doubt." [11]

The 1965 prize was awarded to UNICEF.

* The alphabetical list of those who wrote letters is as follows: Clement Attlee, David Ben-Gurion, René Cassin, Horace Bishop Donegan, Paul H. Douglas, Sir Alec Douglas-Home, Orville L. Freeman, Arthur J. Goldberg, Nahum Goldmann, Arthur L. Goodhart, W. Averell Harriman, Hubert H. Humphrey, Henry A. Kissinger, Eugene J. McCarthy, Charles W. Malik, Mike Mansfield, Jean Monnet, Reinhold Niebuhr, Philip J. Noel-Baker, J. Robert Oppenheimer, Walter P. Reuther, Nelson A. Rockefeller, A. L. Sachar, the Baron Salter, Margaret Chase Smith, Yasaka Takagi, who wrote jointly with Shigehabu Matsumoto, Harry S. Truman, Stewart L. Udall.

Appendix B: Mrs. Roosevelt and the Sultan of Morocco

Eleanor Roosevelt's support of Israel was a continuing one. In 1956 Judge Justine Wise Polier came to her, distressed over the plight of more than ten thousand Moroccan Jews who had reached Casablanca in order to go to Israel and who were now being prevented from leaving. They were living in conditions of misery with the danger of an outbreak of epidemic ever-present. The World Jewish Congress, organizer of the exodus which it thought had the support of the sultan of Morocco, was distraught.

Mrs. Roosevelt listened and, "with the smile that lighted her face when she felt she could be of help to others," told Justine that the latter had come at an opportune moment. She could help, she thought. She had recently received the ambassador from newly independent Morocco, who had come as an emissary from Mohammed V, the sultan, to Hyde Park to lay a wreath on FDR's grave. The ambassador had arrived with such a large entourage from his embassy and from the State Department that Mrs. Roosevelt had not even had enough food for tea and had to send out for more. When tea was over the ambassador had asked for a few moments alone with her. The sultan had directed him to convey to her his deep appreciation of President Roosevelt's advice to him in North Africa in 1943. The president had counseled him to protect Morocco's underground waters when concessions would be given for exploration of oil after the war. The sultan would never forget Roosevelt's consideration for the Moroccan people, and he wanted her to know that he was agreeing to the continuance of United States air bases in Morocco because of his gratitude.

This was an ideal time for her to write the sultan, Mrs. Roosevelt said, her eyes twinkling. A few days later she dispatched the following letter:

July 31, 1956

Your Majesty:

I wish to acknowledge your kind message transmitted to me through your representative. It is very gratifying to know that you remember my husband's visit to you. He often told me of that visit and of his hopes that some day you would bring back much of your desert into fertile land through the use of underground water which might be found, and he recalled his advice to you never to give away all of your oil rights since you would need a substantial amount of those rights to bring this water to the surface. To have you remember this and his interest in the welfare of these areas was very gratifying to me.

As you know, my husband had a great interest in bringing to people in general throughout the world better conditions for living. We tried to do this for the people of the United States, but he was also anxious to see it come about in the world as a whole.

I have had an appeal to bring to your attention the fact that there is a group of very poor Jewish people now in camps in Morocco who were to have been allowed to leave for Israel. They are of no value to the future development of Morocco as they have not succeeded in building for themselves a suitable economy. However, Israel can perhaps help them to develop skills and to improve their lot. Your government has given assurances that they would be allowed to leave but when it has come to a point in the last few months the actual necessary deeds to accomplish their departure have not been forthcoming.

I am sure that it is Your Majesty's desire, as it was my husband's, not only to see better conditions for your own people but to see people throughout the world improve their condition. I hope Morocco will show the world that she is committed, as I believe she is, to the freedom of people who are living there which must include the freedom of people to emigrate. The Jews who had no country now have Israel where they can take their less fortunate brethren and help them to a better way of life. It seems to me that the Arab states would be forwarding their own interests if they were to make this transfer possible. It would relieve the Arab states of indigent people and would show the world that they did have an interest in helping unfortunate people to improve themselves. I, therefore, bring this situation to your attention in this note which primarily expresses my gratitude for your memory of my husband, since I believe that you would not have remembered my husband if you did not have somewhat similar aims.

Very sincerely yours,
Eleanor Roosevelt

Within a few days of the receipt of Mrs. Roosevelt's letter the Jews in Casablanca were released to go to Israel.[1]

References

I. CHAMPION OF HER HUSBAND'S IDEALS

1. Letter from Eleanor Roosevelt to Walter Nash, July 8, 1945.
2. *New York Times,* April 13, 1945.
3. Eleanor Roosevelt, "My Day," syndicated column, April 16, 1945.
4. Letter from Eleanor Roosevelt to Maude Gray, April 29, 1945.
5. E. Roosevelt, "My Day," *op. cit.,* April 16, 1945; letter from Mrs. Kermit Roosevelt to Eleanor Roosevelt, June 24, 1946, and Eleanor Roosevelt's reply, June 25, 1946.
6. Eleanor Roosevelt, *This I Remember* (New York, 1949), p. 68.
7. Interview with Anna Roosevelt Halsted.
8. E. Roosevelt, "My Day," April 24, 1945.
9. Letter from James Roosevelt to Margaret Suckley, April 24, 1945.
10. E. Roosevelt, "My Day," May 8, 1945; *New York Times,* May 9, 1945; letter from Eleanor Roosevelt to Harry S. Truman, April 25, 1945.
11. *New York Times,* May 9, 1945.
12. This conversation was reported to the author by Freeda Franklin.
13. Eleanor Roosevelt, *On My Own* (New York, 1958), p. 5.
14. Letter from Lucy Mercer Rutherfurd to Eleanor Roosevelt, May 2, 1945.
15. Letter from Eleanor Roosevelt to Elliott Roosevelt, May 17, 1945.
16. *Ibid.,* June 6, 1945; letter from Eleanor Roosevelt to Trude W. Lash, June 12, 1945.
17. Letter from Eleanor Roosevelt to Maude Gray, Aug. 2, 1945; letter from Eleanor Roosevelt to Joseph P. Lash, July 9, 1945.
18. Letter from Eleanor Roosevelt to Joseph P. Lash, Aug. 9, 1945.
19. Memorandum from Eleanor Roosevelt to her children, undated.
20. Geoffrey T. Hellman, "Mrs. Roosevelt," *Life,* Feb. 5, 1940.
21. John Morton Blum, *From the Diaries of Henry Morgenthau, Jr.* (Boston, 1968), p. 424.
22. E. Roosevelt, "My Day," April 18, 1945.
23. Letter from Harold Ickes to Eleanor Roosevelt, May 21, 1945.
24. Letter from Eleanor Roosevelt to Harold Ickes, May 26, 1945.
25. Letter from Trude W. Lash to Joseph P. Lash, April 15, 1945.
26. Letter from Harry S. Truman to Eleanor Roosevelt (May 10, 1945).
27. Letter from Eleanor Roosevelt to Harry S. Truman, May 14, 1945.
28. Letter from Harry S. Truman to Eleanor Roosevelt, May 18, 1945.
29. Letter from Eleanor Roosevelt to Grace Tully, June 10, 1945; letter from Eleanor Roosevelt to Robert Hannegan, June 3, 1945.
30. Letter from Eleanor Roosevelt to Joseph P. Lash, June 5, 1945; letter from Izetta Jewel Miller to Eleanor Roosevelt, July 28, 1945.
31. Letter from Eleanor Roosevelt to Harry S. Truman, June 3, 1945; E. Roosevelt, "My Day," June 10, 1945; letter from Trude W. Lash to Joseph P. Lash, July 26, 1945.
32. Letter from Eleanor Roosevelt to James Roosevelt, June 27, 1945.
33. Joseph P. Lash, *Eleanor and Franklin* (New York, 1971), pp. 702–4; E. Roosevelt, "My Day," June 22, 1945.
34. Letter from Eleanor Roosevelt to Joseph P. Lash, July 20, 1945; letter from Eleanor Roosevelt to Sidney Hillman, July 27, 1945.
35. Letter from Eleanor Roosevelt to Joseph P. Lash, July 5, 1945; letter from Harry Hopkins to Eleanor Roosevelt, June 26, 1945, and Eleanor Roosevelt's reply, June 30, 1945; letter from Harry Hopkins to Eleanor Roosevelt, July 2, 1945.
36. Letter from Eleanor Roosevelt to Harry S. Truman, July 2, 1945.
37. Letter from Esther Lape to Eleanor Roosevelt, Nov. 8, 1944.
38. E. Roosevelt, *On My Own, op. cit.,* p. 7.
39. Chester Bowles, *Promises to Keep: My Years in Public Life, 1941–1969* (New York, 1971), p. 122; letter from Eleanor Roosevelt to Harry S. Truman, Nov. 1, 1945, and Truman's reply, Nov. 6, 1945.
40. E. Roosevelt, "My Day," Oct. 16,

1945; S. J. Woolf, "Eleanor Roosevelt of Washington Square," *New York Times Magazine,* Sept. 23, 1945.
41. Letter from Clark Eichelberger to Eleanor Roosevelt, Oct. 3, 1939; memorandum from Franklin D. Roosevelt to Eleanor Roosevelt, Oct. 11, 1939; letter from Eleanor Roosevelt to Clark Eichelberger, Oct. 13, 1939.
42. Lash, *Eleanor and Franklin, op. cit.,* pp. 704–7.
43. Letter from Eleanor Roosevelt to Joseph P. Lash, Aug. 6, 1945; Alice Kimball Smith, *The Peril and a Hope: The Scientists' Movement in America, 1945–47* (Chicago, 1965), pp. 103–4; E. Roosevelt, "My Day," Aug. 14,

1945; *New York Times,* Aug. 10 and 19, 1945.
44. Letter from Eleanor Roosevelt to Harry S. Truman, Sept. 11, 1945, and Truman's reply, Sept. 14, 1945; letter from Eleanor Roosevelt to Harry Hopkins, Nov. 23, 1945.
45. James F. Byrnes, *All in One Lifetime* (New York, 1958), p. 373; interview with Franklin D. Roosevelt, Jr.
46. United Press, Dec. 14, 1945; *New York Times,* Dec. 19 and 20, 1945; Thomas L. Stokes, in the *New York World-Telegram,* Dec. 21, 1945.
47. E. Roosevelt, "My Day," Dec. 21, 1945.

II. THE HARDEST-WORKING DELEGATE

1. Memorandum of press conference, Jan. 3, 1946.
2. *New York Times,* Oct. 24, 1945; letter from Eleanor Roosevelt to Trude W. Lash, Jan. 13, 1946.
3. Eleanor Roosevelt, Diary, Jan. 2, 1946; memorandum of press conference, Jan. 3, 1946.
4. Interview with Ralph Bunche; E. Roosevelt, Diary, Jan. 2, 1946.
5. E. Roosevelt, Diary, Jan. 4, 1946.
6. James Reston, in the *New York Times,* Jan. 6, 1946.
7. Westbrook Pegler, in the *Washington* (D.C.) *Times-Herald,* Jan. 28, 1946; letter from Eleanor Roosevelt to Malvina Thompson, Jan. 13, 1946.
8. E. Roosevelt, Diary, Jan. 6, 1946; letter from Eleanor Roosevelt to Trude W. and Joseph P. Lash, Jan. 6, 1946.
9. E. Roosevelt, Diary, Jan. 7, 1946.
10. *Ibid.,* Jan. 9, 1946; James Reston, in the *New York Times,* Jan. 10, 1946.
11. Interview with Durward Sandifer.
12. Trygve Lie, *In the Cause of Peace: Seven Years with the United Nations* (New York, 1954), p. 10; letter from Eleanor Roosevelt to Trude W. Lash, Jan. 22, 1946.
13. *Verbatim Record of the First United Nations General Assembly.*
14. Letter from Eleanor Roosevelt to Gerald Morgan, Jan. 24, 1946; letter from Eleanor Roosevelt to Maude Gray, Jan. 22, 1946.
15. E. Roosevelt, Diary, Jan. 13, 1946.

16. Letter from Eleanor Roosevelt to Trude W. Lash, Jan. 13, 1946.
17. E. Roosevelt, "My Day," cited (Ch. I), Jan. 16, 1946.
18. Letter from Eleanor Roosevelt to Trude W. Lash, Feb. 10, 1946; E. Roosevelt, Diary, Jan. 20, 1946.
19. E. Roosevelt, Diary, Feb. 4, 1946; letter from Eleanor Roosevelt to Joseph P. Lash, Feb. 3, 1946.
20. E. Roosevelt, Diary, Jan. 21, 1946; E. Roosevelt, "My Day," Jan. 21, 1946.
21. Letter from Eleanor Roosevelt to Joseph P. Lash, Jan. 20, 1946.
22. E. Roosevelt, Diary, Jan. 23, 1946; E. Roosevelt, "My Day," Feb. 8, 1946.
23. E. Roosevelt, "My Day," Jan. 28, 1946.
24. E. Roosevelt, Diary, Jan. 16 and 27, 1946, and Feb. 2, 1946.
25. *Ibid.,* Jan. 29, 1946; E. Roosevelt, "My Day," Jan. 25, 1946; *ibid.,* Feb. 1, 1946.
26. E. Roosevelt, Diary, Jan. 9, 1946; letter from Eleanor Roosevelt to Maude Gray, Jan. 30, 1946.
27. E. Roosevelt, Diary, Feb. 6, 1946.
28. *Ibid.,* Feb. 8, 1946.
29. Letter from Eleanor Roosevelt to James Green, Feb. 26, 1954.
30. Interview with Benjamin V. Cohen.
31. Interview with Durward Sandifer.
32. *Verbatim Record of the First United Nations General Assembly.*
33. Letter from Eleanor Roosevelt to Joseph P. Lash, Feb. 13, 1936.

III. A MAGNA CHARTA FOR MANKIND

1. Interview with James P. Hendrick.
2. Interview with Durward Sandifer.
3. Doris Fleeson, in the *New York Post,* March 8, 1946; Arthur H. Vandenberg, *The Private Papers of Senator Vandenberg,* ed. A. H. Vandenberg, Jr., and J. A. Morris (Boston, 1952), p. 240.
4. Letter from Eleanor Roosevelt to James Byrnes, March 8, 1946.
5. Interview with James P. Hendrick.

6. E. Roosevelt, *On My Own,* cited (Ch. I), p. 73.
7. *Ibid.;* E. Roosevelt, "My Day," cited (Ch. I), May 11, 1946; Eleanor Roosevelt, speech to the National Citizens Political Action Committee, Oct. 7, 1946; *United Nations Records,* E/HR/ 24.
8. E. Roosevelt, "My Day," May 15, 1946.
9. Letter from Harry Hooker to Eleanor Roosevelt, April 18, 1946.

10. Lash Diaries, Sept. 2, 1946; Frances Perkins, *The Roosevelt I Knew* (New York, 1946).
11. E. Roosevelt, "My Day," Aug. 14, 1946.
12. Fern Marja, in the *New York Post*, Oct. 30, 1946.
13. Eleanor Roosevelt, speech in Committee III, *Verbatim Record of the First United Nations General Assembly*, Pt. II, Nov. 9, 1946; S. J. Woolf, in the *New York Times*, Dec. 15, 1946.
14. E. Roosevelt, "My Day," Feb. 3, 1947.
15. *United Nations Records*, E/CN.4/SR.14; *ibid.*, E/CN.4/SR.9; *New York Times*, Feb. 4, 1947.
16. Interview with James P. Hendrick.
17. *Ibid.*
18. *Ibid.*; notes from James P. Hendrick to Eleanor Roosevelt, in the Eleanor Roosevelt Human Rights Commission, file, undated.
19. E. Roosevelt, "My Day," Feb. 12, 1947.
20. Letter from James P. Hendrick to Eleanor Roosevelt, Feb, 18, 1947; letter from John P. Humphrey to Joseph Lash, April 20, 1972.
21. *United Nations Records*, E/CN.4/SR.49; Eleanor Roosevelt, speech on "The Struggle for Human Rights," Paris, Sept. 27, 1948; letter from John P. Humphrey to Joseph Lash, April 20, 1972.
22. Marjorie M. Whiteman, "Mrs. Franklin D. Roosevelt and the Human Rights Commission," *American Journal of International Law*, Oct., 1968; *New York Times*, June 12, 1947.
23. Memorandum from James P. Hendrick of conversation between Eleanor Roosevelt and Sen. Warren R. Austin, July 3, 1947.
24. Letter from Walter White to Eleanor Roosevelt, Oct. 21, 1947, and Eleanor Roosevelt's reply, Oct. 22, 1947.
25. Woolf, "Eleanor Roosevelt of Washington Square," cited (Ch. I).
26. Letter from James P. Hendrick to Eleanor Roosevelt, Oct. 1, 1947.
27. *Ibid.*, Nov. 20, 1947.
28. *New York Times*, Dec. 8, 1947.
29. E. J. Kahn, Jr., "The Years Alone," *New Yorker*, June 12 and 19, 1948.
30. E. Roosevelt, "My Day," Dec. 8, 1947.
31. Interview with James P. Hendrick.
32. *United Nations Records*, E/CN.4/SR.34.
33. Interview with Durward Sandifer.
34. Eleanor Roosevelt, speech on "The Declaration of Human Rights," 1949.
35. Letters from Eleanor Roosevelt to David A. Gurewitsch, Dec. 13 and 15,

1947; E. Roosevelt, "My Day," Dec. 16, 1947.
36. Interview with James P. Hendrick; letter from Eleanor Roosevelt to David A. Gurewitsch, Dec. 18, 1947.
37. *New York Times*, Dec. 16, 1947.
38. Interview with James P. Hendrick; letter from Eleanor Roosevelt to Robert A. Lovett, Jan. 16, 1948, and Lovett's reply, Jan. 19, 1948.
39. Letter from Eleanor Roosevelt to George C. Marshall, May 11, 1948, and Marshall's reply, May 19, 1948; letter from Eleanor Roosevelt to David A. Gurewitsch, May 12, 1948.
40. *New York Times*, May 3, 1948; E. Roosevelt, speech on "The Struggle for Human Rights," *op. cit.*
41. *New York Times*, May 24, 1948; *United Nations Records*, E/CN.4/SR.46; letter from George C. Marshall to Eleanor Roosevelt, July 12, 1948.
42. Letter from Eleanor Roosevelt to Walter White, Jan. 20, 1948; *New York Times*, June 9, 1948.
43. A. M. Rosenthal, "On Dealing with the Russians," *New York Times Magazine*, Jan. 18, 1953.
44. *New York Times*, June 18, 1948; *For Fundamental Human Rights* (United Nations, 1948), p. 21.
45. Letter from Eleanor Roosevelt to David A. Gurewitsch, Aug. 26, 1948; E. Roosevelt, speech on "The Struggle for Human Rights," dispatch from Paris to the State Department, No. 1214, Sept. 29, 1948.
46. *Our Rights as Human Beings* (United Nations, 1955), p. 9; interview with Durward Sandifer.
47. Interview with Durward Sandifer; letter from Eleanor Roosevelt to Maude Gray, Dec. 9, 1948.
48. Letter from Charles Malik to Joseph P. Lash, Sept. 15, 1970; letter from Helen Keller to Eleanor Roosevelt, undated; letter from Clark Eichelberger to Eleanor Roosevelt, April 7, 1949, and Eleanor Roosevelt's reply, undated; letter from John Foster Dulles to Eleanor Roosevelt, Feb. 2, 1949.
49. Herbert G. Nicholas, *The United Nations as a Political Institution* (New York, 1960), p. 132; *For Fundamental Human Rights, op. cit.*, p. 59.
50. Egon Schwelb, *Human Rights and the International Community: The Roots and Growth of the Universal Declaration of Human Rights, 1948–1963* (Chicago, 1964), p. 50; letter from John P. Humphrey to Joseph Lash, April 20, 1972.
51. Eleanor Roosevelt, *The Great Question* (United Nations, 1958).

IV. RELUCTANT COLD-WARRIOR

1. Letter from Harry Hopkins to Eleanor Roosevelt, Nov. 23, 1945.
2. *New York Times*, Feb. 16, 1946.
3. Memorandum from Eleanor Roosevelt to Harry S. Truman, March, 1946.
4. Letter from Eleanor Roosevelt to Joseph P. Lash, Jan. 27, 1946.
5. E. Roosevelt, "My Day," cited (Ch. I), March 16, 1946.
6. *Ibid.*, May 23, 1946; letter from El-

eanor Roosevelt to Harry S. Truman, April 27, 1946.
7. E. Roosevelt, "My Day," May 23, 1946; Joseph and Stewart Alsop, "The Tragedy of Liberalism," *Life,* May 20, 1946; letter from Joseph Alsop to Eleanor Roosevelt, April 26, 1946, and Eleanor Roosevelt's reply, April 28, 1946.
8. *New York Herald Tribune,* May 17, 1946.
9. Letter from Eleanor Roosevelt to Henry Wallace, April 17, 1945.
10. E. Roosevelt, "My Day," Sept. 21, 1946; letter from Eleanor Roosevelt to Harry S. Truman, May 27, 1946.
11. E. Roosevelt, "My Day," Nov. 11, 1946.
12. *Ibid.,* Aug. 28, 1946, and Sept. 17, 1946.
13. *Ibid.,* Aug. 9, 1946.
14. *Ibid.,* Dec. 19, 1946, and Nov. 1, 1946.
15. Eleanor Roosevelt, Foreword to Elliott Roosevelt's *As He Saw It* (New York, 1946), p. ix.
16. Joseph and Stewart Alsop, "Matter of Fact," column in the *New York Herald Tribune,* Dec. 1, 1946; letter from Eleanor Roosevelt to Joseph Alsop, Dec. 5, 1946, and letters from Joseph Alsop to Eleanor Roosevelt, Dec. 17 and 29, 1946.
17. J. and S. Alsop, "Matter of Fact," *op. cit.,* Dec. 1, 1946.
18. E. Roosevelt, "My Day," Jan. 4, 1947; James Loeb, in the *Roosevelt Day Memorial Journal,* issued by the Americans for Democratic Action, 1963.
19. E. Roosevelt, "My Day," Jan. 25, 1947.
20. Letter from Fiorello H. La Guardia to Eleanor Roosevelt, April 2, 1947, and Eleanor Roosevelt's reply, April 11, 1947.
21. Letter from Eleanor Roosevelt to Max Lerner, Jan. 19, 1947.
22. Telegram from C. B. Baldwin to Eleanor Roosevelt, April 16, 1947, and Eleanor Roosevelt's reply, April 17, 1947.
23. E. Roosevelt, "My Day," March 15, 1947.
24. Letter from Eleanor Roosevelt to Dean Acheson, March 26, 1947.
25. Vandenberg, *The Private Papers of Senator Vandenberg,* cited (Ch. III), p. 345; letter from Eleanor Roosevelt to Arthur H. Vandenberg, April 18, 1947.
26. Letter from Dean Acheson to Eleanor Roosevelt, April 15, 1947.
27. Letter from Eleanor Roosevelt to Harry S. Truman, April 17, 1947.
28. Letter from Harry S. Truman to Elnor Roosevelt, May 7, 1947.
29. Letter from Eleanor Roosevelt to Dean Acheson, April 11, 1947, and Acheson's reply, April 15, 1947; letter from Eleanor Roosevelt to Dean Acheson, April 16, 1947, and Acheson's reply, May 7, 1947; letter from Eleanor

Roosevelt to Harry S. Truman, May 19, 1947.
30. Letter from John Foster Dulles to Eleanor Roosevelt, May 26, 1947, and Eleanor Roosevelt's reply, June 21, 1947.
31. E. Roosevelt, "My Day," April 28, 1947.
32. Letter from Eleanor Roosevelt to Joseph P. Lash, July 28, 1947.
33. George F. Kennan, *Memoirs, 1925–1950* (Boston, 1967), pp. 317, 336, 341.
34. Joseph M. Jones, *The Fifteen Weeks* (New York, 1955), p. 36.
35. E. Roosevelt, "My Day," June 9, 1947; letter from Eleanor Roosevelt to Mrs. von Fluss, July 3, 1947.
36. E. Roosevelt, "My Day," July 5 and 9, 1947.
37. Letter from Eleanor Roosevelt to George C. Marshall, July 18, 1947, and Marshall's reply, July 22, 1947; E. Roosevelt, "My Day," Aug. 4, 1947.
38. Letters from Eleanor Roosevelt to Mr. Wiborg, Sept. 21, 1947.
39. Letter from Eleanor Roosevelt to James Roosevelt, June 27, 1945; letter from Eleanor Roosevelt to George C. Marshall, April 15, 1945.
40. Letter from George C. Marshall to Eleanor Roosevelt, July 23, 1947; E. Roosevelt, "My Day," Sept. 18, 1947.
41. Lash Diaries, Sept. 29, 1947.
42. Letter from Robert Hannagan to Eleanor Roosevelt, Oct. 20, 1947.
43. Lash Diaries, Sept. 27, 1947.
44. E. Roosevelt, "My Day," Oct. 8 and 15, 1947.
45. *Ibid.,* Oct. 27, 1947.
46. *New York Times,* Oct. 29, 1947.
47. Letter from Bruce Gould to Eleanor Roosevelt, undated; letter from George C. Marshall to Eleanor Roosevelt, Feb. 10, 1948, and Eleanor Roosevelt's reply, Feb. 15, 1948.
48. James Forrestal, *The Forrestal Diaries,* ed. Walter Millis and E. S. Duffield (New York, 1951), p. 387; letter from Eleanor Roosevelt to George C. Marshall, March 13, 1948.
49. Letter from Eleanor Roosevelt to Harry S. Truman, March 13, 1948.
50. Letter from Harry S. Truman to Eleanor Roosevelt, March 16, 1948; letter from George C. Marshall to Eleanor Roosevelt, March 17, 1948; letter from Eleanor Roosevelt to Joseph P. Lash, Oct. 16, 1948; letter from Bernard Baruch to Eleanor Roosevelt, Oct. 15, 1948.
51. Letter from Eleanor Roosevelt to Trude W. Lash, Oct. 16, 1948.
52. Letter from Eleanor Roosevelt to Joseph P. Lash, Oct. 26, 1948.
53. Letter from Eleanor Roosevelt to Trude W. Lash, Nov. 17, 1948.
54. *New York Herald Tribune,* Jan. 15, 1949; Elizabeth Janeway, "First Lady of the UN," *New York Times Magazine,* Oct. 22, 1950.
55. Lash Diaries, Oct. 2, 1949.

V. THE UNITED NATIONS AND A JEWISH HOMELAND

1. E. Roosevelt, "My Day," cited (Ch. I), April 12, 1943; letter from Louis Bromfield to Eleanor Roosevelt, June 21, 1943; letter from Eleanor Roosevelt to M. Potter, July 26, 1943.
2. Letter from Louis Weiss to Malvina Thompson, June 3, 1943.
3. Letter from Eleanor Roosevelt to Joseph P. Lash, April 6, 1944.
4. Letter from Eleanor Roosevelt to Dr. Dunner, Jan. 16, 1943.
5. Justine Wise Polier, "As I Knew Mrs. Roosevelt," *Petal Paper* (a monthly published in Petal, Miss., by P. D. East), Jan., 1963.
6. Ben Hecht, *Guide for the Bedevilled* (New York, 1944); letter from Eleanor Roosevelt to Joseph P. Lash, May 18, 1944.
7. Letter from Eleanor Roosevelt to the Mizrachi Women of America, Oct. 28, 1943.
8. Letter from Eleanor Roosevelt to Mrs. Miller, Dec. 21, 1948; letter from Eleanor Roosevelt to Joseph P. Lash, Feb. 12, 1943.
9. Letter from Eleanor Roosevelt to Louis Weiss, May 26, 1943; letter from Rose Halprin to Eleanor Roosevelt, Dec. 1, 1943.
10. Letter from Eleanor Roosevelt to Rose Halprin, Dec. 1, 1943; letter from Isaiah Bowman to Eleanor Roosevelt, Jan. 24, 1944.
11. Letter from Eleanor Roosevelt to Mrs. Levin, Jan. 31, 1944.
12. Letter from Trude W. Lash to Eleanor Roosevelt, March 19, 1945.
13. Letter from Stephen S. Wise to Chaim Weizmann, March 21, 1945.
14. *Ibid.*
15. Letter from Eleanor Roosevelt to Franklin D. Roosevelt Jewish Memorial Book Committee, Nov. 12, 1945.
16. Letter from Trude W. Lash to Joseph P. Lash, Aug. 27, 1945.
17. Letters from Helen Waren to Eleanor Roosevelt, Sept. 29, 1945, Oct. 14, 1945, and Nov. 6, 1945; letter from Eleanor Roosevelt to Helen Waren Oct. 22, 1945.
18. Letter from Eleanor Roosevelt to Harry S. Truman, Nov. 20, 1945, and Truman's reply, Nov. 26, 1945
19. Letter from Eleanor Roosevelt to Mrs. Colestone, Jan. 18, 1946.
20. Letter from Eleanor Roosevelt to Kathleen McLaughlin, Jan. 16, 1946; *New York Herald Tribune,* Feb. 14, 1946; E. Roosevelt, *On My Own,* cited (Ch. I), p. 56.
21. E. Roosevelt, "My Day," Feb. 14, 1946; letter from Eleanor Roosevelt to Carola von Schaeffer-Bernstein, May 11, 1946; E. Roosevelt, *On My Own,* p. 57.
22. E. Roosevelt, "My Day," June 15, 1946.
23. *Ibid.,* June 22, 1946.
24. *Ibid.,* June 24, 1946.
25. Letter from Eleanor Roosevelt to Lady Reading, Aug. 23, 1946.
26. E. Roosevelt, "My Day," Aug. 19, 1946; letter from Eleanor Roosevelt to Miss Siegel, Sept. 5, 1946; letter from Eleanor Roosevelt to *Davar,* Dec. 11, 1946.
27. E. Roosevelt, "My Day," Feb. 27, 1947, April 27 and 26, 1947.
28. *Ibid.,* May 14, 1947.
29. Letter from Eleanor Roosevelt to George C. Marshall, May 26, 1947 (the author has not been able to locate this letter), and Marshall's reply, June 20, 1947.
30. Letter from Eleanor Roosevelt to Miss Zelson, June 28, 1947.
31. E. Roosevelt, "My Day," Aug. 23, 1947.
32. Letter from Eleanor Roosevelt to Harry S. Truman, Aug. 30, 1947; E. Roosevelt, "My Day," Sept. 12, 1947.
33. Herbert Feis, *The Birth of Israel* (New York, 1969), p. 43.
34. Forrestal, *The Forrestal Diaries,* cited (Ch. IV), p. 8.
35. Interview with Durward Sandifer; Lash Diaries, Sept. 29, 1947; memorandum from Eleanor Roosevelt to Harry S. Truman, March, 1946, and Truman's reply, March 7, 1946.
36. Feis, *The Birth of Israel, op. cit.,* p. 45; letter from Eleanor Roosevelt to Lessing J. Rosenwald, Oct. 1, 1947.
37. E. Roosevelt, "My Day," Oct. 15, 1947; letter from Eleanor Roosevelt to Miss Binn, Oct. 24, 1947.
38. Letter from Eleanor Roosevelt to Miss Bacon, Feb. 27, 1948.
39. Feis, p. 51.
40. Letter from Eleanor Roosevelt to Harry S. Truman, undated (but clearly written in Jan., 1948).
41. James Reston, in the *New York Times,* Jan. 27, 1948.
42. Letter from Eleanor Roosevelt to George C. Marshall, Jan. 28, 1948.
43. Letter from Eleanor Roosevelt to Harry S. Truman, Jan. 29, 1948.
44. Letter from Harry S. Truman to Eleanor Roosevelt, Feb. 2, 1948; letter from George C. Marshall to Eleanor Roosevelt, Feb. 16, 1948.
45. Letter from Eleanor Roosevelt to George C. Marshall, Feb. 16, 1948.
46. Letter from Eleanor Roosevelt to Harry S. Truman, Feb. 20, 1948.
47. *New York Times,* Feb. 24, 1948.
48. Letter from Harry S. Truman to Eleanor Roosevelt, Feb. 27, 1948.
49. Interview with Benjamin V. Cohen.
50. Letter from Eleanor Roosevelt to George C. Marshall, March 22, 1948; letter from Eleanor Roosevelt to Harry S. Truman, March 22, 1948.
51. Letter from Harry S. Truman to Eleanor Roosevelt, March 25, 1948.

52. Letter from Eleanor Roosevelt to Harry S. Truman, March 26, 1948; E. Roosevelt, "My Day," April 1, 1948.
53. Letter from Eleanor Roosevelt to Adlai Stevenson, April 28, 1948.
54. Forrestal, pp. 405, 406,, 411; interview with Benjamin V. Cohen.
55. Harry S. Truman, *Years of Trial and Hope,* vol. II of *Memoirs* (Garden City, N.Y., 1955), p. 163.
56. Letter from Harry S. Truman to Eleanor Roosevelt, May 20, 1948; letter from George C. Marshall to Eleanor Roosevelt, May 18, 1948.
57. Letter from Eleanor Roosevelt to David A. Gurewitsch, May 26, 1948.
58. Letter from Eleanor Roosevelt to Bernard Baruch, Oct. 4, 1948, and Baruch's reply, Oct. 15, 1948; interview with Porter McKeever.
59. *New York Times,* Oct. 29, 1948.
60. Memorandum from Eleanor Roosevelt to Harry S. Truman, Dec. 28, 1948.
61. Letter from Eleanor Roosevelt to Miss Miller, Dec. 21, 1948.
62. Letter from Eleanor Roosevelt to Miss Berg, April 25, 1950.
63. Conversation with Ralph Bunche; letter from Eleanor Roosevelt to Trude W. Lash, Feb. 22, 1952; letter from Eleanor Roosevelt to Maude Gray, March 5, 1952.

VI. THE 1948 CAMPAIGN: A NEW PARTY—NOT A THIRD PARTY

1. Lash Diaries, Sept. 2, 1946.
2. Letter from Eleanor Roosevelt to S. V. Feeley, June 24, 1946.
3. Lash Diaries, Sept. 2, 1946.
4. Eleanor Roosevelt, "Why I Do Not Choose to Run," *Look,* July 9, 1946.
5. E. Roosevelt, "My Day," cited (Ch. I), Oct. 16, 1946.
6. Letter from Charl Williams to Eleanor Roosevelt, Nov. 7, 1946, and Eleanor Roosevelt's reply, Nov. 9, 1946; "A Visit with Mrs. Roosevelt Two Years after Her Husband's Death," *PM,* April 6, 1947.
7. Jonathan Daniels, *The Man of Independence* (New York, 1950), p. 22; letter from Eleanor Roosevelt to Harry S. Truman, Nov. 8, 1946.
8. Letter from Eleanor Roosevelt to Harry S. Truman, June 30, 1946.
9. Letter from Joseph P. Lash to Eleanor Roosevelt, July 25, 1946, and Eleanor Roosevelt's reply, Aug. 8, 1946; letter from Eleanor Roosevelt to Fiorello H. La Guardia, April 11, 1947.
10. Letter from Edwin W. Pauley to Eleanor Roosevelt, June 9, 1947, and Eleanor Roosevelt's reply, June 14, 1947.
11. Letter from Eleanor Roosevelt to Harry S. Truman, Sept. 3, 1947.
12. Letter from Eleanor Roosevelt to William O'Dwyer, Sept. 2, 1947; E. Roosevelt, "My Day," Sept. 13, 1947.
13. *Woman's Home Companion,* Feb., 1948.
14. E. Roosevelt, "My Day," Dec. 29, 30, and 31, 1947.
15. Letter from Eleanor Roosevelt to Harry S. Truman, Jan. 16, 1948, and Truman's reply, Jan. 19, 1948.
16. Letter from Eleanor Roosevelt to Harry S. Truman, Jan. 29, 1948.
17. *Ibid.,* Feb. 20, 1948.
18. Letter from Harry S. Truman to Eleanor Roosevelt, Feb. 27, 1948, and Eleanor Roosevelt's reply, March 4, 1948.
19. Lash Diaries, March 30, 1948.
20. *Ibid.*
21. Letter from Eleanor Roosevelt to Harry S. Truman, March 26, 1948.
22. Letter from Eleanor Roosevelt to George C. Marshall, March 27, 1948, and Marshall's reply, April 5, 1948.
23. Letter from Lewis Douglas to George C. Marshall, May 3, 1948; letter from May Craig to Eleanor Roosevelt, May 5, 1948, and Eleanor Roosevelt's reply, May 11, 1948.
24. Letter from Chester Bowles to Eleanor Roosevelt, June 18, 1948.
25. Letter from Eleanor Roosevelt to Chester Bowles, June 23, 1948; Clare Luce statement quoted in the *New York World-Telegram,* June 28, 1948; letter from Mrs. Baxter to Eleanor Roosevelt, July 1, 1948; Doris Fleeson, in the *Washington Star.*
26. *New York Times,* July 1, 1948; Daniels, *The Man of Independence, op. cit.,* p. 349.
27. Irwin Ross, *The Loneliest Campaign: The Truman Victory of 1948* (New York, 1968), p. 115; telegram from Eleanor Roosevelt to William O. Douglas, undated.
28. Letter from Eleanor Roosevelt to Maude Gray, July 28, 1948; letter from Eleanor Roosevelt to Mrs. Mortimer, Aug. 6, 1948; letter from Eleanor Roosevelt to Mrs. Lokken, July 10, 1948; E. Roosevelt, "My Day," June 1, 1948.
29. Memorandum from William L. Batt to Clark Clifford, Aug. 6, 1948; letter from Eleanor Roosevelt to Joseph P. Lash, Aug. 13, 1948.
30. Eleanor Roosevelt explained her position in a letter she wrote to Frances Perkins, Oct. 4, 1948; also, letter from Eleanor Roosevelt to Harry S. Truman, Aug. 19, 1948.
31. Letter from Eleanor Roosevelt to Bernard Baruch, Oct. 4, 1948.
32. Letter from Eleanor Roosevelt to Frances Perkins, Oct. 4, 1948.
33. *New York Times,* Nov. 1, 1948.
34. Letter from Eleanor Roosevelt to Joseph P. Lash, Nov. 5, 1948.

35. Letter from Eleanor Roosevelt to Trude W. Lash, Nov. 17, 1948.
36. Memorandum from Eleanor Roosevelt to Harry S. Truman, Dec. 28, 1948.
37. Letter from Adlai Stevenson to Eleanor Roosevelt, Nov. 6, 1948.

VII. CARDINAL AND FORMER FIRST LADY

1. Westbrook Pegler, in the *New York Journal-American,* July 11, 1949.
2. Carl T. Rowan, "The Life of Eleanor Roosevelt," *New York Post,* March, 1958; letter from Mrs. Westbrook Pegler to Eleanor Roosevelt, Aug. 13, 1953, and Eleanor Roosevelt's reply, Aug. 17, 1953; Eleanor Roosevelt, in *the Ladies' Home Journal,* Jan., 1949.
3. Harold Lavine, "Life with Eleanor," *Newsweek,* Aug. 22, 1949.
4. Letter from Eleanor Roosevelt to Betty Hight, Aug. 15, 1949; letter from Eleanor Roosevelt to Herbert Lehman, Aug. 11, 1949.
5. Letter from Eleanor Roosevelt to Betty Hight, Aug. 15, 1949.
6. E. Roosevelt, "My Day," cited (Ch. I), June 23, 1949.
7. Letter from Francis Cardinal Spellman to Eleanor Roosevelt, July 21, 1949.
8. E. Roosevelt, "My Day," July 23, 1949; letter from Eleanor Roosevelt to Francis Cardinal Spellman, dated July 23, 1949, and released July 28, 1949.
9. Letter from May Craig to Eleanor Roosevelt, July 26, 1949; *Arriba,* Aug. 9, 1949; Associated Press, June 2, 1949.
10. Letter from Eleanor Roosevelt to Betty Hight, Aug. 15, 1949.
11. Letter from May Craig to Eleanor Roosevelt, July 26, 1949; letter from Doris Fleeson to Eleanor Roosevelt, Aug. 7, 1949; *Raleigh News and Observer,* Aug. 8, 1949; letter from William Hassett to Eleanor Roosevelt, July 22, 1949; letter from William Phillips to Eleanor Roosevelt, July 26, 1949; letter from Rose Schneiderman to Eleanor Roosevelt, July 24, 1949.
12. Interview with Mrs. Herbert Lehman; letter from Eleanor Roosevelt to Louis Weiss, July, 1949.
13. Letter from William Hassett to Eleanor Roosevelt, Aug. 5, 1949; letter from Eleanor Roosevelt to George Fischer, Sept. 5, 1949.
14. Letter from Eleanor Roosevelt to Dean Acheson, July 31, 1949.
15. Letter from Harry S. Truman to Eleanor Roosevelt, Aug. 2, 1949; letter from William Hassett to Eleanor Roosevelt, Aug. 5, 1949.
16. Lash Diaries, Aug. 8, 1949.
17. Letter from Agnes Meyer to Eleanor Roosevelt, Aug. 4, 1949.
18. Letter from Eleanor Roosevelt to Agnes Meyer, Aug. 8, 1949.
19. E. Roosevelt, "My Day," Aug. 6, 1949.
20. Letter from Eleanor Roosevelt to Agnes Meyer, Aug. 8, 1949; letter from Eleanor Roosevelt to Cyril Clemens, Aug. 23, 1949.
21. *Newsweek,* Aug. 22, 1949; E. Roosevelt, "My Day," Aug. 24, 1949.
22. Letter from Charl Williams to Eleanor Roosevelt, Sept. 1, 1949; Irwin Ross, "Cardinal Spellman," *New York Post,* Sept. 18, 1957.
23. Lash Diaries, Aug. 8, 1949.
24. Letter from Eleanor Roosevelt to Edward Flynn, Sept. 13, 1949.
25. Letter from Eleanor Roosevelt to Harry S. Truman, Oct. 6, 1949.
26. Letter from Eleanor Roosevelt to Dr. Nussbaum, Feb. 12, 1950; letter from Eleanor Roosevelt to George Barsky, March 4, 1950.
27. Interview with Mrs. Herbert Lehman; letter from Eleanor Roosevelt to George Fischer, Sept. 5, 1949.

VIII. AN AMERICAN PHENOMENON

1. Letter from Eleanor Roosevelt to Josephus Daniels, May, 1947; Kahn, Jr., "The Years Alone," cited (Ch. III).
2. Memoranda from Malvina Thompson to Eleanor Roosevelt, 1949.
3. *Ibid.*
4. Letter from William Bishop Scarlett to Eleanor Roosevelt, March 26, 1951.
5. Letter from John Ihlder to Eleanor Roosevelt, April 8, 1949, and Eleanor Roosevelt's reply, undated.
6. Letter from Eleanor Roosevelt to Werner L. Gundesheimer, Dec. 15, 1953; letter from Eleanor Roosevelt to Maude Gray, Nov., 1949.
7. Letter from Eleanor Roosevelt to her children, Aug. 28, 1947.
8. E. Roosevelt, "My Day," cited (Ch. I), Aug. 19, 1947; Kahn, Jr., "The Years Alone."
9. Letter from Eleanor Roosevelt to Trude W. Lash, March 10, 1947.
10. Letter from Eleanor Roosevelt to Henry Toombs, June 10, 1947; interview with Marion Dickerman; letter from Nancy Cook to Eleanor Roosevelt, Oct. 3, 1947.
11. Letter from Eleanor Roosevelt to Henry Morgenthau, Jr., March 2, 1951.
12. Lash Diaries, Oct. 26, 1949; Westbrook Pegler, syndicated column, Jan. 22, 1945, Dec. 23, 1948, and Aug. 17, 1949.
13. Interview with Franklin D. Roosevelt, Jr.
14. Memorandum by Charles F. Palmer

at Hyde Park, June 23, 1951; "Mrs. R.," *Time*, April 7, 1952; W. H. Auden and Louis Kronenberger, eds., *The Viking Book of Aphorisms: A Personal Selection* (New York, 1962), p. 391.

15. Letter from Eleanor Roosevelt to Maude Gray, Sept. 12, 1948.

16. Interview with Maureen Corr; letter from Eleanor Roosevelt to Ralph Thompson, Jan. 19, 1951; letter from Malvina Thompson to W. Funk, Oct. 22, 1946.

17. *New York Post,* May 18, 1949.

18. Richard L. Wilson, "Two Young Roosevelts Race for the White House," *Look,* Nov. 22, 1949.

19. Lash Diaries, Nov. 11, 1950, and July 19, 1950.

20. Earl Warren's comment quoted in the *New York Times,* Sept. 13, 1950; letter from Eleanor Roosevelt to Betty Hight, Sept. 18, 1950; Lash Diaries, Nov. 6, 1950.

21. Letter from W. J. Vigneault to Eleanor Roosevelt, July 26, 1949, and Eleanor Roosevelt's reply, July 29, 1949.

22. Letter from Eleanor Roosevelt to Betty Hight, Dec. 12, 1950.

23. Lash Diaries, Sept. 21, 1949.

24. E. Roosevelt, "My Day," Sept. 9, 1947.

25. Interview with Elliott Roosevelt; E. Roosevelt, "My Day," Feb. 3, 1958; Eleanor Roosevelt, *Autobiography* (New York, 1961), p. 36.

26. Letter from Eleanor Roosevelt to Maude Gray, July 23, 1948; interview with Anna Roosevelt Halsted.

27. Letter from Lawrence S. Kubie to Joseph P. Lash, June 7, 1964.

28. Interview with David A. Gurewitsch; letters from Eleanor Roosevelt to David A. Gurewitsch, Dec. 13, 1947, and April 17, 1948.

29. Letter from Eleanor Roosevelt to Maude Gray, undated; *Variety* quoted in Alfred Steinberg, *Mrs. R.: The Life of Eleanor Roosevelt* (New York, 1958), p. 344; letter from Robert E. Kintner to Eleanor Roosevelt, July 21, 1949.

30. Lash Diaries, Dec. 10, 1949.

31. Letter from Eleanor Roosevelt to John Golden, June 28, 1951; letter from Eleanor Roosevelt to the Duke and Duchess of Windsor, March 6, 1950; letter from Eleanor Roosevelt to Miss Tucker, Jan. 29, 1949.

32. Letter from Lawrence Spivak to Eleanor Roosevelt, April 12, 1949.

33. "Mrs. R.," *op. cit.;* Howard Taubman, in the *New York Times,* Aug. 12, 1950.

34. Letter from Joseph P. Lash to Trude W. Lash Aug. 19, 1951.

35. Letter from Eleanor Roosevelt to Miss Cummins, Feb. 13, 1951.

36. Letter from Eleanor Roosevelt to Maude Gray, Aug. 5, 1948; letter from Eleanor Roosevelt to David A. Gurewitsch, undated; letter from Bruce Gould to Eleanor Roosevelt, Feb. 2, 1949.

37. Letter from Eleanor Roosevelt to Maude Gray, Feb. 13, 1949; Bruce and Beatrice Gould, *An American Story: Memories and Reflections of Bruce and Beatrice Gould* (New York, 1968), p. 285.

38. Letter from Eleanor Roosevelt to Trude W. Lash, March 11, 1949; letter from Eleanor Roosevelt to Martha Strayer, June, 1949; memorandum from Malvina Thompson on discussion with Bruce Gould, March 9, 1949; B. and B. Gould, *An American Story, op. cit.,* p. 285.

39. Letter from Eleanor Roosevelt to Otis Wiese, March 11, 1949.

40. Letter from George Bye to Eleanor Roosevelt, July 2, 1948; letter from Jonathan Daniels to Eleanor Roosevelt, May 3, 1949; letter from Bruce Gould to Eleanor Roosevelt, June 3, 1949.

41. Elizabeth Janeway, in the *New York Times Book Review,* Nov. 6, 1949; Vincent Sheean, in the *New York Herald Tribune Books,* Nov. 6, 1949.

42. Letter from Eleanor Roosevelt to Maude and David Gray, undated, and David Gray's reply, Dec. 19, 1949.

43. Letter from Eleanor Roosevelt to John Gunther, June 2, 1950.

44. Arthur Schlesinger, Jr., in the *Saturday Review,* Nov. 5, 1949.

45. "Mrs. R," *op. cit.*

IX. AMERICA'S BEST AMBASSADOR

1. Letter from Lewis Douglas to George C. Marshall, May 3, 1948; interview with Durward Sandifer.

2. Letter from Eleanor Roosevelt to Ruth Eidson, March 22, 1950; letter from Dean Rusk to Eleanor Roosevelt, March 31, 1950; letter from Llewellyn Thompson to Malvina Thompson, May 18, 1950.

3. *Svenska Dagbladet,* June 9, 1950; *Dagens Nyheter,* June 9, 1950.

4. Letter from Eleanor Roosevelt to Joseph P. and Trude W. Lash, June 10, 1950.

5. Letter from Eleanor Roosevelt to Trude W. Lash, June 13, 1950.

6. *Ibid.,* June 18, 1950.

7. Letter from Eleanor Roosevelt to Joseph P. Lash, June 20, 1950.

8. Letter from Eleanor Roosevelt to Dean Acheson, June 13, 1950.

9. Letter from Robert Murphy to Eleanor Roosevelt, June 23, 1950, and Eleanor Roosevelt's reply, undated.

10. Letter from Peter Stewart (member of the U.S. delegation to the United Nations) to Eleanor Roosevelt, Nov. 16, 1951.

11. Letter from Eleanor Roosevelt to Betty Hight, Dec. 12, 1950.
12. Memorandum from Eleanor Roosevelt to Harry S. Truman, undated.
13. Letter from Eleanor Roosevelt to Avra M. Warren, Dec. 22, 1951.
14. Letter from Dean Acheson to Eleanor Roosevelt, Feb. 13, 1952; U.S. delegation press release, Nov. 16, 1951; Eleanor Roosevelt, "Voice of America" broadcast, Paris, Nov. 16, 1951.
15. Richard N. Gardner, "First Lady of the Voice of America," *New York Times Magazine,* Feb. 3, 1952; letter from Dean Acheson to Eleanor Roosevelt, Feb. 13, 1952.
16. Letter from Eleanor Roosevelt to Jefferson Caffery, Jan. 30, 1952; letter from Eleanor Roosevelt to Trude W. Lash, Jan. 23, 1952; letter from Harold B. Minor to Eleanor Roosevelt, Jan., 1952; letters from Avra M. Warren to Eleanor Roosevelt, Jan. 3, 1952, and Feb. 4, 1952, and Eleanor Roosevelt's replies, Feb. 1 and 5, 1952.
17. Eleanor Roosevelt, *India and the Awakening East* (New York, 1953), p. 34.
18. Letter from Eleanor Roosevelt to Chester Bowles, Feb. 21, 1952.
19. Interviews with David A. Gurewitsch and Esther Lape.
20. Press clippings; *India Today* (publication of the India League of America), April, 1952; interviews with David A. Gurewitsch and Maureen Corr.
21. E. Roosevelt, *India and the Awakening East, op. cit.,* pp. 182–91; David E. Lilienthal, *Venturesome Years, 1950–55,* vol. III of *The Journals of David E. Lilienthal,* 5 vols. (New York, 1966), pp. 364–65; interview with David A. Gurewitsch.
22. E. Roosevelt, *India and the Awakening East,* p. 171.
23. Letter from Eleanor Roosevelt to Dorothy Bourne, March 16, 1952; interview with Maureen Corr.
24. Letter from Eleanor Roosevelt to Harry S. Truman, March 7, 1952.
25. Interview with David A. Gurewitsch; letter from Eleanor Roosevelt to Dean Acheson, March 7, 1952.
26. Letter from Malvina Thompson to Maude Gray, March 10, 1952; letter from Eleanor Roosevelt to Dorothy Bourne, March 16, 1952.
27. Letter from Eleanor Roosevelt to the U.S. embassy at Taipei, Feb. 2, 1952; telegram from Dean Acheson to Eleanor Roosevelt, March 5, 1952.
28. Memorandum from Dean Acheson to Harry S. Truman, April 10, 1952.
29. Letters from Eleanor Roosevelt to Chester Bowles, April 21, 1952, and May 12, 1952; letter from Walter Bedell Smith to Eleanor Roosevelt, May 9, 1952.
30. Letter from Claude G. Bowers to Joseph Guffey, Jan. 17, 1953; letter from Claude G. Bowers to the State Department, Dec. 5, 1952; *Christian Science Monitor,* Dec. 16, 1952.

X. RESIGNATION ACCEPTED

1. Letter from Eleanor Roosevelt to Joseph P. Lash, Jan. 21, 1952.
2. *Ibid.,* Feb. 7, 1952; Truman, *Years of Trial and Hope,* cited (Ch. V), p. 492; Lash Diaries, April 5, 1952; letter from Eleanor Roosevelt to Chester Bowles, April 21, 1952.
3. Letter from India Edwards to Eleanor Roosevelt, April 1, 1952.
4. Letter from Eleanor Roosevelt to India Edwards, undated.
5. Letter from Cyril Clemens to Eleanor Roosevelt, May 31, 1952, and Eleanor Roosevelt's reply, undated.
6. Letter from Eleanor Roosevelt to India Edwards, June 18, 1952; letter from Eleanor Roosevelt to Harry S. Truman, June 30, 1952, and Truman's reply, July 3, 1952; letter from Eleanor Roosevelt to Harry S. Truman, July 13, 1952; letter from Eleanor Roosevelt to Frank E. McKinney, July 13, 1952.
7. *New York Herald Tribune,* July 22, 1952.
8. *New York Post,* July 23, 1952.
9. Letter from Lily Polk to Eleanor Roosevelt, July 11, 1952; letter from Myron W. Cowen (Brussels embassy) to Eleanor Roosevelt, Aug. 15, 1952;
letter from Herbert Beaser to Eleanor Roosevelt, July 29, 1952; letter from Agnes E. Meyer to Eleanor Roosevelt, July 25, 1952.
10. Letter from Eleanor Roosevelt to Adlai Stevenson, Aug. 6, 1952; letter from Adlai Stevenson to Eleanor Roosevelt, undated.
11. Letter from Eleanor Roosevelt to Joseph P. Lash, Aug. 21, 1952.
12. Margaret L. Coit, *Mr. Baruch* (Boston, 1957), pp. 677, 678; letter from Bernard Baruch to Eleanor Roosevelt, Sept. 3, 1952.
13. E. Roosevelt, "My Day," cited (Ch. I), Sept. 13, 1952.
14. Letter from Eleanor Roosevelt to India Edwards, Sept. 28, 1952.
15. Truman, p. 499; letter from Eleanor Roosevelt to India Edwards, Sept. 28, 1952.
16. *New York Times,* Oct. 6, 1952.
17. E. Roosevelt, "My Day," Oct. 29, 1952.
18. Letter from Eleanor Roosevelt to Mrs. McLean, Oct. 9, 1952.
19. Letter from Mrs. Roosevelt to Mrs. Ives, undated; letter from Adlai Stevenson to Eleanor Roosevelt, Nov. 11, 1952.

20. *New York Times,* Dec. 12, 1948.
21. Letter from Eleanor Roosevelt to John D. Hickerson, Nov. 6, 1952.
22. *New York Post,* Nov. 19, 1952; letter from Bernard Baruch to Eleanor Roosevelt, Nov. 16, 1952, and Eleanor Roosevelt's reply, Nov. 18, 1952.
23. Lash Diaries, Nov. 19, 1952.
24. *New York Post,* Dec. 14, 1952; A. M. Rosenthal, in the *New York Times,* Dec. 21, 1952.
25. Letter from Durward Sandifer to Eleanor Roosevelt, Dec. 22, 1952; letter from Dwight D. Eisenhower to Eleanor Roosevelt, Dec. 30, 1952, and Eleanor Roosevelt's reply, Dec. 31, 1952.
26. Letter from Richard S. Winslow to Eleanor Roosevelt, Jan. 20, 1953.
27. Letter from Eleanor Roosevelt to Harry S. Truman, Jan. 8, 1953.
28. Interview with David A. Gurewitsch.

XI. PRIVATE CITIZEN AGAIN

1. *New York Post,* Oct. 9, 1967; A. M. Rosenthal, in the *New York Times,* Jan. 18, 1953.
2. Letter from Henry Cabot Lodge, Jr., to Eleanor Roosevelt, Feb. 7, 1953; letter from Eleanor Roosevelt to Lord Elibank, Feb. 20, 1953.
3. Letter from Durward Sandifer to Eleanor Roosevelt, March 16, 1953, and Eleanor Roosevelt's reply, March 18, 1953.
4. Doris Fleeson, in the *Washington Star,* April 8, 1953; letter from Eleanor Roosevelt to Mrs. Oswald Lord, April 4, 1953.
5. Letter from Eleanor Roosevelt to Durward Sandifer, May 16, 1953; letter from Eleanor Roosevelt to Irene Sandifer, May 16, 1953.
6. Letter from Harry J. Carman to Eleanor Roosevelt, Aug. 13, 1952; letter from Eleanor Roosevelt to Harry J. Carman, Nov. 6, 1952; letter from John Foster Dulles to Eleanor Roosevelt, Nov. 28, 1952; letter from Harry J. Carman to Eleanor Roosevelt, Dec. 4, 1952.
7. Letter from Eleanor Roosevelt to Trude W. and Joseph P. Lash, May 26, 1953; letter from Eleanor Roosevelt to David Gray, June 12, 1953; letter from Eleanor Roosevelt to John Golden, June 12, 1953.
8. Letter from Eleanor Roosevelt to John Golden, June 12, 1953.
9. Tatsuo Morito, in *Fujin Asahi,* Aug., 1953; letter from Eleanor Roosevelt to Harry J. Carman, June 23, 1953; letter from Kichisaburo Nomura to Eleanor Roosevelt, May 29, 1953, and Eleanor Roosevelt's reply, May 30, 1953.
10. Letter from Eleanor Roosevelt to Harry J. Carman, June 21, 1953.
11. Letters from Eleanor Roosevelt to Harry J. Carman, June 4 and 21, 1953.
12. E. Roosevelt, *On My Own,* cited (Ch. I), pp. 113–14.
13. Interview with Irene Sandifer.
14. Letter from Eleanor Roosevelt to Harry J. Carman, June 24, 1953.
15. E. Roosevelt, *On My Own,* p. 124.
16. Letter from Eleanor Roosevelt to John Roosevelt, June 30, 1953; E. Roosevelt, *On My Own,* p. 131.
17. Letter from Eleanor Roosevelt to John Roosevelt, June 30, 1953.
18. *Ibid.,* July 9, 1953.
19. Interview with David A. Gurewitsch; letters from Eleanor Roosevelt to John Roosevelt, July 9 and 20, 1953.
20. Letters from Eleanor Roosevelt to John Roosevelt, July 9 and 20, 1953; E. Roosevelt, *On My Own,* pp. 152–53.
21. Letter from Eleanor Roosevelt to John Roosevelt, July 23, 1953.
22. Letter from Eleanor Roosevelt to Durward Sandifer, June 25, 1953; letter from Eleanor Roosevelt to John Roosevelt, July 9, 1953; letter from Eleanor Roosevelt to David Gray, June 12, 1953; E. Roosevelt, "My Day," cited (Ch. I), Nov. 28, 1952.
23. Eleanor Roosevelt, speech to the Americans for Democratic Action, April 2, 1950.
24. Westbrook Pegler, in the *New York Journal-American,* November, 1953; letter from Eleanor Roosevelt to Mr. Stojilkovic, July 8, 1953.
25. Letter from Eleanor Roosevelt to Joseph P. Lash, July 18, 1951; letter from Freda Kirchwey to Eleanor Roosevelt, May 26, 1952; Eleanor Roosevelt's remarks in the *Nation,* June 7, 1952.
26. Letter from Eleanor Roosevelt to Trude W. and Joseph P. Lash, Aug. 19, 1952; letter from Eugene Lyons to Eleanor Roosevelt, July 6, 1952.
27. Lash Diaries, May 22, 1953; *New York Post,* May 13, 1953.
28. *New York Post,* May 13, 1953; United Press from Hong Kong, June 25, 1953.
29. Letter from Eleanor Roosevelt to Clark Eichelberger, June 12, 1953; letter from Eleanor Roosevelt to Alice Pollitzer, April 29, 1954.
30. Emma Bugbee, in the *New York Herald Tribune,* Oct. 8, 1954; E. Roosevelt, *On My Own,* p. 107; letter from Lorena Hickok to Nannine Joseph, Feb. 5, 1954; Eleanor Roosevelt, *You Learn by Living* (New York, 1960), p. 85; E. Roosevelt, "My Day," April 13, 1953.
31. Letter from Eleanor Roosevelt to David Gray, Dec. 2, 1952.
32. Letter from Eleanor Roosevelt to her children, June 19, 1954.

33. *New York Times* and *New York Herald Tribune,* Oct. 8, 1954.
34. Letter from Eleanor Roosevelt to Edith Helm, Sept. 22, 1954.

35. Doris Fleeson, in the *New York Times,* Oct. 16, 1954.
36. *New York Times,* Oct. 12, 1954.

XII. "MADLY FOR ADLAI"

1. Lash Diaries, Oct. 28, 1953.
2. Letter from Eleanor Roosevelt to Louise Morley Cochrane, Nov. 24, 1952.
3. Letter from Eleanor Roosevelt to Martha Gellhorn, Nov. 2, 1953.
4. E. Roosevelt, "My Day," cited (Ch. I), Sept. 13, 1952; letter from Eleanor Roosevelt to Marie Schwartz, Sept. 16, 1952; letter from Adlai Stevenson to Eleanor Roosevelt, Nov. 20, 1953.
5. E. Roosevelt, *On My Own,* cited (Ch. I), pp. 160–61; letter from Eleanor Roosevelt to David Gray, Oct. 27, 1955; letter from Eleanor Roosevelt to Allard Lowenstein, Oct. 25, 1955.
6. Letter from Eleanor Roosevelt to Thomas K. Finletter, Feb. 11, 1956; letter from Eleanor Roosevelt to Barry Bingham, Jan. 19, 1956.
7. Letter from Eleanor Roosevelt to Lord Elibank, Jan. 20, 1956.
8. Letter from Eleanor Roosevelt to Gus Ranis, Jan. 23, 1956.
9. Letter from Adlai Stevenson to Eleanor Roosevelt, March 7, 1956; letter from Eugenie Anderson to Eleanor Roosevelt, April 11, 1956; letter from Eleanor Roosevelt to Gus Ranis, April 7, 1956.
10. Letter from Eleanor Roosevelt to Adlai Stevenson, April 2, 1956; letter from Eleanor Roosevelt to Gus Ranis, April 7, 1956; letter from Eleanor Roosevelt to Adlai Stevenson, April 11, 1956.
11. David E. Lilienthal, *The TVA Years, 1939–45,* vol. I of *The Journals of David E. Lilienthal,* 5 vols. (New York, 1964), p. 310, May 15, 1941.
12. Lash Diaries, April 20, 1956.
13. Letter from William Benton to Eleanor Roosevelt, April 11, 1956.
14. Letter from Nancy W. Davis to Eleanor Roosevelt, May 3, 1956; letter from Eleanor Roosevelt to Adlai Stevenson, undated.
15. Letter from Eleanor Roosevelt to Allard Lowenstein, June 8, 1956; letter from Thomas K. Finletter to Eleanor Roosevelt, June 13, 1956.
16. Letter from Adlai Stevenson to Eleanor Roosevelt, June 8, 1956, and Eleanor Roosevelt's reply, June 13, 1956.
17. Eleanor Roosevelt and Lorena A. Hickok, *Ladies of Courage* (New York, 1954), p. 277.
18. James M. Burns, *Roosevelt: The Lion and the Fox* (New York, 1956), p. 21.
19. Letter from Richard Bolling to Eleanor Roosevelt, Jan. 10, 1956, and Eleanor Roosevelt's reply, Jan. 20, 1956.
20. Newspaper clippings, datelined Portland, Ore., Feb. 11 and 12, 1956.
21. Letter from Roy Wilkins to Adlai Stevenson, Feb. 9, 1956.
22. Letter from Eleanor Roosevelt to Roy Wilkins, Feb. 15, 1956; letter from Eleanor Roosevelt to Mrs. Walter White, Feb. 24, 1956; letter from Eleanor Roosevelt to Pauli Murray, Feb. 22, 1956.
23. Letter from Eleanor Roosevelt to Roy Wilkins, undated, and Wilkins's reply, April 2, 1956.
24. Letter from Eleanor Roosevelt to Channing Tobias, April 26, 1956.
25. Letter from Adlai Stevenson to Eleanor Roosevelt, June 15, 1956, and Eleanor Roosevelt's reply, June 20, 1956.
26. Letter from Eleanor Roosevelt to Trude W. and Joseph P. Lash, July 22, 1956.
27. Letter from Joseph Rauh, Jr., to Eleanor Roosevelt, July 24, 1956, and Eleanor Roosevelt's reply, July 30, 1956.
28. Letter from Joseph Rauh, Jr., to Eleanor Roosevelt, Aug. 2, 1956; letter from Eleanor Roosevelt to Joseph P. Lash, Aug. 4, 1956.
29. Letter from Adlai Stevenson to Paul Butler, Aug. 4, 1956; letter from Adlai Stevenson to Eleanor Roosevelt, Aug. 9, 1956.
30. Letter from Eleanor Roosevelt to Joseph P. Lash, Aug. 4, 1956; letter from James Finnegan to Eleanor Roosevelt, Aug. 3, 1956; letter from Eleanor Roosevelt to Estes Kefauver, Aug. 4, 1956.
31. Letter from Eleanor Roosevelt to Paul Butler, July 2, 1956.
32. Letter from Adlai Stevenson to Eleanor Roosevelt, July 16, 1956.
33. E. Roosevelt, *On My Own,* pp. 162, 163; newspaper clippings.
34. Arthur Schlesinger, Jr., in the *National Roosevelt Day Journal* of the Americans for Democratic Action, 1963; E. Roosevelt, *On My Own,* pp. 162, 163; see also footnote 36, below.
35. Interviews with Mary Lasker and Lorena Hickok; Eleanor Roosevelt, speech to the Democratic National Convention, Aug. 13, 1956, in Eleanor Roosevelt speech file, in Franklin D. Roosevelt Library.
36. Thomas Stokes, "Mrs. R's Fight," *New York Post,* Aug. 15, 1956; Andrew Tully, in the *New York World-Telegram,* Aug. 16, 1956; *New York Times,* Aug. 14, 1956; *New York Herald*

Tribune, Aug. 13, 1956; letter from Eugenie Anderson to Eleanor Roosevelt, Aug. 6, 1956; letter from Abba Schwartz to Eleanor Roosevelt, July 31, 1956; letter from James Landis to Eleanor Roosevelt, Aug. 3, 1956.

37. Letter from Eleanor Roosevelt to David A. Gurewitsch, Aug. 17, 1956; letter from Helen Hill Miller to Eleanor Roosevelt, undated; David E. Lilienthal, *The Road to Change, 1955–59,* vol. IV of *The Journals of David E. Lilienthal,* 5 vols. (New York, 1969), p. 108, Aug. 17, 1956; letter from William Benton to Eleanor Roosevelt, Aug. 27, 1956.

38. Letter from Eleanor Roosevelt to Adlai Stevenson, Aug. 28, 1956.

39. Letter from Eleanor Roosevelt to David Gray, Sept. 14, 1956; Lash Diaries, Sept. 19, 1956; letter from Adlai Stevenson to Eleanor Roosevelt, Sept. 16, 1956; letter from Paul Butler to Eleanor Roosevelt, Sept. 19, 1956; letter from Katie S. Louchheim to Eleanor Roosevelt, Sept. 19, 1956; letter from

Agnes Meyer to Eleanor Roosevelt, Sept. 22, 1956.

40. Letter from Eleanor Roosevelt to Adlai Stevenson, Sept. 20, 1956.

41. Memorandum from Bernard Baruch to Adlai Stevenson, Sept. 20, 1956; Lash Diaries, Sept. 19, 1956; letter from Bernard Baruch to Eleanor Roosevelt, Oct. 23, 1956, and Eleanor Roosevelt's reply, Oct. 26, 1956.

42. Letter from Eleanor Roosevelt to James Finnegan, Oct. 12, 1956.

43. Letter from Eleanor Roosevelt to Adlai Stevenson, Oct. 10, 1956.

44. Interviews with Anna Rosenberg and David A. Gurewitsch.

45. Letter from Eleanor Roosevelt to Mrs. Philip Vaughn ("Bennett"), Oct. 24, 1956.

46. Letter from Eleanor Roosevelt to David Gray, Nov. 24, 1956; letter from Eleanor Roosevelt to Adlai Stevenson, Nov. 7, 1956.

47. Carl T. Rowan, "The Life of Eleanor Roosevelt," *New York Post,* March, 1958; interview with Samuel I. Rosenman.

XIII. TWO BOSSES—KHRUSHCHEV AND DE SAPIO

1. Letter from Eleanor Roosevelt to Charl Williams, Dec. 8, 1956.

2. Letter from Eleanor Roosevelt to Paul Butler, Dec. 6, 1956.

3. E. Roosevelt, *On My Own,* cited (Ch. I), pp. 194–95; letter from Dorothy Schiff to Eleanor Roosevelt, Jan. 11, 1957.

4. Press conference release, July 1, 1954; letter from Eleanor Roosevelt to David A. Gurewitsch, July 1, 1954.

5. Letters from Eleanor Roosevelt to Trude W. and Joseph P. Lash, Sept. 6, 17, and 20, 1957.

6. E. Roosevelt, *On My Own,* p. 200.

7. Letters from Eleanor Roosevelt to Trude W. and Joseph P. Lash, *op. cit.*

8. E. Roosevelt, *On My Own,* pp. 206, 207.

9. *Ibid.,* p. 232.

10. *Ibid.,* p. 217.

11. Transcript of Eleanor Roosevelt's interview with Nikita S. Khrushchev; E. Roosevelt, *On My Own,* pp. 228–29.

12. E. Roosevelt, *On My Own,* pp. 230–31; interview with David A. Gurewitsch.

13. *New York Post,* Oct. 21, 1957; letter from Eleanor Roosevelt to Queen Juliana, Feb. 14, 1958.

14. Letter from Arthur Schlesinger, Jr., to Eleanor Roosevelt, Nov. 1, 1958; letter from Eleanor Roosevelt to Nikita S. Khrushchev, Nov. 5, 1958.

15. *New York Post,* Sept. 18, 1959; *New York Times,* Sept. 19, 1959; letter from Eleanor Roosevelt to Nikita S. Khrushchev, Sept. 21, 1959.

16. *New York Times,* Oct. 15, 1960; interview with David A. Gurewitsch; letter from Eleanor Roosevelt to Mrs. Broome, Nov. 5, 1960.

17. Interview with Elizabeth Drewry.

18. Interview with Franklin D. Roosevelt, Jr.; letter from Eleanor Roosevelt to David Gray, Nov. 18, 1954.

19. Eleanor Roosevelt, on "Meet the Press," Oct. 26, 1958; Lash Diaries, Nov. 8, 1958.

20. *New York Post,* Nov. 5, 1958.

21. Eleanor Roosevelt, "If You Ask Me," column in *McCall's,* March, 1961; James M. Burns and Janet Thompson Burns, "Mrs. Roosevelt a Remarkable 75," *New York Times Magazine,* Oct. 4, 1959.

22. *New York Post,* July 16, 1959; Lash Diaries, Dec. 31, 1961.

XIV. A NEW GENERATION TAKES OVER

1. Postcard from Adlai Stevenson to Eleanor Roosevelt, July 25, 1959, and Eleanor Roosevelt's reply, July 28, 1959.

2. E. Roosevelt, "If You Ask Me," cited (Ch. XIII), March, 1957.

3. Letter from Eleanor Roosevelt to Chester Bowles, Feb. 14, 1958.

4. Letter from Eleanor Roosevelt to Paul Butler, Jan. 24, 1958.

5. *New York Times,* Dec. 8, 1958; Lash Diaries, Oct. 25, 1958.

6. Eleanor Roosevelt, interview, "College News Conference," ABC-TV, Dec. 7, 1958.
7. Lash Diaries, Nov. 11, 1958.
8. *Ibid.*, Feb. 21, 1960.
9. The author was one of those whom Mr. Johnson regaled with these stories.
10. E. Roosevelt, "My Day," cited (Ch. I), Sept. 27, 1952.
11. Eleanor Roosevelt, "Of Stevenson, Truman and Kennedy," *Saturday Evening Post*, March 18, 1958; interview with Justin Feldman, law partner of James Landis; E. Roosevelt, interview, "College News Conference," *op. cit.*
12. Letter from John F. Kennedy to Eleanor Roosevelt, Dec. 11, 1958, and Eleanor Roosevelt's reply, Dec. 18, 1958.
13. Letter from John F. Kennedy to Eleanor Roosevelt, Dec. 29, 1958, and Eleanor Roosevelt's reply, Jan. 6, 1959.
14. Letter from John F. Kennedy to Eleanor Roosevelt, Jan. 10, 1959, and Eleanor Roosevelt's reply, Jan. 20, 1959.
15. Letter from John F. Kennedy to Eleanor Roosevelt, Jan. 22, 1959.
16. E. Roosevelt, interview, "College News Conference," *op. cit.*; letter from Mary Lasker to Eleanor Roosevelt, Jan. 11, 1960, and Eleanor Roosevelt's comment written on the margin of Mrs. Lasker's letter.
17. E. Roosevelt, "If You Ask Me," Nov., 1959.
18. E. Roosevelt, "My Day," Oct. 23, 1959.
19. *New York Times, New York Herald Tribune,* and *New York Post,* Dec. 8, 1959.
20. Arthur Schlesinger, Jr., *A Thousand Days: John F. Kennedy in the White House* (Boston, 1965), p. 20.
21. E. Roosevelt, "My Day," Feb. 1, 1960, and April 17, 1960.
22. Interview with David A. Gurewitsch; letter from Eleanor Roosevelt to Lord Elibank, April 1, 1960.
23. Lash Diaries, April 12, 1960.
24. *Ibid.*, April 24, 1960; letter from Eleanor Roosevelt to Walter Reuther, April 25, 1960.
25. Letters from Eleanor Roosevelt to Walter Reuther and G. Mennen Williams, April 25, 1960.
26. Lash Diaries, May 31, 1960.
27. Letter from Eleanor Roosevelt to Mary Lasker, June 1, 1960.
28. Letter from Eleanor Roosevelt to Joseph P. Lash, June 7, 1960.
29. Letter from Adlai Stevenson to Eleanor Roosevelt, June 10, 1960.
30. Eleanor Roosevelt called on Stevenson to clarify his position on June 11,

1960, and Stevenson replied on June 12, 1960; E. Roosevelt, "My Day," June 13, 1960.
31. *New York Times,* June 13, 1960.
32. Letter from Adlai Stevenson to Eleanor Roosevelt, June 13, 1960.
33. Arthur Krock, column in the *New York Times,* June 14, 1960; Stevenson comment to Eleanor Roosevelt, June 15, 1960.
34. Letter from Eleanor Roosevelt to Joseph P. Lash, June 15, 1960.
35. Letter from Eleanor Roosevelt to Edmund Brown, June 10, 1960; letter from Eleanor Roosevelt to Michael DiSalle, June 21, 1960.
36. Letter from Eleanor Roosevelt to Agnes Meyer, June 21, 1960.
37. Letters from Eleanor Roosevelt to Trude W. and Joseph P. Lash, June 19 and 29, 1960.
38. *Ibid.*, July 5, 1960.
39. Letter from Eleanor Roosevelt to Gus Ranis, July 9, 1960.
40. N. R. Howard, in the *Cleveland Plain Dealer,* July 13, 1960.
41. Lash Diaries, July 17, 1960.
42. Norman Mailer, *The Presidential Papers* (New York, 1963), p. 36; letter from Eleanor Roosevelt to LeRoy Collins, July 29, 1960.
43. Letter from Nannine Joseph to Cass Canfield, July 19, 1960; David E. Lilienthal, *The Harvest Years, 1959–63,* vol. V of *The Journals of David E. Lilienthal,* 5 vols. (New York, 1971), p. 103; Lash Diaries, July 17, 1960.
44. Lash Diaries, July 17, 1960.
45. Letter from Adlai Stevenson to Eleanor Roosevelt, Aug. 7, 1960.
46. Interviews with Mrs. Herbert Lehman, David A. Gurewitsch, and Maureen Corr.
47. Letter from Eleanor Roosevelt to Adlai Stevenson, Aug. 11, 1960.
48. William Walton, in *As We Remember Him,* ed. John K. Jessup and others (New York, 1965), p. 88.
49. Letter from Eleanor Roosevelt to Stevenson's friends, Aug. 15, 1960.
50. Letter from Eleanor Roosevelt to John F. Kennedy, Aug. 15, 1960; letter from John F. Kennedy to Eleanor Roosevelt, Aug. 26, 1960.
51. Letter from Eleanor Roosevelt to John F. Kennedy, Aug. 27, 1960.
52. *Ibid.*, Oct. 24, 1960.
53. Letter from Eleanor Roosevelt to Peter Kamitchis, Oct. 21, 1960.
54. E. Roosevelt, "My Day," Jan. 2, 1961.

XV. TO THE END, COURAGE

1. Miss Perkins's attitude was described to me by Prof. Maurice Neufeld of Cornell University, who arranged for Miss Perkins to come to Cornell. David Gurewitsch told me the Morgenthau story.
2. Gallup Opinion Index, Report No. 19; Eleanor Roosevelt, financial papers, 1961.
3. Letter from Eleanor Roosevelt to Mr. Horne, Feb. 19, 1960.
4. Emma Bugbee, in the *New York Her-*

ald Tribune, Oct. 11, 1961; *New York Post,* Oct. 11, 1961.

5. *New York Times,* Oct. 6, 1959; interview with Maureen Corr.
6. Emma Bugbee, "My Most Unforgettable Character," *Reader's Digest,* Oct., 1963; Thomas L. Stix, "Mrs. Roosevelt Does a TV Commercial," *Harper's,* Nov., 1963.
7. E. Roosevelt, *You Learn by Living,* cited (Ch. XI); interview with Nannine Joseph.
8. Letter from Anna Roosevelt Halsted to David A. Gurewitsch, April 7, 1960; *New York Post,* Dec. 7, 1961.
9. Interview with the late Mrs. Gerald Morgan.
10. Interview with the Reverend Elliott Lindsley.
11. Mr. and Mrs. Arthur Vervaet told me this story.
12. Interview with Maureen Corr.
13. *Ibid.;* Adlai Stevenson, eulogy, delivered Nov. 17, 1962.
14. Lash Diaries, July 4, 1962.
15. Recollection of the author; E. Roosevelt, "My Day," cited (Ch. I), Aug. 10, 1960.
16. Letter from Eleanor Roosevelt to Franklin Roosevelt III, Jan. 15, 1962.
17. Interview with Anna Roosevelt Halsted.
18. Lilienthal, *The Road to Change, 1955–59,* cited (Ch. XII), p. 299.
19. *New York Times,* March 11, 1961.
20. Letter from Eleanor Roosevelt to Adlai Stevenson, April 19, 1961; letter from Eleanor Roosevelt to John F. Kennedy, April 10, 1961.
21. "List of Women Eligible for Appointment," Eleanor Roosevelt files, in Franklin D. Roosevelt Library; her changed attitude toward the Equal Rights Amendment reported in the *New York Times,* May 8, 1961; message from the Commission on the Status of Women to Eleanor Roosevelt, Oct. 29, 1962.
22. Letter from Eleanor Roosevelt to John F. Kennedy, Feb. 19, 1961.
23. Letters from Eleanor Roosevelt to John F. Kennedy, March 14, 1961, and April 21, 1961, and Kennedy's reply, April 28, 1961.
24. Letter from Eleanor Roosevelt to John

F. Kennedy, July 22, 1961, and Kennedy's reply, July 28, 1961.
25. Letter from Eleanor Roosevelt to John F. Kennedy, Nov. 2, 1961, and Kennedy's reply, Nov. 21, 1961.
26. Letter from Eleanor Roosevelt to John F. Kennedy, Aug. 15, 1962.
27. Letter from Robert F. Kennedy to Eleanor Roosevelt, Dec. 19, 1961.
28. Letter from Eleanor Roosevelt to Jacqueline Kennedy, Dec. 1, 1960.
29. E. Roosevelt, "My Day," May 29, 1962.
30. *New York Post,* April 7, 1959.
31. Interview with Anna Roosevelt Halsted.
32. Lash Diaries, March 16, 1960.
33. Ruth G. Michaels, in *Hadassah,* Dec., 1962; interviews with Maureen Corr and David A. Gurewitsch.
34. *New York Times,* May 25, 1962; Lash Diaries, June 8, 1962; letter from Eleanor Roosevelt to Thomas L. Stix, May 10, 1962.
35. Interview with Anna Roosevelt Halsted; letter from Eleanor Roosevelt to David A. Gurewitsch, undated; Elinore Denniston, "A Recollection," in Eleanor Roosevelt, *Tomorrow Is Now* (New York, 1963), p. x.
36. E. Roosevelt, "My Day," Aug. 14, 1962.
37. Lash Diaries, Aug. 6, 1962.
38. Interview with Maureen Corr.
39. Letter from Trude W. Lash to Paul Tillich, Nov. 18, 1962.
40. Lash Diaries, Sept. 7, 1962.
41. *Ibid.;* E. Roosevelt, *Tomorrow Is Now, op. cit.,* p. 138.
42. Lash Diaries, Sept. 20, 1962.
43. Letter from Trude W. Lash to Paul Tillich, Nov. 18, 1962.
44. Letter from Adlai Stevenson to Eleanor Roosevelt, Sept. 30, 1962.
45. Letter from David A. Gurewitsch to Joseph P. Lash, Dec. 15, 1962; letter from James Halsted to James Roosevelt, March 25, 1966.
46. Lash Diaries, Oct. 30, 1962; letter from Anna Roosevelt Halsted to David Gray, Nov. 1, 1962.
47. Edward P. Morgan, ed., *This I Believe* (New York, 1953), pp. 155–56.

APPENDIX A. THE NOBEL PEACE PRIZE

1. Letter from Adlai Stevenson to Gunnar Jahn (chairman of the Nobel Committee of the Norwegian Parliament), Feb. 21, 1961.
2. Letter from Adlai Stevenson to Gunnar Jahn, Jan. 15, 1962; letter from John F. Kennedy to August Schou, Jan. 23, 1962.
3. Letter from Ralph Bunche to Gunnar Jahn, Nov. 22, 1962.
4. Letter from Lester Pearson to Gunnar Jahn, Aug. 13, 1964; letter from

Andrew W. Cordier to Gunnar Jahn, Sept. 2, 1964.
5. Letter from Sivert A. Nielsen to August Schou, Sept. 5, 1964, and Schou's reply, Sept. 8, 1964; letter from Sivert A. Nielsen to Nils Langhelle, Sept. 21, 1964, and Langhelle's reply, Oct. 28, 1964.
6. Letter from the Organizing Committee to Gunnar Jahn, Jan. 10, 1965.
7. Letter from Harry S. Truman to Gunnar Jahn, Nov. 20, 1964.

8. Letter from Clement Attlee to the Nobel Committee, Oct. 29, 1964.
9. Letter from Jean Monnet to August Schou, undated.
10. Letter from Henry A. Kissinger to the Nobel Committee, Dec. 9, 1964.
11. Letter from Esther Lape to David A. Gurewitsch, Dec. 30, 1964.

APPENDIX B. MRS. ROOSEVELT AND THE SULTAN OF MOROCCO

1. Letter from Justine Wise Polier to Joseph P. Lash, Feb. 29, 1972.

Index

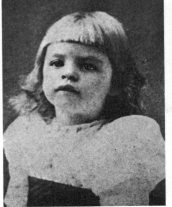

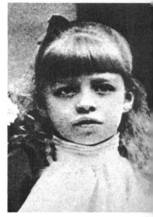